LEE HARVEY OSWALD

AS I KNEW HIM

Lee Harvey Oswald
as I Knew Him

George de Mohrenschildt

Edited and Annotated by

Michael A. Rinella

University Press of Kansas

Published by the University Press of Kansas (Lawrence, Kansas
66045), which was organized by the Kansas Board of Regents and is
operated and funded by Emporia State University, Fort Hays State
University, Kansas State University, Pittsburg State University, the
University of Kansas, and Wichita State University

Library of Congress Cataloging-in-Publication Data

Mohrenschildt, George de.
Lee Harvey Oswald as I knew him / George de Mohrenschildt ;
edited and annotated by Michael A. Rinella.
pages cm
Includes bibliographical references and index.
ISBN 978-0-7006-2013-5 (cloth)
ISBN 978-0-7006-2054-8 (ebook)
1. Oswald, Lee Harvey—Friends and associates. 2. Kennedy, John F.
(John Fitzgerald), 1917–1963—Assassination. 3. Mohrenschildt,
George de. I. Rinella, Michael A. (Michael Anthony) II. Title.
E842.9.M557 2014
364.152'4092—dc23
2014026622

British Library Cataloguing-in-Publication Data is available.

For George and Jeanne

Contents

Illustrations

Acknowledgments

Untying the Gordian knot that is George de Mohrenschildt's manuscript would not have been possible without a small ocean of primary documents now easily accessible in digital form, the most important of which were the following: the Warren Commission's Records Relating to Key Persons (particularly folders 7460466, 7460467, and 7460468) found in the JFK Assassination Records of the National Archives; the HSCA Segregated CIA Collection (microfilm—reel 5) and Russ Holmes Work File available at the Mary Ferrell Foundation; and the thirty-one volumes of Willem Oltmans's *Memoires* now available through the Digital Library of Dutch Literature. Additional assistance was provided by the JFK Presidential Library, the Office of University Publications at the University of Texas, Arlington, Willis Library at the University of North Texas, the Pan Am Historical Association, and the La Fonda Hotel. I would like to thank reviewers Lock K. Johnson and John Prados for their comments and everyone at the University Press of Kansas for their professionalism in preparing the final manuscript for publication.

Editor's Introduction

Let us hope that this book, poorly written and disjointed, but sincere, will help to clear up our relationship with our dear, dead friend Lee.

—George S. de Mohrenschildt

Thus concludes an unpublished manuscript by George Sergei de Mohrenschildt. Readers would be justified in asking themselves: who was this man, what does it matter that he wrote a book at all, and why bother to edit and annotate a text that was, by his own admission, both disorganized and badly composed? While trained as a scholar and a published author myself, I am an acquisitions editor by trade. An acquisitions editor is, in essence, a talent scout who secures worthy manuscripts for his or her publisher. Evaluating manuscripts for both intellectual merit and marketability consumes a major portion of my time each day. Why is that important? It means I'd like to think I am better qualified than most to know a manuscript with potential when I see it. When I began reading the de Mohrenschildt text that was included in an appendix volume of the House Select Committee on Assassinations (HSCA),[1] I very quickly realized there was something special about the material, possibly even something extraordinary. This was an author with an interesting and entertaining story to tell. The author also just so happened to be the man who was, many have argued, the closest friend Lee Harvey Oswald had in the final months of 1962 and the early months of 1963. Oswald, of course, has long been presumed to be the individual who assassinated President John F. Kennedy in Dallas, Texas, on November 22, 1963.

A definitive single-volume biography of de Mohrenschildt, who was born in 1911 and died in 1977, does not exist. Such a work remains to be written; it is surprising after all the time and attention paid to his life, and by so many, many, writers, that one *hasn't* been written. As his friend of some two decades Sam Ballen said, "George had one of the most fascinating and complex life journeys that can be imagined."[2] On the one hand, this lack of a biography is somewhat of a shame given that so many individuals who personally knew de Mohrenschildt, including his fourth wife, Jeanne, his brother Dmitri, his daughter Alexandra, and best friend Ballen survived into the 1990s and beyond. On the other hand, given the fact that so many secret documents relating to de Mohrenschildt's activities between the 1940s and 1960s have only recently been declassified and made available to researchers, perhaps this delay was for the best. The biographical material the reader will find within this introduction and sprinkled throughout the hundreds of annotations that accompany the manuscript cannot substitute for this still-unwritten biography.[3] Its purpose is simply to give the reader unfamiliar with George de Mohrenschildt's oversized and cinematic life a better sense of the author behind the manuscript he left behind.

Diderot's Nephew

George de Mohrenschildt in his final years was a professor of French and Russian in the Literature Department of Bishop College, a small, predominantly black institution in Dallas. The manuscript you are about to read abounds with references and allusions to writers and classics from both French and Russian literature. If there is a single work one could turn to in order to gain an understanding of who George de Mohrenschildt was, particularly in the late 1950s and early 1960s, it would certainly be *Le neveu de Rameau* (Rameau's Nephew), a unique and incomparable work written in the eighteenth century by that leading figure of the Enlightenment, Denis Diderot.[4] In the story the narrator, identified only as *Moi* (Me), recounts his recent encounter with *Lui* (Him) in the Palais-Royal. Lui is introduced with the following description:

> He is a compound of the highest and the lowest, good sense and folly. The notions of good and evil must be strangely muddled in his head, for the good qualities nature has given him he displays without ostentation, and the bad ones without shame. Moreover he is blessed with a strong constitution, a singularly fervid imagination, and lung power quite out of the ordinary. . . . Nothing is less like him than himself.[5]

Lui complains bitterly that the low value society assigns to learned men of talent such as himself leaves no better option than to adopt a parasitical relationship with the wealthy, living at their expense by any means necessary, however repugnant, whether it be self-abasement, flattery, or dishonesty. When it is all over the reader cannot be certain whether anything Lui has said is sincerely held or simply provocative; Lui is simultaneously ironic, self-contradicting, and seemingly unreliable, yet skillfully embedded in his complaints there appear to shine deeper truths. The manuscript contained herein, I would argue, is much the same. George de Mohrenschildt was a living, breathing Lui, a mid-twentieth-century European émigré of innumerable personas including, but by no means limited to: petroleum geologist and strategic resources entrepreneur and hustler; irreverent iconoclast and teasing comedian; refined cosmopolitan and social chameleon; physical fitness buff and devoted tennis aficionado; cystic fibrosis foundation fundraiser and friend to young people; ardent anti-segregationist and liberal professor in the middle of conservative Texas; and finally, Old World European and old-school male.

Many details regarding de Mohrenschildt's personality, worldview, and conduct in life may be gleaned from his own Warren Commission testimony, the testimony of his fourth wife, Jeanne, as well as that of their friends and acquaintances in Dallas. This view may now be supplemented, thanks to the passage of the John F. Kennedy Assassination Records Collection Act of 1992, with a seemingly endless stream of declassified government documents including not only decades of FBI investigation but also intense interest from the CIA, Office of Naval Intelligence, the Assistant Chief of Staff, Intelligence, the Department of the Army, the State Department, and the Civil Service Commission.[6] These declassified documents reveal how deeply baffled and bewildered de Mohrenschildt's life left these federal bureaucrats, hopelessly mired in their institutional arrogance and Manichean Cold War fantasy worlds. De Mohrenschildt was suspected of being, alternately and simultaneously, an *agent provocateur* for French nationalists; Germans fascists; Polish, Yugoslav, and/or Russian Communists; and both a Haitian dictator and the dictator's leading political opponent. He and Jeanne—herself suspected of being either an anarchist, a Bohemian, or somebody's agent—were seemingly always broke or possessing mysteriously acquired wealth, driving everywhere in convertibles with a pair of Manchester Terriers who appear to have antagonized and/or traumatized everyone they came in contact with. He was summed up by informants—who seemed to have been perpetually in his company—as "eccentric, irresponsible, conceited, an adventurer fond of exaggeration, and overly aggressive," while socially he was "known to associate with persons of questionable loyalty, reputation, and moral character."[7] It would be the stuff of some film *noir* or dark comedy, were it not for the tragedy of President John F. Kennedy's assassination and the fact that the agencies seeking to investigate it had managed to convince themselves de Mohrenschildt and his wife possessed some kind of clandestine information—knowledge these same agencies were desperate to acquire.

The Manuscript and the Edit

> Genealogy is gray, meticulous, and patiently documentary. It operates on a field of tangled and confused parchments, on documents that have been scratched over and recopied many times.
>
> —*Michel Foucault*

In addition to dabbling in documentary film and his accomplishments as a talented watercolor artist, George de Mohrenschildt was an avid writer throughout much of his life.[8] Government reports have him working as a journalist for the Polish government press, the *Polish Agency Telegraph*, between 1934 and 1938; de Mohrenschildt had some hope of becoming a journalist after his arrival in the United States. He claimed to have published a number of articles, both in Europe and in the United States. Most of these are now difficult to verify. The manuscript itself mentions an article on the motion picture industry in Europe that was published during the 1940s in *Variety*.[9] There were in addition several articles published in *Oil and Gas Journal* including one titled "Yugoslavia, Young Oil Province with Undeveloped Prospects" that was published in 1958 after his trip to Yugoslavia the previous year under the auspices of the International Cooperation Association.[10] Prior to writing the present manuscript, he authored at least three other book-length works and had hoped to publish them. While he was living in Mexico with the lovely *señora* Larin in 1941, he was working on a bawdy tale called *Adventures of a Young Man in Mexico*. He described it as "more or less a romantic dissertation, a romantic book based on some of my experiences."[11] The manuscript was submitted to at least one publisher but was rejected, apparently on account of de Mohrenschildt's limited command of written English. He began a second book, a work on his early life called *A Son of the Revolution*, and apparently hired a stenographer to assist him.[12] The fate of these two manuscripts and whether either still exists is unknown.

By the time he testified before the Warren Commission in April 1964 de Mohrenschildt had completed a third work, possibly titled *Trois et le Mule* (Three and a Mule),[13] a 600-page draft manuscript describing "the day-by-day adventures" of his walk through Central America with Jeanne in 1960–1961.[14] He approached a number of high-profile individuals to write a foreword to the book, including President Kennedy.[15] All, as far as we know, politely declined. He claimed in his Warren Commission testimony the manuscript "is now in the hands of a publisher in France, and they may publish it."[16] While the manuscript may have intrigued this French publisher, it was turned down, though probably not due to de Mohrenschildt's command of French, which was apparently excellent.[17] As described by de Mohrenschildt this manuscript was written almost like "a diary" and needed to be developed into a unified and compelling narrative. "Someday," he said, "when I have more time, I will make it a bit more colorful."[18] Such a task was beyond de Mohrenschildt's abilities and was certainly incompatible with his extremely restless and impatient nature. As Jeanne said, he couldn't sit still.[19] Despite being "professionally rewritten" and submitted to several publishers, the manuscript was never accepted for publication.[20] The fate of this third manuscript and whether it still exists is also unknown.

The manuscript presented here, the fourth completed by George de Mohrenschildt during his lifetime, appears to have had its genesis in January 1969, at the urging of Dutch journalist Willem Oltmans. In his enormous multivolume *Memoires*, Oltmans's entry for January 26, 1969, reads: "The past few days with George and Jeanne were useful in that I have now convinced them to write about their experiences with Lee Harvey Oswald."[21] Like its predecessors the new manuscript was also intended for publication, though it appears the de Mohrenschildts never seriously entertained the idea of hiring a literary agent, preferring to leave such details to their Dutch friend. Oltmans's memoirs indicate that he spoke to Random House on February 6, 1969, and the publisher had shown "enormous interest" in a book "by George and Jeanne de Mohrenschildt about Lee Harvey Oswald."[22] That same day a letter from de Mohrenschildt written on January 29 arrived, informing Oltmans that thanks to Jeanne's "extraordinary memory" he had "the plan and two chapters completed."[23]

On February 14 and 15, 1969, a series of audio-taped readings from the draft manuscript were made in the company of Oltmans at the CBS studios in Dallas. Large portions of the final manuscript are based on these tapes, and de Mohrenschildt alludes to them in the manuscript's final sentences. Oltmans's exceptionally long entry in his memoirs for February 15, 1969, which summarizes these recording sessions, contains noticeable parallels to much of the material found in Chapters 1, 2, 3, and 4. In a letter he wrote to Oltmans dated May 10, 1976, de Mohrenschildt would say, in his sometimes ambiguous English, "As I listened to the tapes and tried to transcribe them, I realize[d] that they can be of a little help, just to remind me of certain details. OK, so I just sat down and tried to reconstruct Lee's personality. Jeanne was of great help. Several books are being written on about the same subject, but the most serious [Edward J. Epstein's *Inquest*] will be next to mine, I hope."[24]

Oltmans attempted to shop the tapes around but, to his clear frustration, encountered a mixture of uninterest and hostility. The timing was exceptionally bad. New Orleans businessman Clay Shaw had been arrested in 1967 and charged by New Orleans District Attorney Jim Garrison with conspiring to assassinate President Kennedy. On March 1, 1969, a jury in New Orleans had acquitted Shaw after less than an hour of deliberation. The managing editor of *Look* magazine, William Arthur, told Oltmans on March 13 he had no interest in listening to any of the tapes. "Oswald was just crazy," he told Oltmans, and Garrison's case had been a fiasco; interest in the assassination was finished.[25] Doubleday indicated on March 26 that it, too, had no desire to become involved with yet another book about Lee Harvey Oswald. Public interest in Oswald's story, the publisher informed Oltmans, had been exhausted and it was time for the country to move on. When a draft of the entire manuscript was finally finished in the early summer of 1976 the de Mohrenschildts did not actively push to see it published. Jeanne, apparently, was too concerned they'd be prosecuted for mentioning the names of FBI and CIA agents. In his increasingly fragile physical and mental state, George was inclined to agree with her.

During the winter of 1977 some negotiations with "Dutch television and publishing executives" did occur in Amsterdam between March 3 and March 4, during the brief time de Mohrenschildt spent in Europe with Oltmans.[26] Oltmans, who had come to Dallas in February, had convinced de Mohrenschildt to travel to Holland with him when de Mohrenschildt told him in the Bishop College library that he "felt responsible" for what Oswald had done, and that his actions had "guided" Oswald's behavior. Oltmans, who had harbored hopes of some kind of "confession" for years, interpreted this as the beginning of a major revelation. On several occasions de Mohrenschildt had jokingly suggested to Oltmans he might have organized Kennedy's assassination in Dallas. For example on February 16, 1969, while driving Oltmans to the Dallas airport at Love Field he surprised the Dutchman by saying "How would you like it, Willem, if it became known that I am indeed the one who organized the assassination of JFK?"[27] Carel Enkelaar[28] of Dutch NOS Television had urged Oltmans to secure an admission of involvement or guilt from de Mohrenschildt.[29] Now the moment finally appeared to be at hand.

In one version of the meeting in Amsterdam Enkelaar was offering "a month's stay in a fine hotel plus a staff to write the story for book, film, and television versions."[30] When a phone call to the de Mohrenschildts' Dallas lawyer, Patrick S. Russell Jr., confirmed a complete manuscript *already* existed both Oltmans and Enkelaar became even more determined to have a contract signed granting them exclusive rights to the material; as enticements they offered the possibility that "Italian and French publishers might also be very interested in some rights to serialization and a book."[31] In an article he later published in *Nieuwe Revu*, Oltmans claimed the discussion was mainly about "worldwide publication of his book and he agreed in principle to the terms proposed by the Strengholt Publishing House."[32]

In the end, however, the negotiations for the manuscript fell through; it became apparent to de Mohrenschildt the two parties were discussing quite different books. "With Oltmans's growing excitement, de Mohrenschildt understood that the only chronicle of events would be a sensational one. He knew that the document . . . did not contain any such revelations [and] grasped the compromising position in which he had placed himself."[33] He fled the next day while he and Oltmans were on a weekend trip together in Brussels. Print articles appearing in the days after de Mohrenschildt's death on March 29 expressed an awareness of the manuscript and speculated about its possible content.[34] A copy was donated with Jeanne's consent to the HSCA on April 1. The contents must have led to considerable disappointment, as they yielded no pat "smoking gun" revelations. Interest in the manuscript quickly waned, but not before *Time* magazine ran a contemptuous article branding de Mohrenschildt both a lunatic and an opportunist seeking to cash in on the Kennedy assassination.[35]

I have been an editor for close to fifteen years. Occasionally, but only with the most deserving projects I have acquired, I have also performed what is known in the book business as developmental editing. The work of the developmental editor consists of redrafting, revising, and otherwise improving and polishing a manuscript for authors who are otherwise unable to do so for themselves. Such work is meant to accentuate and amplify the author's own words, ideas, and thoughts—*not* change them. Developmental editing is far more common in the world of trade publishing, less so in scholarly publishing. Academic authors have areas of specialization so narrow only another expert would be qualified to recommend improvements and otherwise develop their manuscript. The de Mohrenschildt manuscript, while written by someone with scholarly credentials, is, however, a trade book. It is meant for a general audience. Developmental editing was simply a matter of care, patience, and meticulous attention to detail.

What does this mean? It means I'd like to think I'm better qualified than most to describe the problems found in the de Mohrenschildt manuscript, propose developmental editing solutions to those problems, and then carry them out. It is essential to remember that the de Mohrenschildt manuscript was not even what might be called a first draft. It is more like a very rough first draft of a first draft. Had a book contract been signed and had the manuscript been turned over to any publishing house in operation during the late-1970s, as certainly seems to have been de Mohrenschildt's hope, the material would have required major developmental editing and copy editing in order to become a publishable work. What follows is a list of the manuscript's most significant problems *as a manuscript*—leaving aside for the moment its accuracy *as history*—and some discussion of the developmental editing solutions undertaken to remedy them.

First, even the work's title—*I Am a Patsy! I Am a Patsy!*—is a misnomer and hence problematic. It appears to have arisen out of a 1967 conversation de Mohrenschildt had with the liberal owner/editor-in-chief of the *Midlothian Mirror*, William Penn Jones Jr.[36] As recounted in Chapter 6 by de Mohrenschildt, Jones told him "I shall never forget Lee Harvey Oswald's face, beaten brutally to a pulp, of his terrified expression when he was being led by beefy policemen the day of President Kennedy's assassination. And this young man kept shouting 'I am a patsy!' 'I am a patsy!'"[37] Jones's comments apparently left de Mohrenschildt with the impression Oswald had been continually beaten during the short hours he was in Dallas police custody, and from all indications it was Jones who was the source of de Mohrenschildt's belief that the twice-repeated sentence was Oswald's "last words" in public. In truth Oswald was not beaten while in custody, appeared controlled and slightly defiant rather than terrified, and when asked by a reporter at roughly 7:55 CST on November 22, 1963, whether he had killed the president, Oswald responded, "They are taking me in because I lived in the Soviet Union. I'm just a patsy." The "patsy" self-reference made by Oswald was uttered just once, not twice and, while said emphatically, was not shouted in terror.

The title has therefore been changed to *Lee Harvey Oswald as I Knew*

Him. The reason should be abundantly clear to anyone who has actually taken the time to carefully read the complete manuscript from beginning to end. The *primary* focus of the text is a series of recollections about the man Lee Harvey Oswald himself. The majority of the material is an attempt to "humanize" our view of Oswald through a retelling of the brief time that de Mohrenschildt and his wife, Jeanne, befriended him and his wife, Marina. And the time was quite short, shorter than much of the Kennedy assassination literature seems willing to admit. The de Mohrenschildts were in close contact with the Oswalds for something in the neighborhood of perhaps sixty days, from roughly mid-September through mid-November 1962. Thereafter contact diminished considerably but did not completely end until Easter of 1963. A *secondary* focus of de Mohrenschildt's text consists of several meditations on the corrosive effects knowing the Oswalds had on the professional and personal lives of the de Mohrenschildts, first in Haiti, then in Dallas after their return in 1966, and then finally echoing across the years up until the time of the draft's completion in 1976. Only in a *tertiary* sense—and even then only in an embryonic, rudimentary form—is the manuscript in any way concerned with Oswald's guilt or innocence regarding the Kennedy assassination. Yet this last aspect is what, largely based on use of the word "patsy" in the title, the manuscript is presumed by most everyone to be about. In the publishing business editors routinely change their authors' titles. The new title, I think any objective reading will agree, more accurately reflects the manuscript's true and actual contents.

Second, there is a nearly endless profusion of grammatical and punctuation errors within the manuscript. Spellings, too, are often wrong or wildly inconsistent. The document suffers greatly from what in scholarly publishing we call the "English as a second language" problem. In other words while the author might be highly intelligent, the text itself is not written in a native tongue. The prose in de Mohrenschildt's manuscript, depending on one's level of generosity, reads like a mediocre to below-average translation of Russian into English. Russian and English are quite dissimilar languages. The system of grammar within each, for example, is quite different. In English grammar the rules for word order are fairly fixed. Meaning is expressed through the addition of words. Auxiliary verbs, for example, are used to help express grammatical tense, aspect, mood, and voice. Grammatical rules in Russian, in contrast, convey meaning largely through changes in the composition of words, for example by inflections or the addition of prefixes and suffixes. Word order in Russian is very fluid. Russian and English also convey meaning through their verb systems in drastically different ways.

The Russian system is based on the concept of the aspect: actions are either completed or not completed. There are few auxiliary verbs. This contrasts with English which has progressive and perfect tense forms, and avoids the need for affixation or inflection by the extensive use of auxiliaries. Russian furthermore has no articles. This causes significant problems because the whole concept of article use is alien to Russian learners of English, and the English article system itself is extremely complex. Russian is also largely phonetic—pronunciation can be predicted from spelling and spelling from pronunciation; English most definitely is not. When Kennedy assassination researchers puzzle over de Mohrenschildt misspelling "Oswald" as "Osvald" in written correspondence, to give perhaps the most obvious example, it simply demonstrates their ignorance of these linguistic differences.

All of the aforementioned issues have, therefore, been editorially addressed. The entire manuscript has been thoroughly cleaned and polished to eliminate the many artifacts of de Mohrenschildt's limited command of written English. Where there was even a slight chance that the reader might conclude a revision had altered the meaning of the original material—for example, de Mohrenschildt says "motif" where "motive" is plainly meant—an endnote has been provided and the original word, phrase, or sentence included in the note for comparison. At the same time I did want to retain the *flavor* of his prose, particularly conversations we may assume were as often as not occurring in Russian. Spoken quotations by George, Lee, Jeanne, and Marina have been kept unchanged and intact, except for obvious misspellings arising from the limitations of de Mohrenschildt's English and simple typographical errors.[38] Quotes by native English speakers, in contrast, have been edited so as to flow as if spoken in English. For example, in Chapter 3 Admiral Bruton says, "I'm being made into a salesman" rather than "I am made to be a salesman." No italics exist in the original manuscript and have been added throughout the text to emphasize certain points. Where de Mohrenschildt is "quoting" from a published document, such as the single-volume *Warren Commission Report* or the multivolume *Warren Commission Hearings and Exhibits*, only obvious misspellings have been corrected and the original document, if available, is quoted verbatim for the sake of comparison and accuracy in the notes.

Third, the manuscript is a mess organizationally. While the text refers to itself as having "chapters," there are in fact no chapters, at least as far as the word is traditionally understood in book publishing. De Mohrenschildt misunderstands the word in at least two different ways, using "chapter" to denote what would ordinarily be considered sections within a single chapter, and to indicate a simple paragraph-length passage within a single section.[39] The crude draft manuscript is probably best described as a series of vignettes, that is, short impressionistic scenes each just a few pages in length. While some do manage to transition into one another in a relatively smooth manner, others jump back and forth both topically and chronologically in a distracting and jarring fashion, not only *between* vignettes but even *within* them. The arc of the narrative meanders confusingly back and forth between the early 1960s and the mid-1970s, occasionally interrupted by a digression covering a topic before 1960 or from the later 1960s and early 1970s. There is also a fair degree of repetition in the material, with descriptions of the same event repeated a second and sometimes even a third time in only slightly modified form in different portions of the manuscript. These duplicate passages have been combined using the best elements of each.

Chapters are therefore called for. The chapter names were chosen to reflect their content and may be summarized as follows. Conversations between de Mohrenschildt and Oswald in the late summer and early fall of 1962 about Lee's time in Minsk as well as political topics and events have been placed in Chapter 1. Conversations regarding the troubled marriage between Lee and Marina have been located in Chapter 2. The more limited contact between the de Mohrenschildts and the Oswalds in the winter and spring of 1963 and the preparations for the de Mohrenschildts' move to Haiti constitute Chapter 3. The assassination of President Kennedy and its aftermath, including the de Mohrenschildts' 1964 Warren Commission testimony and the consequences that followed because of it, are the focus of Chapter 4. Their return from Haiti and the 1967 discovery of the now well known "hunter of fascists" photo by Jeanne in their stored belongings is the basis of Chapter 5. Finally de Mohrenschildt's mid-1970s musings about the possible existence of a conspiracy to assassinate President Kennedy, and the question of Oswald's possible guilt or innocence, is the subject matter of Chapter 6.[40]

For the most part, I should emphasize, the edited material still proceeds from beginning to end exactly as de Mohrenschildt wrote it, but with a few notable exceptions. A few vignettes have been relocated. The material titled "Why Lee and I Disliked the FBI" appears near the end of the original manuscript in what is now Chapter 6 but, given how valuable this material is in establishing both men's negative views of bureaucratic authority, it has been relocated to Chapter 1. Similarly the vignette "Marina and the Walker Incident" appears well after the de Mohrenschildts' discovery of the "hunter of fascists" photo but given that Oswald's alleged attempted shooting of

General Walker is directly tied to the photo it makes sense to pair the material together in what is now Chapter 5. Most of the original vignette names have been retained as headings within each chapter, though a few have been renamed to better reflect the content of the material linked to them and, in a handful of instances, new headings have been created where none previously existed but where the text was marked by a major shift in subject matter. Any competent editor working with de Mohrenschildt circa 1977 to develop the manuscript would have insisted on precisely these sorts of changes.

Fourth, the manuscript reflects the life of an extraordinary, larger than life character who seemingly knew everyone.[41] The manuscript is a veritable cornucopia of name dropping, something both de Mohrenschildts were notorious for doing in conversation. Sometimes de Mohrenschildt supplies the reader an individual's name, but frequently there is no name, merely a mention of the individual's occupation, employer, or some other feature felt to be adequate enough for identificaton.[42] The most important information from de Mohrenschildt's perspective is the level of friendship they shared with him; either a good friend, a slight acquaintance, or a stranger. Occasionally some biographical detail might be attached to the individual, but more often than not the surrounding historical context is utterly lacking. To assist the reader full names have been inserted into the text whenever the individual could be confidently identified. Short biographical summaries of each individual have also been placed in the notes, including birth and death dates and details of importance, especially if they relate to the Cold War, the Kennedy assassination, or the world of Port-au-Prince in the early 1960s.

Two additional things also need to be said about the "voice" of de Mohrenschildt's manuscript. First, the reader will notice that the text more often than not refers to its narrator in the plural, for example, by use of "we" rather than "I," "*our* dear, dead friend Lee," rather than "*my* dear, dead friend Lee," and so on—it speaks for *both* George and Jeanne. Second, to avoid possible confusion when reading the notes, I have used "de Mohrenschildt" when referring to George only and "the de Mohrenschildts" when referring to both George and Jeanne. Similarly when I indicate "Oswald" I am referring only to Lee while "the Oswalds" refers to both Lee and Marina. When, more infrequently, the note is about only Mrs. de Mohrenschildt or Mrs. Oswald "Jeanne" and "Marina" have been used, respectively.

Interpretation of the Text

> Hear me! For I am such and such a person.
> Above all, do not mistake me for someone else!
>
> —*Friedrich Nietzsche*

In the fall of 1888 the German philosopher Friedrich Nietzsche, toiling in the twilight of sanity, completed his final original work. It was an autobiographical essay whose title consisted of the Latin words supposedly used by Pontius Pilate when he presented the scourged Jesus to the hostile crowd: *Ecce homo*.[43] Behold the man. A central preoccupation of the document was Nietzsche's own posterity. *"Have I been understood?"* the text practically cries out.[44] Days after completing the work Nietzsche was gone, the abyss he had so frequently peered into having finally swallowed him.[45] The de Mohrenschildt manuscript also commands that we behold a man and understand him, in this case de Mohrenschildt and his association with Lee Harvey Oswald. In de Mohrenschildt's case, as in Nietzsche's, time was beginning to run out. His persecution complex, in evidence since at least the late 1950s, intensified into debilitating fear and paranoia. Depression had also been a growing problem. His behavior became increasingly disturbed and self-destructive during 1976, especially its final quarter, so much so that on November 9 Jeanne and family lawyer Russell filed court papers with the Dallas County Mental Illness Department to have him committed to Parkland Hospital for psychiatric treatment.[46] He would remain there until the end of the year.

Inevitably, then, the question of the author's mental state while writing the manuscript has been raised in some quarters. Is the author sane; is he in command of his faculties? In general, he is. Yes, he is deeply frustrated about the ongoing and seemingly never-ending invasion of his privacy. Yes, he is clearly bitter about lost income in general and about the failure of his long-planned Haitian venture in particular. Yes, he takes some embarrassing swipes at people, some of them perhaps deserving, others not. Yes, he definitely has a sizeable grudge against the insensitive methods of bureaucratic agencies within the American government, especially the FBI. Yes, he deeply regrets his failure to realize that a young man whom he saw almost as a surrogate son was on a path to self-destruction, and that through both his actions and inactions he did not prevent that self-destruction from occurring. But the author of the manuscript is rational. There is no doubt in my mind the authorial "voice" that speaks from the manuscript is virtually identical to the voice found in de Mohrenschildt's Warren Commission testimony given twelve years before. Readers are free to compare the edited manuscript with Appendix B and draw their own conclusions.

To which we may add that by the beginning of the summer of 1976, possibly as early as the middle of July, the manuscript begun in 1969 was already finished. There are no internal references that can be pinpointed beyond that date.[47] The handwritten letter sent to CIA director George H. W. Bush on September 5, reproduced as Appendix D, refers to writing about Oswald in the past tense, that is, "I *tried* to write . . . about Lee H. Oswald" not "I am *trying* to write . . . about Lee H. Oswald." The narrative you will encounter is not the work of the despondent soul teetering in confusion between fact and fancy during the opening months of 1977, being pushed ever closer to the abyssal edge by a host of unscrupulous individuals whose motives were anything but noble. Only a combination of de Mohrenschildt's own difficulty writing in the English language, a failure to understand the differences between inductive and deductive reasoning, and the self-serving desire to cherry-pick from the manuscript in an effort to validate or invalidate certain explanations as to what happened in Dallas on November 22, 1963, could lead to the conclusion that the text is a product of mental illness and therefore easily dismissed.

Having disposed of the question of the author's sanity, this brings us to the Kennedy assassination literature itself. This cottage industry, still going strong after a half century, routinely mines the HSCA's version of de Mohrenschildt's manuscript, selecting a sentence here, extracting a passage there, and rarely to good effect. I am not interested in what these books have to say about Kennedy's assassination.[48] What I am concerned about is what they have to say about George de Mohrenschildt in general, and the manuscript you are about to encounter in particular. Even when these works do not have the misfortune of blundering over de Mohrenschildt's rather limited command of written English, the material is usually taken so out of context with regard to both the manuscript as a unified argument and de Mohrenschildt's life as a unified totality that their analysis—whether unintentionally or intentionally—winds up skewed and distorted, when it is not completely useless. George de Mohrenschildt has become a sort of *tabula rasa* onto which authors may project almost any kind of fantasy. Since his death the denizens of Kennedy assassination research have, to put it bluntly, bequeathed us an imaginary de Mohrenschildt.[49] The manuscript you are about to read has been exploited to support any number of theories, theories the author himself never expressed or espoused, from the sublime and the plausible to the implausible and ridiculous. The errors these writers commit, whether by omission or commission, may be summed up as follows: (1) misunderstanding the author and *his* limitations, (2) misunderstanding the text and *its* limitations, (3) and misunderstanding the contextual history *behind* the text.

Regarding (1), they misread problems arising from an individual struggling to communicate in a non-native language, everything from the phonetic spellings to sentences with an almost surreal word order. The author himself, de Mohrenschildt, was aware of this very danger nearly forty years ago: "Maybe the contradictory nature of Marina's deposition was the result of the testimony being poorly translated. As I have said, Russian is a difficult language."[50] Read through the separate testimonies of the Dallas–Fort Worth White Russians in the *Warren Commission Hearings and Exhibits* and you will find two cultures, and two languages, struggling to make themselves understood to each other. Even so simple a matter as the Eastern Orthodox and Roman Catholic Christmas holidays occurring a week apart appears to have been confused and misunderstood at times. The questioning of transplanted Russians such as George Bouhe (born in St. Petersburg), Valentina Ray (Stalino), Igor and Natasha Voshinin (Labinsk), Anna Meller (Belgorod), Elena Hall (Tehran, Iran, to parents from Baku), Natalie Ray (Stalingrad), Lydia Dymitruk (Rostov), Jeanne de Mohrenschildt (Harbin, China, near the Siberian border), and George de Mohrenschildt (Mozyr, in southeastern Belorussia) veers between comprehension and miscomprehension, sometimes breaking down completely into incomprehension and *aporia*, as both sides struggle to comprehend what the other is trying to communicate to them. The Kennedy assassination literature should exhibit the greatest sensitivity in this regard, but for the most part it impatiently turns a blind eye.

Regarding (2), anyone looking to apply the standards of analytic philosophy to de Mohrenschildt's manuscript in the hope of finding unambiguous "truth" is sure to come away with the impression that the author, even if he *is* sane, is at best absent-minded, more probably concealing some larger truth through digression and a focus on trivialities and possibly just dissembling *ad nauseam*. The problem here is that de Mohrenschildt's mind was continental, not Anglo-American, a difference he himself points out on more than one occasion within the manuscript. He did not interpret the world, and what counted as "truth" for that matter, through the sort of interpretive prisms Anglo-Americans customarily use. His mode of argumentation is less formal, less deductive, and more narrative, more inductive. An example that comes to mind here would be the French historian Fernand Braudel.[51] The whole, the *longue durée*, far exceeds any of the single parts that, taken singly, do not appear to amount to much and sometimes do not even appear to signify much of anything at all.[52] Another example worth citing is the memoir of French UN official Jean Richardot, *Journeys for a Better World*.[53] Living in Haiti during roughly the same time as de Mohrenschildt, Richardot exemplifies the perspective that the professional and personal parts of one's life were intertwined and inseparable. Thus he is as comfortable elaborating on his admiration of Haiti's gingerbread architecture and the beauty of the country's Caribbean sunsets as he is describing the savage and often irrational violence of Duvalier's dictatorship.

Regarding (3), it is simply a mistake to apply, as so much of the Kennedy assassination literature appears to do, present-day sensibilities to someone who grew up in the turmoil of World War I, the Russian Revolution and Russian Civil War, and postwar Poland. The de Mohrenschildt family lost nearly everything to the Bolshevik regime. The precariousness and uncertainty of life in the Old World at this time is scarcely comprehensible to anyone living in today's developed world. When he left Poland to study in Belgium in 1931, Europe was awash in political instability and ideological extremism. By the time de Mohrenschildt departed Belgium for America at the age of twenty-seven the pattern for the rest of his life was already laid: profound suspicion of authority, ambivalent cynicism toward any ideology or religion, and at-all-costs survival in the midst of seas of chaos. Judged externally his personal and professional conduct often suggested a life without any plan, living each day as if it were possibly his last. This would be an exaggeration, of course, but it does grasp an essential quality common to the refugee mind.[54] Trust largely extended to those de Mohrenschildt could look in the eye and work with one-on-one. Everyone else, with trust unverifiable, could be treated as largely disposable. Respect was shown with a handshake, disrespect with its refusal.[55] His professional conduct is amply discussed in the manuscript's annotations, but by way of summation, in addition to his very considerable charm de Mohrenschildt wasn't unwilling to raise his voice, to use intimidation, and both threaten and use legal action to get what he wanted. Regarding his personal life, though it is largely concealed in the present manuscript, written by a man well over sixty and on the cusp of retirement, evidence suggests that right up until his fifties de Mohrenschildt had the sexual appetite of a satyr and his conduct toward women, including his first three wives, was at times abysmal.[56] To judge these behaviors as an indication of an amoral, sinister human being without redeeming qualities while, for example, viewing President Kennedy's many sexual escapades and ongoing drug use, or Robert Kennedy's infidelity and almost breathtaking Machiavellian ruthlessness, as mere foibles—is the worst sort of presentism, even when it isn't simply being hypocritical.

What is the manuscript *really* about then? When one looks at the material with sufficient care and patience, I would argue, the following four conclusions emerge.

First, it appears as if de Mohrenschildt was attempting to re-create or reenact the testimony he had provided to the Warren Commission in 1964. More than half the material—what is organized here as Chapters 1, 2, 3, and 4—covers largely the same ground as de Mohrenschildt's two-day testimony, particularly the second day. This material is reproduced in Appendix B. I have pointed out examples in the notes and the reader is invited to discover additional parallels. The narrative in the manuscript is, of course, somewhat revised and amplified. De Mohrenschildt draws additional material and details from the testimony of his wife, Jeanne, and daughter Alexandra, and his enduring friend Sam Ballen, but it is clear that he also incorporates snippets from many of the other members of the Dallas–Fort Worth White Russian community whose testimony he claimed saddened him, such as George Bouhe, Igor and Natasha Voshinin, Max Clark, Paul Raigorodsky, and, yes, Marina Oswald. He even tips his hand concerning this strategy within the manuscript itself:

> Reading all of this dirty laundry being aired in public I even had the perverse idea of writing a short book, assembling all these opinions and giving the book the title *I Arranged Kennedy's Assassination*.

Stylistically the approach of the manuscript that was completed in the summer of 1976 is, I would argue, precisely this hypothetical book that de Mohrenschildt mentions in jest. The manuscript is a series of vignettes that blend and merge de Mohrenschildt's thoughts—much like one of the watercolor paintings he was known for—with all these other testimonies into a narrative arc.

Second, and following from the first conclusion, the text is most definitely *not* meant to be a joke and is *not* a confession. It is a "retelling" of the Warren Commission testimony he came to regret more intensely with each passing year. In April 1964 the entire Haitian venture, a project years in the making, was at stake. Confident the whole matter of Oswald and the assassination would soon be forgotten and behind him, de Mohrenschildt for the most part was all too willing as we now say to throw Oswald under the bus. Twelve years later, with his days as a high-profile wheeler-dealer well behind him, he wanted to provide a more realistic portrait. The conscious goal of the manuscript is to humanize Oswald, its unconscious goal to exorcise the despair that de Mohrenschildt felt was threatening to consume him. With regard to former, the text succeeds remarkably well. We read here an Oswald who lives and breathes, who possesses surprising nuance and is not the petrified caricature that over the last half century has assumed the status of a cultural cliché. Leaving aside the question of the accuracy of every last detail, it is a compelling alternative portrait. With regard to the latter, unconscious goal, time would demonstrate that writing the manuscript did little to comfort its author, who would outlive its completion by just a few months.

Even some fourteen years after first meeting Oswald, de Mohrenschildt was hesitant to acknowledge the warning signs that were present to the effect that his young friend was capable of committing murder. He sees the symptoms, but diagnosis eludes him; for the most part Lee's background, personality, marriage, and politics appear to him as individual pieces to completely different puzzles. In the 1960s and 1970s the motives of a Lee Harvey Oswald could only be visualized through the funhouse mirrors of Cold War paranoia. De Mohrenschildt himself laments how these cookie-cutter cutouts—"Communist, traitor, misfit, insane killer"—had transformed Oswald the man into a dark, irrational, and incomprehensible menace of near-demonic proportions, but he could not articulate an alternative. In recent decades we have come to know a great deal more about how combinations of crushing poverty, preexisting mental health issues, marital and family stress, and/or social isolation can combine to trigger murderous outbursts, especially in young men. In today's world Lee Harvey Oswalds are depressingly common. In the last decade alone one can cite as examples the homicidal rampages of Seung-Hui Cho at Virginia Tech (thirty-two dead, seventeen wounded), James Eagan Holmes in Aurora, Colorado (twelve dead, seventy injured), or Adam Lanza at Sandy Hook Elementary School in Newtown, Connecticut (twenty-six dead). Looking back now over a half century, with the Cold War long since tossed into the dustbin of history, we are left with a young man whose wife had just given birth to a second baby, who had a history of job insecurity and terminations, and whose unemployment insurance had previously run out in a time before food stamps, Medicaid, or a host of other social services for the poor. On top of which he was a self-professed Marxist and anti-segregationist living in Dallas, Texas— arguably the beating heart of ultra-conservative America.[57] Had it not been for a presidential motorcade passing through town he probably would have wound up being just another "going postal" incident that would have been fortunate to receive more than thirty seconds on local television news.

Third, while de Mohrenschildt reserves judgment with regard to who was ultimately responsibility for events in Dallas—whether Oswald alone, a conspiracy, or Oswald as part of a conspiracy—he emphasizes the Bay of Pigs as a *starting point* for understanding the Kennedy assassination.[58] In 1976 there was far less primary source material available to a professor teaching at a small private college in the middle of Texas. Even the most studious and dedicated writers of the era faced significant hurdles accessing primary documents, many of which remained unknown and/or classified. To the ends of their lives George and Jeanne rejected the idea of Oswald being Kennedy's assassin. Knowing Oswald as they did, as someone with no animosity toward the president, they could not envision a valid motive that would place him and his war-surplus Italian rifle[59] in a sixth-floor window of the Texas School Book Depository. Without a motive to kill Kennedy, they reasoned, Lee could not have pulled the trigger on November 22, 1963. Having exhausted the possibility of explaining a logical motive, the de Mohrenschildts had reached an impasse. Initially, they drew on their memories to speculate that Oswald had simply snapped, that something they knew all too well—namely, Marina's nagging and materialism—had pushed him over the edge. All they got for their efforts to express this hypothesis in their disjointed English was skepticism and derision, soon thereafter to be lampooned as the dimwitted proponents of the "washing machine theory" of the assassination. Eventually, like so many others before them, they too drifted toward explanations based in conspiracy. Influenced by foreign periodicals such as the left-wing *L'Express*, published in Paris, they had almost from the beginning spoken of a possible conspiracy.[60] Originally, it was something akin to a joke, more of the outrageously incorrect antics of the anarchic Jeanne and jester George. But over time it was no laughing matter, and their assertions grew in seriousness. Once *that* happened the assassination conspiracy vultures were sure to circle over their heads without pause, looking for a meal. The manuscript, in its halting prose, criticizes these "scavengers from a poor man's death"—little did its author realize that over the decades his own life, and death, would become similar carrion.[61]

Fourth, the manuscript provides, though largely unconsciously, an alternative explanation that breaks the impasse of Oswald's motive. The text suggests on multiple occasions that Oswald's identity—never secure, always in flux—was exceedingly fragile. When he did not perceive himself as threatened, as he apparently did with the de Mohrenschildts and especially George, Oswald was almost remarkably ordinary, and familiar: a young man looking to understand the most important social and political problems of the time, searching to find a suitable occupation, a father who had perhaps married unwisely but who still loved his children. The manuscript at the same time clearly identifies those for whom Oswald reserved his wrath when his fragile identity *did* perceive a threat: those who presented a challenge to his masculine authority (Marina, FBI agent Hosty); those who represented an ideological danger to his idiosyncratic brand of Marxism (General Walker, former vice president Nixon); and those who represented insult or disrespect to his phantasmagorical self-constructed life narrative (Governor Connally, the Dallas–Fort Worth White Russians). President Kennedy, the manuscript emphasizes, was not threatening in *any* of these ways. With the answer to his impasse staring up at him from the text, de Mohrenschildt cannot bring himself to accept it:

> Only some more logical and cynical writers mentioned the fact that there was no reason whatsoever in Lee's action; but they approve the thesis that Lee was aiming at Governor Connelly [*sic*], whom he had reasons to dislike, but being a usual flop and f--- up, he killed Kennedy instead and only wounded Connelly [*sic*].

The thesis is too cold, too clinical, and too relentlessly cynical: the very sort of Anglo-American reasoning the mind of an Old World European such as de Mohrenschildt would have trouble fathoming, much less accepting. Unfortunately it may also be the most plausible answer.[62] If Oswald *was* trying to kill anyone on November 22, 1963, it was most likely John Connally, not President Kennedy.[63] He was at best a mediocre shot using an inferior weapon, one he had to rapidly assemble and whose scope there wasn't time to properly sight. Only the fact that the vehicle was moving so slowly, in almost a straight line away from him, and innumerable, inexcusable security gaffes allowed the unthinkable to happen. From there, the many wheels of local, state, and federal bureaucracy went into full motion, largely to cover their own arrogance and careless ineptitude—and even *that* was a botched rush to judgment.[64]

This, I would think, is the answer de Mohrenschildt's manuscript was pointing toward though he himself was unwilling to concede it, out of friendship. Now whether or not that answer is *correct* is something readers will have to decide for themselves. From the beginning there have been plenty of "disagreeable fools and dangerous question marks" surrounding November 22, 1963.[65] Bertrand Russell's "Sixteen Questions on the Assassination" left wide swaths of the official narrative in tatters, and it was merely one of the opening salvos.[66] Fifty years later the findings of the Warren Commission are still the subject of intense criticism. But were its findings part of a conspiracy? De Mohrenschildt himself didn't think so.[67] What one sees in the aftermath of Kennedy's death are not the immoral machinations of a grand and sinister alliance trying to, as de Mohrenschildt puts it, "promote a deliberate lie." What one sees instead are, arguably, the machinations of an amoral superpower trying to conceal from its own people that alliances with organized crime, betrayal and murder of other heads of state, and the destruction of foreign governments, including democratically elected ones, regardless of the cost and the naked brutality involved had, by the early 1960s, become a matter of everyday policy and organizational routine. Death was the high cost of maintaining American global hegemony and the affluent style of living its citizens enjoyed. George de Mohrenschildt's manuscript, with its direct discussion of the financial costs of Vietnam and the political costs of Watergate, along with its indirect references and allusions to then-in-progress investigations—such as the Church Committee, which was in the process of revealing the cold-blooded and murderous duplicity of agencies such as the FBI and the CIA—contains an embryonic understanding of this. Today, after two even more expensive wars in Afghanistan and Iraq, CIA assassination drone strikes in several countries, "enhanced interrogation," the Patriot Act, Guantanamo Bay, Plan Columbia, NSA "data mining" of phone records, etc., etc., we know better. The empire wears no clothes.

Finally, this manuscript is the closing act in a personal tragedy. If there is a "patsy" in the text it is none other than George de Mohrenschildt himself. In today's world the distance between the mainland United States and Haiti would have been no obstacle to a ravenous media—the aftermath of a presidential assassination would have seen journalists of every ilk descending on Port-au-Prince in a matter of hours, exposing and devouring in perhaps a few weeks every detail of the de Mohrenschildts' lives and every statement they had ever made. If George and Jeanne had been so foolish to suggest the FBI was behind Kennedy's murder, as they apparently did at an embassy function in Haiti shortly after the assassination, it would have wound up on someone's Twitter account five minutes later. George would have quickly "lawyered up," as we now say, and would never have been so foolish as to testify before the Warren Commission without legal counsel. And he would have found an agent and a publisher for this manuscript, of that I am sure. He would have signed a contract with a major commercial press, received a hefty advance, gone on a book tour, given lectures on CSPAN and Book TV, made guest appearances on PBS and BBC America, and basked in the attention he so clearly enjoyed. Nero and Poppaea, the de Mohrenschildts' Manchester Terriers, would probably have had their own Facebook account, with legions of fans following their every doing. Maybe the Oswald "hunter of fascists" photo winds up in an auction house, or even on eBay. The media, whose attention span grows ever shorter, would have become satiated and moved on, leaving the now-wealthy de Mohrenschildts free to build the house in northern California they had once hoped and planned to make their permanent home.

Sadly, the pace of life in the 1960s and 1970s was far, far slower than it is today. The attention the de Mohrenschildts received after Kennedy's assassination was like a continuous background murmur, rising and falling and rising again in volume but never entirely granting them complete silence. George had persecution issues dating back to at least the late 1950s. Jeanne had serious issues of her own and a confrontational personality that was probably the last thing her husband needed in the wake of Kennedy's assassination. Their behavior in Haiti after the assassination was imprudent in the extreme. Everyone who knew de Mohrenschildt in the early 1960s described his son's death in 1960 from cystic fibrosis as psychologically devastating. The sense of loss after his daughter succumbing to the same disease in 1973, scarcely ever mentioned in the Kennedy assassination literature, can only have been equally strong.[68] We can see indications her death was the catalyst for what would transpire during the final six months of his life. The remorse and despair slowly became cognitive static, the static grew and expanded until, in 1977, it blocked the voice of reason; hypothesis and then sheer fantasy began to blend and merge with memories, fact, and reality. And even at *this* late stage the limitations of de Mohrenschildt's spoken English were being misunderstood, misinterpreted, and, in the case of Willem Oltmans and others, exploited. By March 29, 1977, the pressure, real and imagined, had become too much. "George told me he was tired of being hounded by the press on the Kennedy matter and was thinking of suicide," Sam Ballen recalled in the late 1990s. "We spoke about depression as a defined illness. I convinced him to come to Santa Fe where we would hike the

Sangres, and a date was set. When he did not show up, I was prepared for the worst. The similarity to Hemingway's final days was inescapable."[69] One is reminded of Tolstoy's *Memoirs of a Madman*: "I am running away from something dreadful and cannot escape it. I am always with myself, and it is I who am my tormentor." George de Mohrenschildt had defiantly sown the wind his entire life; while he could not ever fully accept it, in Lee Harvey Oswald he had reaped the whirlwind.

PREFACE

❦

"I'm Just a Patsy!"

These words,[1] among the last uttered in public by my friend Lee Harvey Oswald,[2] still echo in my memory and remind me of the terrible injustice that would have us believe he was the "lone assassin" responsible for killing President John F. Kennedy in November of 1963. That fateful month was a fairly uneventful one in Haiti, where I worked with my young geologist assistant Alston Boyd[3] in an office located on Boulevard Harry Truman[4] in the heart of Port-au-Prince. The office occupied a large room within a Quonset building[5] belonging to the Haitian government, and we were kept there virtually incommunicado due to the presence of government maps and other "strategic information."[6] The tropical heat in Haiti dictated we begin our chores early in the morning and finish by two in the afternoon.

Alston and I drove to my beautiful house, the Villa Valbrune, overlooking Port-au-Prince in the area called the Lyle Estates,[7] located just a block away from the presidential retreat.[8] Like any self-respecting Haitian we ate a meal and took a siesta, then later in the afternoon changed and in the company of my wife Jeanne departed for a reception being held at the Lebanese Embassy.[9] The usually animated streets were eerily deserted. "I feel trouble in the air," Jeanne said. The air was balmy and still, the soldiers and Tontons Macoutes,[10] or TMs as we used to call them, were absent. We could not hear any shots.[11] Arriving at our destination we greeted the Lebanese ambassador and joined the crowd. George Morel,[12] head of Pan American Airways in Haiti, walked directly up to us. "Didn't you know the President was killed?" he said in a strained voice. At first we thought he was speaking of the President of Haiti, Docteur François Duvalier, who was my nominal boss.[13] Noting our still blank expressions Morel explained, "President Kennedy was assassinated today." My heart hoped it hadn't happened in Texas and especially in our hometown of Dallas, but as Morel summarized what had transpired it became clear that it had indeed been in Dallas.

We left the embassy some time later, ourselves gloomy, but those around us did not seem to be too badly concerned with President Kennedy's fate. As we drove away I said angrily, "If Kennedy had had his Tontons Macoutes around, this would not have happened." It was the first but not the last time I would be critical of the services supposedly employed to protect the President of the United States. We traveled to the American Embassy, which was located near the seashore not far from my own office.[14] The doors were wide open, and two marines stood opposite a book of condolences where American residents could sign their names as a gesture of reverence to the dead head of state. Approaching, we found the page blank; we were the first to sign it. We did not stay long, instead driving to the house of an old friend of mine, Valentin "Teddy" Blaque,[15] who was an attaché at the American Embassy.[16] His house was similar to ours, only more opulent with a large terrace overlooking the sparkling waters of Port-au-Prince Bay.[17] The beautiful view belied the somber atmosphere. Several mutual friends were standing around, each looking at the other with stunned expressions that seemed to reflect my own feelings: "Why him? Why Kennedy?"

"For the first time we had a president who was young and energetic. And he was trying to solve the problems of the world," Jeanne said sadly. "And he had to go . . ."

"And in *Dallas*," I mused. Dallas was a conservative and somewhat provincial city, but successful and proud.[18] We knew the mayor, the charming Earle Cabell,[19] and many of the city fathers. Why there? "Who did it?" I asked Teddy.

"I just listened to the radio and a suspect was arrested already," he replied.

An image flashed before my eyes, and I remembered Lee and his rifle with the telescopic site. Before I knew it the words had escaped my lips, "Could it be Lee?" No, it couldn't be. Not Lee. It was impossible. But that was the name Teddy would say: Lee Harvey Oswald. And driving back home, in stunned silence, we thought of Lee and the predicament he must now be in.

We thought of Lee and the predicament he must now be in.
Guards escorting Lee Harvey Oswald after his arrest. © CORBIS

Later, my wife and I made our deposition at the American Embassy.[20] We did know the man who had been officially identified as the main suspect. We were also aware he owned a rifle. We would be happy to testify what we knew about him and about our relationship with him and his wife, Marina Oswald.[21] But neither of us believed he was the assassin. And it was then that strange events began to transpire.[22] A letter was sent by someone in Washington to the officials of the Haitian government urging them to drop me from the payroll and exile me as quickly as possible.[23] Fortunately the existence of the letter became known to me, and thanks to good friends nothing happened. Later, little by little, my wife and I were ostracized by American Ambassador Timmons,[24] followed by the American businessmen and government employees we had previously been on very good terms with and, finally, we learned that all our friends and even acquaintances in the United States were being investigated.

Then an FBI agent named Mr. W. James Wood appeared, wearing a gray flannel suit and sporting bright white teeth, trying to scare us off.[25] Eventually in February 1964 we were officially invited to Washington, DC, to help the Warren Commission in its investigation.[26] Although we felt we could contribute little, we went to testify. Despite assurances our long depositions were to remain confidential all three hundred pages, most of it irrelevant conversation, was printed and distributed.[27] The text provided by myself and my wife exceeded the depositions of Marina and Lee's mother, Marguerite,[28] put together. Why? There are two possible explanations. The first was simply to waste the taxpayer's money with boring and useless details, a cornucopia of gossipy, irrelevant stuff related to our private lives, half of which had nothing at all to do with our relationship with Lee. The second was to distract the attention of the American people away from those truly involved in the assassination of President Kennedy. Whatever the explanation, the story was just beginning.[29] And all this occurred simply because my wife and I liked Lee and tried to defend him, and because Lee had said "I liked and admired George de Mohrenschildt."[30]

ONE

·❀·

First Conversations with Lee

Early in the summer of 1962 rumors began to spread among the Russian-speaking people of Dallas and Fort Worth of an unusual couple—the Oswalds. The husband was supposedly a former American marine[1] who had defected to the Soviet Union and lived in Minsk, the city where I had spent my childhood.[2] He had returned to the United States, now married to a Russian wife. Although he supposedly had a reputation for being an unfriendly and eccentric character, I was curious to meet both of them and discover what their life in Minsk had been like.

Meeting Lee and His Wife

George Bouhe,[3] an elderly refugee considered the "father superior" of all Russians in the Dallas–Fort Worth area, gave me the Oswalds' address, and one September[4] afternoon a friend of mine, retired air force colonel Lawrence Orlov,[5] and myself drove from Dallas to Fort Worth. Fort Worth is a little more than thirty miles west of Dallas. Texas does have some lovely open spaces, but in the summer of 1962 the stretch of road separating the two cities was unpleasant and polluted, frequently smelling of sewage. After some searching we found the address, which turned out to be a shack on Mercedes Street[6] in a semi-industrial, slummy area near a Montgomery Ward.[7]

I knocked on the door and was met by a clean if tawdry young woman, who turned out to be Marina Oswald. Introducing myself and the colonel I explained that I had obtained their address from George Bouhe. Marina invited us inside and offered us some sherry, saying that Lee would soon be over. She spoke beautiful, melodious Russian, quite different from the bastardized version, full of Anglicized intonations and words, used by those of us who had lived in America for many years. We made small talk for a few minutes, sharing a few jokes; she had a pretty good sense of humor, yet beneath her charm I found the opinions she expressed pedestrian, even trite. We learned the couple had a baby daughter, named June.[8]

It was then that Lee Harvey Oswald appeared and though I did not realize it at the time, my life would henceforth be forever intertwined with his. He wore overalls and clean workingman's shoes. His job I would later learn was at the Leslie Welding Company.[9] Yet even in this modest attire there was something extraordinary about him, and only someone who had never met Lee could have called him insignificant. I remember thinking, "There is something outstanding about this man." Although he was average in appearance, medium sized with no distinguishing features save for attractive gray eyes,[10] he showed in conversation both concentration and thoughtfulness. One could detect immediately a very sincere and forward man, one who had the courage of his convictions and who did not hesitate to express them. I was glad to meet someone such as him, as he reminded me of my youth in Europe where, as students, we discussed world affairs and our own ideas happily over beers, not caring about the time.[11]

We spoke English first, and then, somehow, we switched to Russian. Lee spoke it very well, with only a slight accent.[12] From time to time he glanced at the baby, and the tender expression he exhibited told me he loved her. Marina did not say very much.

"Doesn't your wife speak any English?" I asked Lee.

"No, and I don't want her to know English. I want her to continue speaking her own language. Russian is beautiful and I don't want to forget it," Lee explained, before adding with a deep conviction, "Russian literature is marvelous and the people I met in the Soviet Union were so warm and nice to me. I made many friends there."

"And how about the Soviet government," I asked.

"Well, that's another story. The trouble with me is I always look for an ideal which probably does not exist."

Lee glanced at Colonel Orlov. "Maybe your friend does not understand Russian. Let's speak English then. You know I was a marine and I have respect for the brass."[13] He smiled and added a few kind words in English to my friend.

"My wife speaks Russian and she would like to spend time with you, Marina, and the baby of course," I said.

"I would like to but it will depend on Lee," Marina answered.

"I am sure Lee will let you visit, and will come himself," I replied. I felt a bond of friendship was already forming between the Oswalds and myself.

After this short conversation we shook hands and left. On the drive back to Dallas the colonel indicated he thought Marina beautiful and charming, though I found her less so. "But I found the ex-marine so much more interesting," I said. I got the impression that my friend, while sympathetic to Marina, resented Lee's offhandedness, his ironic smiles and especially his ferocious spirit of independence.

First Meetings with Lee

A few days after the trip to Fort Worth I received a call from Lee.

"Marina and I will come over tonight, if you don't mind," he said.

"Maybe I could drive to Fort Worth and pick you up?" I offered.

"No, thank you, we will come by bus," he answered laconically.

At the time my wife and I lived in a pleasant area of Dallas called University Park, located a few blocks from Southern Methodist University, a conservative stronghold.[14] The Oswalds, so different from the local society we were accustomed to, stepped off the bus along with their infant daughter, and we welcomed them into our home. Jeanne liked Marina immediately and offered to help her with her English. "Yes, I have to know the language," Marina agreed. Her eyes darted about the décor of our modest home and then she added unexpectedly, "People have asked me why I like Lee, and I answer them: why did Lee like me?" Jeanne liked the humble nature of her remark and her sympathy for Marina increased.

Jeanne often participated in our discussions.[15] Let me explain her background a little and clarify why she got along so fabulously well with Lee.[16] Jeanne was a famous fashion designer before I met her and half-ruined her career with my frequent travel and adventurous deals as a petroleum consultant, not to mention our nearly year-long walking trip through Latin America.[17] Jeanne's childhood was spent in China, where her father had built a railroad—her family was well-to-do.[18] Even though she had lived a luxurious childhood, she had from the beginning preferred to give rather than to receive. Social attitudes are unpredictable and do not depend on your parents or on your environment. She remembered the Chinese as humble and kind people, dismally poor, who hated to fight and rather insulted each other and stamped their feet. Even in huge families, violence was seldom seen. Far-Eastern subjects, both past and present, were interesting to Lee, who enjoyed discussing them with my wife. She told him of the Japanese invasion, formation of the puppet state of Mǎnzhōuguó[19] and the ensuing cruelties,[20] and, finally, of her subsequent flight from the Japanese to the United States. Lee contrasted her experiences of militaristic Japan with the present Japanese democracy,[21] which he knew so well.

In the meantime Lee and I sat on a comfortable sofa and talked all evening. Now I want to tell you something which may seem foolish to anyone who isn't a dog lover.[22] At the time we had two lovely black Manchester Terriers, Nero and his faithful wife Poppaea. Nero had accompanied us on our long trip over the mountains of Mexico and Central America and saved our lives on several occasions; I can scarcely exaggerate how much intuition Nero developed during our travels and how easily he recognized friends from enemies. Poppaea was bought for him upon our return to the United States. Many of our friends and even our own children complained to us that our dogs were either unfriendly or totally indifferent to them. Well, during that first evening with the Oswalds our dogs did not express any interest in Marina or in baby June, but they *were* fascinated by Lee. Nero especially showed his complete confidence and affection for him. He snuggled up to Lee and looked at him with affection, something he seldom did with anyone, not even to our close friends. He sensed that Lee was an utterly sincere person and was devoid[23] of hatred. Poppaea also licked his hand in a rare display of affection.

Naturally I do not recall every last detail of our first long conversation,[24] but in general I asked questions and he answered them. Lee did not have a trace of nasal Southern drawl—his was the voice of a thinking, refined individual.[25] I never heard Lee use any profanity, in either English or in Russian. This was most unusual for a man of his background, i.e., the slums of New Orleans and Fort Worth and the United States Marine Corps. But do not conclude he was some effete weakling, as I know there is a wide-spread belief that if you do not swear, you are not a red-blooded American male. I myself am guilty of constantly cussing, but despite that the students with whom I associate happily these days at Bishop College[26] consider me OK and a good guy.

I wanted to know what had made him go to the Soviet Union. He answered by telling me of his youth in New Orleans. Since his childhood he had been keenly aware of social and racial injustice. While his classmates were busy playing such red-blooded American sports as basketball or baseball, he read voraciously. Among the books that had made a deep impression on him was Marx's *Capital*,[27] a work that, he said, he borrowed from the Loyola University Library.

"What did you like about it?" I remember asking him.

"It made clear to me the intolerable fact of the exploitation of the poor by the rich," was his reply.

"But," I said, "Lee, you must have seen it all over the world: the weak and the poor are everywhere exploited by the powerful and the rich. Listen to this: two dogs meet at the crossing point between East and West Berlin. One is running away from capitalism, the other from communism. The capitalist dog asks, 'why are you running away?' and the Communist dog answers, 'Because I can eat but I cannot bark.' The Communist dog then asks, 'why are you running away?' and the capitalist dog answers, 'If I bark I cannot eat.'"

Here I want to dispel any impression that Lee did not have a keen sense of humor.[28] He laughed at my joke and offered a few that must have been circulating during the time he was in the Soviet Union.[29]

"A Russian doctor had a parrot who was able to say 'how do you do,' 'good night,' etc. One hot evening the doctor left the parrot on the windowsill to cool off. A Russian *mujik*[30] passes by and hears the parrot's greetings. He takes his hat off and says: 'excuse me, comrade, I thought you were a bird!'"

He continued, "A strip-tease joint was opened in Moscow for the tourists. It was decorated and run just like in Paris, and lots of money was spent on this establishment. Yet it did not attract much trade. A state Economic Commission questioned the worried director. He explained: 'I did my best, hired the best decorators, and imitated a place in Paris.' 'How about the girls?' asked a member of the commission. 'No trouble with them, they are all at least for thirty years good party members.'"

"As you know," he said, "Russians grab all they can from their satellite countries. So one day at the meeting of the Communist Party in Rumania, one of the workers stood up and said: 'Comrade Secretary, may I ask you three questions?' 'Go ahead,' was the Secretary's reply. 'I want to know: what happened to our wheat, our petroleum, and our wine?' 'Well,' said the Secretary, 'It's a very complex economic question; I can't answer it immediately.' A few months later the workers are holding the same type of meeting, and another comrade raises his hand and asks: 'Comrade Secretary may I

If you want to be a revolutionary, you have to be a fool or have an inspiration.
Oswald (wearing sunglasses) in the courtyard of the Gorizont Electronics Factory,
summer of 1960. US National Archives and Records Administration (Commission
Exhibit 2625)

ask you four questions?' 'Shoot,' says the Secretary. 'I want to ask you: what
happened to our wheat, our petroleum, our wine, and also what happened
to the comrade who asked the three questions some time ago?' Silence."

We both laughed. "At least here in America we do not have to worry
about being sent to a concentration camp," I said.

"You are wrong," answered Lee seriously. "Most of the prisoners, con-
victs in American jail are political prisoners, they are victims of the system."
Writing these words more than fourteen years later, I have read similar opinions in liberal books; Lee, I realize now, was way ahead of his time.[31]

I remember concluding our first long conversation by telling Lee, "If you
want to be a revolutionary you have to be a fool or have an inspiration.
Your actions will be judged by the success and failure of your life."

Lee agreed.

Jeanne served a Russian dinner which Marina found delicious but Lee
hardly touched. He was ascetic in his habits, was indifferent to meals, and
didn't like desserts. While we enjoyed our meal baby June slept quietly in
bed, all wrapped up. Lee looked tenderly at her. That night we learned a lot

about him, for example, that he neither drank nor smoked and objected if others, especially his wife, did. Since neither my wife nor I smoked and we drank very little, he liked us and considered that we were on his side. My wife had an elevated notion of Russian hygienic practices and those of Soviet youth in particular, so she was appalled to learn the baby had received none of the usual injections given to an infant, and that Marina, whose teeth were bad,[32] would pick up the pacifier from the floor and place it in her own mouth before giving it back to the baby. "Your infected teeth have to be removed as soon as possible," she told Marina. When Marina objected that she didn't have any money and couldn't speak English, Jeanne promised to help her.

After dinner Lee and I returned to the sofa.

"I served in the Marine Corps not because I was a patriot, but because I wanted to get away from the drudgery and to see the world," he explained.

"Did you like the service?"

"Not particularly. But I had time to study, to read, and indeed we traveled a *lot*."

"You told me you lived in Japan. How did you wind up being there?"

"Just an accident of Marine Corps duty. The military duty was boring and stupid. But fortunately I moved around, began visiting places where young people meet, and I established contacts with some more progressive thinking Japanese. And it was this that led me to Russia eventually.[33] I also learned of other, Japanese, ways of the rich exploiting the poor. Semi-feudal. The industrial giants act paternalistically yet exploit the workers—proletarians. The wages in Japan were ridiculously low."

"Well, it's changing now," I said. "Say, Lee, was it in Japan that you got your discharge from the Marine Corps?"

Lee became touchy and did not like to elaborate on this subject. "I had to work to support my mother."[34]

But as we all know Lee did not go back to the United States to support his mother but went instead to the Soviet Union. He obviously used the money obtained from his discharge to make this trip. He first went to Western Europe and then drifted to the USSR via Finland, as I recall.[35] Lee's discharge had originally been honorable but was later changed to an undesirable discharge, and he hated to talk about it and considered it unfair to him.[36] This may explain his hatred of John Connally,[37] who was Secretary of the Navy at the time of the discharge.

The subject of his discharge was not a part of our conversation that night. He talked about the Soviet Union. "I got to Moscow and stayed there until the Russians had confidence in me and gave me a permit to work." He did not mention to me that he had tried to commit suicide when the Soviet authorities first refused him entry, cutting his wrists.[38]

Marina joined the conversation, adding, "Lee, you threw your passport in the face of the American consul and you said you renounced your citizenship." Lee went on talking about his impressions of Minsk because he knew of my early childhood experience with the city. He gave me a general description and then added candidly, "I was assigned to work in Minsk without any particular reason, in a television factory,[39] possibly because I had a little electronics training in the Marines."

"Tell me more about the countryside," I asked him.

"Svislach River[40] is pretty clean. We used to go by row-boats to the forest nearby to picnic on the weekends. The forests are beautiful there, huge pine trees, clean grass, full of all kinds of berries."

I remembered the Minsk cathedral and several other picturesque churches as well as the main building, police headquarters, which housed the GPU, NKVD, and MGB.[41] My father[42] had spent several months there and almost died of starvation before finally being sentenced to permanent exile in Siberia. These childhood memories and the resentment that went along with them had disappeared by the time Lee and I spoke. He gave me a perfect description of all these landmarks, still present and unchanged. There were many new factories, however, one of which had been his place of employment.

"Did you like your job?" I asked.

"The pay was sufficient, about a hundred rubles a month, average for the Soviet Union. I could live on it. My apartment and all the utilities were furnished by the factory for a nominal fee, along with my medical insurance, and so on." He went on to recount the prices for bread, produce, milk, and meat, which were reasonable, and for clothing, which were outrageously high. "Sometimes I ran short of meat, but you know I am not a big eater; it was of no importance to me."

Marina listened in and gave more precise information, especially complaining about the high cost of clothing and shoes. I could tell she was the practical one.

"You must have been somewhat privileged," I suggested, "being a foreigner."

"Butter and meat were beyond my reach," Marina said bitterly, "but you foreigners could afford those luxuries."

Lee generally did not complain about his life in the Soviet Union, but Marina quite frequently did. I do not know how sincere she was. She considered me a capitalist and I sensed her complaints were an effort to please me. She was ready to continue talking more but since she was from Leningrad,[43] a town I was not familiar with, I interrupted her to ask, "But how did the other workers, the Russians, live in Minsk?"

"Not too well," Lee replied. "Usually one roof for a couple, community kitchens and lavatories. This led to quarrels, gossip, and jealousy; a rather dismal situation. But what does it matter if everyone is in the same boat, if everyone suffers? No rich exploiters like here in the United States, no great contrasts between the rich and the poor."

That night as I recall Marina announced that Lee was going to be laid off from his job at the welding company.[44] It was a poor job anyway, the hours were long, the wages minimal, and the conditions unhealthy. Lee never complained, rather that duty was left to Marina, who was constantly dissatisfied. While Lee's mind was of a stoical, philosophical type, the air of American prosperity bothered Marina. She was envious of other people's wealth and well-being. I suppose this is why Lee got along so well with the other Russians he met in the Soviet Union. Russians do not mind suffering and will even go hungry yet be happy to spend entire nights talking and speculating on esoteric matters.

Why Lee and I Disliked the FBI

Recently, it was established that the FBI[45] had concealed and destroyed a letter from Lee Harvey Oswald written to their Dallas office before the assassination.[46] I do not think we have an exact text of this letter, but the newspapers reported Lee was extremely angry at the way the FBI kept annoying him and his wife and therefore were making his normal pursuit of life impossible.[47] This explains, naturally, why in our conversations Lee had such a dim view of this "great" institution and its leader, J. Edgar Hoover.[48] I saw Hoover once, in La Jolla, California.[49] I remember that Jeanne and I were there to visit a partner of mine, Colonel Edward J. Walz, who had a ranch nearby and also made some investments in the oil ventures.[50] In the evening, having dinner at one of the best motels, facing the sea, I recognized Mr. Hoover, sitting together with some of our oil magnates and behaving in such an obsequious and distasteful manner, as if he were a servant of these very wealthy people.[51] And he looked like a pompous waiter or, possibly, head waiter. I knew some of the people sitting with him and a meeting could have been very simply arranged, and thus a lot of difficulties would have

I saw Hoover once, in La Jolla, California.
J. Edgar Hoover, Director of the FBI, September 28, 1961. Library of Congress

been avoided for both of us in the future. But something restrained me from approaching the group, and I did not do it.

Jeanne did not have any special reason to like or dislike the man, but I had a previous experience with the FBI which was comically ridiculous and could have ended badly for me. Because of it I, too, have a personal grudge against the FBI. My early scrape with them dates from June of 1941, soon after my arrival in the United States.[52] At that time I was very young, had some money which I brought from Europe, had made a little more in this country, and now I found myself about to be drafted into the US Army. But, instead, the doctors revealed that I had very high blood pressure and declared me unfit for service.[53] I still suffer from this high blood pressure, so really I owe my life to the good American doctors who had discovered it so early. Now I can keep it under control.

Frankly, I was not in a very militaristic mood at the time. The Germans had saved my father from the Russians.[54] We de Mohrenschildts are of so-called Baltic descent, which means a mixture of people of Scandinavian,

German, French, and other lineages, descendants of the knights who had conquered Estonia, Latvia, Finland, and even parts of Russia. Now, many Balts were German oriented, and I had relatives of this type, but personally I was French-oriented.[55] I also had spent two painful years in the Polish Military Academy and later spent time "maneuvering" on horse-back around the Soviet border, a rather dangerous occupation. So I found myself about to be drafted in the United States Army and did not feel very enthusiastic at the prospect of starting in boot-camp all over again.

At that time, I was not yet an American citizen but a resident of New York and madly in love with a young Mexican widow whom we shall call Señora L.[56] After meeting her in New York, I asked a Brazilian friend[57] who knew Señora L., "I am madly in love with her, shall I marry her?"

"If you marry her, you will be unhappy. If you do not marry her, you will be unhappy also," answered my friend smilingly.

Of course, he was absolutely right. But still we were madly in love with each other. She had been brought up in Europe and lived there most of her life, thus she had a lack of knowledge of her own country. And so, she invited me to drive with her across the United States to Mexico, which she would explore with me. She spoke very little English, and I very little Spanish, so we communicated in French, which probably made us most suspicious to the FBI! Or maybe someone denounced us. We both had enemies. Anyway, our delightful trip in a new convertible Chrysler down the Eastern seaboard, then along the Gulf of Mexico, was rudely interrupted. This happened on June 3 near Corpus Christi, Texas, where we had rented an apartment in the Nueces Hotel using fictitious names.[58] We left the hotel at Aransas Pass early to go to the beach at Corpus Christi and spent a delightful day there.[59] I like to paint watercolor landscapes with beautiful female bodies in the foreground, and I made several sketches.

Driving back from the beach, we were stopped on a deserted road by a bunch of people who we plainly thought were American gangsters. We had little money with us,[60] and the car was insured in case it was stolen, so we stopped without too much fright. The characters identified themselves: they were FBI agents who had taken us for German spies observing United States coastal fortifications.

When I was telling the story to Lee, he could not stop laughing. "This is so typical of the FBI. Taking you into custody, at that time you were a reserve officer in an Allied Army, driving along the coast with a beautiful Mexican woman, talking French to her, and painting," he guffawed. "You were a typical 'German' spy."

But, dear reader, do not laugh at the FBI's ingenuity. After having verified our papers and listened to angry Señora L. shrieking in Spanish, they followed us back to the hotel and inspected our luggage. Only then did the agents realize they had made a foolish mistake. I even understood that some of them had followed us all the way from New York (once again at great expense to the American taxpayer), so the mistake was a very cold one. Lacking any evidence I was a German spy, they then accused me of an infraction of the old Mann Act.[61] The Mann Act prohibits, still does, crossing the border from one state to another with a woman who is not your wife for the purpose of committing a licentious act.

Of that we certainly *were* guilty; we had passed through dozens of states on the way to Mexico and committed dozens, maybe hundreds, of licentious acts. However, we were not put in jail. We just had to sign some papers declaring that we were not married. After all that we were finally allowed to proceed to the Mexican border. The two of us felt as if someone dirty put their filthy hands in our very personal affairs. After our return Señora L. registered a strong complaint with the Mexican ambassador in Washington and much later received apologies for the actions of the FBI agents.[62]

As far as I am concerned, five years later, when I was applying for United States citizenship in Denver,[63] an FBI agent came to the hearing and re-opened the case, accusing me of immorality and of a flagrant infraction of the Mann Act. I had already passed my citizenship examinations without a single mistake and was holding an important position with a group of oil companies.[64] So I had to get a lawyer to defend me. My lawyer threatened the FBI agent with a personal damage suit in the amount of a million dollars, for damage done to my reputation. And so, the Mann Act was quickly forgotten, the judge laughed at the FBI story, and I was made an American Citizen. Maybe not first class, because I was naturalized, but a citizen still.

And Lee concluded, "And so you lived forever afterwards as a happy naturalized American citizen."

"You don't realize, Lee, how important it was for me to be a citizen, as I became after the war a man without a country, a 'heimatlos.'"[65]

"I guess it's better to be without a country than to live in a country like this, run by the FBI," was Lee's bitter conclusion.

I guess in these days of open immorality and pornography staring at you from magazine racks and bookstore shelves, nobody would be accused of breaking such an antiquated law as the Mann Act. It's probably buried for good. Even so, I still would like to find out someday what kind of a puritanical, hypocritical, son of a bitch this Mann was.

Further Conversations with Lee, 1962

The next time the Oswalds came to visit us we began speaking of Minsk again. I reminisced that when I was five years old my father used to take me to the forest, and I helped him as best as a child can to cut down large pine trees. It was a tough job and my father, who had never been a physically able man, constantly hurt himself. Once he jammed his finger so badly that the bone broke and the finger remained useless for the rest of his life. Surprisingly, I grew adept at swinging an ax and was a capable tree-cutter.

"Is that lovely forest north of town still in existence?" I asked. Lee confirmed that it was.

"Yes, I used to go there frequently, by bus, with my fellow workers. We took food along and spent the whole day talking freely. I explained the United States to them, and they informed me about life in Russia."

I promised Lee I'd give him introductions to a few influential people because I wanted him and his family to move away from the gruesome part of Fort Worth they were currently living in. It was my hope the other members of the Russian community would help him also, and I told him so.

"Thanks a lot, I can take care of myself, I don't want those creeps. I shall find something," he answered gruffly. This was an example of Lee's independent nature. He refused help, even objected to it when it was offered. Rather than be indebted to someone, he preferred to suffer on his own. While Marina was usually a lot of fun, and laughed easily, Lee was usually serious and did not think life a laughing matter. But if he happened to be in a good mood, he was an excellent companion, quite capable of laughing at your jokes and remembering political jokes, which he told well.

"Do you know the one about an America tourist carrying a small transistor radio in Moscow?" he asked me.

"No, I don't know the story."

"Well, the Muscovite stopped the American and said: 'We make them much better than you do. What is it?'"

We both laughed. I then offered a joke of my own.

"What is the difference between capitalism and socialism?" He did not know. "Capitalism makes social mistakes and socialism makes capital mistakes."[66]

Lee countered with, "A Russian Commissar who has died is asked where he would like to go: to a capitalist hell or a Communist hell. The Commissar answers, 'I would like to go to the capitalist hell, I am so tired of a Communist hell.'"[67]

I then told Lee a few jokes about President Kennedy.

"President Kennedy tells a group of businessmen: 'The economic situation is so good that, if I weren't your president, I would invest in the stock market right now!' And the businessmen answer him in unison: 'So would we if you were not our president.'"

We both laughed. I told another joke.

"Kennedy had a terrible nightmare. He wakes Jackie up: 'Honey, what a terrible thing. I dreamed I was spending my own money, not the government's!'"

Again we laughed but without resentment. We both liked President Kennedy. I told one more joke.

"President Kennedy runs to his mother in the middle of the night. 'Mama, Mama, help! Bobby is trying to run *my* country.'"

Lee did find a job to replace the one at the welding factory. It was at Taggart's Reproduction Company, enlarging photos, posters, and maps.[68] He found it through the Texas Employment Agency without help from anyone. It was a good job for him as he had been interested in photography for a long time. I guessed his interest went back as far as his time in the Marine Corps. He brought a good camera from the Soviet Union and took excellent pictures with it.[69] Later he would show me some very impressive enlargements he had made himself. They were in black and white as he did not have the advanced knowledge needed to develop and enlarge color photographs. The job did not pay well, however, and he began to trust me more, to the point where he accepted an introduction to a successful businessman-banker, Sam Ballen.[70] Ballen owned, among many companies, a large reproduction outfit for maps, electronic logs, and records. Unfortunately, the meeting did not go well and there was a mutual dislike.[71] To my friend, Lee was a radical and a maverick, and to Lee, my friend Sam was an ordinary, bourgeois man with no redeeming features.

Our first evenings with the Oswalds were spent in conversation and discussions, and we got to know each other very well. Before Lee got his new job, I asked my daughter Alex and my son-in-law Gary Taylor to help the Oswalds move to Dallas.[72] The Taylors went to visit the Oswalds in Fort Worth and immediately offered Marina and the baby the opportunity to stay with them. Whatever furniture they had could be stored in their garage. Marina accepted their generous offer. The Russian colony collected a small amount of money for Marina and the care of the baby June. Lee did not know about it, he would not have accepted any charity, so it was done secretly. Lee stayed for a short time in the apartment in Fort Worth and then moved into a small room at the YMCA in Dallas, close to his job. During Marina's stay at my daughter's place my wife Jeanne drove her to Baylor Hospital,[73] where they removed her decayed teeth. But this short separation did not prevent Lee from coming to visit us himself, alone.

At the time my wife and I knew Lee the thought that he might one day be a famous/infamous figure in history was the furthest thing from our minds. His visits at this time were very frequent. Sometimes he would stay for only a short time, while other times he would remain for the entire evening. A few of our half-serious, half-joking conversations remain in my memory.

"You are an extremely sincere person Lee," I told him during one of his visits. "You do not lie, even to yourself.[74] Most of the people I know are the opposite of you. They put up a front, they mislead, they deceive and lie, even when thinking."

"I guess it's dangerous to be that way. I know I make a lot of enemies," he acknowledged. "But what the hell. My position is that I am afraid of a very few things in life. I am not cautious." He smiled. "I am not a turkey who lives only to become fat." And he showed me his emaciated belly. He was becoming very thin.

"Lee, your way of life is so un-American, it scares me to think of what may become of you."

"It is true," he admitted, "I am probably committing a sin in not being interested in possessions or money. When a rich man dies, he is like a prisoner, his possessions chains. I will die free, death will be easy for me."

"Stop talking about death, you are only twenty-two," I told him. "Regarding your attitude towards money and possessions I couldn't agree more with you. You would rather do something remarkable than drive a Cadillac. I am the same way."[75]

"Life for me," continued Lee, "is like a hungry crocodile. I'd better defend myself. I have to defend myself against the stupidity of this world. It is enormous! Life must be the work of a perfect idiot. Or maybe the stupidity, like breaking of the atom, is self-perpetuating?"

Not too bad for a twenty-two-year-old American proletarian and high school dropout, I thought.

"Lee, you have an original mind."

"Thank you," he said. "I do not often hear compliments. But let me tell you another reason why I despise the money-loving middle class. Such people are simply stupid, not serious—they attract crooks and adventurers. And so you hear how often they are sheared of their wool, like sheep, by various financial schemers."

"Diderot,"[76] I said, thinks very much like you. "You have nothing—I have very little now, so a real friendship is possible between us. We are sincere with each other."

Lee agreed.

"Another thing Diderot said," I continued, "was that he was very happy being poor and living in a shack. When he achieved opulence and found a nice apartment in Paris, he knew he was going to die."[77]

"The philosophers talk, but you did it," Lee said, sounding envious. "This trip of yours through Latin America: what freedom! Traveling on foot over 3,600 miles of tough trails. This demanded a complete change in life—willingly, suddenly, and for this you needed an extraordinary moral audacity."

"This time it is me who wants to thank you, Lee. The trip was very satisfying to both Jeanne and me. But do not exaggerate: this was an act of desperation rather than audacity after the death of my only son."[78]

Becoming Close Friends

From time to time my wife would prepare a special Russian or French dinner for the Oswalds, always keeping in mind that both of them were undernourished. I would talk to Lee during these occasions, often late into the night. Although he unquestionably had some unpleasant memories attached to his life in the Soviet Union, such as the slashing of his wrists, Lee was never hostile or upset about his experience there. He spoke of his co-workers in a tone both humble and engaging. "They were hospitable, friendly, and sincere, invited me to their homes, fed me from their meager supplies, and we frankly discussed all the same subjects we do here. He also mentioned there were other foreigners living there, some Cuban students[79] and one family from Argentina; the father of the family was an experienced engineer, and it was apparent Lee had great respect for him.[80]

"Did anyone tell jokes about their regime?" I asked.

"Here is one I remember," Lee said. "An American worker comes to the Soviet Union and he sees big apartment complexes. He asks, 'To whom do they belong?' 'To the state,' comes the answer. 'How about these factories and the big black cars?' 'They belong to the state also.'" Lee smiled. "The Russian worker comes to visit the United States. He asks, 'These huge factories, to whom do they belong?' 'To the capitalists,' comes the fast answer. 'Ah-ha,' says the Russian, 'This is terrible!' Then he notices nice suburban homes and new cars. He asks, 'To whom do these belong?' 'To the workers,' comes an immediate answer."

I then asked Lee, "Did you ever hear the one about a Soviet worker who was wandering from one factory to another asking, 'Is there a place that would pay as little as the small amount of work I intend to do?'"

"That's a rather vicious joke," Lee replied, clearly not amused. "Soviet workers work almost as hard as here and certainly get paid much less." He then added, "Nobody in the Soviet Union tried to intimidate me or influence me. But I encounter these tendencies here in America. Nobody ever tried to make a Communist out of me. I was sympathetic, but I never joined the party." I had no way of knowing if he was telling the truth about not joining the Communist Party, but I thought he was speaking on the level with me.

"And what were your living conditions there," I asked.

"Not bad at all, ample meals, clean surroundings, good companionship."

"And the pay?"

"Sufficient. The apartment cost me five percent of my pay, and I don't eat much, as you know. With Marina's additional salary[81] we could manage quite well. Clothing was expensive but adequate, but I am not interested in stylish clothes. Of course the Cubans dressed to kill," he smiled. I thought that Marina must have missed the good clothes.

"How about transportation," I asked.

"I couldn't afford a motorcycle, but I like to walk and the public transportation system was cheap and good."

Jeanne, who had been listening in, asked a question of her own. "What was most annoying about the Soviet Union?"

"Those endless, endless meetings we had to attend after work, listening to those deadly, monotonous speeches. You were lucky if you were in the back and could take a nap. We listened to those bureaucratic outpourings half-dazed, like children during a boring lesson. Then we voted, rather indifferently, on trivial issues. Later we would file out, exhausted, and return home. And," Lee smiled, "we never received any extra pay for the hours lost, though we certainly deserved it." I nodded in approval, as I would also hate wasting my time on such meetings.

Lee spoke frequently to me of his interest in women, talking mainly of the daughters of the Argentine engineer who "were so pretty" and so friendly to him. He bragged amusingly and somewhat naïvely of his conquests while in the Soviet Union. Here in the United States, however, Lee certainly wasn't a lady's man. He felt depressed and confined. I think he more than occasionally regretted having left Minsk. And why not? He was a foreigner, he acted freely, and he looked pleasant. His interest in the Russian people was warm and genuine. I can see how he might have been a Casanova among the Russian women.

Marina herself admitted one day, "He was something out of the ordinary. He looked like an American, was easygoing, loose and alert—not like the other men." That Lee was a perfectly normal and well-adjusted individual while in Minsk was something she insisted frequently. "The only trouble with him was his interest in books—serious books—politics and discussions, rather than sex."

Now you might find it surprising that Marina would share confidential matters about her relationship with Lee, but she was extremely close with Jeanne; my wife would relay the information to me. "Lee only rarely has sex with me," she admitted, continuing, "about once a month, and he is in such a hurry that I do not get any satisfaction. It's most frustrating."

But for the most part we talked with the Oswalds of their lives in the Soviet Union. We soon acquired the distinct impression that Marina wanted a richer and materialistically more rewarding life than the one they shared in Minsk. It was she who convinced Lee to go to the American Embassy, to ask for the return of his passport and for money to allow them to return to the United States.

I am often asked, with a great deal of suspicion, why someone such as myself, a man with several university degrees,[82] fairly good financial and social standing, someone with friends among the rich of the world, would become a friend of a "maladjusted radical" like Lee Harvey Oswald. As I hope the reader will begin to appreciate there were attractive aspects to Lee's personality. I have already mentioned his straightforwardness, honesty, and desire to be liked and appreciated. I was fortunate to have reached an age advanced enough not to give a damn what others thought of me.[83] I chose my friends because they appealed to me. And Lee did.

It never occurred to me at the time that Lee might be an agent of any country, including the United States, despite his having mastered a difficult language like Russian so well that he had just a trace of an accent. Lee was simply too outspoken and naïve. When I was working in Venezuela in the 1940s for the company owned by William F. Buckley Sr., Pantepec Oil,[84] I met Foma Trebin, the Soviet ambassador.[85] Before World War One he had been a roustabout for Nobel Oil,[86] and my uncle[87] had been a director for that company. He knew my name and was very friendly with me. We spent many an evening talking over vodka. As a result he suggested he would offer me a contract to work in the Soviet Union. But after listening to my frequently outspoken opinions he changed his mind, telling me, "My friend, you talk too much, you criticize too much. You would be a babe in the woods in my country and would end up in Siberia." So in this way, too, I was similar to Lee.

Occasionally Lee's constant search for truth, for the answers to the mysteries of life, seemed tragic and disturbing to me. At the same time these traits led me to believe it would be highly improbable that any government would try to make an agent of such a man. His perpetual self-inquiry, self-denial, and self-doubt, mixed with uncertainty,[88] worried him. But I told him not to worry, in my opinion doubt, uncertainty and constant searching were the essence of youth and indicative of an exuberance of life. A strong desire for adventure was another element that motivated Lee's personality. It was why he became a United States marine, and why he frequently switched jobs. Routine was deadly to him, though when he possessed a job that suited him, he seemed fairly happy.[89]

Even before the assassination I was often asked, "How do you get along so well with Lee Oswald?" I would reply, "In my life I have done many things. I was often a promoter, an originator of ideas. So I like new ideas, even if they appear strange and outlandish. I enjoy meeting people of all stripes, and while I might evaluate their thoughts I do not criticize them." Later, after the assassination and when I was in hot water because of my relationship with Lee, a friend of mine testified, "George always liked stray dogs and stray people."[90]

And it was true: many people considered Lee a miserable misfit, an insult to the American way of life, and completely disregarded him. A Russian refugee living in Dallas told me once "I am scared of this man Oswald, he is paranoid."[91] I defended Lee, replying to him "Paranoid or not, he is as intelligent as you are. Listen to him, there is a lot in what he says."

Probably to annoy Lee, the members of the Russian refugee community, and some ultra-conservative Americans, showered Marina with gifts and gave her a great deal of attention. She received over a hundred dresses, and for their baby June they received a new crib, a carriage, and a lot of toys.[92] Since she could not speak English with Americans, their attention was wasted effort. But the gifts and attention the Russians gave Marina unquestionably annoyed Lee. At the time he did not want Marina to learn English. She knew only two words in English—"yes" and "no"—and if she went shopping on her own, she had to point out the articles she wanted. "It's very egotistical on your part, Lee," Jeanne told him. "You have to let her study English so she can communicate with people other than the Russian refugees. You cannot keep her a recluse." Marina certainly threw oil on the fire, bragging about the gifts and talking about the success of some of the donors, who owned both their own homes and two automobiles. Unquestionably this annoyed Lee, and the more people gave to Marina, the more disturbed, no maddened, he became. He declined invitations to these "benefactors'" homes and was often rude to them. The consequences were very sad for their family. As for ourselves, we continued our good relationship with the Oswalds, even as we saw their relationship gradually deteriorating. I became even nicer to him. Never kick a man who is down, help him—that is what I believe. Yes, Lee's actions and sensitivities annoyed me at times, but I did not show resentment and tried instead to find solutions for him and his wife.

One day Lee brought me a typewritten manuscript of his experiences in the Soviet Union. He was interested in publishing them in the form of an article in a magazine or possibly developing them into a book. The few typed pages[93] did not add much to what he had already told me, and the information held my interest only because I was familiar with the locale; anyone unfamiliar with Soviet Minsk was unlikely to find the material interesting. But he thought it important to seek me out because he knew I had published many articles in Europe, and in the United States I had written some theater reviews for *Variety* magazine.[94] As I looked at the pages, Lee sat on the sofa and looked hopefully at me.

"What do you think of this?" he asked.

"Remember, I'm not a professional writer—I was just lucky enough to have some articles published. Your story is simple and honest, but it is very poorly written. It lacks any sensational revelations, and for any reader other than myself it would be pointless. Personally, I like it, because I know Minsk, but how many people know where Minsk is? And why should they have interest in your experiences? Tell me."

"Not many," Lee agreed mildly.

I didn't mention, in order not to offend him, that his grammar was poor and the syntax was abominable.[95] Not to mention those long, pompous words he used. Lee could be amusing when he used difficult English terms like charisma, politico-mania, extravaganza, elitism, dialectical materialism, etc.[96] We would laugh together about his use of such words, the exact meaning of which eluded him. They were the result of his poor formal education.[97] The one thing that spoke in his favor was his sincerity and his obvious good will to inform correctly.

"If you add some sensational, detective-story-type details, include a beautiful female spy, depraved policemen,[98] and if you depict all Russians as degenerate monsters, *then* your story[99] will be published."

"No thank you," Lee said proudly. "I do not want to tell lies. My purpose is to improve Soviet-American relations." And he added quickly, "People here should know how decent and generous Russians are. How well they treated me, a simple American ex-marine, with kindness and generosity. I did not find anything 'monstrous' in Soviet Russia."

"Personally, I agree with you," I assured him. "You talk about some individuals you met there. It's good and factual, and they are decent people. But who is interested in 'comrade this' or 'comrade that' or in refugees from Argentina or cheerful Cuban students?"

Lee agreed, and I handed him back his manuscript. The same typewritten pages were shown to me, for identification, by the Warren Commission lawyer,[100] and they were printed in the *Warren Commission Report*.[101] So Lee's wish to have them published came true, if only after his death.[102]

TWO

◦◦◦

Lee's Troubled Marriage to Marina

It was a wonderful setting for a Soviet-style romance: the city of Minsk, with its Svislach River, a new apartment building, and an American refugee. "I remember looking at that apartment building," Marina reminisced, "but only high technical and political personnel lived there, as well as some foreigners, Lee among them." Actually, the building belonged to the factory where Lee worked at the time. But for a girl who had lived in crowded rooms with a stepfather and several stepbrothers and sisters, the location seemed a real paradise.

The Oswalds in Minsk

Marina came from a fairly good family from our point of view, since her father belonged to a former Czarist officer group.[1] After his death her mother Clogia Vasilyevna Prusakova married a man named Alexandr Ivanovich Medvedev.[2] When her mother died in 1957 Marina then lived with the family of her stepfather in Leningrad.[3] I remember her amusing response when I asked her if she liked her siblings.

"They were good, normal children, not like me. I was the bad one," she laughed.[4]

Eventually she got tired of living with them and decided to move to

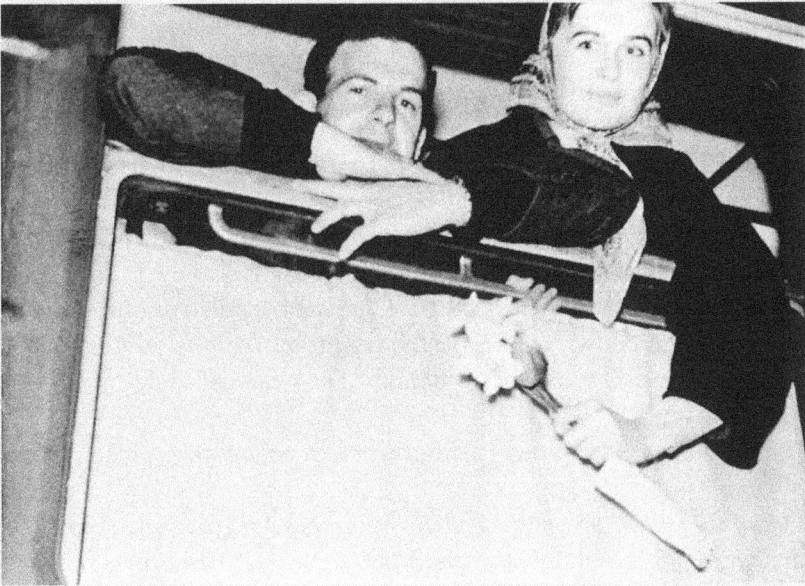

I once asked him . . . "How the hell did you get out of Russia so easily?"
Marina and Lee Harvey Oswald leaving Minsk, bound for the United States. Warren
Commission Document Photos (Commission Document 443—FBI Memorandum
Report of 1 February 1964)

Minsk, where she received a degree as a registered pharmacist.[5] She was working at a hospital where Lee was being treated.[6] She took care of him, flirted with him very nicely, and began conquering his heart. Later he found excuses to keep going to the same hospital. And that's how the romance started and flourished. They began going out together to dances and movies and eventually a bond of affection and love developed between them.[7] They married on April 30, 1961, and moved into his apartment building.

She could have just as easily cohabitated with him; this happened frequently with young couples in the Soviet Union. Why did she marry him? The reasons are known only to Marina: love for Lee, pity for him, or a desire to leave the country and come to the United States. I suspect the last, because soon after their wedding Lee apparently[8] decided that he wanted to return to the United States. He traveled to Moscow without a permit, went to the American embassy, got his passport back and borrowed $500.00 for travel expenses.[9] He had to travel to Moscow a second time to arrange his exit with the Soviet authorities.

One question that has always puzzled Jeanne and I was Marina being permitted to leave the Soviet Union so easily. "Well, I did it," Lee smirked, "because all bureaucrats, all over the world, are stupid." At the time we were indifferent to the matter and so we did not inquire further. Marina had for a period of time lived with an uncle, on her mother's side, who was a colonel in the NKVD.[10] He had been opposed to her marriage with Lee, but later something changed his mind. Maybe this colonel had his own reasons for helping his niece get out of the Soviet Union.[11] Possibly it was just good riddance. Perhaps it was something else.[12] But the permission to leave, uncle or no uncle, was highly unusual. From our reading of the *Christian Science Monitor* we knew of many cases where Americans failed to obtain a permit to allow their Soviet wives to leave the country.[13]

Later, I once asked him point blank, "How the hell did you get out of Russia so easily?"

Lee disliked and even despised bureaucracy in any form, be it American or Soviet.

"Here they are nasty; in the Soviet Union they are naïve and stupid. I outsmarted those Russian bureaucrats. Man, they are an amorphous bunch of people. They make a mistake and go to a concentration camp like a bunch of sheep."

Contrasts between Lee and Marina

Being in a close relationship with the Oswalds we soon noticed the signs of the coming disintegration of their already fragile relationship. Lee seemed to be fond of Marina but he mostly cherished baby June. Maybe he was too secretive a person to show his affection, and Marina's Slavic nature demanded more attention and tenderness. But Lee never spoke badly to us about his wife, he never criticized her but neither did he ever express any deep feeling for her. Even in his typewritten memoirs he spoke very little of her.[14]

Marina, on the other hand, continually annoyed and criticized Lee, possibly due to a perversity of her Russian character. "He is so puny, so dull, he never drinks, only works, tires easily, is only interested in books," she complained to me and my wife. Lee was indeed all wrapped up in his work, books, his ideas about the equality of all people, especially of all races. And Marina said these things both behind his back and to him directly when we were present. Never did we hear from her that she loved her husband. But there was nevertheless an element of strong attachment which tied these two so different people together, but we did not notice it at the time.[15]

We seldom heard Lee talk much about women. Marina, on the other hand, spoke freely to Jeanne and to me about her admiration for strong, sexy men.[16] She spoke enthusiastically about the Cubans she met in Russia. "They were outgoing and gay. Often they carried their guitars with them, sang their catchy Caribbean tunes, and danced so well. They were such fun!" She also confided in Jeanne about her pre-marital experiences, handsome fellows she had met and shared her bed with. There were also parties organized in Minsk by the sons of the richer *apparatchiks* who had comfortable apartments at their disposal. While the parents were away the kids drank and slept together indiscriminately, real Soviet-type orgies. "This was terrific," she reminisced.

"And I also remember a handsome boy who instead of joining us on holidays would take a book and would go all day to the forest to study. Some people are crazy," she concluded. This was an indirect criticism of her husband who did not like music except sad and melancholic Russian tunes, did not play any musical instruments, and who could not dance. And let's face it—he wasn't particularly entertaining in bed with her, either.

Lee was rather neat and orderly while Marina was lazy and devil-may-care about her household and herself. This unusual Russian-American couple was too much for the average Anglo-American. Hence their cohabitation with Lee's brother, Robert Oswald, and his family was short.[17] Marina's attitude became all too clear to my wife as she had more opportunity to observe Marina than I did. This ex-Russian activist and member of the Communist Youth stayed in bed until noon or later and avoided domestic chores. This was what happened when she stayed in our house. The same opinion was shared by my daughter Alex with whom Marina also stayed for a while.[18]

Marina was simply devoid of energy[19] while Lee, though capable of making an effort, was not however an average go-getting type of a person who succeeded in America. I often regretted that Lee did not get a better education because he would have done well in the scholastic world and would have been a useful citizen.

I remember Lee read Russian classics and discussed some of them at length with me, especially the psychoanalytical study *The Idiot* by Dostoyevsky.[20] I never saw him interested in anything except Russian books and magazines. He said he didn't want to forget the language, but it amazed me that he read such difficult writers as Gorki, Dostoyevsky, Gogol, Tolstoy and Turgenev—in Russian.[21] He understood pre-revolutionary life in Russia, which I did not know first-hand but heard about from my parents. Russian classics belong exclusively to the pre-revolutionary or early revolutionary days and modern Russians are fascinated by those tales of extravagant aristocracy, Czarist power and abuses of it, great wealth and great waste, ownership of slaves,[22] and the power and influence of the Greek-Orthodox church.[23] These aspects of the old days Lee observed with distaste, but the elegance and the gaiety of certain occasions also gave him a feeling of nostalgia, as if he were Russian himself.

Marina did not care about any of this. She was utterly materialistic, really predisposed by nature for the mediocrity of middle-class American life: new clothes, buildings with plastic, neutral surroundings, and tall, well-dressed men.

"Lee, when shall we get a car?" she kept on nagging. "Everyone here has one, even the poorest people!" Poor Lee didn't even know how to drive.[24] He took the bus and hitched rides with others. And when Marina was talking to Jeanne, he said: "I never wanted a mediocre, obscure, money-loving middle-class wife who would have the taste of vanity, of luxury, of comfort, of all that bourgeois nonsense."

Well, you have one, I thought!

Marina liked wine; Lee objected to it.[25] She smoked; he detested the smell of tobacco. Whenever he wasn't around and she had the chance she would become a chain-smoker, inhaling deep, asking for drinks, enjoying these forbidden

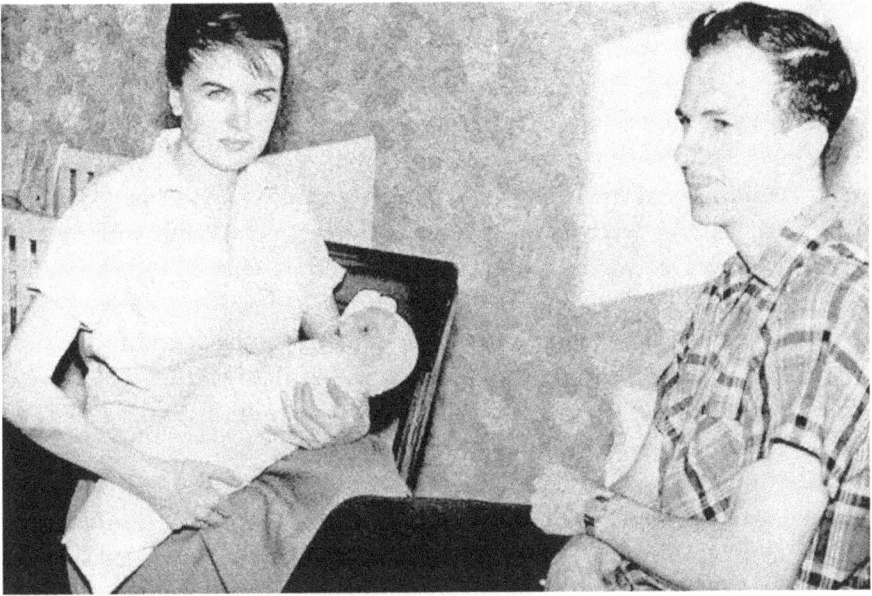

This unusual Russian-American couple was too much for the average Anglo-American.

Lee, Marina, and baby June sometime in the summer of 1962. US National Archives and Records Administration (Commission Exhibit 2622)

pleasures. Lee respected education and knowledge, especially in others; Marina was just the opposite; she didn't even value her degree as a pharmacist.

"It must have been difficult to get it, no?" I asked her once.

"Not for me, I got by easily, used ponies[26] and passed my examinations," she answered breezily.

In my conversations with Lee, I found out that he was an open and straightforward agnostic. Religion simply did not interest him. He said that was probably the case of how he felt since his early childhood. His agnosticism was a type similar to Thomas Jefferson's or Ben Franklin's—and it was fine.[27] He was not an aggressive atheist who wanted to impose his point of view with violence. He must have read Arnold J. Toynbee[28] and Bertrand Russell[29] because his argumentation against organized religion was solid. Only once while discussing this subject did he express his views with cold disdain. "What I dislike," he said, "are the materialistic aspects of the American type of religion, all the large denominations with their ridiculously garish churches, their tax-deductible tricks and finagling." Lee seemed quite well versed on the matter. Here, rather than I instructing him, he was rather instructing me. And I had to agree with him on the greedy aspects of our modern Christianity, so far removed from the original teachings of poverty and humility.

One day he said to me, humorously and with a chuckle, "The doctor sees a man at his weakest, the lawyer sees a man at his wickedest, and the priest sees a man at his stupidest." "I read it somewhere,"[30] he explained before asking, "It's pretty good?" Lee was always very humble with me and he really blossomed when I showed some interest in what he had to say. But aren't we all the same way?

Since I have mentioned Lee's agnosticism, let's go back to Marina's attitude towards religion. We were positive at first that Marina was also an agnostic, even an atheist; after all she was brought up in Soviet Russia in purely Communist surroundings. She did not have the slightest idea of God, nor any interest in anything divine, or so it seemed to us. But soon she realized that being religious in the United States would be advantageous to her, as it usually is. And so she had her child June christened later in the Greek-Orthodox church in Dallas during one of her separations from Lee.[31] This exacerbated their conflict. He told her in our presence "You double-crossed me. You should have consulted me before doing this to my child. This is unforgivable!"

And so religion, too, was another element that added to their disputes.

Personally, I do not criticize faith or religion, but these should be true and profound inner feelings, not just outward manifestations. Lee's faith, his strongest belief, was the rightness of racial integration. He told me on many occasions things like "It hurts me that blacks do not have the same privileges and rights as white America does." And I agreed with him. The early 1960s were still the Segregationist era when blacks had to sit at the back of the bus, couldn't eat in the same restaurants, or stay in the same hotels and motels as whites.[32] It angered and annoyed me. At the time I didn't have much contact with anyone black, except for some artists, teachers, and preachers. But in my profession as a petroleum geologist I couldn't afford to have black friends in the house too often, because I would have been blackballed professionally. Fortunately the situation has now changed for me and I am very happy.[33]

Lee also resented Marina's care of his child, thinking it poor. This led to frequent quarrels and recriminations. Gradually the fights between the Oswalds became more frequent and vicious. Marina would arrive by bus at our home with the baby and would complain to Jeanne, "He beat me up again." As proof of this she showed bruises on her body to Jeanne and a black eye to me.

One day we visited them in their apartment on 604 Elsbeth Street in Oak Cliff.[34] It was on the ground-floor of a dreary red-brick building, the atmosphere of the house and the neighborhood was profoundly depressing.[35] The living-room was dark and smelly, the bedroom and the kitchen facing bleak walls. But Lee was proud of his own place and showed me his books and magazines as well as some letters from Russia which we read together.[36] The place was spruced up by the lovely photographs of the Russian countryside Lee had taken there and later enlarged himself. Trees and fields, charming peasant huts and cloudy skies contrasted strangely with the dreary walls and the lugubrious atmosphere. Some pictures were framed by Lee while others, unframed, were assembled carefully in an album. I also recall artistically taken pictures of Moscow and Leningrad, especially of the river Neva,[37] which I also slightly remembered from my childhood. He was happy his job gave him access to elaborate photographic equipment. "Look at these churches, look at these statues," he exclaimed proudly. Indeed almost all his pictures had a professional touch and he was justly proud of them.[38]

While Lee and I were chatting on that moth-eaten sofa in the living-room, Marina invited Jeanne to come to the kitchen. There she cried and showed a burned spot[39] on her shoulder. "The son of a bitch caught me smoking and he grabbed the cigarette and put it out on my bare flesh."

"This is terrible, this is terrible!" shouted Jeanne, coming out of the kitchen. "Lee, what have you done to your wife?"

"Well, she smoked against my orders," he said sullenly.

"You picked up those customs just living abroad for two years? You could not have picked up this brutality in Russia where women are independent," Jeanne challenged him, with a great deal of anger. "And here you have no right to brutalize a woman just because she smokes occasionally."

Right there we discussed with them very frankly their growing antagonism and tried to find a solution to it. We came up with an idea of a temporary separation but left it up to them.

"Take it easy," I told Lee, "and stop abusing your wife."

"But she enjoys brutality," he answered calmly. "Look at me. I am all scratched up." Indeed, even in the darkened room we could see long red marks on his face—traces of Marina's fingernails. "She is provoking me," he added sadly.

"Still it's no excuse," I said. "Your temperaments obviously clash; it's another reason for separation."

The Oswalds remained silent, wrapped up in their misery.

"Do it," said Jeanne, "before you really hurt each other. And you Lee are more responsible because you are stronger."

"Man, that woman loves to fight," countered Lee seriously.

Marina and Jeanne went back to the kitchen where Marina cried on my wife's shoulder. On the way home Jeanne related the complaints. "He is cold and hostile," said Marina. "He goes to bed with me so rarely now. Once in a couple of weeks. He makes me so god-damn frustrated."

Jeanne was amused by such a frank revelation but could not find a better solution for Marina than advising her to be more feminine, use some perfume in the evening, and occasionally put on a sexy, transparent negligee.

But before leaving I remember taking a close look at baby June, laying in her crib, rather fat and not being yet able to say a word. "She reminds me of someone, of some celebrity," I mused.

And then the answer came to me. "Look at June," I shouted. "Look: she is a baby edition of Nikita Khrushchev!"[40]

I did not mean it as an insult, just the opposite. I rather liked that outgoing, earthy old man, and so did the Oswalds. So we all laughed and assembled around the crib, examining the baby. "Same pinkish color of the skin," observed Jeanne. "Same rare, fluffy hair," said Marina.

"Same round Russian face," agreed Lee smilingly.

And so we left that evening, advising our young friends to talk over their problems and to stop torturing each other. Whatever their decision was, we would be glad to help them in any way we could.

Driving back from the Oswalds we spoke of their problems and laughed at the June/Khrushchev comparison. "Yes, the baby has the same slanting eyes and the same belligerent expression," said Jeanne. "How come I did not notice it before?"

Yes, June was not a pretty baby at the time but perfectly normal and healthy. We have not seen her in a long time, for reasons that shall become obvious later, but I am sure she grew up to be a lovely young girl. She has a stepfather now and probably knows little or nothing about her real father.[41] We remember with sadness how much Lee was devoted to her. "He is an unusually loving and tender father," I mused aloud while driving.

"And he has a very good heart," said Jeanne, "Look how much our dogs love him."

"It's so touching when Lee kisses June and calls her *moia malenkaia devochka* (my little girl). And he never gets mad at her," I concluded while we approached our house.

Growing Animosity

Conflict between married couples develops slowly, confined to just a few areas of their lives and then, like a cancer, the disease metastasizes and attacks the couple's entire relationship with alarming rapidity. Slowly but insidiously the animosity developed in the case of Oswalds.

Lee's relationship with Marina worsened as she became more enticed by American "luxuries." It was a sensuous joy for her to wear silk nightgowns loaned by my wife when she stayed with us. My daughter Alex said that Marina did the same thing when she stayed in her apartment.

As Marina was luxuriating, Lee was reading[42] whenever he could his Russian books (he had brought a lot from the Soviet Union), and his friends kept providing him with new supplies of books and magazines.[43]

Although I did not notice any special signs of jealousy on his part regarding Marina—she could not communicate with Americans and the Russian refugees were too old for her—it obviously annoyed him that his wife kept corresponding with an ex-boyfriend, or an ex-lover, in the Soviet Union.[44] Lee intercepted a letter from this man and became very bitter. I do not remember whether he beat her on that occasion; Marina did not complain of a beating. But he told me that the letter referred to a plan Marina had to return to the Soviet Union without him. It could be that Lee imagined all this, given how tense the situation was, and now things simply became tenser.[45] Lee obviously loved Marina in his own way and did not want to lose her.

Marina's occasional drinking and especially her smoking gave Lee fits, as I just mentioned; he especially hated the smell of tobacco on Marina's breath. Laughingly, I told him to avoid this problem and to approach Marina, when he was in an amorous mood, from the back. He didn't see the humor in my teasing suggestion and did not laugh this time.

June's upbringing also caused bitter disputes between the couple. Lee accused his wife of not paying enough attention to his daughter, failing to change her diapers fast enough and not being tender enough with her. Truthfully Marina was not a bad mother, but Lee was a perfectionist to a fault and it was so very clear he also idolized his daughter. My wife and I felt he spoiled the child too much and we told him so.[46] The Oswalds quarreled in front of us bitterly but without physical violence. But gradually the tempo of their fights increased, and we saw Marina more and more often with bruises and Lee with scratches on his face.

Jeanne tried to convince Lee to change his ways and become more tolerant otherwise his confrontations with Marina would end in a tragedy. I did not believe that Lee would seriously hurt Marina and tried to make a joke out of it, laughing, "even prominent men occasionally beat their wives. The most important thing is not to maim them."[47]

My wife liked Marina and found her amusing and stimulating, but we were both annoyed to hear her regular complaints about "that idiot Lee who does not make enough money."

"Why don't *you* try to make something out of yourself?" asked Jeanne. "I came to America penniless, worked hard and became a successful fashion designer. Go to school, learn English, and revalidate your degree."

Marina was not interested.[48]

When Jeanne had come to America she did not know the language well. To encourage Marina and prevent her from bitching at Lee, Jeanne gave her the language instruction records she had used. My wife had made a superhuman effort to become independent, learned English fast, and then gave an excellent education to her own daughter, Christina. We also gave the Oswalds a phonograph with which to play the records. But instead of learning English she played melancholy Russian tunes and obviously did not cherish the idea of finding a job.

One day both of them were reading to us a letter from Marina's girlfriend in Russia. "Marina," it read, "I knew you would make it, you were destined to be great and your success in America is a proof of it."

Lee smiled sadly, and said, "Marina what were you saying to your friend?"

One day Marina told Jeanne that she always wanted to come to the United States—at any price. Marina did become famous after the assassination. She appeared on the cover of the February 14, 1964, issue of *Time* magazine, received a lot of money from charitable but foolish Americans, and is now well-off financially.[49] At the time it was pathetic to read such nonsense. But is it possible that Marina in her own strange way considered her arrival in America a great success? Did the hundred-odd dresses donated to her go to her head? Who knows?

Brokering a Separation

We were appalled at the Oswalds' marital troubles, which from being bad became desperate. One day in early November Marina came to our house without announcement, crying, badly bruised all over, and carrying baby June along.[50] It would be dangerous for her to leave. Jeanne called one of two families who knew the Oswalds. We discussed the situation with a charming couple—the Mellers[51]—a very kindly couple without children of their own. Teofil had been a professor in eastern Poland and Anna was a Russian displaced person, a refugee. They met in a camp in Germany, fell in love, married, and eventually came to the United States. They met Marina and liked her and at the same time they were not prejudiced against Lee. Though they were not rich, they were generous, and they accepted our request to host Marina and the child until the situation cleared up. They wholeheartedly approved of the proposed arrangement because they thought that Marina would be better off alone than with Lee. And I personally was sure that Lee would be happier without Marina. Since Marina was for this arrangement from the start, it was only Lee we were worried about.

That same day I invited Lee to come to the house to discuss the situation. We spoke very calmly and matter-of-fact about the need for a separation. Both our dogs, Nero and Poppaea, sat snugly next to Lee and were living proof that he was calm, not frantic nor nervous. When it came to the most recent beating arising from the Oswalds' desperate quarrels, Jeanne said, "Separate as fast as you can. Stay away from each other. I will let you know Lee later where Marina will be. But not before some time elapses."

At that Lee became indignant, raising his voice so loudly that Nero and Poppaea bolted from him and hid. "You are not going to impose this indignity on me!" He shouted. "I shall tear up all of June and Marina's clothes and break the furniture." He was incoherent and violent. We had never seen him in this condition before.[52]

"If you did this, you will never see June and Marina again. You are ridiculous," Jeanne said quietly. "There is a law here against abuse."

"By the time you calm down, I shall promise you will be in contact with baby June again," I interceded, knowing that Lee was afraid that someone would take the child away from him. And so he calmed down, promised to think the situation over, and assured us that there would be no more violence. After a while we drove the couple back to their dreary Elsbeth Street apartment.

The next evening Lee was back with us, all alone. He wanted to talk the situation over again. He sat gloomily on our famous sofa, and both of us tried to talk some sense to him.

"I've heard of love accompanied with beating and torture," I said half seriously. "Read Marquis de Sade or observe the life of the underworld—*l'amour crapule* (the bastard love), as they say in France.[53] But your fights seem to be deprived of sex, which is terrible."

"If you think you are fond of each other, cannot you do it without scratching, biting, and hitting?" Jeanne said, taking a completely different tact.

Lee remained glum, and didn't say a word.

"Separation will be a test for both of you," continued Jeanne, "you will see if you can live without each other. If you can, Lee, you will find another woman and will be happier with her."[54]

"If not," I laughed, "you will separate again or divorce. Look at me. I married *four* times until I found somebody who can stand me."

Jeanne kept on talking about finding a nice temporary home for Marina and baby June and the good care both of them would have. We did not mention the Mellers just yet.

"I promise you, Lee, that after a cooling off period, I shall give you the address and the telephone, so you can communicate with your child. Nobody should separate a child from her father."

Lee believed my promise because he knew that in a previous marriage I had been myself a victim of a vindictive wife who prevented me from seeing my children.[55]

That night we separated rather sadly. "You may hate us Lee, or maybe you will be grateful to us one day for forcing[56] this separation," I said. "But I don't see any other way out under the current circumstances. This is Saturday, we are free tomorrow and will come in the morning to help Marina and the baby move out."

Lee agreed, but he was on the verge of tears. "Remember your promise," he said. "You will give me their address and telephone soon."

We shook hands and Lee left.

The next day, a Sunday, we drove to the Oswalds' apartment on Elsbeth Street. Lee hardly said hello to Jeanne, someone to whom he had always been most cordial in the past.

"This is not the end of the world, Lee," she told him. "Cheer up!" And she went to help Marina. I sat on the sofa with him and tried to talk to him. He was gloomy and hardly said a word. He did not try to help us move the crib, the baby's belongings, etc. In the meantime our big white Galaxie convertible[57]—which we kept for years in memory of the Oswalds—was filling up high with all sorts of junk. When it came to Marina's wardrobe, Lee suddenly became infuriated. Seeing all those innumerable items of clothing, Lee grabbed an armful of them and shouted, "I will not permit it! I will not permit it! I shall burn all this garbage."

And so back into the apartment we went, following Lee and the bundle of Marina's clothes.

"You cannot go back on your promise to be calm, Lee!" shouted Jeanne. Disgusted, I wanted to call the police for help. But Lee looked so desperate that I sat with him on the sofa again, grabbed him by the arm and tried to reason with him. "Brutality won't help you, Lee," I said firmly. "If you keep on with these tantrums, Marina and the baby will be gone anyway and you won't see them again. So better submit and keep your word."

He sat there, his face dark, not sure of what he was going to do.[58]

"We are wasting our valuable time helping you kids," I shouted finally losing my patience. "To hell with you and your quarrels!"

Lee then calmed down and agreed to everything. He even helped carrying the clothes given to Marina by her Russian-American benefactors, whom he hated. Our convertible, overloaded, groaned and sank almost to the street.

And so we departed, Jeanne holding up stuff to prevent it from falling out, Marina holding on to baby June. As I was driving I laughed because we looked so obviously ridiculous. But fortunately this was a Sunday and there were few people on the streets. I drove slowly to the Mellers' apartment, avoiding main arteries from Oak Cliff, the far western part of Dallas, to the Lakeview area, in the eastern part of Dallas, a distance of some fifteen miles. When we arrived at the home of that gentle couple, they came out, greeting Marina and the baby, and helped to unload all that junk. Little did they suspect that this kind act of theirs would cause them so much trouble after November 22, 1963, and that their life would be disturbed by the insane suspicions and crazy publicity following President Kennedy's assassination.[59]

Marina complained one last time about "that stupid Lee" and the trouble he had caused all of us. I was worried about him. "Let's get it over with," I said wearily, finishing the unloading. "And then let's get out of here. We have done enough for these crazy kids."

Separation and More Trouble

The separation which we worked so hard to arrange was obviously not the right long-term solution for the couple's problems. It was also a heavy burden on this charitable Polish-Russian couple—the Mellers—who were used to their own ways and who had to share Marina's temperamental problems. She would not help Mrs. Meller with any household chores and behaved like a prima donna. And for Lee the separation was much worse. He missed Marina and the child and came to our house daily, asking how they were, did June miss him, and were they well taken care of. He realized in other words that this separation was not a joke and, to a great extent, had been caused by his own behavior.[60]

Again we had a chance to talk together, in a less cheerful mood than previously. "One can arrive at the truth by trial and error," he said. "In my case I commit so many errors and I still do not know whether I arrive at the truth."

"It is possible, Lee," I countered, "that you take things too seriously. Don't do things which are unpleasant or uncomfortable simply because of some great ideology you may have a belief in. You see the whole mess you are in. You must have read Arthur Koestler's book[61] where he repents for his years as an ideological Communist revolutionary."

Lee remembered the book.

"Stop living miserably, do like a normal person does, live pleasantly and keep your own ideology to yourself. Don't disclose yourself."

"You are right, of course," said Lee. "But this society we live in, it's so disgusting and degrading. How can you stand it?"

"Well, my friend, that's why we have built-in distractions, stupid and moronic things like television, movies, and rock and roll music for most of the people."

"And good books for *us*," concluded Lee, rather aptly.

"Lee, you are too straight, your back does not bend enough. One of these days someone will break your back. You have to learn to bend, be resilient."

"But look at the politicians here, most of them. They want to be praised publicly for their honesty and good will. Connally, the governor of Texas, for example. In reality they will do all their degrading actions and yet try to appear in a good light."

This was the first time he mentioned his loathing for Governor Connally. What caused it, we shall discover shortly.

"What you need, Lee, is a good walk in the jungle, like we did. That would bring you back to the essentials of life—survival."

"Marina is not Jeanne, she will not do anything of the sort. And we have the baby, too."

Later we were asked many times and with great suspicion questions like "why were you wasting your time on this crazy Marxist and his unappealing wife?" The answer is twofold. First, we desired to help a young couple in despair. Second—and this is the more complex answer—I found Lee a most interesting and invigorating individual. I have traveled the world as a petroleum consultant, had several wives, and was part of the quote unquote establishment, mainly for business reasons. So-called jet-set or cafe society people are really very boring, and the same the world over. An eccentric like Lee, in contrast, was of great interest to me. He never bored me.

A sincere conversation calmed Lee down, acted as a balsam[62] for his raw nerves, and under the circumstances talking wasn't bad for *me* either. Fortunately, I remember well so much of what he said. I distinctly recall that during one of those evenings together we talked of John F. Kennedy. Lee liked him and certainly did not include him among those despicable politicians he mentioned in our prior conversations. I once showed him the president's picture on the cover of *Time* magazine[63] and Lee said "how handsome he looks, what open and sincere features he has and how different he looks from the other ratty politicians."

I don't remember his exact language but Lee spoke most kindly of the gradual improvement in racial relations in the United States, attributing them to the president. Like most young people he was attracted by President and Mrs. Kennedy's personalities, but he also knew that Kennedy's father[64] was a rascal who made money off of Prohibition whiskey and being bullish on the stock-market or, in other words, betting against the American economy.[65]

Lee often mentioned that the two-party system of American government did not work well, and that other points of view were not represented. He did not see the difference between a conservative Democrat and a fairly liberal Republican—and in that I agreed with him.

"Both Republicans and Democrats really did not oppose each other," he mentioned one day. "They do not represent different points of view, and they are both solidly against the poor and oppressed."

But regarding President Kennedy, Lee did not have such a gloomy attitude and he hoped that after the Bay of Pigs fiasco[66] Kennedy would accept coexistence with the Communist world.

As I mentioned before, he did not like the Marine Corps and considered it racist and segregationist.[67]

"Do you know that President Truman wanted to abolish this Marine Corps," Lee said. "I would agree with him on that."[68] Lee did not like any militarists, Russian or American; he thought that someday there could be a *coup d'état* in this country organized by the Pentagon and that the country would become a militaristic, Nazi-type, dictatorship.[69]

Maybe this negative attitude was the result of the separation, these days he was downcast and did not smile at my jokes. Yet I tried my best. I remember telling him about the meeting of four girls, French, English, American, and Russian. "The French girl said, 'my lover will buy me a dress.' The

This was the first time he mentioned his loathing for Governor Connally.
Texas Governor John Connally tips his hat as President and Mrs. Kennedy board the presidential limousine at Love Field, Dallas, November 22, 1963. Courtesy Fort Worth Star-Telegram Collection, Special Collections Division, The University of Texas at Arlington Library, Arlington, Texas

English girl said, 'my husband promised to buy me a new coat.' The American girl bragged, 'my boss will buy me a mink stole.' And the Russian girl concluded: 'Girls, I am a prostitute also.'"

One of those evenings Lee spoke for the first time of his discharge from the Marine Corps. "I received an honorable discharge and then those bastards, in the Navy, changed it into an undesirable discharge, just because I went to Russia and threw my passport in the face of the American consul."

"Didn't they do it because you lied? You were supposed to go back to the States to help make a living for your mother."

"Oh, hell, that was just a crooked excuse," he said sullenly. "And Connally signed this undesirable discharge."[70]

Those days Lee was bitter about religion, which in general he seldom mentioned. He explained his avowed agnosticism: "money wasted on these innumerable churches, garish and costly, would be spent much more usefully on hospitals, asylums, homes for the poor and elderly, and on eliminating slums."

But Lee did not like the Communist party either. "In Russia party members are mostly opportunist, carrying their cards proudly in order to get better jobs, or they are forced into the party by their circumstances or families."

Again I tried to cheer up Lee by telling him a joke I heard in Yugoslavia.

"An uneducated Montenegrin Communist arrives in Belgrade where he sees for the first time changing lights in a main intersection. 'Comrade,' he timidly asked a passerby, 'What are these lights for?' The sly answer was: 'the red lights are for the Communists to cross over, the yellow for the Communist sympathizers, the green for all the others.' And so the peasant tried to cross on the red light, almost got killed and was strongly admonished by the policeman who said, 'What kind of fool are you?' The peasant replied 'I am a member of the Communist Party, but I didn't really want to join it, I was forced into it.'"

He did not laugh but conceded that the joke proved his point. "People without any affiliation to the party were the nicest among those I met in Russia," he concluded.

I remember that Lee did not like any political parties, anywhere. He was just a natural-born nonconformist. But he told me that when he used to teach his co-workers English in Minsk, he tried to present the United States in the most favorable light and wasn't too popular with the authorities because of that. In the USSR he defended the USA, and in the USA he defended the USSR!

This type of attitude I like very much. I tried to do the same when I worked in Yugoslavia in 1957.[71] I remember deeply offending the secretary of the Communist party of Slovenia, comparing him to my ex-father-in-law who had been chairman of the Republican Party in Pennsylvania and an extremely rich man.[72] Both of them, super-Communist and a super-capitalist, were made in the same mold. When he heard this, Lee finally smiled.

And so Lee tried to create good feeling in two opposing countries, in two opposing systems of government. This is not an attribute of a violent man, just the opposite. I must say that I never considered Lee capable of a truly violent act. Marina annoyed him, and he beat her up, but she scratched him back and hurt him worse.[73] Lee regretted his acts but Marina did not. Lee threatened to destroy toys and clothes, but he did not do it. Look how he eventually accepted our intervention. I am not a very violent person, but I would not stand for somebody else taking away my wife and my only child, whatever the reasons were.

Many local people, especially the Russian refugees, expressed hostility about Lee because he had "deserted" the United States, the "the land of the free and home of the brave,"[74] and many considered him an outright traitor. Many resented him—and he answered in kind. And we were the only ones who took an interest in him and gave him a chance to express himself.

Unquestionably, Lee was a very sincere person. He meant what he said, even if it was certain to lead to trouble for him. Marina, I remember, had the same feelings regarding religion as Lee. She found all religions absolutely ridiculous, a childish farce. But at the same time she had her baby baptized—just in case. She knew it would create a favorable impression among Americans and Russian refugees. She did it at the time of this separation, we did not know about it, and she did it without Lee's consent.

And so baby June was baptized in the Russian-Orthodox church on October 16, where the priest, father Dimitri Royster, was a good friend of mine.[75] Being a neophyte himself—he had been a strong Baptist—he was somewhat fanatical about his new faith and considered this baptism a great achievement. He did well in Texas and at the present time he is a bishop in California.

When Lee heard of this baptism, he became infuriated, and it led him into more religious or rather anti-religious discussions, which I remember well.

"You know all those theories of immortality leave me cold," said Lee. "And who would be this mysterious judge who would punish or reward me? It's out of sight."

"Yes, I agree with you but becoming just gas after death seems too simple to me."

"Eternity, immortality, what highfalutin ideas," continued Lee. "Anyway I have a hard enough time in this short existence of mine," he smiled bitterly. "What shall I do with immortality?"

"Somebody said," pursued Lee, "this man is not intelligent enough to doubt—he is a *believer*."

"My friend," I said, "hope and religion are a peculiar mixture. They make lots of people happy, but they also made Jewish people go to gas chambers singing Hebrew songs, instead of fighting the Nazis."

"That won't happen to me," said Lee. "I don't need hymns to pep me up when I die. And I don't know where I shall go after death and I don't care. But I shall not be like a rich American who eats, sleeps, drinks, amuses himself and then dies painfully leaving all his belonging and a large bank account. I shall die poor and free."

I have frequently been asked: was Lee a good husband? I don't remember Lee ever saying that he would go back to the Soviet Union, even when his marriage was going on the rocks. We have seen in some detail his unpleasant characteristics. But he often helped Marina with the household work. He gave her all the money he earned. Sometimes he complained that she was too lazy and then he did the job himself, cleaning dishes or even washing clothes. He was always kind and tender to the baby. As far as sex is concerned, while we heard Marina's bitter complaints about Lee, we know that the greatest mystery in the world is what happens between a married couple at night, behind closed doors. Sometimes there is magic, sometimes there is not. And while we listened to Marina, we never looked through *that* keyhole.

If Marina had any brains she should have known that a man like Lee, who was not a big money-maker and was barely even a wage earner thanks to his constant employment switching, would never have provided her with all those desirable consumer goods that America seemed to possess in such limitless quantities. Marina liked to ridicule Lee. She called him a fool, a moron. "You are always thinking of politics instead of making money—you act like a big shot!" She picked at him, annoyed him, as if she *desired* a separation, something she finally achieved through us. For example the letter from Marina's ex-boyfriend or ex-lover that Lee intercepted: why did she keep it?[76] Maybe she wanted to end her unsuccessful marriage?

Marina also had a bad habit of constantly correcting Lee when he was speaking Russian and that really irritated him and me as well. Lee, for a man of his background, had a remarkable talent for Russian, and Marina foolishly tried to blow up his occasional mistakes or ridicule his slight accent. It's difficult to know two languages to perfection, and Lee's English was perfect, refined, rather literary, deprived of any Southern accent. He sounded like a very educated American of indeterminate background. But to know *Russian* as he did was remarkable and to appreciate serious literature written in the language was something really out of the ordinary.[77] He had an affinity for the Russian ways of life, everything from customs, music and food.

Therefore to criticize this remarkable fellow was an act of nastiness or idiocy, especially for Marina who knew only two English words, "yes" and "no." That's how she went around and did her shopping, pointing at the articles with her finger.

Lee once asked me, "What is your philosophy of life? You make *me* talk a lot but *you* tell me jokes instead of being serious."

"Well, jokes sometimes express more than thick, serious doctoral theses," I answered. "Frankly, I am not interested in politics, I lost most of my relatives—and so did Jeanne—through various wars and revolutions. What I believe in most is to live and let live. But let the minorities and the poor live decently. For that type of a government I had voted Republican so far, but I am considering switching to the Democratic Party. There is a guy there by the name of Eugene McCarthy[78] whom I like. I also tend to believe that each country deserves the government it winds up with; let the Communists live the way they want, and the same goes of the socialists or even dictators. For instance the Germans definitely deserved Hitler."

Lee nodded in agreement.

"This country has too many damn problems to intervene in other countries and impose our ways.[79] We must solve our problems first."

The federal government would later annoy me to no end and constantly interfere with my life.[80] It began immediately after the assassination and Lee's declaration that I was his best friend and the only one he respected. Both my wife and I had left Dallas for Haiti eight or nine months *before* the assassination, because I was working on the geological survey of that country I had been hired to carry out. From the start I became marked as a "suspicious" man by the FBI and CIA. Various agents, both in disguise and officially representing their agencies, invaded the lives of my friends and business acquaintances asking questions like: "Is he a Communist? An anarchist? Is he an *agent provocateur*? What country is he working for?"

You can imagine the effect of these endless yet vague inquiries. Some moronic agent finds your friend and asks "Is George a potential killer?" Your best friend begins to worry. Perhaps it is true. The same sort of questions began to circulate about my wife: "Is she a Marxist? Why was she born in China? Is she an agent of Mao Tse Tung?"[81] Stupid, stupid, questions, but your business contacts take notice, begin to worry, and you lose them.

Some even intimated that I was a sort of hypnotist and that I held Lee under my spell.[82] You have to investigate like Scotland Yard or private detectives do, cautiously, quietly, meticulously, and not by innuendo, gossip, or plain brutal imposition. Finally, just assembling a bunch of these semi-salacious depositions into a large number of volumes, all done at large taxpayer expense—and that's what the *Warren Commission Report* and the *Warren Commission Hearings and Exhibits* are—is the height of foolishness and a nightmare of blind bureaucratic logic. But we shall talk about these matters later.[83]

CHAPTER TWO

In 1960 I lost my only son Sergei to a congenital disease, cystic fibrosis.[84] His death was not unexpected once the diagnosis had been made, but when it happened it affected me so strongly that I knew I had to "get away from it all." I asked my wife to give up her successful job in the designing profession and join me on an expedition, on foot, through the trails of Mexico and South America.[85] This effort helped me immensely.[86] Shortly after our return we met the Oswalds. Lee and Marina understood my actions, which were the Russian way of getting back to nature, being alone in the wilderness with the image of the person we had lost in our minds. It was a way to experience a communion with the departed and come to grips with the ordeal of our separation from them.

Walking among the poor and dispossessed of Latin America also opened our eyes to the realities of human life. Before, like most people living in the United States, we were busy carrying on with business and hustling after success and pushed the existence of poverty and inequality from our minds. Perhaps for this reason I became receptive to some of Lee's ideas, listened to them, discussed them freely, and came to look at him as a friend, almost a son. Possibly I identified him with my lost son, unconsciously, of course, and as far as age is concerned he could have been my son.[87] And on Jeanne's part there was the same dynamic with Marina, who was about our daughter Alexandra's age. Our experiences among the poor of Mexico and Central America greatly interested Lee, who asked many intelligent questions. Because of his childhood in New Orleans and his early contact with Latin Americans, he understood the complex, almost feudal problems of the poor in the hemisphere and was searching for solutions.

After the forced separation Lee came to our house every day. "Give me Marina's telephone number," he begged me, "I want to talk to her and the baby." After thinking it over Jeanne and I agreed to give him Marina's number and address, against Marina's wishes. We just did not believe that Marina should be afraid of Lee. Whether the decision was the right one, we don't know, but starting that evening Lee began calling his wife at all times of the day and night, disturbing everyone until the Mellers asked Marina to move out.[88] Marina refused to move back in with Lee and instead moved to the home of Katya Ford, a Russian refugee married to an American geologist named Declan,[89] and still later moved to the home of Valentina Ray, another refugee with an American husband, Frank, who was an advertising executive.[90] Eventually, though, she returned to Lee.[91] Her return, which we did not see, supposedly involved a tearful scene where Lee, while on his knees, swore his love and promised to make some money.[92] The separation was too short to have a positive effect and in the end we were angry with ourselves for intervening in their lives.

Life was catching up with us, and our own time was becoming more precious. Jeanne had to finish some urgent designing jobs and my long awaited geological survey project in Haiti was coming to fruition. That fall I was also chosen to be the chairman of the local cystic fibrosis campaign, which meant writing letters, seeing a lot of people, participating in various kinds of meetings and, above all, raising money.[93] Jeanne pitched in, spent her energy usefully, raising large amounts of money from our rich neighbors and from executives in the clothing industry. The campaign was a great success.[94] Coincidentally, the local cystic fibrosis organization my ex-wife and I had started in Dallas became a national organization with headquarters in Atlanta.[95] At the beginning of our association with the Oswalds,[96] First Lady Jacqueline Kennedy became an honorary chairman of our foundation, something all of us who had lost children were profoundly grateful for. I had told Lee previously that I had known the first lady as a young girl, as well as her mother, father, and all of her relatives, and how charming the whole family was.[97] Lee was aware of this fact and he expressed several times how much he admired our president's wife.

THREE

❧

Final Conversations with Lee

Newspaper journalists and writers wish to attribute to me the part of Svengali,[1] a sinister, evil adviser to Lee. Nothing could be farther from the truth. He was a strong and stubborn man, one hundred percent American, who had made an early decision, in his childhood as a matter of fact, that the American way of life means unabridged capitalism, crooked politics, violence, racism, a pursuit of material luxuries rather than ideals, keeping up with the Joneses,[2] etc. It was these convictions that motivated his defection to Russia in the hope of finding something better. Believe me, on these matters nothing I could have said would have persuaded him to the contrary.

Christmas of 1962

Anyone familiar with Haitian things knows how difficult it is to organize anything worthwhile in that country. But I have always been very fond of Haiti and especially of the people there. Fortunately my many friends were helpful and we were assured now that my survey was developing a firm base. I was also trying to organize the Haitian Holding Company to help develop the sagging economy of this impoverished but beautiful country.[3] Time was becoming scarce for us, and we were seeing the Oswalds rather infrequently as 1962 drew to a close. One night Lee came alone and seemed very depressed.

"Lee, my friend," I told him. "You like Tolstoy, don't you? He said many clever things but this one applies to you: 'Man must be happy. If not he has to work on himself to correct this misunderstanding which makes him unhappy.'[4] I think I know what *your* 'misunderstanding' is."

Lee nodded sadly. "My tragedy," he said, "is that my suffering is inflicted on me by a person whom I want to be close to and from whom I would want to find protection and consolation."

These words, which I remember distinctly, touched me greatly.

"You try to change Marina into your image. It's difficult, if not impossible. You should like her for what she is, not for what you would want her to be. Do you see my point?"

"But she is becoming like an American middle-class wife," Lee fought feebly. "She thinks only of foolish comforts. She is becoming like the rest of them, talking of washers, driers, and other gadgets as if they were the most important things in life."

"Lee, you are too demanding. She is new in this country and is affected by it. Take it easy. Try to be friends with her. Somebody said: 'friendship is a quiet and exquisite servant, while love is a ferocious and demanding master.'"[5]

"I am a fool, and I am very unhappy," Lee said quietly. "But thanks for the advice anyway. You are a very good friend."

When he left I thought to myself, "Here is a good fellow whose *real* tragedy is a complete misunderstanding of himself. He wants love from a woman who does not understand him. And he himself does not squarely face the issues. What is most important to him? In the meantime the despair is like an organism which destroys him. He begins to lose hope."[6]

So Lee went back home, back to his miserable life. But he seemed to be resigned to unhappiness, and we had not received any complaints of physical abuse from Marina for several weeks after her return to Lee—no black eyes and no cigarette burns on her delicate white flesh.

A big party was to be given for Christmas of 1962 by Declan Ford,[7] another geologist such as myself, and his wife Katya, herself a Russian refugee who knew the Oswalds well but tried to steer away from them. They were probably annoyed by Marina's stay with them in November. As far as Lee was concerned they were rather indifferent to him. Being younger than most ex-Russians, Katya was a relatively liberal person.

After we received the invitation, Jeanne called Katya and asked her permission to bring the Oswalds, who were extremely lonesome at the time. Katya was not at all enthusiastic at Jeanne's suggestion but with a little bit of arm-twisting she accepted. She insisted, however, that the Oswalds were not to bring June to the party. The baby may have been a pretext to prevent the Oswalds from attending as they had no money to hire a baby-sitter. So I got on the phone with Katya and said, "The Oswalds are lonesome, isolated, nobody sees them except us and we are not giving a party this year. We will not come without the Oswalds. Marina will not have anyone to speak to if we invite her to another, purely American party. At your party she will find some Russian-speaking people. I have a solution. We shall find a baby-sitter for June."

Fortunately Jeanne's friend Anita, an Italian-American lady, a good Christian, volunteered for the job and stayed with June that whole night.[8]

That Christmas eve[9] both Marina and Lee were well dressed and looked very elegant. Lee didn't always have to be a non-descript individual, he had sometimes a very pleasant appearance and could dress well. The Oswalds, my wife, and myself, chatting pleasantly, departed for the Ford's attractive house in North Dallas. It was a clear, cold night and a slight layer of snow, unusual for Texas, cheered all of us and gave the city a Christmas-like appearance.

When we arrived most of the guests had already consumed a lot of drinks and were chattering away excitedly in what seemed to be a dozen languages. The loveliest girl in the crowd was a Japanese musician, Yaeko Okui, staying in Dallas for a short time with her friends from Tokyo.[10] She was a delicate, elegant, sophisticated girl, restrained and dignified, a little lost in our Dallas society of noisy, self-assertive, aggressive females.

Marina did not look very well at ease; she seemed to be afraid of the crowd. She liked to interact with men one-on-one, and appeared bashful, like a country girl. Lee, on the other hand, blossomed in a group and was the hit of the party. It was the first time that I saw him truly shine in a large group. Naturally a good conversationalist when he wanted to be—in both English and in Russian I might add—he was outgoing and friendly. Possibly because the people were more liberal than usual, his behavior was exemplary. Serious, attentive, and polite, he answered questions intelligently, if the person who asked the question was serious. He reacted well to the surroundings.

Somebody played Russian tunes on the piano and some good singing voices could be heard. Marina unfortunately was not musical, and Lee was engrossed in conversations.[11] I stayed around him and noticed that several women flirted with him and displayed their charms.[12] Some were quite attractive. But Lee's greatest conquest was this Japanese woman I just mentioned, Yaeko. I found her the most interesting woman present. He noticed her also and angled towards her—or possibly it was vice-versa—anyway they were soon engaged in a conversation.[13] Lee had served in Japan and therefore he had learned a lot about the country and the people. He had told me in the past that he had met some interesting leftist youngsters there.

Maybe Yaeko had met American servicemen before, but whatever it was they were soon so engrossed in each other I wisely left them alone. Marina stayed around, but not being able to understand Lee and Yaeko's English, she fretted and did not know what to do with herself. As far as I was concerned, I was delighted with her discomfort. How many times I'd heard her call Lee a bore, a fool, a bookworm, how many times she degraded his masculinity, and yet here was the loveliest girl of the entire party in a trance. Now Marina became jealous to the point she even forgot to smoke cigarettes and to drink wine—both were free and plentiful—she just watched Lee with narrow, jealous eyes. "We should go home," she muttered under her breath to me. "It's getting late. I am worried about June."[14]

"Don't worry, she is well taken care of. And we are having a good time," I answered. It was a bit sadistic, but I was rather enjoying the situation.[15]

Regardless of how Marina felt Lee was not to be budged. He enjoyed the evening and insisted staying there to the end of the party.[16]

The other Russians at the party, unknown so far to the Oswalds, like cultured Russian Jews, were amazed by Lee's almost perfect command of the language. He spoke very fast to an elderly lady and she said: "I have lived here in America thirty years and I cannot speak English as well as you, young man, speak Russian."

The party became even more boisterous and noisy. Lee and Yaeko lost track of each other. But she found me and asked timidly, "What an interesting friend you have. What's his name?"

"Lee Harvey Oswald."

"Oh, what a lovely name."

"I agree with you that Lee is an unusual and intelligent young man, but many others, the majority, disagree with me. They don't seem to understand him."

"I do," said Yaeko. "He had so many true things to say about Japan. He is a very sensitive person and he understood my country. The new Japan is very complex."

"Yes, Lee is not one of those GI's who believes that for the price of a bar of chocolate and a pair of nylons a woman can be conquered, or a whole country for that matter."

"Where does he work?" she asked bashfully.

I gave her the address and the telephone number of Jaggars-Chiles-Stovall and thought something good was at last happening to my friend Lee. Perhaps new horizons were opening for him. Even a new romance!

Unfortunately, I cannot say whether anything romantic ever materialized with Yaeko, as my life became hectic after the party and I did not have much time for the Oswalds, their troubled marriage, or Lee's love life. They did communicate however.[17] I wouldn't have known about it had it not been for Marina, who came over one day and furiously told me, "I found this Japanese girl's address in Lee's pocket. What a bastard, he is having an affair with her."[18]

I did not say anything. "Good for him," I thought smiling inwardly.

"That Japanese bitch," she cried bitterly, "we had a fight over her—and look at the result."

She sported a new black eye.

"She provoked me to a fight," Lee told me later, showing his scratched face. "This time she fought like a mad cat."

The situation was normal again: they were at each other's throats.

Rare Meetings in 1963

This latest incidence of violence, due this time to Lee's contact with Yaeko, showed my wife and me that it was up to them to iron out their difficulties. We even began to agree that the Russian refugees were perhaps right in eliminating this unhappy couple from their lives. We did not show Lee or Marina this change in our attitude, but our meetings became rarer.[19] When we saw each other we spoke mostly about Lee's job, our coming departure to Haiti, and about June's health. Only one evening in early 1963 led to some serious discussion. All four of us were present.

I remember Jeanne complimented Lee for his serious attitude towards life. She was tired of people teasing her and did not enjoy this American pastime. My teasing annoyed her also.

"Excessive vanity is related to jokes and constant teasing," she told Lee. "People who tease are trying to be brilliant at others' expense. That you don't do, Lee, neither to us or to Marina. The teasers and constant jokers," she continued, "want to show themselves superior."

Lee was grateful for the compliment. He sat on that sofa of ours and told us something very touching. "I think that I shall be moving away from here after your departure. When my heart is heavy—and it will be when you will be gone—it will be hard for me to remain in one place."

"Don't impose new changes on Marina and the child, think of them," said Jeanne. "If everything works out well, we shall invite you to stay with us in Haiti."

Then she gave the Oswalds some advice. "You seem to be still in love with each other. Cultivate this love as you would cultivate a fire, adding affectionate actions like little pieces of wood. Otherwise the fire will be extinguished."

I had to add my own piece of advice. "Study, Lee," I said. "Study is the best consolation against worst adversities. Some philosopher said that, it's not my own idea."[20]

"Kids," said Jeanne, "we shall miss you, even though you have been giving us a lot of headaches. We shall be basking in the sun of Haiti, drinking in the beauty of our favorite island and eating mangoes."

"Maybe it won't be so pleasant," I quipped, not wanting to remind the Oswalds too much about their dismal lives on Elsbeth Street in Oak Cliff. "Remember life in America is 'fun-fun-fun' and then 'worry-worry-worry.' Try to have more fun than worry."

As a result of our admonishments Marina promised not to smoke and Lee said, "Since you won't be smoking, I won't put out cigarettes on your arm."

Screening Our Film

One evening with the Oswalds in January of 1963, one fraught with incidents, stands out in our memory.[21] That evening we decided to show the 8-mm movie of our walking trip,[22] which Lee had not seen and had insisted on seeing. A scientist working for the research department of an oil company, Everett Glover,[23] arranged for the projection in his house and invited all his friends, acquaintances, and colleagues.[24] Most scientists and skillful technicians dream of wilderness and free life in the open. And so the large room was full. Our only guests were Lee and Marina, who had found someone to babysit for June.

I did not show this film[25] often as the original was precious to us; there were no copies. Taken entirely outdoors, the film came out amazingly well. It started with our departure from the "civilized" world in October of 1960, at the ranch of my very close friend Tito Harper,[26] and ended a year later

CHAPTER THREE

south of the Panama Canal.[27] What we did was a little walk from the border, all on foot. We did not cheat, even once. During this *hegira*[28] we made a complete breakaway from all comforts, slept exclusively outside, on the ground, ate whatever the Indians had to sell, and I occasionally bartered my knowledge of minerals in exchange for food supplies.[29] We walked freely as much as we wanted, slowly at first, much faster later, guiding ourselves by old mining maps and by compass.

The film, taken periodically, showed this amazing change in us, from slobs to healthy individuals. We lost a lot of disgusting fat in a hurry and after three months became lean and bronzed like savages, able to run up a high mountain without breathing hard. The rest of the footage consisted of beautiful scenery, Indians we met, our wonderful Manchester Terrier Nero, and our unpredictable mule Contessa. We concluded our *hegira* at a ranch south of the Panama Canal and left Contessa there, to be retired from hard work.[30] I hope she ended her life peacefully. We returned from Panama in a more civilized way, flying by plane first to Jamaica and then to Haiti where we took a good long rest and visited Michael Breitman, an elderly friend of my father.[31]

Quite a few of Glover's friends from Dallas and New York, mostly career people, were interested in meeting Lee despite being conservatively inclined. Some were more interested in him than in our movie.[32] They got their money's worth. After the showing they asked Lee some pointed questions and he answered them aggressively and sharply without hiding his feelings. I think he wanted to show these well-dressed and prosperous youngsters, even to the point of exaggeration, that he was radically different from them. I wanted him to stop, hinted at it, but he went on nevertheless, talking of his sympathies for revolutionary movements all over the world, of his respect for Fidel Castro[33] and for Che Guevara.[34] This hardly made him popular with this group, composed mainly of employees of big oil companies, who were dreaming not of revolutions but of advancement of their respective careers.

And there is nobody more conservative and even race conscious than an oil company employee or executive. Lee knew that. "I bet you," he said sharply, "that your companies do not employ any blacks or Mexicans in any positions, not even an average position much less an executive."

Nobody answered Lee's challenge.

"Naturally when you are abroad you act differently, you use natives of all colors. American oil companies are *so* liberal."

But there was an exception in this conservative group—a tall, dark-haired, attractive woman who appeared to be in her late twenties. She took a vivid interest in Marina and did not take offense to Lee's utterances. She asked me if Marina spoke any English.

"No," I said.

"Would you introduce me to her? My name is Ruth Paine."[35]

And so I introduced her to Marina. To my great surprise Ruth began to speak in fluent Russian to an equally flabbergasted Marina.[36]

Mrs. Ruth Paine, an eccentric American, came from a wealthy Philadelphia Quaker family and went to some Eastern college where she took Russian studies very seriously. She was one of those gifted people who learn a difficult language well and are infatuated by the Russian culture. Mrs. Paine was probably bored with the suburban Irving atmosphere and wanted to practice Russian; her husband Michael,[37] being a busy research engineer for Bell Helicopter,[38] left her with a lot of time and energy on her hands. Marina was a real find for her: a native Russian who did not speak any English. Some people accused her later of an infatuation of a different type, but I did not notice it.[39] Anyway, she was more interested in Marina than in Lee who in the meantime continued with his furious and extravagant discussion with our conservative friends.

Thus began a friendship between these two women, a friendship which lasted until shortly after the assassination. Ruth had done more for Marina and June than any other person over the preceding months and yet, for some reason, Marina refused to see her after Lee's death.

All in all the showing of our film was a success. The screen was filled with beautiful scenery, waterfalls, volcanoes in eruption, and outcrops of brilliantly hued deposits. Scientists, being adventurers at heart, love the wilderness. Marina, not being an outdoor woman, could have cared less, but, being polite, she did not express her lack of interest and kept on chatting amicably with Ruth.

Lee, on the other hand, commented excitedly how much he liked the film and that he envied us for having lived for a year so close to nature, an ascetic life of complete freedom.[40]

"You have walked almost four thousand miles to get away from people, comforts, stupid gadgets, and conventions. It would be my dream also to do that. I envy you. I have never been completely free."

"Yes, it was a great privilege," I told Lee, "but it was tough, believe me. We wore out twenty-two pairs of shoes and *guaraches*[41] each."

The subject of our film filled most of our last conversations with Lee and even Marina participated in these discussions.

"How could you have done such a thing at your age?" she asked Jeanne. "And to look so trim, strong and beautiful?"

"Effort and constant exercise. Control over your body," Jeanne would lecture her. But to no avail. Neither was I successful in convincing Lee to be more athletic.[42] "Get the troubles, sadness, and anger out of your systems through hard physical exercise," I advised them both. "It worked so well in our case." Unfortunately, neither of them would follow our advice.

"I would never do anything without paying for food and lodging," said Lee. "And Marina is not an outdoor woman like your wife."

Lee's Views on Latin America

Over the years I had lived in several Latin American countries, where the social injustices were obvious, but back then, before 1960, I was looking at life through the eyes of an eager petroleum geologist, not a sociologist.[43] Our primitive walking trip, in contrast, put us close to simple people, and we lived with them and we began to understand the problems of the poor. On the basis of our trip I began to occasionally look at things like Lee always did. It was much like what had happened to Lee in Japan—hence his close and immediate relationship with Yaeko, who was a sensitive and perceptive woman.

More should be said of Lee's interests in world affairs. Lee's views on Latin America were determined long before we met. Recalling some of my conversations with Lee he was rather an admirer of Fidel Castro and especially the romantic, swashbuckling personage of Che Guevara. Lee liked Fidel as a representative of a small country, an underdog, facing fearlessly a huge and powerful country like the United States. In his mind Fidel was a sincere man who aimed to provide the best for his country, to eradicate racial prejudice and to bring social equality to his people. I do not think he knew very much about Cuba, and his information came through his contact with the Cuban students and technicians he had met in Minsk. Che on the other hand appealed to him as a handsome, brilliant doctor, who had traveled around Latin America discovering basic injustices and who eventually tried to correct them. He did know that in some of the poorest parishes of Mexico the peasants considered him a new Savior. Now Che is dead, and the man who killed him was assassinated recently in Paris.[44] So it's all immaterial.

Regarding the Bay of Pigs,[45] Lee thought it was an utter disaster. He was sure that we should not have gotten involved in the internal affairs of Cuba. He was opposed to the anti-Castro Cuban refugees, but this subject was not

Left: Fidel Castro addresses the United Nations General Assembly, 1960.
Right: Che Guevara after the Battle of Santa Clara, January 1, 1959. Oficina de
Asuntos Historicos de Cuba (Office of Historical Affairs, Cuba)

discussed too much between us. He thought that Cuba before Castro was
a whorehouse for American tourists and headquarters for American racke-
teers like Lansky and company.[46] As far as I was concerned, I was not sure
whether he was right or not. I knew Cuba very slightly myself. I was there
a year or so before Castro's victory over Batista.[47] To me it was a cheerful,
corrupt country; but austerity did not seem to fit the Cuban sunny natures.

Lee thought President Kennedy should not have allowed any invasion of
Cuba, but he was not vehement or violent in his views on this subject. I have
the impression that the matter was not of much interest to him. Lee never
expressed any hatred for Kennedy because of the Bay of Pigs; he just calmly
assessed the whole affair as a very foolish action.

Lee told me that the same phenomenon of awakening to the fate of the
poor had happened with Che Guevara when he carried out his assignment
as a doctor in Central America,[48] sometimes in places we had visited ourselves. The desperate plight of the poor could not be denied by anyone with
open eyes and a little bit of feelings for a fellow-man.

"Che Guevara understood the situation well," Lee said, "although his stay in Central America took place years before your trip. But you still saw dismal poverty in parts of Mexico, in Guatemala, San Salvador, Nicaragua, and Panama, didn't you?"

"Yes we did. But in Costa Rica we found a somewhat different situation. Do you know why?" We knew the answer but asked Lee anyway.

"Simply because," he answered, "this country has never been occupied and corrupted by us, Americans."

Right he was. The ignorant "high-school dropout" knew the history of different United States interventions in Latin America. Costa Rica is like the Switzerland of Latin America, with a true democratic government, limited police force, no army or air force.[49] You can talk freely there and meet the president in the barbershop in San Jose. You can, however, also find refuge for your money in Costa Rica if you steal millions in the USA.[50]

We discussed with Lee the dismal poverty of overcrowded El Salvador, where the wealth of the whole country belongs to twenty-three families, *latifundistas* since the Spanish conquest.[51] What was true when I talked to Lee is still true today.[52] During our walking trip through Guatemala, we just happened to be there shortly before the Bay of Pigs operation.[53] To our surprise the town was full of crew-cut Americans, not speaking a word of Spanish, out of place. I told Jeanne, "but these are marines, or rather marine pilots. What the hell are they doing here?"[54] And then there is the tragicomic history of Nicaragua. The Somoza family owns most of Nicaragua, and this regime was imposed by the wife of an American ambassador during the occupation by the Marines.[55] An elderly Nicaraguan geologist told us the story of a handsome and husky telephone lineman, who seduced the lonesome wife of the Yankee ambassador—the name was mentioned but I forgot it—and his subsequent appointment as chief of police, which was equivalent to a dictator for life.

All these injustices are out in the open now, but thirteen years ago, when I discussed them with Lee, they were not. Today the frequent support provided by the United States to the oligarchs, crooked generals, and ruthless dictators of the world is discussed openly in the House, Senate, and in the United Nations.[56] But back in 1963 such conversations were so out of place they might have been considered subversive. Now, after Vietnam and Watergate, we all see a little clearer and talk more freely.[57]

"Lee," I asked, "how do you understand the Latin American situation so well?"

"I am from New Orleans, as a kid I met a lot of refugees from all these banana republics, no better source of information."[58]

In this way Lee and I were both true non-conformists, even revolutionaries. Being with him took me back to my young days at the University of Liège, when we spent entire conversations[59] discussing various problems of life without any respect for the rules or for the established authorities. My long years of experience in Latin America, followed by my son's death and the ensuing sadness, had led me to commiserate with the fate of the poor and starving. As a young man I was career and money mad: a hustler. I have been in the Social Register,[60] played with the jet-set, knew innumerable rich people, such as the Bouvier family, including both parents and their daughters Jacqueline and Lee when they were young girls.[61] All this foolish activity makes me disgusted with myself today. Now all this is a waste of time, meaningless, but Jeanne, my wife, and Lee had always been on the side of the underprivileged, and she had lived in China and saw new-born babies thrown in the garbage because parents were too poor to feed them. To Lee, commiseration for the dejected came naturally. Poor as his family was in New Orleans, he never really experienced hunger. But through his inner nature he felt sympathy for socially marginalized people. He had remained the same since his childhood, which made him such a beautiful and worthwhile person to me.

In our last meetings Lee often expressed his concern about this country. American origins—according to him—ran from the hypocritical pilgrims through the Indian genocide, to the invasion of the continent by the greedy and hungry European masses that, greeted with the racist attitudes of the Anglos, became even more racist themselves. Even before the bus boycott[62] in this country, Lee said he was keenly aware of the racist cancer eating at America. "All people are SOBs," he often said, "and the strongest and more ferocious always win, physically but not morally."[63]

Since Marina never participated in these political discussions, I would talk with Jeanne about the relationship between this curious couple after their departures from our home.

"Opposites attract," was Jeanne's opinion.

"I think it's sex," was my opinion, "but what type of sex I don't know." There had to have been a strong emotional bond between those two. They always came back to each other, except just before the assassination. Lee had a job with the Book Depository; everything seemed fine. He begged Marina to come and live with him. Marina refused because Lee couldn't afford to buy a washing machine, something she had had access to in the Paine's house. From this incident arose a ridiculous theory attributed to me by some publication, *Esquire*, I think, titled "A washing machine theory of Kennedy's assassination."[64] Supposedly, I compared Marina to a typical Texas woman who would not go back to her husband because he could not afford a new Cadillac. But in poor Marina's case it was a washing machine. The comparison is not bad, but I did not enunciate it since for me Lee is innocent of Kennedy's assassination. I cannot prove it conclusively but the later events, which will be discussed below, tend to prove Lee's innocence.

Lee and Admiral Bruton

Practical issues of life took over. I had to spend virtually all my time on my geological work and on preparations for our coming departure to Haiti. At the same time Jeanne was designing furiously for several companies, trying to make some money. Our finances at that time were almost exhausted.[65] There was a hiatus in our meetings with the Oswalds. In March I flew to Haiti to sign a contract there and then spent some time in New York preparing for the survey.[66] Jeanne, too, did not see the Oswalds because she was finishing her designing assignments and was packing. We intended to take a minimum of things to Haiti, necessitating leaving our furniture and heavy items in a warehouse in Dallas.[67]

Then I came back from New York and asked Jeanne to invite the Oswalds. They arrived immediately and brought baby June along. I remember this was a beautiful, spring day, warm enough to swim. And so Jeanne called Frannie Bruton, the wife of Rear Admiral Henry C. Bruton.[68] Both were good friends of ours and, incidentally, long-time enemies of Richard Nixon, whom they knew from his California days when he made his career ruining good citizens' reputations.[69] We used to call him *Henri*, in the French manner, because he loved to speak French with us, as did Frannie. Both spoke French very well and were well read. Later they went to live in France.[70]

The admiral was a highly decorated submarine hero during the Second World War; I do not recall whether he had four or five Navy Crosses.[71] He never talked about them and was a most humble and charming person. Frannie was an ex-school teacher, an amateur painter, and an admirable woman in many respects. The Brutons were having a swimming party that day and invited us to attend. Jeanne asked her if we could bring a couple of friends along, and mentioned the name of the Oswalds. Although we had spoken to her before about this unusual couple Frannie couldn't recall who they were, but asked us to bring them along anyway.[72]

And so we arrived at the Brutons' lovely place with its huge swimming pool and Frannie was delighted to see us. When I reminded her that Lee was an ex-Marine, she went to get the admiral who was a congenial man and liked[73] to meet the enlisted men.

In the meantime Marina sat by the swimming pool with the baby. She either did not know how to swim or disliked showing her figure, which was not too hot. Jeanne had given her a conservative bathing suit, but she refused to use it. Lee sat quietly, immersed in his thoughts. That was frequent with him when he was in new surroundings. I, however, was eager to get in the water.[74] Before diving in I said jokingly, "Lee isn't that funny that you get punished for your actions—which are only an appearance—but you don't get punished for your thoughts, which are the real thing."

While he was pondering that little jest, I continued, "This is a nice place, makes you think of oppressed workers, etc. You should see the places of the *real* moguls of finance. This is just a poor admiral's retirement home."

Frannie and Jeanne were talking in the meantime with great animation about China. Frannie, herself a world-traveled woman, of most varied interests, knew China, where she spent several years with her husband. She loved the country and the people—so she and Jeanne hit it off fabulously well.

I went back to Lee and told him[75] quietly, so that the ladies could not hear us, "Does the wife of the Admiral strike you as an aristocratic, rich woman?"

He just nodded agreement.

"Do you know that she is the daughter of a tenant-farmer widow from Oklahoma? In her childhood her mother[76] was so poor that she took washing in. Frannie walked to school four or five miles. She couldn't afford to buy paper and used the margins of old newspapers to write on or to do her arithmetic. And the admiral was also a poor farm-boy from Arkansas. He got his education in the navy and is both a lawyer and an electronics engineer."

I do not know why I wanted to talk so much, but on this occasion I wished to impress upon Lee that everything material in this world isn't bad and that comforts obtained honestly are not to be despised.

Lee did not say anything.

At that moment Admiral Bruton appeared. He was not exceptionally tall but had broad shoulders; a typical submariner. "When I was in a submarine in the Pacific," he once jokingly told me in a good-natured manner, "I couldn't turn around in the conning tower[77] because I was constantly excited thinking of all those women back on the mainland. So I had to forge ahead, and that's how I got my Navy Crosses."

CHAPTER THREE

But on this occasion he simply greeted everybody and began talking disgustedly of his new job with the Collins Radio Company,[78] actually an important position he took[79] after his early retirement from active duty three years earlier. He did not like the commercial aspects of his work. "I should have stayed in the Navy a bit longer," he said irritably, "I am being made into a salesman."[80]

Then he began talking warmly to Lee, asking him about his duties in the Marine Corps. Although Henri was kind and continued chatting amicably, my friend remained cool and aloof.

"That Marine Corps was the most miserable period in my life," Lee said disgustedly. "Stupid work, ignorant companions, abusive officers. Boy, was I happy to have gotten out of it. To hell with the Navy."[81]

Here I saw for the first time his profound dislike for the military and especially for the brass. The term "admiral" itself apparently irritated him.

"He is somewhat of a rebel and a little bit a Marxist," I told the admiral, trying to smooth over the disagreeable incident.

I never saw Henri mad before, but now he really was, and I knew that he could hardly restrain himself from ordering Lee to stand at attention and then to telling him to march out of the house. Instead he just walked away.[82] Lee did not continue being insulting and spoke politely with Frannie about his stay in Japan. "You lived in the compounds there, being officers' wives, and didn't have the chance to meet the real people in Japan, like I did."

"I wish I could have," answered Frannie diplomatically.

Marina was the personification of charm that afternoon. We had to translate what she said, of course. But she loved the arrangement of the whole house as we showed her around, including the luxury of the furnishings and Frannie's excellent if amateur paintings.[83] The surroundings were an incredible contrast to the Oswalds' gloomy apartment on Elsbeth Street. She smiled politely and even flirted with the admiral.

Excellent snacks, not a real dinner, were served later by our hosts, and nothing too out of the ordinary happened after that. Henri was a good host and restrained himself while Lee, finally relaxed, told some funny, if slightly derogatory, tales[84] about his Marine Corps life.

"We had a sergeant in the Marines who was as racist as any German SS trooper," he began telling us. "But then his sex habits—"

"Please, Lee," I stopped him.

"I could sing you the Marine anthem but, fortunately, I never learned it," Lee continued, trying to be funny again.

I cannot say that this evening was a great success. But we left quite late, still amicably, because most of the conversation at the end of the evening was carried on in French between the four of us, without Lee and Marina.

Four years later in 1967 we saw the Brutons again in Washington, DC. They had moved out of Dallas and taken permanent residence in Arlington, and we spent a couple of days in their house. Naturally the subject of the assassination came up, and when the Brutons learned who had visited their home they were absolutely flabbergasted.[85] They did not associate the rude young ex-marine with the "presumed" assassin[86] of President Kennedy. They probably did not catch the Oswalds' names when they had met them, and then they had traveled extensively in the meantime.

Frannie became quite excited on learning that she had entertained "that horrible individual." Henri, being an adventurous man, was rather more amused than appalled by this fortuitous acquaintanceship. "Well," he said jokingly, "we met Nixon *and* we also met Lee Harvey Oswald."

Neither of the Brutons was ever approached by the FBI and had never been asked to testify at the Warren Commission, so nobody seems to have known of this strange meeting. It seems to me that I had mentioned it to the Warren Commission, but possibly the assistant counsel did not take me seriously and then it may be that they would not bother an American retired rear admiral.[87] The "so-called foreigners," people like my wife and myself, were to bear the brunt of the suspicions and innuendoes.

Easter of 1963

On April 13, if I remember correctly, we were at last nearly ready to leave. All our light belongings were packed and our furniture was ready to be sent to the warehouse. During the commotion before our departure we saw little of the Oswalds, and we knew that they were practically living like hermits. Nobody visited or invited them to visit, except maybe the Paines. Jeanne and I sat exhausted that evening after playing tennis.[88] "This is a big holiday," she said. "And the Oswalds are alone. Even Marina is abandoned by the conservative refugees as she has gone back to her 'Marxist' husband."

I agreed with Jeanne and commiserated with Marina. Being left alone was a penalty for her because she preferred Lee, notwithstanding all the fights and the beatings.

Jeanne had previously bought a huge toy rabbit, practically June's size, a pink[89] fluffy thing for the poor child. The Oswalds' new apartment was on Neely Street, a few blocks away from their old place on Elsbeth Street.[90] This was our first visit to their new abode which was infinitely better than the previous one. They had the second floor here, all to themselves. Huge trees shaded the structure and in the back yard the climbing roses hung up on the trellises.[91] The house itself had a white frame of the usual type for a Southern structure.

We rang the bell. The lights were off as it was obviously late for our sedentary friends. Although it was about 10 p.m. we had to keep ringing a long time.[92]

"Who is there?" asked Lee's familiar voice.

"Jeanne and George, open up, we have something for June," I answered cheerfully. Lee came down, opened the front door and then led us up a dark staircase.

Now Marina was also up and the apartment lights came on. Everything was clean and spacious but almost devoid of furniture. "Isn't this a nice place?" confided Marina in Russian. "So much better than the old hole-in-the-walls."

We agreed and congratulated them on finding such a good place.

She was cheerful and Lee was smiling also, which hadn't happened often recently.[93] He was happy that they were left alone by the émigrés and even by the rare Americans they knew. Lee's feelings for the émigrés could be compared to those a pro-Castro Cuban might have towards all the refugees now crowding the streets of Miami.

Lee appeared satisfied with his job and proud of being able to provide a better place for his family.[94] This was the first time in quite a while that we did not see any conflict between him and his wife. Of course, what follows will prove that everything wasn't milk and honey[95] for the Oswald family.

Marina served soft drinks and began discussing some domestic affairs with Jeanne. Lee and I walked to the balcony and began to chat. He was very curious about my project in Haiti but up to now neither one of us was sure the work would materialize. Now it was a *fait accompli*.[96] Lee envied my profession and the chance I would have to help an undeveloped country and the poor people living there. He knew Haiti from his readings and was aware it was the oldest, independent black republic in the world. He had learned that Haiti had helped the United States during the War of Independence, a fact not known to many Americans of his age and background.[97] He also had heard about United States intervention in Haiti after World War I—actually at the end of the war—and of the long American occupation of that country.[98] He even learned which part of the Española Island the Republic of Haiti occupied and her size.[99]

"You are very lucky going there, it will be an exciting experience," he said. His opinion was valuable and encouraging to me because most of my friends and acquaintances had a very dim view of my whole project and thought it would be dangerous and a waste of time.[100] It turned out to be one of the most useful and pleasant experiences of our lives.[101] But most of these would-be advisers knew little about Haiti—and I mean well-educated, prominent people. To them it was an insane, tropical, and black locale with a rather ferocious dictatorship.[102] Some had predicted the worst disasters if we lived there.

Then we talked pleasantly of his job, of June who was growing nicely, and we also spoke of the unfortunate rise of ultra-conservatism in America, of the racist movement in the South. Lee considered this the most dangerous phenomenon for all peace-loving people. "Economic discrimination is bad, but you can remedy it," he said, "but racial discrimination cannot be remedied because you cannot change the color of your skin." Of course, he greatly admired Dr. Martin Luther King Jr.[103] and agreed with his program. He frequently talked of Dr. King with a real reverence.

In the meantime Marina was showing Jeanne her bedroom, kitchen, and the living-room. There she opened a large closet, next to the balcony, and began showing Jeanne her wardrobe, which was considerable. On the bottom of the closet was a rifle standing completely in the open.

"Look! Look!" called Jeanne excitedly. "There is a rifle there."

We came in and I looked curiously. Indeed there was a military rifle there of a type unknown to me, something mounted on top.

"What is that thing dangling?" asked Jeanne.[104]

"A telescopic sight," I answered.

Jeanne had never seen a telescopic sight before and probably did not understand what it was. But I did: I had graduated from a military school.[105]

"Why do you have this rifle here," Jeanne asked Lee.

Marina answered instead. "Lee bought it. Devil knows why. We need all the money we have for food and lodging and he buys this damn rifle."[106]

"But what does he do with a military rifle," Jeanne asked again.

"He likes shooting at the leaves."

"But when does he have time to shoot at the leaves, and where," asked Jeanne curiously.

"He shoots at the leaves in the park, whenever we go there."

This explanation did not make much sense to us, but liking target shooting ourselves we did not consider this a crazy occupation.

All this time Lee stood next to me curiously silent.

"Did you take a pot-shot at General Walker, Lee?" I popped the question

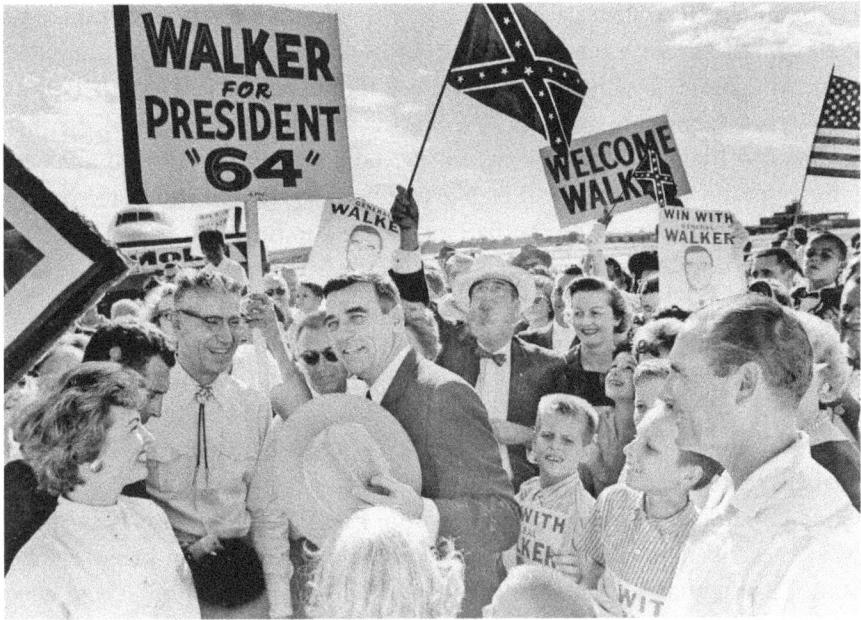

General Edwin Walker lived fairly close to us, on Turtle Creek Boulevard. Supporters greet General Edwin Walker (holding hat) at Love Field in 1962. Joe Laird/*Dallas Morning News*

spontaneously, then a guffaw, thinking this was a pretty good joke.[107] Lee didn't like General Walker and I knew that.

Lee's reaction was strange. I have often tried to reconstruct it in my mind. He did not say anything. He just stood there motionless.

General Edwin Walker[108] lived fairly close to us, on Turtle Creek Boulevard.[109] Everyone knew his house, which had a huge American flag in front, sometimes replaced by a Confederate flag and much later by South Vietnamese and Rhodesian flags.[110] He was a rather notorious character who was asked to resign his post in Germany by President Eisenhower, if I remember correctly.[111] He was an ultra-rightist who had tried to run for governor of Texas in 1962 against John Connally[112] and received a surprising number of votes, some two hundred thousand, on a political platform somewhat to the right of Hitler's. Although he apparently considered me a dangerous radical, I had no real animosity toward him and jokingly called him General Foker.[113]

It was a really foolish joke because a few days before there had been an attempt on Walker's life.[114] As I said, Lee's facial expression remained calm.

He became just a little paler. This was the last time I was with him, and yet I cannot say with precision what his reaction was. I think he mumbled something unintelligibly and I did not ask him to repeat it. For sure he was embarrassed, possibly stunned. And Marina was definitely shocked. Neither Jeanne nor I laughed much at my joke. And certainly not Marina nor Lee. Only later did we learn why this joke had been so stunning and unexpected to them. My attempt at humor had hit the nail on the head.

Marina testified under oath to the Warren Commission that Lee did shoot at General Walker and had missed him narrowly. She also testified that I *knew* Lee shot at General Walker.[115] Marina also testified that Lee indeed considered General Walker a fascist and tried to kill what he thought was the most dangerous man in the country. Marina's testimonies turned out to be contradictory and vague, but there is another thing which makes me believe that Lee did possibly try to shoot General Walker. A man, whose name I do not recall, a Jewish man, whom Lee met at the Fords' Christmas party, described General Walker as the most dangerous man in the United States, a potential neo-fascist leader. I noticed that Lee kept on asking why. And the other fellow explained clearly his reasons. Lee might have been influenced by this statement.[116]

Another possible indication of Lee's involvement is the inscription on Lee's photograph, which we received posthumously, and Marina's inscription on it. I shall return to our discovery of this photograph later.[117] This originally innocuous remark of mine influenced our lives, but we heard later from Albert E. Jenner, assistant counsel to the Warren Commission, that Marina's testimony was even more damaging to me. She supposedly remembered my saying: "Lee, why did you miss him?"[118] That I naturally did *not* say, and Marina was so vague in her recollections that even the Warren Commission did not take her seriously. In the end this single joke cost me a lot of money by damaging my relationship with many of my business contacts.[119]

I now think Marina believed that I somehow knew of Lee's attempted shooting of General Walker and that's why she was so afraid that evening—I might tell the police or FBI about it. Lee, on the other hand, never considered me capable of betrayal, and of course *he* knew that I was completely unaware of his attempt. Had I known *anything* about it in advance, I would have persuaded him *not* to try any such crazy foolishness.

Lee was a little scared of my extra-sensory perception—which I still have with my students now. He often commented with amazement that I could guess his thoughts. And I do believe in the existence of ESP, especially among people closely attuned to each other. It happens to me constantly. For exam-

We were bound first for New York, Philadelphia and Washington,
then from there to Haiti.
Aeroport François Duvalier, Port-au-Prince, Haiti, circa mid-1960s (postcard)

ple, I accurately guess who is on the line when the phone rings. I know when somebody close to me writes me a letter or wants to get in touch with me. It even happened that I thought suddenly of a well-known person—but barely known to me—turned on the TV and there he would be. I remember this happened with Captain Rickenbacker,[120] whom I know slightly but admired a great deal. We were sitting in a living-room with friends in New Orleans and I said suddenly, "turn on the radio, Captain Rickenbacker is going to speak." And he did.

Our meeting on this Easter evening in 1963 ended in an amicable manner. The four of us walked in the small garden and Marina gathered a gorgeous bouquet of yellow roses and gave them to Jeanne in appreciation of the toy rabbit she had brought for baby June. I also think the Oswalds were happy that I did not make any further mention of the rifle or the Walker joke, trying to make an issue out of it. It was our last meeting and a friendly one. We said that June looked less now like Khrushchev, she was growing up. She did not have such a bald head anymore, her eyes had gotten bigger, and she was less chunky.

Lee himself mentioned it, caressing the child. "Look, she is much better-looking now than our great Russian leader."

"I hope she keeps his amusing and friendly personality," said Jeanne.[121]

After this Easter visit things began to move so fast for us that we could not see the Oswalds again, and we did not even talk to them on the phone. Just a few days later, on April 19, 1963, our plane was airborne.[122] We were bound first for New York, Philadelphia, and Washington, then from there to Haiti.[123] I could begin to work on my long-awaited project,[124] which was officially finalized, signed by Haiti's president François Duvalier and published in the *Haitian Congressional Record*.[125]

◈

FOUR

Haiti and the Warren Commission

We arrived in Port-au-Prince, capital of Haiti, on June 2, 1963.[1] For several months we led a delightful existence[2] in our beautiful house overlooking Port-au-Prince Bay,[3] doing useful work with my international group of geologists: one Italian, one Swiss, and one American, as well as our Haitian helpers.[4] But after November 22, 1963, the situation would change completely for us.

Our Move to Haiti

Our move to Haiti ended our personal contact with the Oswalds.[5] Soon after arriving we received a postcard from Lee, giving us his new address in New Orleans. At our last meeting on Easter Sunday, neither of the Oswalds mentioned that they intended to leave Dallas. So, this was a surprise for us.[6] Obviously they had moved from Dallas to New Orleans at about the same time we were in transit to Haiti, we just do not know for certain.[7] Maybe they were just lonesome. Maybe Lee wanted to remove himself and his family from General Walker's neighborhood.[8] It is worth remembering, though, that he did not deny—or accept—his guilt in shooting at General Walker.[9]

And so Lee gave us the now famous address on 4905 Magazine Street[10] in New Orleans, Louisiana, the town where he spent most of his youth. This postcard was, incidentally, written in English. The card got lost somehow, and Jeanne failed to put the exact location in her address book. So we still had Lee's Dallas address at 214 Neely Street and the business address of his reproduction company. We did plan on sending them a Christmas gift, but the tragic events of November 1963 occurred in the meantime.

Whenever we look at this address book now we think of Lee, and wish he were still alive, not only because we liked him so much, but also because he could have proved his innocence or, if he *were* involved in something, to tell the whole truth, even about a conspiracy. He always had enough integrity to tell us the complete truth, even if he had done something wrong.[11] What I have to say here, and it has bothered me for such a long time such that I have never said it before, relates to explaining the type of person Lee Harvey Oswald was, and the reader will have to form his opinion of his guilt, or lack of it. Several new elements will be brought in here, which, in our opinion, are favorable to Lee.[12] Both my wife and I still miss him and are deeply sorry that he met such an untimely death at the hand of such a repulsive individual as Jack Ruby.[13]

Living abroad as we were in the months immediately after the Kennedy assassination and not having any inside information on the case we were "brainwashed" by media coverage which emphasized constantly and repeated over and over[14] that Lee indeed was unquestionably the lone and only assassin. Information began to trickle in from the embassy personnel, and through the *New York Times* and the Miami papers like the *Herald* that we received, that I had been Lee Harvey Oswald's "best friend," and that both Jeanne and I "befriended" the assassin of the president of the United States. We did not hide anything.[15] Of course, we *did* tell the political officer at our embassy that we knew Lee and Marina and that we *were* ready to help in any investigation.

We also wrote to our friends about it—all our letters were, we would learn later, intercepted by the FBI[16]—and finally I wrote a letter of condolence to Jacqueline Kennedy's mother, Mrs. Janet Lee Auchincloss,[17] whom I knew better than her illustrious daughter. Janet, formerly Mrs. Jack Bouvier of New York and Southampton, was a dear friend of my in-laws and mine.[18] In this letter that I composed just twenty days after the assassination[19] I expressed my grief over the death of a great president and a wonderful man. Being under the influence of the barrage of one-sided propaganda in the newspapers and on both radio and television at that time, I added to this letter: "I am deeply sorry I have ever met Lee Harvey Oswald and befriended him."[20] On January 29, 1964, she wrote back to me: "it seems extraordinary that you knew Lee Harvey Oswald and Jacqueline as a child. It certainly is a strange world. And I hope, like you do, that Lee Harvey Oswald's innocent children will not suffer." I then replied on February 2 that we would be in town shortly and would be delighted to visit.[21] Copies of our letters, I would learn, were given to the Warren Commission by Allen Dulles, her close friend.[22]

Without any facts to the contrary and Lee dead, everyone in Haiti considered him the assassin. Even the cynical and well-informed European diplomats in Haiti were of the same opinion. They did, however, begin to grumble, if only under their breath, asking themselves the question: "where is the motive?"[23] Then something unusual happened. Mr. W. James Wood, an FBI agent, arrived in Port-au-Prince.[24] He was wearing a gray flannel suit and sporting the kind of suntan you find in Miami, along with a phony, artificial smile.[25] His sole purpose, I discovered, was to make me deny a statement I had made to my friends and to the political officer at the embassy. What was this disturbing statement? I had contacted[26] a government man in Dallas, the only one I knew personally, probably a CIA agent, or possibly an agent of the FBI, a very nice fellow by the name of J. Walton Moore.[27] Agent Moore had interviewed me upon my return from a government mission to Yugoslavia[28] and we got along well. He had lived in China, was born there as a matter of fact, in a missionary family. So I invited him and his wife to the house, and he got along fabulously well with Jeanne, who had grown up in China herself. I used to see Agent Moore occasionally for lunch. A cosmopolitan character, most attractive. A short time after meeting Lee Harvey Oswald in the summer of 1962, before Lee and I became friends, I was a little worried about his opinions and his background. And so I went to see Agent Moore at his office, in the same building where I used to have my own office, the Reserve Loan Life Building on Ervay Street.[29] I asked him point blank, "I met this young ex-marine, Lee Harvey Oswald, is it safe to associate with him?" And Agent Moore's answer was "Oh, he's OK. He is just a harmless lunatic."[30] That he was harmless was good enough for me. I would decide for *myself* whether Lee was a lunatic.

It was that "harmless lunatic" statement which apparently so greatly disturbed Agent Wood and his superiors. And that same statement would later disturb Albert E. Jenner Jr., the assistant counsel to the Warren Commission, when I later gave my testimony in Washington. As disturbed as Jenner would later be, despite knowing that my testimony was made under an oath to tell the truth, Agent Wood was even more so. He tried to make me deny the statement altogether. We were sitting in a luxurious embassy room, staring with animosity at each other, and this repulsive, replete bureaucrat dared to tell me, "You will have to change your statement."

"What do you mean?" I asked incredulously.

"That false statement of yours, that a government man told you that our president's assassin was a harmless lunatic."

"*False* statement? Man, you are out of your mind!" I answered sharply.

And so the gray-suited man in no uncertain terms threatened me, "Unless you change your statement, life will be tough for you in the States."

"Nuts!" was the only answer I could make.

It was after this meeting with agent Wood that I immediately began having doubts about Lee's guilt. And while I was talking to him—the conversation lasted quite some time—he constantly tried to intimidate me, reminding me I had met a lot of undesirable people in my life and puritanically challenging me on the grounds of moral turpitude, i.e., too many women.

I told this obnoxious FBI agent that either the FBI or CIA or some other agency must be in some way implicated in President Kennedy's assassination. I just took the precaution of saying this, which seemingly backfired.[31] But I did imply that these government agencies were negligent. Still my supposedly false statement was of utter importance to the FBI and Agent Wood and he kept on trying to force me to deny it. I categorically refused to deny anything and we ended this stormy session without shaking hands.[32]

Then my wife went through the same routine. Agent Wood made more threats and alluded to her having belonged to some leftist organization of scouts (imagine—leftist scouts!) which supposedly marred her background. Since she did not have any behavior patterns that would suggest she was guilty of anything, except her "guilt" of having been born in China, she answered Agent Wood in a quiet and icy manner and absolutely refused to influence me to change my statement.[33]

"You don't seem to like the FBI," said Agent Wood with an artificial smile, at the end of our interviews.

"I do not like your methods," I replied. "They are both brutal and naïve. Learn from Scotland Yard, they know how to conduct themselves. When they inquire they do it with discretion, not by innuendo and gossip. You do harm to the people you investigate and don't discover anything useful about the case."

A friend of mine in Dallas, investment banker Sam Ballen, later told the Warren Commission investigators that our emotions were probably tensed up during our interview with Agent Wood.[34] And he was right.

The assurance I received that he was harmless naturally had a positive influence on how I approached my relationship with Lee.[35] I kept asking him many potentially embarrassing questions, for instance, "How did you get to Russia? Isn't it expensive to travel so far? How did you come back to the United States so easily?" His answers were good enough for me, and my opinion of him rose. He did not work for any foreign government, nor for our government—the latter is more doubtful.[36] If I thought he did, he would not have been a good friend of mine. On the other hand, after this interview, my opinion of the FBI under J. Edgar Hoover sank even further.[37] Even today, so many years later, my opinions are being reaffirmed by recent events: the destruction of Lee's letter to FBI agent James Hosty, in which he demanded this agent leave him and his wife alone.[38]

As I have mentioned the whole Bouvier family were very close friends of mine. I met them soon after my arrival in the United States.[39] They were very warm, friendly people. The newspapers all over the country made a big issue out of our relationship. For example on November 24, 1964, the *New York Times* published an article with the headline "Friend of Oswalds Knew Mrs. Kennedy."[40] Some odious insinuations were put forth about me in several newspapers as well, about my life seeming to be full of such "strange coincidences." It's probably in the grave that I shall stop meeting strange people and forming peculiar friendships.[41]

Even the president of Haiti, Dr. François Duvalier, got alarmed by all these goings-on. Let me assure you President Duvalier was no friend of President Kennedy, who cut American aid to Haiti down to almost nothing.[42] But there was another factor: my house was located in the same mountainous development, the Lyle Estates, as the president's palace, and the implication was obvious: when you are the president of Haiti and you are living next to the man who befriended a president's assassin, it presents a problem.

In a small country like Haiti, government people know more about what is going on in the American Embassy than the ambassador himself. This visit by the FBI was blown completely out of proportion. Americans on the island were becoming scared of me, and even the Haitians began to avoid visiting us.

The Warren Commission

As the atmosphere in Port-au-Prince became increasingly oppressive for us, and my work was beginning to suffer from it, we were considering abandoning my survey, disbanding my small group of personnel and returning to the States. But then President Duvalier himself devised a solution to the

He told me firmly, "You are in hot water."
May 22, 1963: Port-au-Prince, Haiti: Ex-President François Duvalier (arm raised) addresses the public from the porch of the Presidential Palace, as armed soldiers and militiamen line the steps. Duvalier told his listeners that Haiti will establish a "new order" that should serve as an example for all black peoples of the world. © Bettmann / CORBIS

situation. He asked Dr. Hervé Boyer,[43] minister of finance—secretary of the treasury—and a good friend of mine who had helped me to get the survey contract, to invite me to his office and to have a chat with me. It was a friendly office which I visited often when some sort of problem had to be solved. Dr. Boyer's secretary, a gorgeous Mulatto girl who was also his mistress, was no less amicable than usual to me when I arrived.

But Dr. Boyer was not so amicable. He told me firmly, "You are in hot water. Everyone is talking about you and your wife. Do not abandon your survey but go back to the States and clear your name somehow. If you cannot, come back, wind up your work and leave the country."

It just so happened that on that very same day our embassy received a letter, addressed to me and my wife, from Mr. J. Lee Rankin,[44] general counsel of the Warren Commission investigating the assassination of President Kennedy. Mr. Rankin invited us to come to Washington, D.C., if we wished, to testify. This letter also stated that if we accepted the invitation to testify, the Warren Commission would pay all our expenses to Washington and back to Haiti. Of course we were most anxious to cooperate as much as we could to solve this crime. But Jeanne refused to travel without our two feisty Manchester Terriers, Nero and Poppaea and so, after the exchange of more wires, Mr. Rankin agreed to our additional "dog expense."[45]

We stayed at the old Willard Hotel,[46] not far from the Veterans' Administration Building, where the commission was located.

I was the first to testify. The man who took my deposition was Albert E. Jenner Jr.,[47] a lawyer from Chicago, who much later became famous in connection with the Watergate case. Jenner was a well-known trial lawyer and I have to admit that either[48] he was much more clever than I was or, perhaps, that I was impressed to the point of being overawed by the whole setting and the situation as it unfolded in Washington at the time. Anyway, as we will see, Jenner played with me as if I were a baby.

The people I met during my testimony were rather impressive. Allen Dulles,[49] former head of the CIA,[50] was there; he did not interfere in the proceedings but remained in the background, a kind of distant threatening figure. Another was Supreme Court Chief Justice Earl Warren, a rather sympathetic, paternal figure who, we found out later, had a weakness for Marina. Representative Gerald R. Ford was also there, friendly and youthful-looking. The last ten years have changed him considerably.[51] And then there were innumerable, hustling lawyers, all of them trying to figure out how a single man, Lee Harvey Oswald, could have done so much damage with his old, primitive, Italian army rifle.[52] Being around such a galaxy of legal and political talent, you wouldn't need to be tortured to allow words to be put in your own mouth,[53] you would simply be impressed and intimidated to the point you would say almost anything about an insignificant, dead ex-marine.

And during my lengthy deposition, I said some unkind things about Lee which I now regret. The pressure we were under was very strong. The reader must recall my situation, sitting there with the possibility of losing my contract in Haiti always in the back of my mind,[54] answering an endless flow of well-prepared and insidious questions for more than two days. Was the sheer length of the proceedings meant to be a kind of intimidation?

"We know more about your life than you yourself, so answer all my questions truthfully and sincerely," Jenner began.[55]

I should have retorted, "If you know everything why bring us all the way from Haiti?" But I did not and began to talk. And talk. And talk. Later I would discover my answers were very nicely edited in the subsequent report.[56]

"Say the whole truth and nothing but the truth," he intoned.

Jenner was a good actor. Very cold and aloof at first, then switching to flattery and smiles when he felt I was getting tensed up and antagonistic.

"How cosmopolitan you are! How many important people you know! Yes, you are great!" said Jenner ingratiatingly. He even complimented my tan.[57] And this flattery had its effect on me, demonstrating Jenner was now such a good "friend" of mine.[58] So I answered all the endless questions to the best of my ability, with utter sincerity, without even asking to have my lawyer present. Jenner, the sneaky bastard, did not say a word about the whole testimony being printed and distributed all over the world. And so my private life was shamelessly violated. During this time Jeanne and our dogs were languishing back at the hotel.

At the end of my long testimony Jenner seemed convinced that I was not involved in any way in this "already solved" assassination. He began showering me with so many compliments I felt like the star of a pornographic movie. Before leaving, I reminded Jenner of the harm this affair was causing me, how it was reflecting negatively on my work in Haiti, and about the attitude of American ambassador Timmons. In response he inserted some nice statements, putting me above all suspicion. Big deal! The harm was already done. How could I have been suspected of anything in the first place, being so far away from Dallas, unless President Duvalier and I used voodoo and inserted needles into or shot at a doll resembling President Kennedy![59] Since everything about me was now known and on the record, Jenner concluded my useless testimony by saying, "You did all right. Keep up the life you have been living.[60] You helped a poor family." But he added as an aside a vague admonishment, "Remember, sometimes it is dangerous to be too generous with your time and help."

There followed one-and-a-half days of testimony by my wife and our two Manchesters. They were not "material witnesses," but Jeanne categorically refused to leave them in the hotel. If our dogs, who loved Lee,[61] could have talked, their testimonies would have been more valuable than ours. Jenner shied away from Nero and Jeanne promised that he would not bite, that he never bit Lee who was a good human being—to which Nero would be willing to swear.[62]

As Jeanne and I later discussed our experiences as witnesses, many details came to our minds. For instance Jenner slyly asked, "Lee Harvey Oswald must have asked you a question about your political philosophy. What did you say?"

"Live and let live," I answered simply. Jenner made some comments on that but generally seemed satisfied.

I said to Jeanne later, "It was an unpleasant experience, but in Russia we would have been sent to Siberia for life." She agreed.

Jeanne's reaction to, and opinion of, our experiences was somewhat different from mine.[63] I was anxious to clear up my name and return to Haiti. "I considered it a favor of mine to come and help the committee," she had said. "I was completely relaxed. The counsel was pleasant and reserved. However, instead of asking *pertinent* questions, for instance, 'When did you meet the Oswalds?' and 'How many times did you talk to Lee and Marina and about what?' they asked me instead 'Where were you born?' and 'Who were your parents?'—I never suspected that my personal life would be broadcast, although I had nothing to be ashamed of. Still it's my property, my life. The whole report was a whitewash,[64] a cover-up." We shall leave the question and possibility of a cover-up by the Warren Commission for the book's final chapter.[65]

"I can never forgive all the checking,[66] asking me how many children I had," Jeanne continued with fire in her voice,[67] "or how many times I changed jobs, and why, whom I had worked for, or how many times I went to Europe on buying trips, and how much I earned. I had expected to speak only of Lee and Marina. I spoke of my wonderful parents, of my life in China, my arrival in the USA. My poverty, hard work, and finally my success. I expressed my hope that this would be a country free of prejudice, of racial discrimination. Financial opportunities in the USA were not the prime reasons for my coming here. My faith, or lack of faith, was all polluted by this porno-exhibitionist questioning. *Finally* we began discussing Lee in a desultory manner." She then concluded bitterly, "So I have a grudge and if I could, I would try to make them pay for the harm and insult they did to me. Where is the privacy we are supposed to have here?"[68]

Naturally our testimonies regarding Lee and Marina coincided. We said the same things in our own way and we never even bothered to read our own testimonies. It should surprise no one that everything coincided perfectly. When you speak the truth, you don't have to "remember" it; we had no need to embellish.[69]

"Finally," remembered Jeanne, "they made me identify the gun. Nero sniffed at the gun; he could have made a better identification than I. For me the gun seemed familiar, but whether it was the same one we saw in the closet, I couldn't say. It seemed to have a telescopic sight. So I told Jenner, 'Ask *Marina*, she could identify the gun!'"[70]

We both felt that the minds of the members of the Warren Committee were already made up. They appeared obsessed with the idea that Lee was the sole assassin. The idea of, for example, anti-Castro Cuban refugees with a mortal grudge against Kennedy, did not interest them.[71] We both were interviewed in the same way: anytime we said anything favorable about Lee, they passed over it.[72] And Jenner, like a Jesuit,[73] kept asking questions which were incriminating to Lee.

Both of us felt that Jenner was displeased whenever he heard some favorable facts about Lee. We discussed something we had heard from the committee members themselves: most other witnesses were nervous and contradicted themselves, probably intimidated by the awesomeness of the proceedings and the fact that many were not even naturalized citizens.[74] And so some good people spoke very unkindly and untruthfully about Lee just because they were frightened and they wanted to please the commission. They really should be forgiven.

All the favorable facts we mentioned about Lee were subsequently read out of context[75] in the abridged edition of the report read by most of the general public, or not mentioned in it at all. We asked ourselves: why did the Warren Commission spend all that money bringing us to Washington and back to Haiti, keep us in an expensive hotel, conducting all that hellishly expensive investigation about us all around the world, and even pay *our dogs'* travel expenses?[76] Why such an extravagant waste of the taxpayers' money if they did not want to hear the truth?

We also wondered why the Warren Commission paid so much attention to the testimony of people who had not known Lee and Marina in Dallas, or who had known him long before the assassination. The answer: just to fill up sixteen volumes worth of pages and tranquilize the American populace.[77] Thus the minds[78] of not only the seven Warren Committee members but even the president's family were made up.

Jenner constantly kept asking me, "Why did Oswald like you and didn't like anybody else?"[79] It was as if he thought there was some kind of kinky homosexual link between us.

"I don't have the slightest idea, maybe because I liked him."

"Maybe he liked you because you were a strong person?" Jenner asked, again intimating that maybe I was a predatory "wolf" or a devil influencing him to do evil. "Maybe he identified you as an internationalist?" he asked intimating yet again some dark connections I might be keeping hidden.

"Maybe," I answered. "I am no admirer of any particular flag."

"You and your wife were the only ones who remained his friends?" continued Jenner's line of inquiry.

The question was asked of both of us. And we both answered in about the same terms: "to us they were warm, open, young people, responsive to our hospitality."

Jenner then brought to my attention a part of the December 12, 1963, letter I had written to Mrs. Auchincloss from Haiti. He used this as my admission of Lee's guilt though I have explained already under what circumstances this letter was written. "Since we lived in Dallas we had the misfortune to have met Lee Harvey Oswald and his wife Marina. I do hope that Marina and her children (now she has two by Lee) will not suffer too badly through life and that the stigma of the assassination will not affect her and the innocent children."[80] This was my foolish letter and my speculation, not Jeanne's.

And again, after the impact of this letter read to me, Jenner very cleverly bamboozled me into a possible motive of Lee's guilt. "The only reason for Lee's criminal act," I continued, "would be that he might have been jealous of a young, rich, attractive president who had a beautiful wife and was a world figure. Lee was just the opposite; his wife was bitchy and he was a failure."

Now, away from the pressure of the Committee, I consider what I said in this testimony[81] of mine most unfair. It would not have made him a hero[82] to have shot a liberal and beloved president, especially one beloved by minorities. Neither was Marina such a bitch, or Jacqueline quite so beautiful.[83]

If you read the *Warren Report*, there is another leading question by Jenner: "As a humanitarian person you cannot imagine anyone murdering another person?"

It was a childish and naïve question, of course. I stupidly answered, "I cannot imagine doing it myself." At least I did not express an opinion about Lee's guilt. Lee, being an ex-marine, trained to use a rifle in the manner of a soldier,[84] was capable of killing but only if the motive were a very strongly held ideological one, or in self-defense.

Visiting the Auchincloss Home

After our ordeal in front of the Warren Commission we were invited to the luxurious house of Jacqueline Kennedy's mother Janet and her step-father, Mr. Hugh Auchincloss.[85] Being quite tired out by our testimony we were happy to accept. This luxurious home was located in Georgetown[86] and Auchincloss's money originated through some association of Hugh's family with John D. Rockefeller Sr. of oil fame. Allen Dulles, who as I just mentioned was a long-time friend of Janet's and a member of the committee heading up the Warren Commission, was there also.

During our visit the conversation turned to the coincidence in our lives. Once, I had been on a flight from Dallas to Washington and Janet happened to be on the same plane.[87] She was returning home from some health-farm in Phoenix, Arizona, where rich women stay on a diet and exercise program and put themselves in an acceptable shape again. The time was 1960, the year of the presidential election, and Janet—a staunch Republican—was for Nixon and was sure that her son-in-law, John, did not have the slightest chance to win the elections. I, on the other hand, was sure that Kennedy would win the election and was going to vote for the Democratic Party[88] for the first time.[89] I explained to her that the mood of the country was for her charming son-in-law, and she answered that I did not understand American politics.

Sadly, we eventually had to talk about the assassination. Dulles asked me a few astute questions about Lee. One of them was, I remember, did Lee have a reason for hating President Kennedy? However, when I answered that he was rather an admirer of the dead president, everyone took my answer with a grain of salt. Again the overwhelming opinion was that Lee hated the president and was the sole assassin. Without the hate, in their eyes, there was no motive.[90]

Sitting there among all that opulence I couldn't help but recall Lee, comparing his life of poverty with the life of these multi-millionaires. I tried to reason with them, but to no avail. It seemed to me that I was facing a different sort of conspiracy here, one of stubbornness and silence. Finally both Jeanne and Janet got very emotional, embraced each other and cried together, one over the loss of her son-in-law, another over the loss of a great president she admired so much.

"Janet," I said before leaving, "you were Jack Kennedy's mother-in-law, and I am a complete stranger. I would spend my own money and lots of my time to find out who were the real assassins or the conspirators. Don't you want any further investigation? You have infinite resources."

"Jack is dead and nothing will bring him back," she replied decisively.

"Since he was a very beloved president, I wouldn't let a stone go un-turned to make sure that the assassin be found and punished," implored Jeanne. "We both have grave doubts in Lee's guilt. Why don't you conduct a real investigation as to who was the rat who killed him?"[91]

"But the rat was your friend Lee Harvey Oswald," was the cold answer.

Later Jeanne and I had long discussions regarding why those so close to the slain president, neither Janet, nor Robert and the rest of Kennedy family (as we discovered later), would be so adamant on this subject.[92] Could it be

The Auchincloss home, located at 3044 O Street, N.W., Georgetown, in 2008.

possible, as much as it sounds like sacrilege, that Lee was a "convenient" assassin to all concerned, including the relatives and friends of the late President Kennedy? Convenient not in any derogatory sense but because he was a scapegoat, a patsy, while the assassination was an act of revenge arising out of President Kennedy's biggest and costliest mistake: the Bay of Pigs.[93]

We were about ready to leave the Auchinclosses' luxurious mansion.

"Incidentally," said Mrs. Auchincloss coldly, "my daughter Jacqueline never wants to see you again because you were close to her husband's assassin."

"It's her privilege," I answered diplomatically.

Hugh, who was a very silent man, asked me suddenly, "And how is Marina fixed financially?"

"I do not know, I just read that she received quite a lot of money from the charitable American people—maybe eighty thousand dollars."[94]

"That won't last her long," he said and, almost without transition, pointed out an extraordinary antique chess set. "This is early Persian, valued at sixty thousand dollars."

We said our goodbyes amicably and drove off, back to our hotel.

"That son-of-the-gun Hugh has an income running into the millions," I told Jeanne thoughtfully.

"Such figures are beyond my comprehension," she said sadly.

Our Return to Haiti

When we had received J. Lee Rankin's letter inviting us to come to Washington and testify before the Warren Commission, we felt certain that we would be of poor help,[95] as we had been out of contact with Lee for over seven months[96] prior to the assassination. We could not say what happened to him and Marina after we had left Dallas. We only knew Lee was in New Orleans, because of the postcard. But, naturally, I was anxious to testify in order to clear my name and to be able to continue work on my survey.

But the American colony in Port-au-Prince was in an uproar when they were told that we were going to Washington for this purpose.

"How horrible!" some said.

"Aren't you afraid?" said others.

Even my old friend at the American Embassy Teddy Blaque said, "But he was an assassin and you were so deeply involved with him."

Many thought that we would be put in jail and would never come back to our lovely house in Port-au-Prince.

Fortunately, the Haitian ambassador in Washington was reassured by the Warren Commission that we were decent people, the ambassador transmitted this message to President Duvalier, and we could return safely to Haiti. But in the long run my contract became hopelessly harmed by the on-going[97] publicity and by the peculiar attitude the American embassy took towards us. And President Duvalier, the astute Papa Doc, got wind through his many informants that our embassy would not protect my rights any more, and the sly old fox was absolutely right. The payments for my survey began drying up and despite years of effort on my part I never received any cooperation from anyone at our embassy in Haiti or in the State Department in trying to recover the large balance of my contract still due to me.[98]

The Impact on Our Lives

The publication of the *Warren Commission Report* in the fall of 1964 brought an immediate and drastic change to our lives in Haiti.[99] Only the close and true friends understood the real reasons behind our involvement with the "presumed assassin" of the generally beloved President Kennedy. In this manner the phony friends were weeded out of our lives, but regardless too many people we knew, thanks to the publicity caused by the *Report*, were contacted by FBI agents at various times asking imbecilic and insulting questions, implying grim and terrible suspicions[100] about us. A good friend of Jeanne's, who I will not name here, recalls that an FBI agent asked for a whole day of his precious time just to talk about us. Discussing Jeanne's background in China, the agent asked our friend, "Is she loyal to the United States?"

Our friend answered without hesitation, "Yes, she is, in my opinion."

"Who are you kidding?" was the agent's sarcastic reply.

People began offering us money for interviews, which we refused to accept. Overseas telephone service in Haiti was inadequate. Very few people on the island in the mid-1960s had private telephones. I happened to be one of the few with a telephone in my office, but not at home. The office telephone kept buzzing, month after month, and on the other end I would hear unknown voices asking insidious questions like "What was your relationship with Oswald? What did you think of him? Did you have the same convictions as he did? Did he kill Kennedy? Why are you hiding in Haiti?" Some man from Hong-Kong called me just to ask a single question: "Who *are* you?" The very notion we were in "hiding" in Haiti was absurd, because I had been working on my contract with the Haitian government a whole year before we met the Oswalds and we had been living on the island nine months and without interruption before all hell broke loose in Dallas.[101] A few especially persistent reporters[102] kept on calling me, spending their evil money on the long-distance charges; I would simply hang-up on them.

Appearing on NBC

After our return to Haiti we were offered the opportunity to be interviewed for a television program being produced by NBC.[103] The name of the journalist who contacted us was George McMillan,[104] an experienced newsman, and he asked if he could come all the way to Haiti to visit us. He sounded like an intelligent man and had been provided with a good recommendation by a mutual friend.[105] We were not sure whether he wanted to talk to us about Oswald or about the situation in Haiti, because the country was very much in the international spotlight at the time.[106] I was in charge of the geological survey and the only American working independently in Haiti at that time. I thought that McMillan wanted an interview with me because I certainly knew the situation well and my take might be different from what the American press had described. I did not commit myself to being interviewed on television but told McMillan that he was welcome to visit us in Haiti.

Unfortunately a gruesome incident took place the day of his arrival at the old Port-au-Prince airport. It had been a season full of invasions: a group from Cuba had landed on the island and created havoc all over eastern Haiti.[107] They were well armed, familiar with the terrain, and murdered indiscriminately. Eventually all of them were executed by Duvalier's faithful Tontons Macoutes. One of these invaders was brought to Port-au-Prince and publically executed to show the Haitian populace that it wouldn't pay to threaten "Papa Doc" and his government. The dead body was exhibited on the plaza near the airport with all the individual's supplies and ammunition.[108] The corpse was attached to a chair and the swarm of flies around it was so thick it resembled a funeral smoke. When McMillan arrived he saw the commotion and the crowds surrounding the body. I didn't want him to dwell upon something like the gruesome sight of a dead man attached to a chair without being able to give him some facts surrounding the execution. What an impact his report would have on the public in the United States if he began it talking about a dead body and flies. Haiti, as I often tried to explain to people not familiar with the country, wasn't usually like this.[109] I drove around the scene at full speed without making a comment.

We brought McMillan to our house because he seemed to us a very pleasant individual. He had told us that he defended equal rights for black Americans and that somewhere in the Carolinas, where he lived, the KKK had burned crosses on his lawn and forced him to leave. He said he wanted all our friends who came to visit us in Haiti to know the true facts about the regime—the good and the bad. It was my opinion Dr. Duvalier was an advocate of the poor Blacks against the rich, French-educated Mulattoes.[110] This was a simplified version of the situation, but it was better than the full condemnation of the Duvalier regime in Graham Greene's book *The Comedians*.[111]

This evening like so many others in Haiti the sky was aflame with rose and gold, a glorious sunset. Below, as the evening began to envelop Port-au-Prince, the city suddenly began to shine with light, giving the illusion of dancing and twinkling candles in the warm atmosphere of ever deepening darkness. Every

George de Mohrenschildt at the time of his NBC interview (November 25, 1964).
Argenta Images / Rogers Photo Archive

so often the faint hum of an approaching plane could be heard, growing in intensity as the lone craft flew over the bay before projecting a beam of light to guide its sharp descent to the airport.[112] Later, as we sat on our terrace listening to the delicate tinkling of anolis lizards and looking at the fantastic evening view of the city and the dark waters of Port-au-Prince Bay, McMillan mused aloud, "Why didn't you want me to see the cadaver?"[113]

"Very simple: I didn't want you to see the dead guerilla, not without telling you the facts surrounding his death first," I explained. "After all, Papa Doc is my employer."

But instead of listening to me, or even answering, McMillan suddenly switched subjects. He launched into a monologue[114] about the great program NBC and he were preparing, to be called "The Warren Report," that Jeanne and I would be the main personalities in it, etc. He even offered to fly in the whole television crew, if we accepted. But sick of all the unwanted publicity, we firmly refused.

McMillan was polite about it and turned out to be a good tennis player.[115] His trip was not a complete waste of time and we, being boycotted by the

Americans in Haiti, were glad to have with us a liberal, independent person. He left Haiti two days later asking us to reconsider our decision and mentioned a substantial fee.[116]

I asked several friends for advice regarding his offer, and they all answered that remaining silent and invisible would only harm us further.

"You are the only ones who could say a few kind words about Oswald," wrote one of my best friends who had met Lee and wasn't entirely convinced of his guilt.[117]

"This national TV appearance would dispel the dangerous aura of mystery in your relationship with Lee," wrote another.

And so, after battling back and forth on the matter, we reconsidered our decision. I called McMillan and arrangements were immediately made by NBC to bring us and our faithful Manchesters to New York City.

The weather around New York City was stormy and we had to circle for two hours before landing, but finally the ordeal was over and we landed safely. NBC reserved for us a suite[118] at the Plaza Hotel and the next day we spent the whole afternoon in front of the cameras.

And again, as the interview progressed, it became increasingly obvious that the producer and McMillan were trying to make me say something derogatory about Lee, to drag out of me some insidious, damaging comment.[119] To them he was definitely the assassin and we, possibly, the conspirators or his secret advisers. As Jeanne and I refused to take the bait and remained positive in our non-sensational answers to their questions, the whole interview did not make any sense. We were invited to New York with the hope[120] that either we would produce some inside information or would prove to millions of Americans who would watch the show that Lee was the only assassin. Since the Warren Commission, slanted as it was, could never find any reason in Lee's involvement in this crime "of the century," the promoters of the NBC show hoped that I, as his best friend, would finally explain his insane action.

For Jeanne and I, who did not have any more information regarding the assassination than anyone reading newspapers and magazines, Lee remained the same person we knew—an eccentric, interesting, warm, and close friend, someone we never seriously considered as President Kennedy's assassin. Of course, a sudden onset[121] of insanity is a possibility. But all of our previous incidents and conversations with Lee did not suggest impending insanity. Neither was he ever to us a poor loser, a stupid high-school dropout, or a book-thirsty revolutionary, nor was he a person jealous of other people's success and money. Such people exist[122] on the streets of any American city, and in droves.[123] The photo included in Chapter 5, of Lee with the rifle along with Marina's inscription on the back, would indicate that he *might* have been considering hunting fascists—and in his mind General Walker was one—but certainly not our President Kennedy.

A few days later, while we were still in New York, I saw a complete forty minute preview of our appearance.[124] Again it was clear to us what a poor job we had done trying to present Lee's side. And later, the worst parts of these forty minutes were cherry-picked for use during the hour-long "The Warren Report" that so many millions saw. It aired at 6:30 p.m. on Sunday, September 27, 1964, the same day that the Warren Commission's final report was made available to the public.[125] It was as if we were witnessing a never-ending witch-hunt, only this time instead of it being the McCarthy era, the campaign was against a dead defenseless man.[126]

Our Return to the United States

Upon returning to Haiti after our interview in New York we knew immediately that something had gone awry in our until-then cordial relationship with the Haitian government. Usually we sailed through customs,[127] cheerfully greeted by Mr. Jolicoeur, a charming clown-like public relations man for the Duvalier government.[128] He would meet us with the jovial saying "*Bonsoir, cheri.* Mr. Haiti at your service!"[129] This time our luggage was searched, while militia examined our papers in different parts of the building.[130] When we were reunited with our belongings I discovered the bulk of the maps and other information I had carried with me were missing. Since they were my property, I lodged a strong protest with our embassy and Duvalier's cabinet.

Both parties laughed at me. What maps? What search? Where were you? How naïve can you be? Worst of all was the attitude of the American Ambassador, Benson E. L. Timmons III,[131] along with the *chargé d'affaires* Curtis and all the other sycophants working for them.[132]

"I hate you. You cause me nothing but trouble!" Ambassador Timmons declared hysterically.[133]

"I am a Christian, Mr. Timmons, I don't hate anybody," I replied.[134] "But I do wish you would help me recover my maps."

The stolen maps destroyed my desire to continue working for the Haitian government.[135] Before this incident, Duvalier's regime had insisted that I try to develop some of the resources I'd discovered in Haiti: copper, titanium, bauxite, and excellent oil possibilities. Whenever I left the country I took the bulk of the information (not all, fortunately) with me and each time I acted as an agent for Haiti. Most of my work was completed.[136] Now, with the maps gone, my trust was destroyed and I began preparing for departure.[137] Since the Haitians owed me a large amount of money for the survey, I dispatched, through friends, my most valuable information to a safe place in the States.

Naturally, I began worrying that the Haitians would detain me as a hostage, with the information as the ransom. Just recently an American citizen living in Haiti, an ex–air force officer, was accused by Papa Doc of dealing with the president's enemies abroad. The poor fellow sought[138] asylum in our embassy but was refused (embassies usually grant asylum to political refugees; ours didn't). The chief of police came and assured Ambassador Timmons that nothing would happen to the poor ex-officer. And so the man was carried out screaming and shouting and nothing was heard of him again. My friends in the know told me that he was beaten to death in the dungeon of the presidential palace.[139]

Such a fate was not to our taste. Since nobody expected our immediate departure, we made a very secret deal with a small German cruise line plying the trade in the Caribbean islands, using the good offices of the German ambassador.[140] Late in the evening the only person who came to say good-bye to us was the delightful ambassador and his charming Austrian wife; we shared a few glasses of champagne. Now, you might be wondering: if we had such trouble with customs on our way in, how did we avoid them on our way out? I still had a *laissez-passer*[141] from President Duvalier and nobody bothered to stop the truck with our furniture and supplies and our personal car.

The little ship allowed us to board late in the evening and, unhindered, we sailed into the Caribbean night. Incidentally, we entered our names on the ship manifest as "sailor" and "cook."[142] The crew, most international, was composed of a German ex–submarine commander, a young Norwegian engineer who was a genius and could repair anything on board, and a medley of Haitians, Jamaicans, Trinidadians, and other picturesque Caribbeans. Jeanne decided to cook some delicious European meals for the captain and the crew, and I, in excess of energy, painted the whole deck. Having skirted very close to the Cuban Coast, we landed in Miami, where we received a pleasant surprise. When I asked the captain for the bill, not only for us but also for shipping the car and our luggage, he answered, "It was a pleasure having you on board. You earned more than the price of your transportation." The only way to reciprocate this generous act was to invite the officers to a sumptuous dinner before we went our separate ways.

From Miami we drove back to Texas in our Galaxie convertible.[143] Our pace was slow. We breathed in the fresh marine air and wanted to forget the whole tragic incident. As we were passing Florida's Lake Okeechobee late in the evening on a deserted road, a brilliant comet crossed the dark, tropical sky, lighting the weird scenery around us and even scaring Nero and Poppaea. A comet for some is considered a good omen, but for us it foretold very bad times indeed.

Arriving back in Dallas on November 10, 1966,[144] we hoped to be reunited with some good, old friends. Quite a few had come to Haiti and enjoyed our hospitality. Instead we encountered suspicion and an outright hostility. Surprised at first, we soon discovered the reason: the *Warren Commission Report* published in the fall of 1964. We had signed the transcripts immediately after our testimonies, without even bothering to read them. Why would we? It was supposed to be "the truth and nothing but the truth" and who would want to quibble over the words? After our lengthy depositions we were so sick and tired of the whole affair. We put the matter of the intrusive inquiries by these various agencies and even our own testimonies completely out of our minds.

But back in Dallas we had to face the situation once more.[145] The aura of suspicion, of innuendoes, of gossip, of half-truths and semi-lies, began to pollute the very air around us.

"Have you read the *Warren Report*?" a lawyer, a good friend of ours, asked us.

"No," I answered. "I heard there is a comprehensive resume of various depositions."

"Aren't you going to read it? It contains some sixteen volumes and one of them is almost exclusively about the two of you."[146]

We had postponed reading these dry, bureaucratic, insipid pages until, compelled by the circumstances, we were forced to read what we had said in Washington and especially what has been said about us in these sixteen enormous volumes. One day we saw some friends in Fort Worth—they had known Lee and Marina also but had avoided testifying[147] by some hook or crook—and they loaned to us the volume in which we figured so prominently.

"Read it carefully and don't miss a word," they told us. "Actually, you should read *all* the volumes and you will understand the attitude of many people towards you."

And indeed, after reading several depositions, I was ready to vomit.

I now understood what Assistant Counsel Jenner, our "inquisitor" at the Warren Commission, had mentioned.

"You will be the only people in the world to know exactly what others think about you," he said. He did not dwell further on these words and did not indicate that our depositions and those of other people we knew or had even remote relations with, would be printed, after careful editing, to probe the nebulous point that Lee was the sole assassin.[148] Apparently some of the decent people who volunteered to testify did so on the condition that their testimonies would remain secret and available only to Warren Commission members. But the FBI insisted that all depositions should be printed and distributed to the public. The ghost[149] of J. Edgar Hoover must regret that decision because in time the public discovered how many falsehoods his organization was involved in.[150] There were a few good and truthful facts scattered about. For instance, a friend of mine, Sam Ballen, an investment banker in Dallas, testified that he met Lee and that he found him intelligent and alert.[151] Another young man, who had lived in Fort Worth, also had some kind words for my friend. But these were exceptions.[152]

It was saddening to read many things. An old business associate, Paul Raigorodsky, offered the opinion that "he never trusted me completely."[153] My ex-secretary Natasha Voshinin divulged that I had made many suspicious and intriguing trips to—in her mind at least—such exotic and mysterious places as Houston, Texas.[154] An old Russian émigré, George Bouhe, a buddy whom we never considered to be very bright but considered harmless, made a scurrilous remark about Jeanne to the effect, "that Chinese woman never even believed in God."[155] As if religion was not a very personal matter. "He always wanted to be the commissar of Texas," was an opinion of a slight acquaintance.[156] And finally there was the testimony of my ex-son-in-law, Gary Taylor, who unbelievably said "If anyone had finagled this assassination or had influenced Lee Harvey Oswald in that direction, that person would obviously be George de Mohrenschildt."[157] Reading all of this dirty laundry being aired in public I even had the perverse idea of writing a short book, assembling all these opinions and giving the book the title *I Arranged Kennedy's Assassination*. Or maybe a title that would be sure to attract customers, such as *My Affair with the Teen-age Jacqueline Bouvier and How I Got Rid of Her Husband*.

The same people who had detested or ignored Lee and Marina, Russian refugees and Americans alike, began to make money off of them, especially off of the resulting incomprehensible elevation of "poor Russian Marina— that defenseless, God-fearing, miserable wife of that brutal monster Lee Harvey Oswald."[158] Newspapermen kept on calling us; they were geniuses at discovering our whereabouts even though we did not have a listed number and stayed with some friends. The owner of the apartment house on Gillespie, an eccentric lady who, like us, was extremely fond of Haiti—she almost had a fit when she saw Haitian licenses on our car—asked discreetly for police protection for us. These media people *should* have been using their talents to look into Lee's activities in Atlanta, New Orleans, and Mexico City just before the assassination.[159] Jim Garrison, the New Orleans district attorney, tried and his career as district attorney was ruined.[160] People who had the slightest connection with Lee and whose testimonies were not exactly "kosher" as far as the official version of events was concerned, began to die mysteriously.

Notwithstanding these superficial conclusions, favored in the United States, the general opinion in other countries began to swing the other way; many stopped accepting the thesis of Lee's guilt. Some suspected Vice President Lyndon Johnson, a party which had profited directly from the assassination and who always thoroughly disliked the cold-shoulder treatment given to him and his wife by the whole Kennedy clan. It's not for us to judge, but the latest discoveries of the FBI's finagling add some credence to this theory.[161] After all LBJ was a most devious man, and rather ignorant.[162] They say that he was not even sure of the location of Vietnam.

And so, little by little, even naïve and credulous Americans, annoyed by this constant harping on Lee's guilt, by the platitudes and repetitious statements served up from official sources, began to disbelieve Lee's guilt, or at least they began to doubt the nonexistence of any conspiracy. After all, Americans are business-minded; if somebody performs an act such as assassination, without any rhyme or reason and without any financial reward, something must stink in Denmark.

As for Jeanne and I, we personally retained our doubts but kept them to ourselves, saw fewer people than before, restrained our social life and eliminated false friends and acquaintances. A dear friend of ours, a staff writer for the *Dallas Times Herald*, insisted on interviewing us.[163] I pointed out in this interview my deep-felt opinion about how harmful it is for the United States to believe the simple tale that a lone lunatic killed the president and then, another lunatic killed him.[164] And then, shortly afterwards, the brother of the President was murdered in cold blood by another "lunatic," without any apparent reason. What is this,[165] a country of homicidal maniacs? If a reasonable theory of a plot or plots was ever finally substantiated, I think it would be beneficial to this country. Until then, Lee Harvey Oswald will remain the most convenient patsy.[166]

FIVE

⤎⤏

A Ghost Visits:
Finding a Photograph

In February of 1967 we finally found a suitable place to settle down. Before that we had moved from one place to another[1] and visited our children in California and Mexico.[2] The new location, conveniently called La Citadelle, suited our needs exactly because it[3] was ample enough to accommodate all the furniture and other goods which had been stored in the warehouse since the beginning of 1963. It was about time we removed everything anyway, because the cost of four years storage at the Great Southwest Warehouses in Dallas was beginning to exhaust us financially.[4] I thought of abandoning the junk altogether and just leaving everything to the warehouse—it's good sometimes to start from scratch—but there were all our books. . . .[5]

A Message from Lee

And so we went to the warehouse with an old, faithful friend, Everett Glover, one always ready to help (and pick up some old junk for himself). Before our furniture was taken out, we began looking through the accumulation of various and sundry items that could be thrown in the trash.[6] I was less interested in this task, so I chatted with my friend, a good guy who had followed us on many of our trips, while Jeanne was finishing the selection of things to take and to discard. Suddenly, she rushed out of the warehouse with a crazy look on her face.

"Look, look, what I found!" she shouted excitedly.

She dragged me to a pile of open crates and I saw inside a slightly familiar-looking green box.

"What the hell is this?" I asked.

"This is the box with the records I gave Marina before our departure," she said.[7]

"How did they get there? We left them such a long time ago?"

"I haven't the slightest idea, I considered them lost." Jeanne was short of words—this was so weird. "I had used them myself to learn English when I came to this country. They served me well. Then I loaned them to Marina long before our departure for Haiti."

"Remember how punctiliously[8] honest Lee was," I said. "He would not keep any of our belongings. But how the hell did the records get into this warehouse? Perhaps he remembered where we were planning to store our furniture? Or, possibly, maybe he had handed the package[9] over to Glover, because he knew we had loaned him some of our furniture[10] and it was Glover who finally added them to the rest of the stored boxes at the Southwest Warehouse?"

This remains a mystery to this day, because we lost track of Everett, a good guy who apparently got so frightened by his very slight acquaintanceship with the "president's assassin" that he moved somewhere without leaving a forwarding address.[11]

My wife began taking the albums out of the box and as she opened each of them to see if the records inside were broken or not, she shrieked[12] almost hysterically.

"Look, there is a picture of Lee Oswald here!"

This was the same, very controversial picture of Lee, the one which appeared on the February 21, 1964, cover of the now-defunct *Life* magazine.[13] Many newspapermen and Kennedy assassination "investigators" had assumed and had written hundreds of pages claiming that this picture was a fabrication, a "fake," a photograph of Lee's face superimposed on another person.[14] Frankly we had not cared up until this point. But now, right in front of us, there was proof that the picture was genuine.

We stood there, literally frozen stiff. In the photo Lee was staring at us in his martial pose, the famous rifle in his hands. Like in a marine parade. It was a gift to us from beyond his grave.

"Look, there is a picture of Lee Oswald here!"
Lee Harvey Oswald poses with rifle, pistol, and copies of *The Militant* and *The Worker*. US National Archives and Records (Commission Exhibit 134)

"What did he mean by leaving this picture to us?" I wondered aloud. "He was not a vain kind of a person."

Jeanne slowly turned the photo over and became excited again. "Look, there is an inscription here." It read: *"To my friend George from Lee Oswald"* and was dated April 5, 1963, at a time when we were thousands of miles away in Haiti.[15] I kept looking at the picture and the inscription and was deeply moved, my thoughts going back to when Lee was alive.

There was also an epitaph, seemingly in Marina's handwriting, in Russian. In translation it read: *"This is the hunter of fascists! Ha! Ha! Ha!"*

Here Marina was again making fun of her husband, jeering Lee's very serious anti-fascists feelings, which we knew so well and described to the reader in earlier chapters.[16]

It's hard to describe the impact of this discovery on us, especially Lee's dedication and Marina's joke.[17] This message from beyond the grave was amazing and shocking. I say from beyond the grave because we did not even dare to visit his burial place; the FBI was suspicious of anyone who went there.[18] The confirmation that Lee considered me his best friend flattered me, but Marina's message expressed a chilling scorn for her husband. In any event if Lee was "a hunter of fascists"—and we agree with such a description—who was *she* making fun of him?[19] First of all it leaves no doubt[20] regarding her assertion that Lee tried to shoot General Walker, and second, for any Soviet Russian refugee the word "fascist" is not a laughing matter—some fifteen million people lost their lives fighting Germany and its allies between 1941 and 1945. And how many millions more died of disease, cold, and hunger?

We reserved this photograph just for ourselves and showed it to only a few close friends. Their reactions were interesting: to some the photograph indicated that Lee was a maniac, a killer. It constituted a proof of his aggressiveness, of his guilt. To others, just the opposite sort of reaction occurred— it gave him the aura of a militant idealist. The man of such anti-fascist inclinations *could not* be the assassin of the most liberal and race-conscious president in the history of the United States.

We did not bring the photograph to the attention of any authorities. To them Lee Harvey Oswald's case was closed and we did not want any further involvement with them. Neither did we show it to any investigators or reporters in the United States.[21] But I did write a letter to a friend, Dick Billings, one of the editors of *Life* magazine,[22] explaining that I had a message from Lee Harvey Oswald and I did ask him to keep the matter confidential.[23] I added to my letter a short résumé of the facts, explaining how this picture got into our possession. Immediately, I received a call from my friend saying that *Life* had a team working on Oswald's case, a team of investigators, because the magazine had doubts about the Warren Commission's conclusions.[24]

The next day a reporter[25] assigned to the assassination case called me and we talked for a long time. He was intimately familiar with all the details, psychological and technical, of this unbelievably complex case, having worked on it since November 1963. He listened to my description of Marina's epitaph and gave it the same interpretation as we ourselves had.[26]

"We shall use it as a main feature of our special edition if and when we know something more definite about Oswald's involvement or of his innocence," he said.

Again I asked the man to temporarily keep this matter confidential and he promised to do so.

Obviously, either people at *Life* were talkative or, more probable, our telephone was tapped. Later on, we had reason to believe on several occasions someone was listening in on our calls.[27] We now know much more about "Watergate" type tactics on the part of our government agencies, especially the FBI, but at the time we felt we did not have anything to conceal—except the existence of this picture—and this only for our own sentimental reasons.[28] Whenever we heard a suspicious noise on the telephone, we laughed, spoke in foreign languages, or made offensive remarks at whoever was listening in. Some voluminous files must be hidden somewhere containing "transcripts," translations and obliterations of our conversations.[29] Again, being faithful taxpayers year after year, we could but marvel at the unbelievable waste of our money. But what was tapping one phone line compared to the 140 billion U.S. dollars spent in Vietnam?[30] But in a culture of bad ideas one bad habit just leads to another. And another. And another.

More Unusual Visitors

The photograph we found in the record album is identical to one appearing in the *Warren Commission Hearings and Exhibits* and the one *Life* magazine published shortly after the assassination. Marina took it, at least she so testified.[31] Only the dedication to me and the inscription by Marina constitute new elements. This picture unquestionably did a lot of damage to Lee in the eyes of the public. It shows him in a militaristic pose,[32] holding a rifle, a pistol visible on his right side.

But let's not forget that Lee was trained by the Marine Corps to hold, show, and respect weapons. In another bow to the United States Marine Corps the .38 Smith and Wesson Special[33] we saw in his apartment was well oiled and immaculately clean. But whatever later testimony may have tried to prove, I knew that he was not a particularly good shot. He did not have that cold stare in his eyes,[34] and he did not have a very steady hand and a stiff stance which indicate to anyone familiar with military things the character of a good marksman. He also did not have the ugly expression of a killer, and Jeanne and I knew professional killers: Jeanne in China during the Japanese occupation, I in other parts of the world.[35] He owned a pistol but we never discussed why. I assumed for self-defense, as he lived in a very disreputable part of Dallas. Maybe Lee liked to shoot at the leaves, such as Marina claimed, but he did not have a decisive, self-assured, automatic attitude of a sharpshooter. On the contrary, he was a nervous, jittery, poorly coordinated type. Not to mention, as I said earlier, he was completely non-athletic. He was also devoid of any mechanical ability. I had observed boys and men of that type in my own regiment in Poland and they were totally unfit for military performance—and usually very poor shots.

We tried to keep the existence of Lee's photograph as secret as possible; a few friends were aware of it and *Life*'s reporter knew of it. Something, however, leaked out and about two weeks after my conversations with writers at *Life* I received a strange telephone call. A slightly accented voice said, and I quote, "We are from *Life* magazine," and he mentioned the name of the reporter I had spoken to. "We are here in Dallas and would like to see you. May we?"

"Certainly," I immediately agreed. "Come over."

They knew the address, and an hour later two men appeared in our house. A strange pair they were: a slight, Latin-American fellow who introduced himself as "Fernandez" and a big bruiser, a beefy, powerful, Anglo named "Smith."[36] They sat down, announced that they represented *Life* magazine, the Latin mentioned his reporting[37] qualifications while the Caucasian character said he was a photographer. Indeed he was loaded with cameras[38] of all types. Smith mentioned that he was also a staff photographer for *Fortune* magazine, which put me completely at ease.[39]

"We would like to ask you a few questions the other *Life* reporter failed to discuss with you," said Fernandez.

I obliged him. These questions were unimportant, mostly about Lee's habits and his character. Then they became more specific. Was he sociable? Whom did he know well? What were his relations with his fellow workers in this country and in the USSR? Did he have many friends in addition to us? What did he do in Mexico? Whom did he meet there? Could he speak Spanish? Why did he go to New Orleans? Could he drive a car? And many other questions which I do not recall now. I answered these questions to the best of my ability, but naturally many had to remain unanswered, since I was out of the country and did not have any contacts with Lee during that time.

The question may well arise in the reader's mind: why was I so frank with these *Life* magazine people and let myself be interrogated[40] so naïvely? The answer is that one of my most admired friends used to be a staff writer for *Life* and he had performed an extremely kind and difficult intervention on behalf of my father, who was stranded in Europe during the war.[41] Incidentally, I felt very much at ease with these two characters because I had a visitor at the time, an economist from the east, a very athletic fellow and a good friend and he was there the entire time.[42]

Later in the afternoon, Jeanne arrived, very surprised to see the unusual guests. I explained who they were. "But you have a very strong Spanish accent," she told Fernandez.

"Yes, of course, I am of Spanish origin and I had worked as a reporter for *Life*, mostly in Latin America. So, excuse my poor English."

This sounded reasonable enough.

Then Smith, the photographer, produced a series of excellent, very clear photos of some twenty men, mostly of Latin appearance, and asked pointedly if we had ever met any of them.[43]

We both looked carefully at these strange, sometimes brutal, faces.

"I am not sorry not to have met any of them," I quipped. "They look rather disreputable. Who are they?"

Somehow this question remained unanswered.[44]

"I have an excellent memory for faces and I am positive not to have ever seen any of them," I added.

Jeanne, in a more cheerful and confident mood, pointed out three better-looking ones: "This one has a cute moustache! That one has an interesting look about him. And this one is so handsome! Oh, I would like to meet these three men," she concluded laughingly.

This cheerfulness was met by a stony silence, a kind of hostile attitude. Fernandez did not say a word. He seemed disappointed. Smith broke the awkward silence and asked, "May I take a few pictures of you and the dogs?"

The mentioning of Nero and Poppaea[45] conquered Jeanne and we obliged again. Many photographs were taken.

The conversation lingered for a while longer. Fernandez became more amiable and called Nero, in Spanish, Señor Neron, which pleased Jeanne to no end. Finally, the two strangers left, promising to contact us again from New York, to honor my request to give our regards to my friend there and to send us copies of the pictures.

A few days went by. We both were busy and didn't have time or occasion to discuss this visit. One evening, lying in bed, I asked Jeanne, "What did you think of those two characters who came to visit us the other day?"

"Rather suspicious," she said. "I was thinking of them at this very moment. This is ESP. How did you know they were from *Life*? Did they have any identification?"

"None," I mused. "And I did not ask for any. But they knew exactly what I had been talking about with the *Life* reporter in New York. Fernandez remembered all the questions and all my answers."

"You were very careless," said Jeanne convincingly. "Don't you know that the house has been bugged on and off? More on than off."

She was absolutely right. These men turned out to be imposters. The next day I checked with the *Life* office in New York.[46] Smith and Fernandez did not exist as far as *Life* was concerned.

It is very possible that my naïveté and certainty that we did not know any of the men in the photographs put these two men at ease, otherwise we might have joined the other twenty or thirty people who had died mysteriously just because of their accidental knowledge of some details or people which might have contradicted[47] the official version of Oswald's guilt.

We never communicated to anyone, except to a few very selected and faithful friends, what had occurred. The government agencies would have made their usual mess out of this situation and we might then have become victims of an eventual revenge.

But to our minds, this visit was very significant: people that we had glanced at so casually were, unquestionably, in some way involved in President Kennedy's assassination. Now they have disappeared into the rest of the population[48] or, possibly, they had left the country altogether. The question of who the real criminals were remains a mystery to solve, but not for our bureaucratic mass of officials who carry on their business like unsophisticated, under-educated clods.[49]

Lee's opinion, mentioned earlier, comes clearly to my mind once again: "The bureaucrats all over the world are the same." To which I add my own definition: most of them would not be able to make an honest living in the world of business and free competition.

Marina and the Walker Incident

We are now convinced of Lee's innocence or his being just a patsy in a larger conspiracy. And we can now speak more objectively of the reasons for our having this conviction. Our very lukewarm performance before the Warren Commission was not decisive enough to alter the overwhelmingly negative portrayal of Lee into something more favorable. The general atmosphere prevailing in the United States in the wake of the Kennedy assassination created a pressure capable of warping your judgment and changing your words. How that oppressive weight influenced my testimony can be seen so clearly by me now, looking at it after so many years, as if it were somebody else's deposition, deprived of any nuance, any warm feelings for Lee, full of my own stupid jokes, which make me sad now.[50] I was not expressing myself to the fullest extent and I didn't defend Lee vigorously and passionately enough, which I am sure would have happened if *he* had to defend *me* in a similar situation. My testimony should have been more useful, as I had known him well, better than anybody else and, at least if the length of our depositions is the measure, better than his mother and his wife.

I was cleverly led by the assistant counsel for the Warren Committee, Albert E. Jenner Jr., into saying some things I had not really wanted to say, to admit to certain defects of character Lee possessed, which I wasn't sure were his. In other words, I consider myself a coward and a slob who did not stand up proudly to defend a dead friend. That big, clever boy, the trial lawyer, handled me like a baby: first he bullied me, then led me to tell him carefully all about my life by saying "don't conceal anything, we know more about yourself than you do."[51]

During these unbearably long sessions Jenner asked me, "Didn't you know that Oswald tried to shoot General Walker?"

You already know from previous chapters what actually happened,[52] and what Marina had said later.

"Of course not," I answered, "my pot-shot joke was in dubious taste but only a joke nevertheless."

"But Marina said," continued Jenner, "you knew about it, you said it yourself."

Now, after all these years, reading for the first time the text of the Warren Commission, which had been too repulsive for me to touch, I have reviewed her statement.

She quotes me as saying, "How is it possible, Lee, that you missed?" (page 23).[53]

This is what I was supposed to have said that Easter night when my wife and I arrived to give a stuffed toy rabbit to little June. And I was supposed to have said that before entering the apartment and seeing the rifle. This statement of course made me appear to be Lee's co-conspirator. However, soon afterwards, in her deposition she affirmed in these words: "George de Mohrenschildt didn't know about it, he was smart enough to have guessed it."[54]

As a result of such contradictory testimony the government of the United States ordered the FBI to complete a costly and most useless investigation of Jeanne and myself.[55] FBI agents were sent far and wide, to all those innumerable places we lived in, in various countries and different continents, where they received what information they did through interrogation, bribery, or subterfuge. So much American taxpayer dollars wasted . . . and, naturally, the incident with the rifle initiated[56] all this insane activity.

But now, looking at the *Warren Commission Report*, I think that there must have been other reasons that millions of dollars were spent on the unimportant lives of my wife, our children, and myself, with the final result that our depositions were more voluminous than Lee's own wife, Marina. Could it be that Marina was told by someone in the government, especially in the FBI, to use this inane accusation, then to change it? Maybe Marina someday will admit how all this nonsense came about. Generally, she speaks well of both of us in the remainder of her deposition, calling Jeanne a good friend, and me "a strong man" and a "liberal."[57]

Considering how foolish any large bureaucracy can be, maybe the contradictory nature of Marina's deposition was the result of the testimony being poorly translated. As I have said, Russian is a difficult language. Jenner and Dulles told us that Marina had made innumerable mistakes—perjuries if you wish—being under tremendous pressure and frightened out of her wits. There was gossip going around in the committee building that Chief Justice Warren liked Marina so much that he advised her to incriminate us, to take the pressure off herself.[58] After all, we were these "mysterious foreigners,"[59] living abroad and leading a strange life. Shifting the blame to us would take away the sting of her guilt, because *she* did know the truth about whether or not Lee tried to shoot General Walker and missed. If it were true, he would have been taken out of circulation.

The second version of Marina's deposition was different again. I would like to quote it exactly: "De Mohrenschildt did not know anything about the shooting. Simply he thought that this was something he thought Lee was likely to do. He simply made a joke and the sting of it hit the target."[60]

And finally, by this extremely circuitous route,[61] we come to the correct version of the incident.

And then Mr. Rankin asked her: "from your knowledge were they [Lee and I] close enough so that your husband would make George de Mohren-schildt a confidant of anything like that?"

"No matter how close he might have been to anyone," answered Marina, "he would not have confided such a thing."[62]

And thus, again, we came to a reasonably true answer.

It's hard to say whether Lee would have confided in me had we not left for Haiti;[63] this is pure speculation and I tend to agree with Marina. Had he done so, I would have *certainly* persuaded him not to repeat[64] such a foolish enterprise. As much as I dislike fascists, I would have been against such a violent action against such an insignificant man like General Walker, someone we used to call "General Foker" just for laughs.

Marina is the only one who knows whether Lee actually shot at General Walker. If he did, if it is really true, his mind had been firmly made up.[65] He would have remained secretive about it. Lee wasn't a fool: if he *had* shot at anyone, he would not have left his rifle right in front of the closet for anyone to look at it. Not when he had a large apartment with a lot of hiding places. He would have put his rifle in a well secreted spot.[66]

In conclusion, poor Marina was so mixed up in her testimonies that she did not even remember the incident I have described in Chapter 2, when we took her away from Lee's apartment on Elsbeth Street[67] and carried her, the baby and their belongings to live at the Mellers' place. She had probably not[68] forgotten the burned flesh on her arm and, if anything, she must have been terribly frightened when she testified in 1964. Thanks to her initial, extremely damaging testimony, we got investigated through and through at a great expense to American taxpayers but, fortunately for us, we came out somewhat unscathed, just damaged morally and financially.

Marina after Lee

Now something should be said as to why we did not contact Marina regarding the picture of Lee.[69] After all, she took it. Naturally she became aware of the photo's discovery from our mutual friends, the Fords. But as this book[70] clearly indicates, there is no love lost between Marina and us. It is true: we did not treat her very nicely in our Warren Commission depositions.[71] We were, however, utterly honest. We had helped her with the baby care, with her own health, and finally made a supreme effort trying to solve

There was really nothing to dislike, there was simply no substance to her.
Marina Oswald arrives to testify at the Warren Commission hearings, June 11, 1964. © Bettmann / CORBIS

her unsolvable conflicts with Lee. We never received a word of thanks from her. But this is not important; we helped her when she was poor and desperate. Marina should have recognized it and would have, had she taken the trouble of reading our depositions carefully. She might have reached a more accurate conclusion[72] about both herself and her relationship with her dead husband.

I remember talking to my wife about Lee and she mentioned that we both treated him on a perfectly equal basis, and never scorned him, while other people who helped the Oswalds did it only for Marina, or for the child. Lee did not like any help, especially the type of donations they were receiving. He was occasionally rude to the people who interfered in their lives, being intrinsically a very independent, self-sufficient person. As I said before, he was almost quintessentially the rugged American individualist. And so he began refusing invitations, which infuriated Marina.[73]

Unfortunately, after Lee's death Marina showed herself to be a real "operator." She did nothing to discourage others perceiving her in the role of a helpless victim[74] or of a woman "searching for God," and naturally God-fearing Americans sent her substantial contributions or donations, all tax-free. We heard from some reporters[75] that donations were frequently sent to her in the form of cash stuck between the pages of a Bible; she would grab the money and cast the Bible aside.[76] Her dreams were of an America bristling with high rises, crisscrossed with high-speed interstates, and blessed with all sorts of consumer luxuries, especially fast automobiles.[77] The short sketches of various incidents involving Marina presented in earlier chapters will help prove to the reader these peculiarities of her character which may, admittedly, appear *admirable* to many readers, though not to us.

Another reason we did not contact Marina about the photo was her attitude towards Mrs. Ruth Paine. Ruth was a perfectly charming, charitable Quaker, a Christian in the true sense of this word who, like us, helped the Oswalds out of pure humanitarian impulses. Actually, she did more for them than anyone else. Marina lived with her for months and often took advantage of her hospitality.[78] Ruth drove her to New Orleans and back. She showed utter kindness to her, occasionally to Lee, and especially to baby June. She and her husband Michael were simply admirable people. Yet Ruth had her own family to take care of as well as her teaching profession. Her only reward consisted of lessons in conversational Russian.

Lee, on the other hand, seldom accepted hospitality and certainly did not ask for it. And yet Ruth's and Marina's great friendship ended abruptly after the assassination. As Ruth told us later, upon our return from Haiti, Marina said that she never wanted to see her again, ever.[79] It is possible that Marina was advised by the authorities to shy away from her former independent-minded friends, and she must have been scared stiff of them. Time will tell. Many years have passed and she still does not see Ruth. And Mrs. Paine is too proud a person to insist otherwise.

Well, she is remarried now, to a man named Porter.[80] When we see each other we say "hello" politely but there is no question of having a serious conversation with her. As a matter of fact, the last time we saw her I did not even recognize her. She looked prosperous and spoke excellent English. We never *disliked* Marina. There was really nothing to dislike, there was simply no substance to her.[81] She was amusing sometimes, witty, most naïve yet, like some Russian peasants, with a great deal of shrewdness underneath. My wife used to call her affectionately "that rascal Marina" and that description fitted her perfectly.

CHAPTER FIVE

SIX

꧁

Who Were the Real
Criminals?

Over twelve years[1] have passed since the tragic events of November 22, 1963. With the passage of time my wife and I became more and more convinced that the whole story of Lee Harvey Oswald had not been told. We have spent many an agonizing moment thinking of Lee, ashamed that we did not stand up more decisively in his defense. But who would have listened to us at the time, and who would have published anything true and favorable to him? No one, probably. In the short chapters of this book I have tried to correct the distorted image of this good friend of ours. I hope too this book will correct the generally low opinion people in this country have of Lee. Maybe this attempt of mine to cast him in a different light[2] will have some influence on the final judgment as to where the responsibility lies for the assassination of President John F. Kennedy.

Looking Back

Looking back now at Lee we can remember his reactions, how he suddenly became standoffish, sometimes supercilious, and spoke only to people whom he liked and trusted. And there were not many of them. Lee was not close to his mother and seldom spoke of her. But neither did he criticize her. He hardly spoke of his brother Robert and not at all about Robert's wife,

Vada. Yet the Oswalds stayed with them for a short time immediately after their arrival in the United States in 1962. We never met any of the other members of Lee's family and we are sorry not to have met his mother, Mrs. Marguerite Oswald, who has tried desperately to clear up her son's name and reputation. Even Marina spoke nicely of her. We wish Marguerite the best of luck.

What fiendish names were given our friend Lee Harvey Oswald—Communist, traitor, misfit, insane killer! I hope he will forgive us, and I hope also that Marguerite will forgive us. One of the reasons we agree that her son was probably innocent of Kennedy's assassination—and we insisted on this during the Warren Commission interviews (although it was never brought up publicly)[3]—was the following: Lee actually admired President Kennedy, if only in his own reserved way. Let me give an example. One day Jeanne and I discussed with Lee Kennedy's efforts to bring peace to the world and to end the Cold War.[4]

"Great, great," exclaimed Lee. "If he succeeds, he will be the greatest president in the history of this country."

We constantly hear shouts of "it's the Communists' fault" or "it's a Marxist conspiracy"—omitting the fact that most of our foreign policy[5] mishaps come from our own mistakes whether or not they are committed with good or bad intentions. We wasted $140 billion and 45,000 American lives in Vietnam to prove that "democracy is right."[6] Our top capitalist, the late Harold Lamar Hunt,[7] called President Kennedy a "traitor" and the confrontation between the United States and the Soviet Union, during the Cuban Missile Crisis, a "dispute between two Communist states."[8] Everything is relative, I suppose, if one is going to adopt *that* kind of view.

Kennedy's efforts to alleviate and to end racial segregation in America were also admired by Lee, who was sincerely and profoundly committed to a complete integration of blacks and saw it as the future[9] of the United States. "I am willing to fight for racial equality and would die fighting if necessary," he told me once. I naturally agreed with him. Marina, on the other hand and as we have seen, was not interested in anything except acquiring possessions. Her crass materialism, envy of the success of the other local refugees, compared to Lee's idealism, inevitably led to confrontations.

Because of his poor, miserable childhood, Lee may have compared himself to the blacks and the American Indians and commiserated with them. In this he was a noble and striking contrast to[10] the Southern white trash and rednecks, whose support for segregation stems from their fear of the blacks, of their strength and of the possibility of their prominence in every field of

CHAPTER SIX

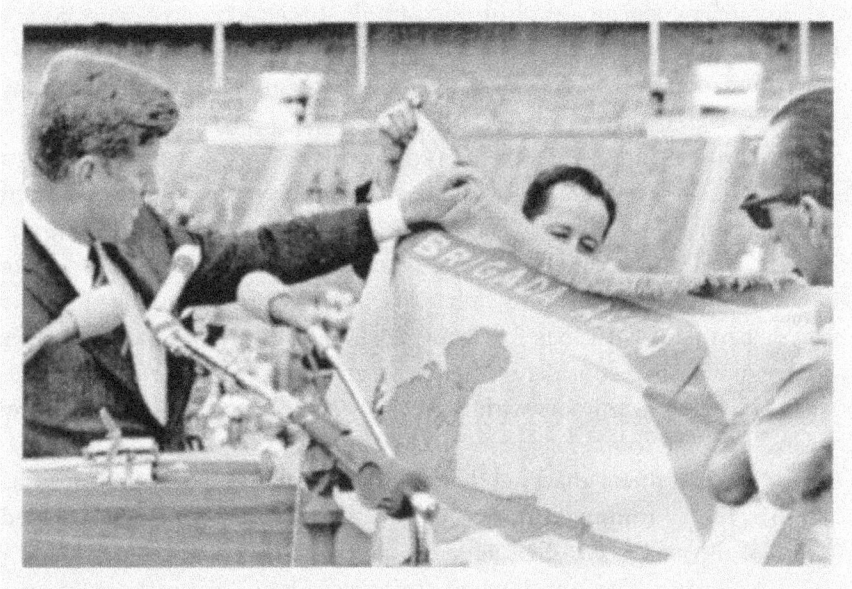

The Bay of Pigs resulted in unbelievable hatreds and desires for revenge.
President Kennedy is presented the Brigada Asalto 2506 flag during a ceremony held at Florida's Orange Bowl Stadium on December 29, 1962. Argenta Images / Rogers Photo Archive

human endeavor. Education for black Americans was anathema for them, while Lee was whole-heartedly for it. He loved black children and admired their cute and outgoing ways. He also was fond of black music and folklore with which he was familiar from his childhood days in New Orleans.

Lee without any doubt despised reactionary groups, the white supremacists and all the other so-called "hate groups" and did not hide his feelings. It was strange indeed for a poor white boy from New Orleans and Texas, purely Anglo, to be so profoundly anti-racist.

"Segregation in any form, racial, social or economic, is one of the most repulsive facts of American life," he often told me. "I would be willing any time to fight these fascistic segregationists—and to die for my black brothers."

He obviously intended to do just that: *fight fascism*, a trait we saw in earlier chapters and exhibited in Marina's written inscription on the back of the picture of Lee that we discovered in 1967. The Warren Commission also completely disregarded this strongly anti-segregationist aspect of Lee's character and eliminated comments I made about it from the report.[11] It was easier to simply assert that the assassin of President Kennedy was a crazy, semi-literate, ex-marine with an undesirable discharge; some screwed-up, Marxist lunatic with a poverty-stricken childhood, unsuccessful in all his pursuits whether in the USSR or the USA, and a man with a failed marriage verging on disastrous.[12]

It was a better option for them, and for the rest of the country, than to find out that the assassination was a devilishly clever act of revenge caused by the Bay of Pigs disaster.[13] The Bay of Pigs resulted in unbelievable hatreds and desires for revenge among Cuban refugee groups in places like Miami and New Orleans. Remember that many Cuban refugees and their relatives had paid with their lives during the failed invasion, and the ones who remained alive considered the disaster Kennedy's fault.[14] I cannot visualize Lee being in cahoots with these anti-Castro Cuban refugees in New Orleans, as some sources suggest, but he *might* have played his own game, meeting some of them, checking them out just for the hell of it to determine what their motivations were, just as he had attended a meeting that included General Walker.[15] On the other hand, I *can* very easily visualize Lee joining a pro-Castro group. The amusing and attractive side of Lee's personality was precisely this: he liked to manipulate his own life; he was an actor among an audience.[16] A very curious individual.

But the desire for revenge among the Cuban refugee groups here was covered up and whenever somebody like Jim Garrison[17] in New Orleans would try to establish a connection between the assassination and the Bay of Pigs, he would be put down as a drunkard, an incompetent, and silenced. Garrison was completely discredited and lost his district attorney's position.[18] His latest book *The Star Spangled Contract* is a work of fiction dealing with the assassination.[19] And now I am sorry to cast an accusation at the Kennedy family, especially on his brother Robert, who wanted to sanctify the late president's memory and to make us all—all American citizens—forget our president's biggest mistake, the Bay of Pigs.

Robert Kennedy was himself assassinated in June of 1968, carrying to the grave the reason for the strange warning about me that he had given to my friend Willem Oltmans.[20] The Reverend Dr. Martin Luther King Jr.[21] had been shot just weeks before, in a cowardly way by an ignorant redneck, James Earl Ray,[22] possibly encouraged by another redneck—one more clever and powerful—J. Edgar Hoover of the FBI, who hated and despised blacks. The Nobel Prize for Peace awarded to King in 1964 was the ultimate insult for Hoover, who was trying to convince everyone King was a dangerous Communist.[23] Hoover, too, is dead now, having outlived RFK and King by just five years.[24] Lee once said something about the FBI which did not strike me at the time as very clever, but history proved his judgment correct. "Knowledge is a great power, especially if you know it about very important people." Obviously J. Edgar Hoover's files come to mind.[25]

The shrewd[26] and unscrupulous agents of the CIA and their associates amassed[27] large fortunes by illicit profits in Korea, Vietnam, Thailand, Cambodia, and Laos.[28] And I am sure the discoveries will continue to be forthcoming: of deals, corruption, double crosses. They irritate me as they ought to irritate any taxpayer who has been paying their federal taxes for years. And in this manner American money will soon become Chinese money.[29] It is ironic that the high-school dropout, that "inferior" American, Lee Harvey Oswald, had foreseen, if dimly, all of this when he called our bureaucracy stupid but crooked.[30] But knowing him the way I did he would have understood *Gulag Archipelago* and would have approved of Solzhenitsyn's indignation.[31]

President Kennedy's widow remarried in October of 1968. Questions arose in some decent people's minds: did Jacqueline know what type of an individual she chose as her spouse[32] or was it a huge bank account she desired, not a real person?[33] Nancy Thorpe, the dean of women at the University of Texas, Arlington, where I had been lecturing at the time was pale with indignation when she heard the news.[34] Some will say that the introduction of Aristotle Onassis[35] at this late juncture may be in bad taste, others may find it interesting, significant and of relevance.[36] Conscience is the most stretchable substance—Ari's friends found him cheerful, amicable, cosmopolitan, intelligent—although his education was not more advanced than Lee's, and he danced well and sang Greek and Argentinian folk songs.[37] Consider, though, the articles in the French publication *Le Canard enchaîné*.[38] You will learn that the Onassis fortune made during the war was based on a very simple formula: old tankers are over insured, duly sunk by the Nazi submarines, their motley, ignorant crew members drown and their no less ignorant poor families receive peanuts in the way of compensation.[39] Repeat the operation dozens, maybe hundreds, of times. Later, after already having acquired a huge fortune he negotiated exclusive rights for transportation of Arab oil, becoming wealthier still.[40] His end in March of 1975 was somewhat gruesome,[41] and Mrs. Onassis became a widow again. If you believe in just punishment, Aristotle Onassis's rotten soul will remain forever in the fires of Greek-Orthodox hell.[42]

Let me say a few final words about the FBI.[43] The FBI should be reformed and then more closely controlled by Congress.[44] This institution should adopt the more modern ways of European agencies such as the Sûreté nationale in France[45] or Scotland Yard in Great Britain in order to become less secretive, more sophisticated, and less naïvely vicious. Frankly, next to the FBI I even prefer the straightforward methods of the Haitian paramilitary police, those bogey men[46] with dark glasses the Tontons Macoutes,[47] who protected the life of President "Papa Doc" Duvalier before his death and who still protect his son "Baby Doc." Why would I say this? The FBI, despite its expensive budget and great size,[48] could not protect the lives of President Kennedy, nor his brother Senator Robert Kennedy, nor, most important of all I think, the life of Dr. Martin Luther King Jr.

The FBI also did a great deal of damage to us simply because, while still in Haiti, I often expressed my opinion to the effect that Lee was a patsy and he was neither interested in nor preparing to assassinate a man he liked and respected. I was also an open critic of our government agencies like the CIA because J. Walton Moore, whom I had contacted regarding Lee, told me that he was a "harmless lunatic."[49] As a result of this frank criticism, the FBI did its best to crucify us in Haiti, to damage my business contract with the Duvalier government, all with the connivance of the American Embassy. In the final analysis I lost a lot of business contacts and a great deal of income because the FBI had pried too much into my brief association with Lee[50] and exposed it in the wrong light.

A New Friend: Willem Oltmans

After our return from Haiti in 1967 we were constantly assailed by a great number of journalists, all wanting to interview us.[51] The most interesting among them was a Dutchman, Willem Oltmans.[52] Educated in the United States—a Yale graduate[53]—Oltmans was the United States representative of NOS Television (Dutch State Television) with headquarters in New York.

Oltmans told me how he became interested in the president's murder, while we were still in Haiti and before my Warren Commission testimony in Washington. He flew to Dallas on March 9, 1964, on American Airlines from Kennedy airport in New York to address the next day the Criterion Club in Wichita Falls, Texas.[54] At the counter in New York he ran into Lee's mother, Marguerite Oswald. The two sat together during the following dinner-flight and it was during this journey that Oltmans first began to doubt the truth of the claim that Lee Harvey Oswald had killed President Kennedy all by himself. It was Marguerite who informed him that the chief of police in Dallas interrogated Lee for forty-eight hours, without making a tape-recording of the hearing or even keeping his notes.[55]

Upon returning to the Netherlands Oltmans discussed his conversation with Marguerite with the famous clairvoyant, Gerard Croiset,[56] who lived in the city of Utrecht and who has been solving crimes and murders all over the world, including in the United States. Doubleday published a biography of this amazing Dutchman, *Croiset the Clairvoyant*, in 1964.[57] It was Croiset who first described my existence to Oltmans in a tape-recorded interview (kept at the Institute of Parapsychology at the University of Utrecht). Croiset told Oltmans that Lee had a friend in Dallas, in his fifties. He described to Oltmans a man whose name contained the word "de" and also the letters "sch."[58]

Oltmans immediately consulted the chief of programs of National Dutch Television in Hilversum, Carel Enkelaar. He received an assignment to return to Dallas and try to locate this mysterious friend of Oswald's who, according to the Dutch clairvoyant, was both of noble descent and a geologist. This mysterious Mr. X was, according to Croiset, the architect of the ambush that had killed President Kennedy. Oswald, Croiset claimed, was only the fall-guy.[59]

Oltmans returned to Fort Worth and visited Marguerite Oswald on March 11, 1967.[60] It was Lee's mother who, following Croiset's description, pointed to a volume of a complete set of the *Warren Commission Hearings and Exhibits* and indicated our name and existence to the Dutch journalist. Oltmans reported back in Hilversum that Croiset's indication had been correct. There was a friend, in his fifties, who fit Oltmans's description precisely, and his name was George de Mohrenschildt.

NOS Television then instructed Willem Oltmans to phone me and ask for an interview. When he called me at home on March 31[61] I replied that I had to attend the World Petroleum Congress in Mexico City[62] and that he should contact me in two weeks.[63] As things would transpire, however, I did not hear from him again until later that year. When Oltmans first reported to Hilversum that he had contacted me, the Dutch television presidium immediately instructed him to contact the office of Robert F. Kennedy, at the time the senator of the state of New York. He had an office located at the US Post Office building, near 43rd street. They reasoned that so many people directly or indirectly connected with trying to unravel the Kennedy assassination had been killed, or mysteriously disappeared, that Oltmans was in grave danger.

Oltmans returned to his apartment in Kew Gardens, New York, and on April 3[64] saw Tim Hogan, Senator Kennedy's press assistant, and explained the entire situation, including Croiset's analysis, that President Kennedy had

Left: Willem Oltmans, November 12, 1973, holding a copy of his book *Den Vaderland Getrouwe*. Dutch National Archives
Right: Robert F. Kennedy in the Cabinet Room of the White House, Washington, D.C., January 28, 1964. LBJ Library

been killed in a plot and that I was the engineer of the ambush. Hogan said the senator was upstate making a speech in Albany that morning[65] and was flying back at 1 p.m. in the "Caroline." He would immediately relay to the senator Oltmans's request whether he could have some protection from the FBI. NOS Television had figured that Senator Kennedy, being former attorney-general of the United States and the slain president's brother, was as safe a person as any to ask for help in this delicate manner.

Hogan called Oltmans back and informed him that RFK had personally picked up the phone and talked to J. Edgar Hoover in Washington, D.C. FBI agents would contact him later that day. Indeed, at 4 p.m. two agents called at Oltmans's apartment. They stayed two full hours, but Oltmans only revealed to them that he was instructed to interview my wife and I in Dallas and that, at the same time, NOS TV had told him to contact Robert Kennedy.

When the agents left Oltmans's apartment they assured him that from that moment on he would be under 24/7 FBI surveillance and there would be nothing to worry about. The next evening[66] Oltmans wanted to visit an Indonesian friend in Greenwich Village, an architect, who was designing a cover for a book Oltmans was writing about Sukarno, the former president of Indonesia.[67] Driving southward on Westside Drive at around 8 p.m. in a Sunbeam Tiger (a convertible sports car) with a V-8 motor and aluminum racing wheels, at a speed of about sixty miles per hour, Oltmans was overtaken by a cab with a passenger riding in the back-seat. The cab cruised parallel to Oltmans's car until they reached the 53rd Street exit. Then the cab suddenly accelerated, and Oltmans's car was cut off in such a way that he crashed in the rails. His car was a total loss. His head was injured and bleeding. He was brought to the Kew Gardens hospital, where he was examined, bandaged, and sent home. In less than ten days the insurance awarded him a new car, which Oltmans quickly shipped off to the Netherlands. He himself left the United States a few days afterwards.

Two months later, Oltmans received in his country bungalow near Utrecht a telephone call from a certain Glenn Bryan Smith, attorney from Fort Lauderdale, Florida.[68] Smith announced that he was conducting an investigation into the JFK murder for Robin Moore,[69] the author of *The Green Berets*. He wanted to discuss with Oltmans the Dallas affair and compare notes. Oltmans agreed to a meeting in Hotel Terminus in Utrecht, but only in the presence of Carel Enkelaar, the head of NOS TV. It so happened. During the conversation, however, Smith slipped in some threats. He cautioned Oltmans in the presence of Enkelaar to stop investigating President Kennedy's assassination because "you would not be the first person to die or disappear in this matter. What they do is, they will kidnap you in a New York street, drive you to a private airport, and dump you over the Atlantic Ocean. You would not be the first person to die this way either." Oltmans says that he remained unperturbed. He waited a few months more before publishing an extensive report on his automobile accident in the leading weekly magazine the *Haagse Post* on September 30, 1967,[70] showing on the cover pictures of John F. Kennedy and myself.

Oltmans returned to the United States in October 1967 and came to film us in our Dallas apartment with the local CBS TV crew on Sunday the 15th.[71] It was a very pleasant meeting for us. From that moment on this Dutch journalist, who initially approached us because he had received indications that we might be involved indirectly through Oswald with the Kennedy assassination, became a very personal friend. He has visited us every year since 1967 and is now convinced that we had nothing whatsoever to do with the assassination of President Kennedy. As a matter of fact, he told us that despite Gerard Croiset's great gifts for solving crimes, some forty percent of his indications and prognoses turn out to be false. Nevertheless, Oltmans relayed to us that as recently as the summer of 1976, this famous Dutch clairvoyant is still convinced and deadly serious[72] that I am the man who tricked Lee Harvey Oswald, and who set up, financed by the Dallas oil lobby, the assassination of John F. Kennedy.[73] I am supposed to have done it from Haiti—probably through some voodoo trick! I should have sued that Dutch clairvoyant, but I presume that he is broke and an international lawsuit would be very costly.

Lee: One Last Assessment

As we saw earlier, in the preface of this book, I had a premonition the day of President Kennedy's assassination, three thousand miles away in Haiti, that Lee was involved in some way and that he was in deep trouble. It's strange how these feelings work. I cannot tell you who assassinated President John F. Kennedy. In time someone will prove who fired the fatal shots, will prove or disprove a conspiracy to commit the assassination, and will prove or disprove Lee's involvement, or lack thereof.[74] I *can* tell you that Lee was not jealous of the Kennedy's and Bouvier's wealth, nor was he envious of their social standing; of that I am sure. Wealth and society were not a source of resentment but rather big jokes to him.[75] If there are good Catholics involved in this affair, maybe a confession will solve the problem.[76] It would be good for their souls.

With the exception of the European press, the majority of the American books and articles have accepted an almost preposterous thesis introduced by some lawyer of the Warren Commission named Arlen J. Specter[77] that the same bullet passed through President Kennedy and then at the same time gravely wounded Governor John Connally.[78] Yet, Connally himself distinctly remembers two consecutive shots and he has never changed his testimony.[79] Our dear President Ford's book, *Portrait of an Assassin*, was ghostwritten, inept, and uninteresting.[80] I have to give credit to the American people; the book was a failure. As I mentioned in Chapter 4 the superficial conclusion favored in the United States—the thesis of Lee's guilt as the lone assassin—has been rejected in most other countries. Many people suspect Vice-President Lyndon Johnson, being as he was a party which profited directly from the assassination and who always resented the cold-shoulder treatment he and his wife had received from JFK and the whole Kennedy clan.

Recall the inscription on the picture we had discovered in 1967, in our stored belongings.[81] How could a hunter of *fascists* be the assassin of a young and *liberal* president? Would Lee address this photograph so endearingly to me, knowing well how much I liked the president, had he intended to assassinate him? Would even his wife call him, with sarcastic humor, "the hunter of fascists" on the same photograph if her husband was preparing to assassinate the most liberal president America ever had? Only some more logical and cynical writers mentioned the fact that there was no reason whatsoever in Lee's action; but they approve the thesis that Lee was aiming at Governor Connally, whom he had reasons to dislike, but being a usual flop and f--- up, he killed Kennedy instead and only wounded Connally.

Now let us ask ourselves a question: was there a conspiracy on the part of the Warren Commission members, this powerful and impressive group of people, to promote a deliberate lie, to inculcate an innocent person? No, I don't think so.[82] They acted naïvely and sheepishly for a purpose which seemed right to them and good for the country. The country was in an upheaval, it was necessary to pacify public opinion. And the dead eccentric is the easiest subject to condemn.[83] Personally, I think that such a mentality is tragic and detrimental to this country. On American politics Lee expressed the following opinion to me: "Under dictatorship people are enslaved but they know it. Here the politicians constantly lie to people and they become immune to these lies because they have the privilege of voting. But voting is rigged and democracy here is a gigantic profusion of lies and clever brain-washing."[84]

Lee denied that he was the assassin to the last moment of his life. Despite being questioned by the Dallas police for forty-some hours, he never admitted anything. Knowing Lee and his truthfulness, my wife and I believe that if Lee had been given the chance to speak, he would have told the truth. *If* he had even some part in the assassination, he would have proudly presented to the world his reasons for it. Unfortunately, Dallas police captain Fritz[85] never released to the Warren Commission investigators any notes of this interrogation and he denied that the interrogation had been tape-recorded. The entire Dallas police department, supposedly, had not one tape-recorder at the time. As primitive as the Dallas police force may have been in 1963, such negligence is hardly credible. The city of Dallas was certainly rich enough at the time to have acquired a tape recorder for its police department. Chief Justice Warren, while interrogating Captain Fritz, asked acidly: "Wasn't it worthwhile to borrow a tape recorder when the assassination of the President of the United States was being investigated?"[86]

And so any record of Lee's interrogation either does not exist today or has mysteriously disappeared.[87] William Penn Jones Jr.,[88] the editor[89] of the *Midlothian Mirror*,[90] a Texas newspaper, and a simple honest man, told me upon my return to the United States from Haiti: "I shall never forget Lee Harvey Oswald's face, beaten brutally to a pulp, of his terrified expression when he was being led by beefy policemen the day of President Kennedy's assassination. And this young man kept shouting 'I am a patsy! I am a patsy!'" And, continued this elderly newspaperman, "I swear to God I knew that he was telling the truth." In my opinion Lee *would* have told the truth during this lengthy interrogation, during which he must have been beaten and maybe tortured. Anyone would have broken down, perhaps cracked,[91] but his defiant last words were "I am a patsy!"[92] Lee Harvey Oswald might have been violent sometimes, like almost anyone amongst us is at one point or another, and he might even try to kill a person he truly and intensely hated, for example a General Walker or someone racist or someone who might want to hurt him and his family.[93] But to assassinate a president he expressed admiration for in my presence so many times, just for the attention-seeking glory of it, as some have claimed, was entirely foreign to his personality.

In my humble opinion, as indicated by some of the events and conversations in this book, the Kennedy family did not want to pursue the matter of finding the real, unquestionable assassin nor a conspiracy. And they could have done it with their own, immense, private resources. If somebody killed my son or my brother, I would certainly want to know for sure who did it. But possibly a personality like that of Lee Harvey Oswald perfectly suited the political purposes of the Kennedy family.[94] In the end Lee was led around, from one place to another, by the Dallas police, the movements were announced, the crowds were there and, as if on cue, he was shot and killed. Lee was a "lunatic" and a "Marxist" who killed John F. Kennedy without any reason; Kennedy, for his part became a national martyr. And so, the matter was closed forever. Why look for the truly responsible people? Jeanne and I, independently of each other, both asked Assistant Counsel Jenner "Why don't you send good detectives to New Orleans and to Mexico, find out who Lee's contacts were at that time, and what he was up to at the time of the tragedy?" It seems that a senate committee is going to do just that now, in the summer of 1976.[95]

I can still hear his voice: clear, sincere, simple, without affectation. Listening to Lee describe his experience in the Soviet Union, one saw clearly that the Soviet Union was not a paradise but just another livable country, enormous, with endless problems, full of people both good and friendly and many other people who were stupid, cruel, and limited. As everyone knows Russian is a complex language and he was supposed to have stayed in the Soviet Union only a little over two years. He must have had some previous training and that point had never been brought up by the Warren Commission—and it is still puzzling to me. In my opinion Lee was a very bright person but not a genius. He never mastered the English language yet he learned such a difficult language! I have taught Russian at all levels in a large university and I never saw such a proficiency in the best senior students who constantly listened to taped Russian and spoke to Russian friends. As a matter of fact, American-born *instructors* never mastered the spoken Russian language as well as Lee did.[96] Had Lee remained in the Soviet Union I am convinced he would have wound up in a labor camp for his outspoken opinions—for his loose tongue.

In earlier chapters I spoke of Lee's occasional, clever repartees, his frequent outbursts of justifiable anger at the existing situation in this rotten world of ours, his deep concern for the starving and those poorer than himself, his worry and his pity for the racially segregated, and for any masses deprived of their just rights by clever manipulators. Of all the material I have gathered here the one point I would hope to make, more than any other, was that Lee was *above all* an anti-segregationist, opposed to anyone[97] who chose to discriminate against minorities or anyone underprivileged.

Lee cared for freedom in this country, and he hoped for the improvement of the world tensions. Some other aspects of Lee's personality have, I hope, emerged from this book. I have sought to show that Lee was not a harmful person, on the contrary, he was a rather inspiring individual. He possessed a deep desire to improve relations between the United States and the Soviet Union. Lee subscribed to *Krokodil*,[98] a Soviet satirical publication, somewhat similar to the American *New Yorker* or the British *Punch* magazines. *Krokodil*, which we often read together, featured mainly Russian self-criticism in the form of short stories or cartoons. Local politicians were depicted as animals and, in the manner of Krylov's fables,[99] these cartoons emphasized the foibles of the Soviet bureaucracy. As one would expect the magazine also took swipes at the bourgeois world quite sharply.

At last the latent animosities between these superpowers are starting to dissipate.[100] It took twelve years and a man like Henry Kissinger[101] to at least partially achieve this purpose. But Lee would have hoped for more than just *détente*. He hoped that these two powerful countries would become friends and he tried[102] to achieve it in a naïve and maybe foolish, but sincere, way. He wanted to improve our image around the world in his own way, humanizing the United States, for example, with his defense of American ways during his stay in Minsk. It is clear now that war between these two countries would end in a nuclear[103] holocaust. And so, Lee Harvey Oswald had dreamed and hoped for peace[104] and for friendship—not so bad for a high-school dropout from a New Orleans slum.

It is my firm opinion that Lee was never sure he was right, but he was always groping for truth, for a way into the light. Comparing the Soviet Union to the United States, he told me once, "Both sides have made a lot of mistakes, enormous mistakes, but which side is right and which side is wrong, I'll be damned if I know."[105] It is always better for nations[106] to be friends than to fight wars, only insane people would want conflict now with the thousands of weapons available in the world's nuclear arsenal. It is insane that people believe modern weaponry can provide a decisive edge anymore. These insane people are forcing others to believe in the superiority of any weaponry. We can kill the entire Russian population hundreds of times over and they can do the same to us. So what purpose does nuclear "superiority" serve?

Both Lee and I firmly believed that subservience to any dominant political idea is wrong; people should try to discover an ideology which fits them, even though it might be unpopular, and follow it. If not, we would become the same fools[107] Russians were during Stalin's time. Their servility backfired and they became victims of it. "They did not try to find out who was right and who was wrong," Lee told me during one of our conversations, which often dealt with the Stalinist times in Russia. He had learned a lot in Minsk. "Free people," he had said, "should not remain mere pawns in the world game of chess played by the rulers."

Some time ago I saw a program, sponsored by some safety razor firm, which featured Lee talking in New Orleans on the radio.[108] This was regarding his pro-Cuban activity. The program was taped and Lee's photos were inserted. Lee spoke rather intelligently, but the inserted photos made him look ugly and threatening. It was a nasty way to portray a dead man. Technically, the program did not make much sense and was awful, but its purpose was to brainwash the American people into believing ever more firmly that Lee was the sole and only assassin.

Regarding Lee's real or imaginary attempt at General Walker's life, the truth will remain a mystery.[109] There are additional stories going around that, according to Marina, Lee also wanted to shoot Nixon, whom he considered a reactionary of the same type as Walker. This was at the time when Nixon was vice-president.[110] But Lee never even spoke to me about Nixon, so it remains pure speculation.[111]

CHAPTER SIX

I did not know Lee to be a dangerous man, a man who would kill like a maniac without any reason—with reason *any* man is a potential killer—and we have seen in the preceding pages ample proof that he was rather an admirer of Kennedy. Lee's convictions[112] when we knew him were fairly liberal, equalitarian; I would not even call them Communist but a set of rather vague Marxist beliefs.[113] One day Jeanne asked Lee, very straightforwardly, "Why did you decide to go to the USSR—answer frankly! You risked never returning."

"I was looking for an ideal," Lee answered with a note of sadness.

"And why did you decide to return to the United States?" Jeanne demanded.

"Because I did not find my ideal. Obviously utopia does not exist. I could travel and change countries the rest of my life and never find it."

We liked this answer, and agreed with him.[114] Maybe, had he lived longer, he would have fitted better into the scheme of American life. He would have joined the flower children, grown a beard and certainly would have been among those protesting the war in Vietnam. He did not try to influence me in any way nor did I try to exert any influence on him. "That's why it's so easy to be with you," said Lee one day, "everyone tries to influence me one way or another, in the Soviet Union, in Japan, here, but you leave me strictly alone." Whether you were responsible, even partially, or just involved, even as a patsy, in the conspiracy to assassinate President John F. Kennedy, I do hope that this book will help you sleep in peace.[115]

A Final Word

It must be acknowledged that our brief friendship with the Oswalds had strange and adverse effects on our lives. Almost everything I have done in my life since the Kennedy assassination has become suspicious and been distorted thanks to the actions of unscrupulous reporters and book-writing rumor-mongers. I cannot even begin to give a complete accounting of the incongruous theories and suppositions which evolved—and are still evolving today—in the feverish minds of various writers and reporters as a result of my past friendship with Lee. Usually they do little more than rehash the information about me found in the *Warren Commission Report*.[116] Some are completely ridiculous.[117] Some, though, go further. Insulting and stupid articles continue to appear in newspapers and magazines all over the world, calling Jeanne and I the "mysterious associates of Lee Harvey Oswald." The latest intrusion[118] into my privacy came just a few months ago when articles

It must be acknowledged that our brief friendship with the Oswalds had strange and adverse effects on our lives.
George de Mohrenschildt—Bishop College professor, with wife, Jeanne (circa 1974).
Argenta Images / Rogers Photo Archive

appeared in both the *San Francisco Chronicle* and in the *Chicago Tribune* snidely suggesting that I had gone to the Bahamas after the assassination to be paid off there by someone, to keep some dark and terrible secrets regarding Lee Harvey Oswald. A shyster in Washington by the name of Bernard Fensterwald Jr. assured a European newspaperman, Henk Leffelaar, of a similar monetary operation.[119] And what can you do about it? Suing is not my style and I have no time for it.[120] And so I write to these journalists and receive letters of apology. But the damage to my public reputation, with public opinion, is done.[121]

People read the *Warren Report* too superficially, focus on the gossipy aspects of our sprawling testimony, and wonder who these strange foreign people called the de Mohrenschildts are. They call us on the phone at all hours, asking us foolish questions. Even now, long after giving our testimony, insidious articles appear claiming that we were bribed ("bribed" by whom?) to hide the truth about Kennedy's assassination. Subsequent publicity makes us appear controversial and even more gruesomely threatening.

Books, too, have spread bizarre idiocies about myself. An example is a work published in 1968 in French titled *L'Amérique Brûle* (*America Is Burning*).[122] The "author," James Hepburn, is actually a pseudonym for a group of European newspapermen.[123] The publishers are in Luxembourg where they cannot be sued. In this book I am alleged to have been a CIA agent assigned to Lee Harvey Oswald. Let me translate a passage[124] regarding my supposed relationship with Lee: "Oswald was put under supervision by the CIA and interrogated as well as tested by one of the specialists utilized by the CIA in Washington D.C. and by its Houston Branch. He was an oilman, whose *nom de guerre* (operative name) was George S. de Mohrenschildt."[125] I certainly should have chosen an easier *nom de guerre*! I cannot prove that I was never a CIA agent because it is impossible to prove a negative. I cannot demonstrate either that I ever was. Nobody can. Only recent disclosures[126] have made known names of the CIA agents who were at the same time employees in our State Department and who worked in our embassies and consulates in various capacities. Before this the fact of belonging to the CIA was a well-kept secret.[127] But enough of this nonsense.

At present we are alive, fairly healthy,[128] and enjoying a very different way of life.[129] We moved away from the business world to the academic world and the latter is more rewarding.[130] I have returned to teaching and am happy to be with young people.[131] We have not lost our real friends.[132] And we do not complain: life is interesting and exciting for us. Often we wish Lee were here with us to share some of the progressive[133] changes we

are seeing in this country and in the world. But we also think frequently about the shadier aspects of this gruesome "investigation" of President
Kennedy's murder, of the harm done to this country, and especially of the
damage to the memory of Lee, my dead friend. In this book I have been trying to concentrate on presenting to the reader the personality of Lee Harvey
Oswald as I knew him, based on what I have remembered, taped and noted,
of his opinions, his jokes and his remarks in our conversations.[134] I offer you
no easy solution, no criminal served up on a platter.[135] Judge the man for
yourself. Make up your own mind. As for myself, I often miss Lee and his
stimulating presence. He died much too young.[136]

APPENDIX A

·∞·

Letter from George
de Mohrenschildt to
Mrs. Janet Lee Auchincloss

EDITOR'S NOTE: *The following letter was published in the* Warren Commission Hearings and Exhibits *as "De Mohrenschildt Exhibit 14." It sheds light on de Mohrenschildt's state of mind at a time almost immediately after the Kennedy assassination and before he had been contacted to testify before the Warren Commission. The reader will note, as I have pointed out in the Editor's Introduction, the difficulties written English presents for someone whose native language is Russian. The phonetic spellings (even of Oswald's name), odd sentence constructions, and other mistakes within the letter are typical of someone thinking in Russian but writing in English. The reader may also note some interesting similarities between the content of the letter, the manuscript's preface, and the vignette in Chapter 4 I have named "Visiting the Auchincloss Home." The postscript is yet another indication of how deeply his son Sergei's 1960 death impacted de Mohrenschildt. Note that Sergei died at the age of seven; he would have been ten had he still been living at the time this letter was written.*

Port-au-Prince, Haiti, Dec. 12, 1963
c/o American Embassy

Dear Janet:

We are appaled [*sic*] and deeply disgusted by President Kennedy's cowardly assassination. We were ashamed that it happened in our home town. May I ask you to express my deepest sympathy to your daughter and tell her that both my brother and I will always remember her as the charming little girl from East Hampton. So many sorrows have been ruining her young life.

Since we lived in Dallas permanently last year and before, we had the misfortune to have met Osvald [*sic*] and especially his wife Marina sometime last fall. Both my wife and I tried to help poor Marina who could not speak any English, was mistreated by her husband; she and the baby were malnourished and sickly. We took them to the hospital.

Sometime last fall we heard that Osvald [*sic*] had beaten his wife cruelly, so we drove to their miserable place and forcipby [*sic*] took Marina and the child away from the character. Then he threatened me and my wife but I did not take him seriously. Marina stayed with the family of some childless Russian refugees for a while, keeping her baby, but finally decided to return to her husband. Somehow then we lost interest in the Osvalds [*sic*].

It is really a shame that such crimes occur in our times and in our country. But there is so much jealousy for success—and the late president was successful in so many domains—and there is so much desire for publicity on the part of all shady characters that assassinations are bound to occur. Better precautions should have been taken. Remember our discussion one day on the plane from Dallas to Washington? We spoke of criminal children and the terrible problem of delinquency in the South. Osvald [*sic*] was just an expression of that cancer which is eating American youth.

You will excuse this rambling letter but I was just sitting in my office thinking of the strange fate which made me know Jackie when she was a little girl—and which made me also know the assassin (or presumable assassin) his wife and child. And your daughter has been of such help to the Cystic Fibrosis Research Foundation which he [*sic*] had started in Texas several years ago. She was an honorary chairman of the Foundation.

I do hope that Marina and her children (I understand she has two now) will not suffer too badly throughout their lives and that the stigma will not affect the innocent children. Somehow, I still have lingering doubt, notwithstanding all the evidence, of Osvald's [*sic*] guilt.

I just received a letter from my brother and he also recalls our friendship with you and extresses [*sic*] his deepest sympathy to you and your daughter. Please acdept [*sic*] my feelings of respect and consideration.

Sincerely,
/s/   G. de Mohrenschildt
George de Mohrenschildt

I also had a great tragedy three years ago, my only son died of Cystic Fibrosis at the age of ten and I understand the impact of the sudden death and the ensuing horrible shock.

APPENDIX B

༄

Excerpts from George de Mohrenschildt's Warren Commission Testimony

EDITOR'S NOTE: *The testimony of George S. De Mohrenschildt was taken April 22 and April 23, 1964, at 200 Maryland Avenue N.E., Washington, D.C., by Mr. Albert E. Jenner Jr., assistant counsel of the President's Commission. Dr. Alfred Goldberg, historian, was also present. Readers will note how closely de Mohrenschildt's unfinished manuscript parallels portions of the excerpted material. As noted in the Editor's Introduction, substantial portions of the manuscript appear to be a "retelling" of de Mohrenschildt's Warren Commission testimony. When de Mohrenschildt is reading from documents placed into exhibit—such as the reply he received from Mrs. Auchincloss to his letter of December 12, 1963 (see Appendix A)—the text has been italicized and indented, to better distinguish it from his spoken testimony in response to Jenner's questions.*

[April 22, 1964]

* * *

MR. JENNER: Now, this brings us to the summer of 1962.

MR. DE MOHRENSCHILDT: Yes.

MR. JENNER: Now, in due course you met Marina and Lee Harvey Oswald.

MR. DE MOHRENSCHILDT: Yes.

MR. JENNER: Give me—I am going to pose a hypothetical to you. Let us assume that a Russian couple would come to Dallas, let us say right now—no friends, not know anybody in Dallas. What would normally happen? As soon as you became acquainted with the fact, or the community—the Russian group became acquainted with the fact that there was a Russian couple?

MR. DE MOHRENSCHILDT: They would be exceedingly interested, naturally.

MR. JENNER: Curious?

MR. DE MOHRENSCHILDT: Exceedingly curious.

MR. JENNER: Now, if you were there, would that include you?

MR. DE MOHRENSCHILDT: Yes.

MR. JENNER: And your wife?

MR. DE MOHRENSCHILDT: Yes. Well, aside from us—the most curious would be George Bouhe, because he actually met us first—the first in Dallas—he told us about Oswald, as far as I remember. Because he is curious by nature. He wants to know what is going on. He wants to convert them to the Greek Orthodox Church, and so on.

MR. JENNER: Would there be any effort to help these people become acquainted throughout the community?

MR. DE MOHRENSCHILDT: If they—if that couple came from Soviet Russia, from the Soviet Union, you mean?

MR. JENNER: Well, let's assume that.

MR. DE MOHRENSCHILDT: Well, the old guard would not do anything. They would be curious, but—they might meet them and very soon afterwards they would get disgusted with them, because what they would say to them would not fit with their beliefs. And we know that Soviet Russia is a going concern. To them it is not, it does not exist. It just isn't there.

MR. JENNER: All right. Now, when did you first meet either Marina—I will put it this way: When did you first hear—

MR. DE MOHRENSCHILDT: The first time—

MR. JENNER: Of either of these people—Marina Oswald or Lee Harvey Oswald?

MR. DE MOHRENSCHILDT: As far as I remember, George Bouhe, who is a close friend of mine, and a very curious individual, told me that there is an interesting couple in Fort Worth, and that the Clarks know them already—Max Clark and Gali—they know them already. Somebody read about them in the paper—I don't know exactly, I don't remember the exact wording anymore that somebody read about them in the paper, maybe Mr. Gregory, and discovered them, made a discovery.

MR. JENNER: Now—

MR. DE MOHRENSCHILDT: But we heard from George Bouhe the first time.

MR. JENNER: At this time were you aware that there had been an American who had gone to the Soviet Union and attempted to defect to the Soviet Union?

MR. DE MOHRENSCHILDT: Yes.

MR. JENNER: And that he had returned to the United States?

MR. DE MOHRENSCHILDT: That is what I heard from George Bouhe.

MR. JENNER: That was the first you ever knew anything at all about—

MR. DE MOHRENSCHILDT: I never heard about them, never heard anything about them before.

MR. JENNER: Now, is that likewise true of Mrs. De Mohrenschildt?

MR. DE MOHRENSCHILDT: Same thing. I think we were both together when this conversation took place.

MR. JENNER: When did it take place?

MR. DE MOHRENSCHILDT: I could not tell you the date. I think in the summer of 1962.

* * *

MR. JENNER: You were curious to find out more about them, were you not?

MR. DE MOHRENSCHILDT: Yes.

MR. JENNER: What did you do?

MR. DE MOHRENSCHILDT: Again, now, my recollections are a little bit vague on that. I tried, both my wife and I, hundreds of times to recall how exactly we met the Oswalds. But they were out of our mind completely, because so many things happened in the meantime. So please do not take it for sure how I first met them.

MR. JENNER: We want your best recollection.

MR. DE MOHRENSCHILDT: My best recollection—I even cannot recall who gave me their address in Fort Worth. I don't recall that. Either George Bouhe or the Clarks, because the Clarks knew them already, Max and Gali Clark, because they were from Fort Worth, you see. And I think a few days later somebody told me that they live in dire poverty. Somewhere in the slums of Fort Worth. I had to go on business to Fort Worth with my very close friend, Colonel Orlov.

MR. JENNER: What is his first name?

MR. DE MOHRENSCHILDT: Lawrence Orlov—he is an American, but he has a

Russian name for some reason—maybe his great-grandfather came from Russia. And to my best recollection, Lawrence and I were on some business in Fort Worth, and I told him let's go and meet those people, and the two of us drove to this slum area in Fort Worth and knocked at the door, and here was Marina and the baby. Oswald was not there.

MR. JENNER: This was during the daytime?

MR. DE MOHRENSCHILDT: Late in the afternoon, after business hours, 5 o'clock.

MR. JENNER: You and Colonel Orlov?

MR. DE MOHRENSCHILDT: Colonel Orlov.

MR. JENNER: She answered the door.

MR. DE MOHRENSCHILDT: Yes.

MR. JENNER: You identified yourself?

MR. DE MOHRENSCHILDT: Yes; I said a few words in Russian, I said we are friends of George Bouhe. I think he was already helping them a little bit, giving them something for the baby or something. I think he had already been in—he helps everybody. He has been helping her especially. And so the introduction was fine. And I found her not particularly pretty, but a lost soul, living in the slums, not knowing one single word of English, with this rather unhealthy looking baby, horrible surroundings.

MR. JENNER: Now we are interested in a couple of things. You found that she knew substantially no English?

MR. DE MOHRENSCHILDT: No English at all at that time. I think she knew, maybe I remember that I asked her, "How do you buy things in the store," and she said, "I point with my finger and I can say 'yes' and 'no.'" That is all.

MR. JENNER: Did you go into the home—was it a house or apartment?

MR. DE MOHRENSCHILDT: It was a shack, near Sears Roebuck, as far as I remember—near that area. I don't know if you went down there. A little shack, which had only two rooms, sort of clapboard-type building. Very poorly furnished, decrepit, on a dusty road. The road even was not paved.

MR. JENNER: What did you talk to her about?

MR. DE MOHRENSCHILDT: Just asked her how she likes it here, and how she was getting along, does she get enough food, something like that—completely meaningless conversation. And I think Lawrence was there, you know, but he did not understand what I was saying. He doesn't know Russian.

MR. JENNER: Did you ask about her husband?

MR. DE MOHRENSCHILDT: I said, "Well, I would like to meet your husband." She said he should be back from work soon. She asked me to sit down, offered me something to drink, I think—she had some sherry or something in the house. This is the best of my recollection. And Lawrence sat down, and found her very nice. And then after a little while, Oswald, Lee appeared.

MR. JENNER: You say Lee appeared?

MR. DE MOHRENSCHILDT: Yes, Lee appeared.

MR. JENNER: Lee appeared. You had never seen him before?

MR. DE MOHRENSCHILDT: Never seen him before.

MR. JENNER: And he came in?

MR. DE MOHRENSCHILDT: He came in.

MR. JENNER: What happened, and what was said?

MR. DE MOHRENSCHILDT: Well, he loved to speak Russian.

MR. JENNER: Did you introduce yourself? And explain why you were there?

MR. DE MOHRENSCHILDT: Yes, I said, "I'm a friend of George Bouhe, I want to see how you are getting along."

MR. JENNER: Did you speak in Russian or English?

MR. DE MOHRENSCHILDT: In English at first, and then he switched to Russian.

MR. JENNER: What was your impression of his command of Russian?

MR. DE MOHRENSCHILDT: Well, he spoke fluent Russian, but with a foreign accent, and made mistakes, grammatical mistakes, but had remarkable fluency in Russian.

MR. JENNER: It was remarkable?

MR. DE MOHRENSCHILDT: Remarkable—for a fellow of his background and education, it is remarkable how fast he learned it. But he loved the language. He loved to speak it. He preferred to speak Russian than English any time. He always would switch from English to Russian.

MR. JENNER: Did you discuss life in Russia, how he got there?

MR. DE MOHRENSCHILDT: I don't think the first time. I don't think the first time I said anything at all, you know. Possibly he told me that he had been in Minsk, and that got me curious, because I had lived in Minsk as a child, and my father was the so-called nobility marshal of Minsk. He got me curious, you know. But I do not recall for sure whether it was the first time I met him or the second time or the third time. I don't remember. I think it was a very short meeting the first time, because Lawrence Orlov was there, and he wanted to get back home, so we just said, "Well, we will see you," and possibly Marina had mentioned that her baby needed—

that she needed some medical attention with her teeth, and that the baby had not been inoculated. Possibly that was that time. But I am not so sure.

MR. JENNER: At least there was a time when that did arise?

MR. DE MOHRENSCHILDT: Yes, yes.

MR. JENNER: Her need for dental care, some attention needed to be given to the child?

MR. DE MOHRENSCHILDT: Yes.

MR. JENNER: Your impression was the child looked rather on the sickly side?

MR. DE MOHRENSCHILDT: Yes; very much so. It was kind of a big head, bald big head, looked like Khrushchev, the child—looked like an undergrown Khrushchev. I always teased her about the fact that the baby looked like Khrushchev.

MR. JENNER: I don't want to prod you, because I want you to tell the story in your own words. Now, you had this visit, and you returned home?

MR. DE MOHRENSCHILDT: I think the first visit was very short, and we drove back with Lawrence, and I remember on the way we discussed that couple, and both had a lot of sympathy for her especially. But he also struck me as a very sympathetic fellow.

MR. JENNER: Yes. Give me your impression of him at that time, your first impression.

MR. DE MOHRENSCHILDT: The first impression and the last impression remain more or less the same. I could never get mad at this fellow.

MR. JENNER: Why?

MR. DE MOHRENSCHILDT: Sometimes he was obnoxious. I don't know. I had a liking for him. I always had a liking for him. There was something charming about him, there was some—I don't know. I just liked the guy—that is all.

MR. JENNER: When you reached home, you reported on this—

MR. DE MOHRENSCHILDT: You know, he was very humble with me, he was very humble. If somebody expressed an interest in him, he blossomed, absolutely blossomed. If you asked him some questions about him, he was just out of this world. That was more or less the reason that I think he liked me very much.

MR. JENNER: Yes; he did. It is so reported, and Marina has so said. Well, that first visit didn't give you any opportunity to observe the relations between Marina and Lee, I assume?

MR. DE MOHRENSCHILDT: I already noticed then that the couple that they were not getting along, right away.

MR. JENNER: What made you have that impression?

MR. DE MOHRENSCHILDT: Well, there was a strained relationship there. You could feel that. And, you know how it is—you can see that the couple, that they are not very happy. You could feel that. And he was not particularly nice with her. He didn't kiss her. It wasn't a loving husband who would come home and smile and kiss his wife, and so on and so forth. He was just indifferent with her. He was more interested in talking to me than to her. That type of attitude.

MR. JENNER: But you did notice throughout all your acquaintance with him that he blossomed when you paid attention to him, let us say?

MR. DE MOHRENSCHILDT: Exactly.

MR. JENNER: You drew him into conversation or situations—especially when you asked something about him?

MR. DE MOHRENSCHILDT: Yes; exactly. I think that is his main characteristic. He wanted people to be interested in him, not in Marina. And she remained quite often in the background. Later on, even in conversation she would remain in the background, and he would do the talking.

MR. JENNER: Did he have an arrogant attitude?

MR. DE MOHRENSCHILDT: No; with me he has never been arrogant. Even when we came to the incident, you know, when we took the baby away from him, and Marina away from him later—you know that?

MR. JENNER: I want to get that in sequence. But you did it yourself, did you?

MR. DE MOHRENSCHILDT: My wife and I; yes.

MR. JENNER: Now, why do you not just go along and tell me as things develop. And how attitudes changed, and everything.

MR. DE MOHRENSCHILDT: Well, then we started getting reports, you know, from George Bouhe and the Clarks about them. We didn't see them very often.

MR. JENNER: Please, I don't want you to say you didn't see them very often. Maybe you didn't.

MR. DE MOHRENSCHILDT: Yes.

MR. JENNER: I want to know how this developed.

MR. DE MOHRENSCHILDT: Well—

MR. JENNER: When next did you see them, after this initial event?

MR. DE MOHRENSCHILDT: That I don't remember. I don't remember. But I do know that we saw Marina very soon afterward, because either my wife went to get her or my daughter went to get her—I don't remember that anymore—to take her to the hospital. Or maybe George Bouhe brought her to our house so that my wife, who was free at the time, could take her to the dental clinic. I think that was the next time that we saw Marina. Maybe a few days later.

MR. JENNER: In any event, it was before Marina went to live with the Mellers?

MR. DE MOHRENSCHILDT: Yes.

MR. JENNER: And it was before Marina went to live with the Taylors?

MR. DE MOHRENSCHILDT: Yes. She never lived with the Taylors. I think she spent a night with them, and that is all. She lived, I think—I think both of them lived somewhere in the neighborhood. I think she spent a night with my daughter, when she happened to be in Dallas for this medical care. And since they are about the age of my daughter—she is a little bit older, but about the same age I don't remember how it happened, but either I or my wife introduced Marina to my daughter, and also Lee. This is very vague in my mind, what happened there.

MR. JENNER: Well, your recollection is that within a few days George Bouhe brought Marina to your home?

MR. DE MOHRENSCHILDT: I think so.

MR. JENNER: For the purpose of having your wife take Marina to get some dental care?

MR. DE MOHRENSCHILDT: That is right.

MR. JENNER: And where was she taken?

MR. DE MOHRENSCHILDT: She was taken to the Baylor Dental Clinic.

MR. JENNER: That is located where?

MR. DE MOHRENSCHILDT: It is right in the center of Dallas, near the Slaughter Hospital—what a name for a hospital. It is the name of the man who founded it. Well, the dental clinic is right there next door. They give you dental care gratis, or almost for nothing. George Bouhe was giving her money, by the way.

MR. JENNER: He was giving her money?

MR. DE MOHRENSCHILDT: I mean small amounts of money, you know, either for injections or something like that—because she didn't have anything.

MR. JENNER: She was destitute, was she?

MR. DE MOHRENSCHILDT: Completely destitute—because Lee was at the time losing his job. I don't recall when he told me that—maybe already at the first meeting. He told me that he was about to lose his job. He was working somewhere in Fort Worth as a manual laborer, some ironworker.

MR. JENNER: Leslie Welding Co.?

MR. DE MOHRENSCHILDT: Yes; I don't know the name of it. This company was going bankrupt, or that he was going to lose his job. At least that was his version. Maybe he was fired.

MR. JENNER: That was his version. That wasn't the fact.

MR. DE MOHRENSCHILDT: It was a fact?

MR. JENNER: It was not. Your wife also took the baby for some medical care?

MR. DE MOHRENSCHILDT: Now, this I am not so sure. She told Marina where to go, and told her, "You have to give the baby such and such injections." And this I remember well—that she didn't do it. She didn't go to that children's clinic, because of pure negligence. She is that type of a girl—very negligent, poor mother, very poor mother. Loved the child, but a poor mother that doesn't pay much attention. And what amazed us, you know, that she, having been a pharmacist in Russia, did not know anything about the good care of the children, nothing.

MR. JENNER: How did you find out she had been a pharmacist in Russia?

MR. DE MOHRENSCHILDT: Well, that eventually came—the second time or the third time that we met her—she told us the story of her life.

MR. JENNER: Do you have a recollection as to what she told you?

MR. DE MOHRENSCHILDT: Yes. Well, she said exactly her story of her life as she told me, that she comes from a family of ex-Czarist officers. That her father had been a Czarist officer of some kind—you see what I mean? I don't remember whether it was navy or army. I don't recall it any more. That her mother remarried, and that her stepfather did not treat her well. That they moved—I think they lived in Leningrad when she was a child. That eventually they moved to Minsk. I don't remember what her father's profession was. One thing I remember—that one of her uncles was a big shot Government official, something like that—colonel or something like that. That I remember she told me. And then she went to this school of pharmacists, I think in Minsk, and graduated as a pharmacist. And one day she was walking by this river, which I also remember, in Minsk—the River Svislach, which crosses the whole town, and where there are some new apartment buildings built, and in one of those apartment buildings there were very nice apartments, and that is where the foreigners lived. She said it was her dream someday to live in an apartment like that. And that is where Lee Oswald lived. And eventually when they met—I remember they met at some dance or I think he was ill, something like that, after that dance, and she came to take care of him. That is something I have a vague recollection of—that she took care of him, and from then on they fell in love and eventually got married. But she said it was the apartment house that was one of the greatest things she desired to live in, and she found out later on that Lee Oswald lived in that apartment house, and she finally achieved her dream. It sounds ridiculous, but that is how in Soviet Russia they dream of apartments rather than of people. She told us a tremendous amount of things which will come to me as things go on.

MR. JENNER: Go ahead.

MR. DE MOHRENSCHILDT: Naturally I was talking to her and to him—I was trying to find out what is the life of young people in Soviet Russia, what are the prices on food, what can you get for your money, what salary you get, what amusements you get.

MR. JENNER: Tell us what they said.

MR. DE MOHRENSCHILDT: The salaries—she was getting an equivalent of $60 a month. He was getting something like $80 a month. That almost all of it had to be spent on food. The lodging was very cheap, almost nothing, because it was provided by the Government. That the food was rather plentiful, you could get it—but it was rather monotonous. Sometimes you could not get meat. They used to have discussions between them all the time, always they quarreled about—Lee Oswald and Marina always quarreled between themselves as to what actually were the prices, what actually were the conditions of life in Soviet Russia.

MR. JENNER: Tell me about the differences here.

MR. DE MOHRENSCHILDT: Yes.

MR. JENNER: The attitudes she had, and the attitude he had.

MR. DE MOHRENSCHILDT: He liked Russia more than she did. I think he liked the conditions in Russia more than she did.

MR. JENNER: Why?

MR. DE MOHRENSCHILDT: Because he was a foreigner there, and he had a privileged position. He had a nice apartment. He said that people were interested in him, you see. That very often—he worked in a TV factory— the workers would come to him and ask him questions about the United States and so on, and that pleased him very much, because he was that type of an individual who needed attention. Marina was more inclined to criticize the living conditions there than he did—as far as I remember. Yet she was not too critical, you see. It was a livable way of life. Actually, they came to think that possibly their life was better there than in Fort Worth. In other words, both were disappointed in what happened to them after they came back to the United States. And I think that Lee more than Marina. Because as the time went on, Marina was getting more and more things from people, people like the Clarks, like ourselves, like George Bouhe, started giving her gifts, dresses and so on and so forth. She had some hundred dresses.

MR. JENNER: A large number of dresses?

MR. DE MOHRENSCHILDT: About a hundred dresses. When we carried them out to live with the Mellers, my car was loaded with her dresses. It was all contributions from the various people, in Fort Worth and Dallas.

MR. JENNER: In addition to dresses and clothing, what other things?

MR. DE MOHRENSCHILDT: Well, mainly baby things. She had two cribs, I remember. She had a baby carriage. I think George Bouhe gave it to her. Toys for the baby. Many things like that.

MR. JENNER: Now, you say you carried her out and took her to the Mellers?

MR. DE MOHRENSCHILDT: Yes. This was already possibly two weeks after we met them.

MR. JENNER: Now, what was the occasion that you did that, and why did you do it? That was a pretty forward thing to do, was it not?

MR. DE MOHRENSCHILDT: Yes. In the meantime, Lee lost his job and George Bouhe told him that he should move to Dallas, he will give him an introduction at the Texas Employment Agency—he knew somebody there. And eventually he got a job through that Texas Employment Agency. I don't remember the name of the person who was there, some Texas lady whom George Bouhe knew. And I told him that I would help him, too, to find a job, and even spoke to Sam Ballen about it, can he give him a job. And that is probably the only time that Sam Ballen met Oswald. I told him to go to Mr. Ballen's office—he has a reproduction business, a very large one in Texas.

MR. JENNER: Reproduction?

MR. DE MOHRENSCHILDT: Reproduction, electric log reproduction service. When they reproduce electrical logs from the oil wells. And also, they print catalogs and things like that in his office. It is quite a large business that he has—with branch offices all over Texas, and even in Denver, Colorado. I said, "Why don't you see if you can give him a job?" And I remember that Sam saw Lee Oswald and found him very interesting. I remember I saw him the next day and said, "How did you like Lee Oswald?" and he said, "Nice fellow, very nice fellow, very interesting fellow."

MR. JENNER: But he did not have any work for him?

MR. DE MOHRENSCHILDT: He didn't have a job for him. And at the same time he received a job at some other outfit—I forgot the name of it—the traffic outfit, and they moved from Fort Worth to Dallas.

MR. JENNER: You said you entered and took Marina out of the house, and the baby?

MR. DE MOHRENSCHILDT: That was a little bit later on—when he already moved to Dallas, he already had the job. But now I am trying to recall who moved him from Fort Worth to Dallas, and I think that was Gary Taylor, my ex-son-in-law, and Alex, my daughter. I think they both drove to Fort Worth. I told them to do so—"Go to Fort Worth and help them, they have no car, they have no money—help them to move." I think in the meantime Lee found a job at Jaggars, and was looking for a place to live, and found a place to live himself in Oak Cliff, this address which I don't remember now—the first address in Oak Cliff. He had two addresses. I forget the exact address. My wife will remember that. Anyway, my daughter and her husband went there and moved them.

MR. JENNER: When was this?

MR. DE MOHRENSCHILDT: Well, maybe two weeks after we met the Oswalds.

MR. JENNER: September of 1962?

MR. DE MOHRENSCHILDT: About that time, about September. A little before that, I think, because in September we started the campaign on the cystic fibrosis, and we completely lost track of them—we were very busy on that. And I think it was in September that this campaign started.

MR. JENNER: And before you started your campaign on cystic fibrosis, they had already moved to Dallas?

MR. DE MOHRENSCHILDT: They already moved to Dallas. We already had moved them—had taken Marina away from her husband. And she already had returned back to her husband.

MR. JENNER: All right. Now, you say you had already taken Marina away from her husband. Tell us how that occurred.

MR. DE MOHRENSCHILDT: In the meantime, George Bouhe became completely disgusted with Lee.

MR. JENNER: Why?

MR. DE MOHRENSCHILDT: Because I don't know exactly why—because he liked Marina very much.

MR. JENNER: Bouhe?

MR. DE MOHRENSCHILDT: Bouhe he is an elderly man.

MR. JENNER: Yes, I appreciate that.

MR. DE MOHRENSCHILDT: He wanted—almost like a daughter, you see. To him she was a poor girl whose father was an ex-officer, and she needed help. And he really gave her money. He would give her $30, $40, I think, all at once.

MR. JENNER: Did he ever collect money from you and others to contribute?

MR. DE MOHRENSCHILDT: I don't think so.

MR. JENNER: Did you ever give Lee Oswald any money?

MR. DE MOHRENSCHILDT: No.

MR. JENNER: Did you ever give Marina any money?

MR. DE MOHRENSCHILDT: Not as far as I remember. Maybe a dollar—maybe 50 cents, something like that, for a bus. But never any money. I was in a very difficult financial condition myself at that time. I don't think I gave her even 50 cents. Sometimes we would invite them to eat a little bit, you see, in the house.

MR. JENNER: You invited them to your home to eat?

MR. DE MOHRENSCHILDT: Yes. I think maybe once or twice they came to the house to eat.

MR. JENNER: Your home on Dickens Street?

MR. DE MOHRENSCHILDT: Yes.

MR. JENNER: All right, tell us the circumstances—

MR. DE MOHRENSCHILDT: Of how we took her away?

MR. JENNER: And why.

MR. DE MOHRENSCHILDT: Well, George Bouhe, started telling me that "George, Lee is beating Marina. I saw her with a black eye and she was crying, and she tried to run away from the house. It is outrageous." And he was really appalled by the fact that it actually happened. And Jeanne and I said, let's go and see what is going on. George Bouhe gave me their address, as far as I remember, there in Oak Cliff, because, I didn't move them—it was my daughter who moved them, I think. So we drove up there to that apartment, which was on the ground floor, and indeed Marina had a black eye. And so either my wife or I told Lee, "Listen, you cannot do things like this."

MR. JENNER: Was he home at this time?

MR. DE MOHRENSCHILDT: I think he was. Or maybe he wasn't. I just am not so sure. Maybe he was, maybe he wasn't. But anyway, he appeared a little later.

MR. JENNER: While you were still there, he appeared?

MR. DE MOHRENSCHILDT: Yes.

MR. JENNER: And when you entered that apartment on the first floor, you observed that she had a black eye?

MR. DE MOHRENSCHILDT: A black eye, and scratched face, and so on and so forth.

MR. JENNER: Did you inquire about it?

MR. DE MOHRENSCHILDT: Yes.

MR. JENNER: What did she say?

MR. DE MOHRENSCHILDT: She said, "He has been beating me." As if it was normal—not particularly appalled by this fact, but, "He has been beating me," but she said, "I fight him back also." So I said, "You cannot stand for that. You shouldn't let him beat you." And she said, "Well, I guess I should get away from him." Now, I do not recall what actually made me take her away from Lee.

MR. JENNER: Now, Mr. De Mohrenschildt, there has to be something.

MR. DE MOHRENSCHILDT: Yes, I know. I do not recall whether she called us in and asked us to take her away from him or George Bouhe suggested it. I just don't recall how it happened. But it was because of his brutality to her. Possibly we had them in the house and discussed it, and I told him he should not do things like that, and he said, "It is my business"— that is one of the few times that he was a little bit uppity with me. And then again George Bouhe told me that he had beaten her again. This is a little bit vague in my memory, what exactly prompted me to do that. My wife probably maybe has a better recollection. Anyway, on Sunday, instead of playing tennis, we drove to Marina's place early in the morning and told Oswald that we are going to take her away from him, and the baby also, and we are going to take her to Mr. and Mrs. Meller. I think George Bouhe made the previous arrangement, because he was closer to the Mellers than I was. Or maybe I called them. I don't remember exactly. Anyway, they were ready to receive her. And Lee said, "By God, you are not going to do it. I will tear all her dresses and I will break all the baby things." And I got very mad this time. But Jeanne, my wife, started explaining to him patiently that it is not going to help him any—"Do you love your wife?" He said yes. And she said, "If you want your wife back some time, you better behave." I said, "If you don't behave, I will call the police." I felt very nervous about the whole situation—interfering in other people's affairs, after all. Well, he said, "I will get even with you." I said, "You will get even with me?" I got a little bit more mad, and I said, "I am going to take Marina anyway." So after a little while he started— and I started carrying the things out of the house. And Lee did not interfere with me. Of course, he was small, you know, and he was a rather puny individual. After a little while he helped me to carry the things out. He completely changed his mind.

MR. JENNER: He submitted to the inevitable?

MR. DE MOHRENSCHILDT: He submitted to the inevitable, and helped me to carry things. And we cleaned that house completely. We have a big convertible car, and it was loaded, everything was taken out of that house.

And we drove very slowly all the way to the other part of the town, Lakeside, where the Mellers lived, and left her there.

MR. JENNER: Did Lee accompany you?

MR. DE MOHRENSCHILDT: No; that was it. The next day or a few days later—I don't remember exactly when—George Bouhe called me and said, "George, you should not give Lee the address of where Marina is." I think he came to see me about that—"because he is a dangerous character, and he has been threatening me, and he had been threatening Marina on the telephone."

MR. JENNER: He knew where Marina was?

MR. DE MOHRENSCHILDT: Maybe I am confused a little bit. He knew George Bouhe's telephone number. He had been threatening him, and wanted to know the telephone number or the address of where Marina was. And this time my wife and I said we do not have the right not to let him know where she is, because she is his wife, and we should tell him where Marina is. Now, I do not recall how it happened—maybe Lee came over to our apartment in the evening. Anyway, we gave him the address of the Mellers, you see, and told him that the best way for him to do is to call ahead of time if he wants to see Marina, talk to her on the telephone, and if she wants to see him, she will see him. And he was very happy about that—because I thought it was a fair thing for the fellow to do. I repeat again—I liked the fellow, and I pitied him all the time. And this—if somebody did that to me, a lousy trick like that, to take my wife away, and all the furniture, I would be mad as hell, too. I am surprised that he didn't do something worse. I would not do it to anybody else. I just didn't consider him a dangerous person. I would not do it to somebody else. Well, anyway, later on—this is from hearsay again, now—Marina moved to Declan Ford's house, because I think the Mellers got tired of her, and then she moved eventually to somebody else's house, the name you mentioned here before a Russian girl who married an American—Thomas something.

MR. JENNER: Ray?

MR. DE MOHRENSCHILDT: Ray. She moved to Ray's house, and then—

MR. JENNER: Excuse me. You took her to the Mellers?

MR. DE MOHRENSCHILDT: Yes.

MR. JENNER: And she went from the Mellers to the Halls?

MR. DE MOHRENSCHILDT: That I do not remember anymore. I do not recall that. I thought she moved from the Mellers to Mrs. Ford, and from Mrs.

Ford to the house of the Rays. What I recall now is that she had moved before to Mrs. Hall's house.

MR. JENNER: You learned that she had already been at Mrs. Hall's home?

MR. DE MOHRENSCHILDT: Something like that is in my mind—that she had already tried to go away from Lee, and stayed with Mrs. Hall. But I am not one-hundred percent sure. I know that for the second time she was at Mrs. Hall's house, a little bit later.

MR. JENNER: What was your understanding of the difficulties they were having?

MR. DE MOHRENSCHILDT: Why was he physically beating her? The difficulties were this: She was—just incompatibility. They were annoying each other, and she was all the time annoying him. Having had many wives, I could see his point of view. She was annoying him all the time: "Why don't you make some money?" Why don't they have a car, why don't they have more dresses, look at everybody else living so well—and they are just miserable flunkies. She was annoying him all the time. Poor guy was going out of his mind.

MR. JENNER: And you and your wife were aware of this, were you?

MR. DE MOHRENSCHILDT: Yes.

MR. JENNER: And had discussed it.

MR. DE MOHRENSCHILDT: We told her she should not annoy him—poor guy, he is doing his best. "Don't annoy him so much." And I think I mentioned before one annoying thing. She openly said he didn't see her physically—right in front of him. She said, "He sleeps with me just once a month, and I never get any satisfaction out of it." A rather crude and completely straightforward thing to say in front of relative strangers, as we were.

MR. JENNER: Yes.

MR. DE MOHRENSCHILDT: I didn't blame Lee for giving her a good whack on the eye. Once it was all right. But he also exaggerated. I think the discussions were purely on that basis—purely on a material basis, and on a sexual basis, those two things—which are pretty important.

MR. JENNER: Yes; they are.

MR. DE MOHRENSCHILDT: In politics they agreed more or less. See they were both somewhat dissatisfied with life in Soviet Russia. I had that impression. They wanted a richer life. And as far as I remember, it was Marina who convinced Oswald to leave Soviet Russia, and go back to the United States.

MR. JENNER: You have a definite—

MR. DE MOHRENSCHILDT: I have a definite recollection of that. I do not recall in exact words how it was said. But either one of them told me that—that it was Marina who wanted to come to the States, and made him go to the—back to the United States Embassy, and ask for his passport. And I remember very distinctly what he told me, that he illegally took a train from Minsk to Moscow, because being a foreigner, he was not supposed to leave town without notifying the police. He did that illegally, and went to Moscow, and presented himself at the United States Embassy.

MR. JENNER: Did it come to your attention, or did he ever say to you that—even before he was married, that he had determined to return to the United States, and had taken some steps to do so?

MR. DE MOHRENSCHILDT: No; I don't recall any of that.

MR. JENNER: Your distinct recollection, however, is that she did tell you that she desired to come to the United States, and she pressed him to do so?

MR. DE MOHRENSCHILDT: Yes; and possibly he was disgusted by that time also, because he was the fellow who needed attention, he was a new fellow in Minsk, a new American, so they were all interested in him. And then they lost interest in him eventually. So he became nothing. Again. So he got disgusted with it. And Marina told him, "Let's go back to the States, and you take me to the States." Now, what is not clear to me—and I never inquired into it, because I was not particularly interested—how she got the permission from the Soviet Government to leave. That I don't know.

MR. JENNER: You never discussed that with her?

MR. DE MOHRENSCHILDT: Never discussed that. Somehow I was not interested to ask her that question. I should have, possibly.

MR. JENNER: Did you ever ask him about it?

MR. DE MOHRENSCHILDT: Never asked him this question.

[April 23, 1964]

MR. JENNER: On the record. Mr. De Mohrenschildt, you testified yesterday it was your then recollection that Marina did not live with your daughter, Alexandra, then Mrs. Gary Taylor.

MR. DE MOHRENSCHILDT: That's right. I think she spent one night with them, but never lived with them, as far as I know.

MR. JENNER: Maybe that's it. Now, perhaps to refresh your recollection, Marina testified—this question was put to her. "Did you have anything to do with the Gary Taylors?" "Answer: Yes; at one time when I had to visit the dentist in Dallas, and I lived in Fort Worth, I came to Dallas and I stayed with them for a couple of days."

MR. DE MOHRENSCHILDT: She probably is right. I think she spent only one day. But I could not swear to that.

MR. JENNER: Now, I want to stimulate your recollection in another respect. Your daughter has made a statement that in September of 1962, "My father asked me to allow Marina Oswald and her child to reside with me at my then home at 1512 Fairmont Street, Dallas. My father explained that Lee Harvey Oswald and his wife Marina had recently arrived in Dallas, Tex. They had no money and Lee Oswald was unemployed. He told me that while Marina resided with me, Lee Oswald would reside at the YMCA." Does that serve to refresh your recollection?

MR. DE MOHRENSCHILDT: I frankly do not remember. I have the impression that I said "Help her as much as you can," but I do not recall saying that she would live with them. I do not think I would have imposed that on my daughter.

MR. JENNER: Well, that testimony of Marina that she did live with your daughter for several days, and your daughter's statement, does not—

MR. DE MOHRENSCHILDT: I do not know about it. Maybe they did, maybe they did not I just do not recall that.

MR. JENNER: All right.

MR. DE MOHRENSCHILDT: I repeat again that they were out of my mind—completely—after the last time we saw them.

MR. JENNER: Well, this is September of 1962.

MR. DE MOHRENSCHILDT: 1962, sure. They were out of my mind. I forgot the Oswalds.

MR. JENNER: No; 1962, sir.

MR. DE MOHRENSCHILDT: No, no. Now the Oswalds were out of my mind.

MR. JENNER: You mean you have not been thinking about them.

MR. DE MOHRENSCHILDT: Yes; I have not been thinking about them. May I say a few things here that I remember? As I told you before, we met the Oswalds through Bouhe, and then we talked about them to Max Clark, and again to Bouhe. And I asked Mr. Bouhe "Do you think it is safe for us to help Oswald?"

MR. JENNER: You did have that conversation.

MR. DE MOHRENSCHILDT: Yes.

MR. JENNER: Why did you raise that question?

MR. DE MOHRENSCHILDT: I raised the question because he had been to Soviet Russia. He could be anything, you see. And he could be right there watched day and night by the FBI. I did not want to get involved, you see. And I distinctly remember, number one, that George Bouhe said that he had checked with the FBI. Secondly, that in my mind Max Clark was in some way connected with the FBI, because he was chief of security at Convair—he had been a chief of security. And either George Bouhe or someone else told me that he is with the FBI to some extent. You never ask people "Are you from the FBI?" And to me it is unimportant. But somehow in my mind I had this connected. And so my fears were alleviated, you see. I said, "Well, the guy seems to be OK." Now, I am not so clear about it, but I have the impression to have talked—to have asked about Lee Oswald also Mr. Moore, Walter Moore.

MR. JENNER: Who is Walter Moore?

MR. DE MOHRENSCHILDT: Walter Moore is the man who interviewed me on behalf of the Government after I came back from Yugoslavia—G. Walter Moore. He is a Government man—either FBI or Central Intelligence. A very nice fellow, exceedingly intelligent, who is, as far as I know—was some sort of an FBI man in Dallas. Many people consider him head of FBI in Dallas. Now, I don't know. Who does—you see. But he is a Government man in some capacity. He interviewed me and took my deposition on my stay in Yugoslavia, what I thought about the political situation there. And we became quite friendly after that. We saw each other from time to time, had lunch. There was a mutual interest there, because I think he was born in China and my wife was born in China. They had been to our house I think once or twice. I just found him a very interesting person. When I was writing this book of mine, a very peculiar incident occurred.

MR. JENNER: Which book?

MR. DE MOHRENSCHILDT: The last one: the travelogue. One day we left for Houston on a business trip, and I left all my typewritten pages, some 150 typewritten pages, in my closet. When I returned from the trip and started looking through the pages, which had not been touched, supposedly, by anybody I noticed small marks on the pages—"No. 1" after five pages, "2"—small marks with a pencil, another five pages, No. 3, and so on and so forth. I told my wife, "Jeanne, have you fiddled around with my book?" She said, "Of course not." I said, "That's impossible." And I forgot it for a while. In the evening we got back home, and we stayed in bed, and all of a sudden the idea came back to me that somebody must have been in my apartment and checked my book and read through that and took photographs. And it was such a horrible idea that Jeanne and I just could not sleep all night. And the next morning we both of us went to see Walter Moore and told him, "Now, look what happened to us. Have you Government people"—and I think I asked him point blank, you know— "Have you FBI people looked through my book?" He said, "Do you consider us such fools as to leave marks on your book if we had? But we haven't." I said, "Can't you give me some protection against somebody who has?" He said, "Do you have any strong enemies?" I said, "Well, I possibly have. Everybody has enemies." But I never could figure out who it was. And it is still a mystery to me. So I am not so sure whether I asked point blank Clark or Walter Moore about Oswald. I probably spoke to both of them about him. My recollection is, and also my wife's recollection is, that either of them said he is a harmless lunatic. Later on Max got disgusted with him and said that he is a no-good b - - - - - d, a traitor, and so on and so forth. But by that time we already forgot Oswald—got Oswald out of your lives, you see. This is one point. The second point is as you can see the whole of the Russian colony in Dallas were interested in the Oswalds one way or the other, because they represented somebody who had been to their old country just recently, and could give them the latest information on what was going on. As I said, the old guard were naturally against them right away. The others were just curious. But this particular couple, Natasha and Igor Voshinin, refused to see them. And I insisted several times, "Why don't you see them? You love all the Russians. Why don't you meet Marina Oswald?" And she said, "We don't want to, and we have our reasons for not meeting them." And it kept on in my mind. I did not want to raise that question. But why didn't they want to meet them?

MR. JENNER: Well, tell me what is your speculation as to why they did not want to meet them?

MR. DE MOHRENSCHILDT: I do not have the slightest idea. Maybe they knew something about Oswald, of some connection.

MR. JENNER: Or maybe they were alarmed, and didn't want to take any chances.

MR. DE MOHRENSCHILDT: Maybe just that.

MR. JENNER: But they were pretty firm in not having any traffic with them.

MR. DE MOHRENSCHILDT: Absolutely firm. The only ones. Maybe they were just more recently arrived in the United States and they were not so secure like we were, you see. And possibly they were just alarmed of meeting somebody who just came from Soviet Russia.

MR. JENNER: I think I will ask you at this point, Mr. De Mohrenschildt, you are a man of very superior education and extremely wide experience and acquaintance here and in Europe, South America, West Indies—you have lived an extremely colorful life. You are acquainted to a greater or lesser degree with a great variety of people.

MR. DE MOHRENSCHILDT: Yes.

MR. JENNER: Did there go through your mind speculations as to whether Oswald was an agent of anybody?

MR. DE MOHRENSCHILDT: No.

MR. JENNER: Why? Before I put it that way—when you say "No," am I correct in assuming that you thought about the subject and you concluded he was not an agent of anybody? Is that what you meant?

MR. DE MOHRENSCHILDT: I never thought even about it. I will tell you why I thought he never was—because he was too outspoken. He was too outspoken in his ideas and his attitudes. If he were really—if he were an agent, I thought he would have kept quiet. This would be my idea.

MR. JENNER: You say he was outspoken. What do you base that on?

MR. DE MOHRENSCHILDT: For instance, he showed me his—he discussed very freely with me, when he showed me his little memoirs.

MR. JENNER: I am going to show you those papers in a little while.

MR. DE MOHRENSCHILDT: Those memoirs I think are very sincere. They explain more or less the sincere attitude of a man, sincere opinion of a man.

MR. JENNER: Before I show you any papers, I want you to finish this reasoning of yours.

MR. DE MOHRENSCHILDT: I did not take him seriously—that is all.

MR. JENNER: I know you didn't. Why didn't you?

MR. DE MOHRENSCHILDT: Well—

MR. JENNER: You are a highly sophisticated person.

MR. DE MOHRENSCHILDT: Well, he was not sophisticated, you see. He was a semi-educated hillbilly. And you cannot take such a person seriously. All his opinions were crude, you see. But I thought at the time he was rather sincere.

MR. JENNER: Opinion sincerely held, but crude?

MR. DE MOHRENSCHILDT: Yes.

MR. JENNER: He was relatively uneducated.

MR. DE MOHRENSCHILDT: Oh, yes.

MR. JENNER: Quite, as a matter of fact—he never finished high school.

MR. DE MOHRENSCHILDT: Yes; I did not even know that.

MR. JENNER: Did you have the feeling that his views on politics were shallow and surface?

MR. DE MOHRENSCHILDT: Very much so.

MR. JENNER: That he had not had the opportunity for a study under scholars who would criticize, so that he himself could form some views on the subject?

MR. DE MOHRENSCHILDT: Exactly. His mind was of a man with exceedingly poor background, who read rather advanced books, and did not understand even the words in them. He read complicated economical treatises and just picked up difficult words out of what he has read, and loved to display them. He loved to use the difficult words, because it was to impress one.

MR. JENNER: Did you think he understood it?

MR. DE MOHRENSCHILDT: He did not understand the words—he just used them. So how can you take seriously a person like that? You just laugh at him. But there was always an element of pity I had, and my wife had, for him. We realized that he was sort of a forlorn individual, groping for something.

MR. JENNER: Did you form any impression in the area, let us say, of reliability—that is, whether our Government would entrust him with something that required a high degree of intelligence, a high degree of imagination, a high degree of ability to retain his equilibrium under pressure, a management of a situation, to be flexible enough?

MR. DE MOHRENSCHILDT: I never would believe that any government would be stupid enough to trust Lee with anything important.

MR. JENNER: Give me the basis of your opinion.

MR. DE MOHRENSCHILDT: Well, again, as I said, an unstable individual, mixed-up individual, uneducated individual, without background. What government would give him any confidential work? No government would. Even the government of Ghana would not give him any job of any type.

MR. JENNER: You used the expression "unstable." Would you elaborate on that?

MR. DE MOHRENSCHILDT: Well, instability—his life is an example of his instability. He switched allegiance from one country to another, and then back again, disappointed in this, disappointed in that, tried various jobs. But he did it, you see, without the enjoyment of adventure like some other people would do in the United States, a new job is a new adventure, new opportunities. For him it was a gruesome deal. He hated his jobs. He switched all the time.

MR. JENNER: Now, let's assume he switched jobs because he was discharged from those jobs. Does that affect your opinion? That is, assume now for the purpose of discussion that he lost every one of his jobs.

MR. DE MOHRENSCHILDT: Well, frankly, if I—you always base your opinion on your own experience. If I had my own country since my childbirth, and my government, I would remain faithful to it for the rest of my life. He had a chance to be a marine. Here was a perfect life for him—this was my point of view. He was a man without education, in the Marines—why didn't he stay in the Marines all his life? You don't need a high degree of intelligence to be a marine corporal or a soldier.

MR. JENNER: That is, it was your thought—

MR. DE MOHRENSCHILDT: That was my idea.

MR. JENNER: That if he had an objective that he could have had, it would be to stay in the Marines and become a marine officer, and have a career in the Marines.

MR. DE MOHRENSCHILDT: That is right. Well, instead of that he disliked it and switched to something else. I do not know the details of all his jobs, you see, but I certainly can evaluate people just by looking at them—because I have met so many people in my profession—you have to evaluate them by just looking at them and saying a few words.

MR. JENNER: Did you form an impression of him, Mr. De Mohrenschildt, as to his reliability in a different sense now—that is, whether he was reasonably mentally stable or given to violent surges of anger or lack of control of himself?

MR. DE MOHRENSCHILDT: Of course, he was that. The fact that we took his wife away from him, you know, was the result of his outbursts and his threats to his wife.

MR. JENNER: What kind of threats?

MR. DE MOHRENSCHILDT: Well, that he will beat the hell out of her. I think Marina told me that he threatened to kill her. It comes back to my mind, you see. You asked me yesterday a question, what actually precipitated us taking Marina and the little child away from Oswald.

MR. JENNER: You actually took Marina and the child away?

MR. DE MOHRENSCHILDT: Yes. So what actually precipitated that? Something must have precipitated it. I cannot recall what it was. But now I seem to vaguely remember that Marina said that he would kill her, that he will beat her sometime so hard that he will kill her. So that is the reason we went out there and said—well, let's save that poor woman.

MR. JENNER: Where were they living then?

MR. DE MOHRENSCHILDT: They were living then at the first address in Oak Cliff—Ruth Street, I think. It is a two-story brick building.

MR. JENNER: Mercedes?

MR. DE MOHRENSCHILDT: Ruth Street. I do not remember Mercedes Street.

MR. JENNER: Elsbeth?

MR. DE MOHRENSCHILDT: Elsbeth—yes.

MR. JENNER: He never lived on any street by the name of Ruth.

MR. DE MOHRENSCHILDT: No.

MR. JENNER: Yesterday you adverted, I thought, to a concept that this man seemed—he responded when you would bring him into a conversation or situation.

MR. DE MOHRENSCHILDT: Yes.

MR. JENNER: That he was somewhat egocentric in that respect?

MR. DE MOHRENSCHILDT: Very much so. And that is probably the reason that he was clinging to me. He was clinging to me. He would call me. He would try to be next to me—because, let's face it, I am a promoter and a salesman. So I know how to talk with people. I usually do not offend people's feelings. When I talk to people, I am interested in them. And he appreciated that in me. The other people considered him, well, he is just some poor, miserable guy, and disregarded him.

MR. JENNER: Now, I would like to go into that a moment. It gradually developed, did it, that the people in the Russian colony, their curiosity—they had curiosity at the outset and they had interest at the outset.

MR. DE MOHRENSCHILDT: That's right.

MR. JENNER: They met him at your home and other homes?

MR. DE MOHRENSCHILDT: Yes.

MR. JENNER: I take it you now suggest that after a while their interest in him waned?

MR. DE MOHRENSCHILDT: It disappeared mainly; yes.

MR. JENNER: And was it replaced by something else?

MR. DE MOHRENSCHILDT: Dislike, mostly dislike, and fear.

MR. JENNER: What was the fear?

MR. DE MOHRENSCHILDT: Especially on the part of a scary individual, like George Bouhe—he was actually physically afraid of him.

MR. JENNER: George Bouhe was?

MR. DE MOHRENSCHILDT: George Bouhe. He was actually physically afraid of him. He told me, "I am scared of this man. He is a lunatic." I said, "Don't be scared of him. He is just as small as you are."

MR. JENNER: Yes, but George Bouhe is a small man. You are a well-built, athletic, six-foot-one. What did you weigh then?

MR. DE MOHRENSCHILDT: 185 pounds. I was not afraid of him, naturally, but George Bouhe was.

MR. JENNER: And that is not your nature, anyhow, that is not your personality as I observe you testifying.

MR. DE MOHRENSCHILDT: Yes; he was that way, you know. Now, Max Clark naturally was not afraid of him because Max Clark himself is an athlete, an ex-colonel in the Air Force, I think. He just disliked him, and he said to hell with that fellow, because Lee was rude to him.

MR. JENNER: Who was rude?

MR. DE MOHRENSCHILDT: Lee Oswald was rude to Max Clark and to his wife. They invited him on some occasion—this I remember vaguely— they invited him at some occasion to come to their house. And Lee said, "Well, I will come if it is convenient to me." Imagine that—an answer of that type.

MR. JENNER: Now, the Clarks, certainly Mr. Clark—I do not know too much about Mrs. Clark—but Mr. Clark is an educated man.

MR. DE MOHRENSCHILDT: Very educated man.

MR. JENNER: And a man of attainment. He is an attorney, is he not?

MR. DE MOHRENSCHILDT: Yes.

MR. JENNER: Did it occur to you that here is a person who is relatively uneducated, of limited capacity—I think this man had intelligence—

MR. DE MOHRENSCHILDT: Yes.

MR. JENNER: Being invited to the home socially of a man of capacity?

MR. DE MOHRENSCHILDT: Yes.

MR. JENNER: A lawyer, a leader in the community with a fine service record. What was your reaction to that?

MR. DE MOHRENSCHILDT: Well, Max invited him purely because his wife was Russian and she would like to speak Russian once in a while.

MR. JENNER: You think Lee resented that, do you—that the interest was in Marina and not in Lee Oswald?

MR. DE MOHRENSCHILDT: Yes; definitely. Oh, that is an exceedingly important point, you know. Lee resented the interest that people would take in Marina. He wanted the interest concentrated on himself.

MR. JENNER: And did he exhibit that in your home and at other gatherings where you saw him? Did he interrupt so that the attention might be drawn to him and away from her?

MR. DE MOHRENSCHILDT: Yes; he was not—

MR. JENNER: I do not want to put the words in your mouth.

MR. DE MOHRENSCHILDT: Yes, I understand what you mean. I am trying to think of a particular case that I would remember. I do not remember any particular case, but I always took him and considered him as an egocentric person. I do not remember any particular incident, but I knew that he wanted the attention to himself, always. Not in any particular case, but always. And he would rather disregard what Marina would say. And this is possibly the reason for his not wanting to—for Marina to learn English, so she would stay completely in the background.

MR. JENNER: Now, you opened that subject which I want to inquire of you about. Did you people in the Russian colony—did you consider that? Did you regard that as unusual?

MR. DE MOHRENSCHILDT: Right from the very first day my wife told Marina, "You have to learn English, you have to be able to communicate, and especially since you do not get along with your husband and you are going to leave him some day—you have to be able to support your child and yourself. You have to learn English and start immediately on it." We gave her some records to study English—not mine, but my wife's and her daughter's records, of Shakespearian English, how to learn English, and they obviously still have those records.

MR. JENNER: Yes, they were found in Mrs. Paine's home.

MR. DE MOHRENSCHILDT: We even gave them a phonograph, I think, a cheap phonograph, to play the records.

MR. JENNER: You gave them records?

MR. DE MOHRENSCHILDT: Yes.

MR. JENNER: You also gave them an instrument to play them on?

MR. DE MOHRENSCHILDT: A cheap phonograph, to play those records.

MR. JENNER: What else do you recall giving them—dresses?

MR. DE MOHRENSCHILDT: I do not—

MR. JENNER: Toys for the baby?

MR. DE MOHRENSCHILDT: Toys for the baby, definitely. And I am sure that my wife had given some dresses. But she will remember better than I do. But we never gave them one cent of money. This I recall—never—and Lee would not take money, you see. I might have given him a little bit if he had asked. But he was very proud about it. He resented when people gave something to Marina. Marina would take anything, you see—she would take anything from five cents up to anything. And the more the better. But Lee did not want to take anything. He had a very proud attitude. That is one of the reasons I sort of liked him, because of that. He was not a beggar, not a sponger.

MR. JENNER: Did you notice over the period of time you knew him developments of resentment on his part of, say, these people in the Russian colony who had come here and had established themselves to a greater or lesser degree?

MR. DE MOHRENSCHILDT: Yes; it was a very strong resentment on his part. It was almost an insane jealousy of people who succeeded where he could not succeed.

MR. JENNER: Did you ever have any discussions with him on that? How did you acquire this feeling?

MR. DE MOHRENSCHILDT: That was again through my understanding of human nature, rather than from direct conversation. From hearsay, rather. You see, number one, for instance, the fact that he was so rude to the Clarks, because they lived very well. It is an insult in his face, the house that the Clarks have—very luxurious home, two cars, and so on and so forth. It is a slap in his face. This same thing that George Bouhe, a refugee, would give Marina $30 or $40 or a new baby crib, like that, like nothing. That was a slap in his face. The fact that I had a new convertible was a slap in his face. But he was not stupid enough just to say so. But you can feel that.

MR. JENNER: Well, it might have been—

MR. DE MOHRENSCHILDT: And maybe George Bouhe unfortunately annoyed him unintentionally with that.

MR. JENNER: Well, that might be possible. George Bouhe, my impression of him is that he is a direct man.

MR. DE MOHRENSCHILDT: George Bouhe's intention was to take Marina away from Oswald very soon—not for himself, but to liberate her from Oswald. That is a fact.

MR. JENNER: You had discussions with George Bouhe?

MR. DE MOHRENSCHILDT: Yes; he said, "We have to take this girl away from him," and this is one of the things that prompted us to take Marina and the child away from Oswald. We discussed all that with George Bouhe— to make her a little bit happier—maybe she will make another life for herself, and especially for the baby. I had lost my child, you know, just a year and a half before, or 2 years before. I am fond of babies. I wanted this baby to be happy and have some sort of a future.

MR. JENNER: Did you discuss with Oswald this subject of Marina acquiring a greater facility in the command of the English language?

MR. DE MOHRENSCHILDT: Yes.

MR. JENNER: And what was—

MR. DE MOHRENSCHILDT: He said, "I don't want her to study English because I want to speak Russian to her, I will forget my Russian if I do not practice it every day." These are the words which I remember distinctly. And how many times I told him, "You have to let your wife learn English. This is a very egotistical attitude on your part."

MR. JENNER: Very selfish.

MR. DE MOHRENSCHILDT: Very selfish. He would not answer to that.

MR. JENNER: Did it occur to you as a possibility, or among others in the Russian colony, that he might have had another objective, and that is that she would return to Russia?

MR. DE MOHRENSCHILDT: Never. That never occurred to me. I do not think that. Knowing Marina, she would never go back to Russia. She liked the United States. She liked the facilities of life here. Of course, you never know people. You cannot vouch for them. But that was our opinion. Maybe we simplified too much the matters. I do not know.

MR. JENNER: Did there come a time in the spring or the midwinter of 1963, latter part of January, and in February, in which there was any discussion, or you learned that Marina had made application to the Russian Embassy to return to Russia?

MR. DE MOHRENSCHILDT: No.

MR. JENNER: No discussion?

MR. DE MOHRENSCHILDT: No discussion of that.

MR. JENNER: And except for my now uttering it, you have been wholly unaware of it?

MR. DE MOHRENSCHILDT: Wholly unaware of it. Totally unaware of that, never heard of that. What we learned, at that period—that she had her child christened in the Greek Orthodox Church against Oswald's strong objections.

MR. JENNER: Were you personally aware of those objections?

MR. DE MOHRENSCHILDT: No. I just heard that he objected to Marina doing it—and she took the child to church anyway and had the child christened. But I do not recall the circumstances. Somebody told me that.

MR. JENNER: But you are unaware of any discussion of her returning to Russia in the spring or late winter of 1962–1963, that winter?

MR. DE MOHRENSCHILDT: No.

MR. JENNER: And she never appealed to you that he was forcing her to make application to the Russian Embassy?

MR. DE MOHRENSCHILDT: I do not recall anything of that kind.

MR. JENNER: Mr. De Mohrenschildt, it appears to be the consensus in that Russian colony, that community, that Oswald reached a point where he resented all the people other than you; that he had a liking for you.

MR. DE MOHRENSCHILDT: Well, I explained to you that I do not know whether he had a liking or not.

MR. JENNER: Or respect, or something.

MR. DE MOHRENSCHILDT: I treated him nicely. My wife treated them like human beings, disregarding their bad qualities. Because that is our way of treating poor people. My philosophy is—you may object to that—but my philosophy is not to bend in front of the strong and be very nice to the poor—as nice as I can. And they were very miserable, lost, penniless, mixed up. So as much as they both annoyed me, I did not show it to them because it is like insulting a beggar—you see what I mean. Well, the other Russians obviously do not have such a charitable attitude. I do not think he has ever been, for instance—I am trying to think whether he had a resentment against all of the Russian colony or not. I would not say so. I do not know how was his attitude toward Mr. Gregory. I think they remained pretty—not close, but on speaking terms.

MR. JENNER: That seems to be so.

MR. DE MOHRENSCHILDT: Because Mr. Gregory is a very fine person—very fine person, who is an elderly man, who is nice to a poor person.

MR. JENNER: Your impression is that he, to use the vernacular a little bit—he was sort of eating on himself, he wanted to amount to something, and he appeared to be unable to, and was constantly groping.

MR. DE MOHRENSCHILDT: Yes. That is his main—his makeup—trying to do something. One conversation I had with him—I asked him, "Would you like to be a commissar in the United States," just teasing him. And he said—he sort of smiled—you could see that it was a delightful idea. To me it was a ridiculous question to ask. But he took me seriously. I laughed with the guy. Sometimes I would laugh, I would tease him. And it was amusing. But I tried not to offend him, because, after all, he was a human being. And in addition to that—in my case we had a point of contact which was the fact that he lived in Minsk, where I lived when I was a child also, where my father was this marshal of nobility. And later on in life I lived in Poland, very close to that area, I was interested in how the peasants were getting along, what does he find in the forest there, what kind of mushrooms you find, that type of conversation went on sometimes.

MR. JENNER: Did he appear to have knowledge and recollection of things in which you were interested in the community, the countryside?

MR. DE MOHRENSCHILDT: Very much so. That was a likable characteristic he had. For instance, he liked animals. My dog was sort of friendly with him. When he would come, my dog would not bark. He liked walking. He told me that around Minsk he used to take long walks in the forest which I thought was very fine. Those are contacts that possibly brought a certain understanding between us. He spoke very interestingly about the personalities of fellow workers there at his factory.

MR. JENNER: I want you to keep ruminating in this fashion, because these things will come to you. What did he say about his work there?

MR. DE MOHRENSCHILDT: Well, he said that the work was all right, not too hard, not too well paid, [but] that it was very boring. That later, after the work, he had to be present at all sorts of meetings, political meetings. He said he got bored to death. Every day he had to stay for an hour at some kind of a meeting, the factory meeting. And this is a thing I thought was very intelligent because that is one of the points that is really hateful in a Communist country—the meetings after work. That I noticed through my own experience in Yugoslavia, that the engineers and the plain workers just hated that—a political meeting after working 8 hours. And Lee Oswald also resented that in Russia. And I thought it was a rather intelligent—one of the intelligent remarks that he made. And he repeated that very often—that is the thing he hated in Russia; resented, rather than hated. Well, he described the personalities of some of the people that he knew there which I do not recall anymore. But some of them were nice, and some of them less nice, and some of them very much interested in the United States, some of them unfriendly—that sort of vague recollection.

MR. JENNER: Did you engage him in conversation respecting Communism as a political ideal and his reactions to that?

MR. DE MOHRENSCHILDT: He kept on repeating that he was not a Communist. I asked him point blank, "Are you a member of the Communist Party?" And he said no. He said, "I am a Marxist." Kept on repeating it.

MR. JENNER: Did you ask him what he meant by that?

MR. DE MOHRENSCHILDT: I never frankly asked him to elaborate on that because again, you know the word "Marxism" is very boring to me. Just the sound of that word is boring to me.

MR. JENNER: What impression did you get in that connection as to whether he was seeking some mean or middle ground between democracy and what he thought Communism was?

MR. DE MOHRENSCHILDT: Possibly he was seeking for something, but knowing what kind of brains he had, and what kind of education, I was not interested in listening to him, because it was nothing, it was zero.

MR. JENNER: I see. It was your impression, then, he could contribute nothing?

MR. DE MOHRENSCHILDT: No, he could contribute absolutely nothing except for a remark like that about the meetings, which was just an ordinary remark a person of his intelligence could understand. But when it comes to dialectic materialism, I do not want to hear that word again.

MR. JENNER: Did discussions occur as to his attempted defection?

MR. DE MOHRENSCHILDT: From the United States to Russia?

MR. JENNER: Yes.

MR. DE MOHRENSCHILDT: How it happened?

MR. JENNER: Yes.

MR. DE MOHRENSCHILDT: Why it happened and how it happened?

MR. JENNER: Yes.

MR. DE MOHRENSCHILDT: Yes.

MR. JENNER: Tell me about that.

MR. DE MOHRENSCHILDT: A few words I remember now. He said that while he was in Japan he saw tremendous injustice. By that he meant, I think, the poverty of the Japanese working class or the proletariat, as he called them, and the rich people in Japan. He said it was more visible than anywhere else. Now, I have never been in Japan, and I cannot vouch for that. But that is what he told me. And he also told me that he had some contacts with the Japanese Communists in Japan, and they—that got him interested to go and see what goes on in the Soviet Union.

MR. JENNER: Just concentrate on this, please. Tell me everything you can now recall as to what he said about—you used the term, what we lawyers call a conclusion. You said he had some contacts with the Communists in Japan. Now, try and recall what he said or as near—

MR. DE MOHRENSCHILDT: I see what you mean. Since it was so removed from my interest, I did not insist. I just heard that.

MR. JENNER: Just give me your best recollection.

MR. DE MOHRENSCHILDT: That is all I recall—that he said, "I have met some Communists in Japan and they got me excited and interested, and that was one of my inducements in going to Soviet Russia, to see what goes on there."

MR. JENNER: Did you form any opinion that this man, because of his meager boyhood, on the verge of poverty, or in poverty all during his youth and up to the time he went into the Marines at least, that he had some groping for a ready solution that would not permit that sort of thing?

MR. DE MOHRENSCHILDT: Naturally. That's the whole point. I could understand his point of view, because that is what happens exactly in the whole world with dissatisfied people. If they are constructive, they study more and try to get good jobs and succeed. The others try to form a revolutionary party. And he was one of them.

MR. JENNER: The others try to do it overnight, by force of arms.

MR. DE MOHRENSCHILDT: That's right.

MR. JENNER: Did you ever discuss with him that there are many great men and women who have come from poverty?

MR. DE MOHRENSCHILDT: Oh, yes. You could not discuss it with Oswald because he knew it all.

MR. JENNER: He always knew what the answer was.

MR. DE MOHRENSCHILDT: He always knew what the answer was. And possibly that is why he was clinging to us, to my wife and me, because we did not discuss it with them, because we did not give a damn. After we found out what was going on in that town of Minsk, what was the situation, what were the food prices, how they dressed, how they spent their evenings, which are things interesting to us, our interest waned. The rest of the time, the few times we saw Lee Oswald and Marina afterwards, was purely to give a gift, to take them to a party, because we thought they were dying of boredom, you see—which Marina was.

MR. JENNER: She was?

MR. DE MOHRENSCHILDT: She was, because he never would take her any place. That was the reason we invited them twice; once to a party at Declan Ford's—and that was, I think, a Christmas party—another time a party at Everett Glover's, where I was showing my movie to the whole group. Because I thought they would be exceedingly—Marina was dying of boredom there.

MR. JENNER: Let me get to that party at Declan Ford's. That was—was that a New Year's Day or New Year's Eve party?

MR. DE MOHRENSCHILDT: I think it was right at Christmas or New Year's Eve.

MR. JENNER: The party went on for a couple of days, didn't it?

MR. DE MOHRENSCHILDT: A couple of days?

MR. JENNER: Yes.

MR. DE MOHRENSCHILDT: I did not know that the party ran for a couple of days. But we arrived at 9 o'clock and left around 1 or 2, and it was still going strong.

MR. JENNER: Well, I suppose when a witness said it lasted a couple of days, maybe the witness was thinking it started in the early evening of one day and did not end until well into the next day.

MR. DE MOHRENSCHILDT: No; it was not any of those wild parties. It was a very friendly, very good party.

MR. JENNER: I'm not suggesting the party was wild. There is no intimation of that.

MR. DE MOHRENSCHILDT: No on the contrary, there are very hospitable people invited, and always had a congenial crowd there. And that is why we suggested, let's bring that miserable Marina and Oswald there, so they would meet some people. And I think if people continued doing that, if people did that, maybe this tragedy might not have occurred.

MR. JENNER: Or it might have become worse, his resentment.

MR. DE MOHRENSCHILDT: Maybe so.

MR. JENNER: Did Marina smoke?

MR. DE MOHRENSCHILDT: Yes. Oh, boy, this is an interesting question. She loved to smoke and would smoke as many cigarettes as she could lay her hands on. And you know, Oswald did not smoke and forbade her to smoke. This is the reason—one of the reasons they fought so bitterly— because he would take the cigarette away from her and slap her.

MR. JENNER: In your presence?

MR. DE MOHRENSCHILDT: In my presence, would take the cigarette away from her and push her, "You are not going to do that," in a dictatorial way. So I would say, "Now, stop it, let her smoke." And then he would relax. But that is the type of person he was. But not in our presence when we were away, Marina said he would not let her smoke nor drink, I think. He refused to let her drink either. And she liked to have a drink. With all her defects, she is more or less a normal person, and rather happy-go-lucky, a very happy-go-lucky girl.

MR. JENNER: What about his drinking?

MR. DE MOHRENSCHILDT: I never saw him drink. Maybe he would take a very little, but I never saw him drink more than half a glass—as far as I remember. I didn't pay too much attention. Maybe that is why he was tense, because he did not drink enough. He was always tense. That guy was always under some kind of pressure.

MR. JENNER: You have that impression?

MR. DE MOHRENSCHILDT: Yes; always some kind of a pressure.

MR. JENNER: And this was an inward pressure, you thought?

MR. DE MOHRENSCHILDT: Yes; some inward pressure.

MR. JENNER: See if I can refresh your recollection a little about that party, the first of the parties. I am going to ask you about the second one as well in a moment.

MR. DE MOHRENSCHILDT: Yes.

MR. JENNER: Do you remember being present at that party Mr. and Mrs. Thomas Ray?

MR. DE MOHRENSCHILDT: Yes. If they are the people whom I identify as he being a man in the advertising business and she a girl of Russian origin—a friend of Mrs. Ford.

MR. JENNER: He married her when he was in Germany.

MR. DE MOHRENSCHILDT: Yes; that's it—something like that. You know, in this group of the Russian émigrés, there were two people who came from Soviet Russia—there were Mrs. Ford and this lady, an entirely different type of individual—the new blood. They were younger and they were brought up in Soviet Russia.

MR. JENNER: Yes; they were people—

MR. DE MOHRENSCHILDT: They were so-called—what do you call—displaced persons, who were grabbed by the Germans and displaced in Germany, and then the American soldiers grabbed them and married them. Both of them were the same type. Very nice people, but they had a different background.

MR. JENNER: Now, this party occurred on the 28th and 29th of December.

MR. DE MOHRENSCHILDT: As far as I remember, it was around New Year's Day.

MR. JENNER: And it was at the Declan Fords?

MR. DE MOHRENSCHILDT: Yes.

MR. JENNER: Was George Bouhe there?

MR. DE MOHRENSCHILDT: I think so.

MR. JENNER: And Mr. and Mrs. Meller?

MR. DE MOHRENSCHILDT: I think so, too. And a lot of other people.

MR. JENNER: There is another Ray couple, Mr. and Mrs. Frank Ray.

MR. DE MOHRENSCHILDT: That I do not know.

MR. JENNER: Mr. and Mrs. C. E. Harris?

MR. DE MOHRENSCHILDT: I think I recall this person. Grayish hair.

MR. JENNER: From Georgetown, Tex.

MR. DE MOHRENSCHILDT: A tall man with grayish hair.

MR. JENNER: His wife was Russian born.

MR. DE MOHRENSCHILDT: I don't know them well. I probably would recognize them if I saw them.

MR. JENNER: Were there some people by the name of Jackson at that party who had a very lavish house?

MR. DE MOHRENSCHILDT: Jackson? I know a Jackson who has a very lavish house. He is a geologist also. But I do not recall seeing them at the party.

MR. JENNER: There is some testimony that in the early morning hours the party adjourned to the Jacksons' house.

MR. DE MOHRENSCHILDT: Well, we had already left.

MR. JENNER: John and Elena Hall. They were there.

MR. DE MOHRENSCHILDT: I do not recall that. I met them, I think, only once. I met her twice or three times. I recall her pretty well. But I do not recall him.

MR. JENNER: Tatiana Biggers.

MR. DE MOHRENSCHILDT: That is the person I could not identify. I don't know who she is.

MR. JENNER: Also present, Lydia Dymitruk.

MR. DE MOHRENSCHILDT: I think so. I think I remember her.

MR. JENNER: A single person, divorced.

MR. DE MOHRENSCHILDT: Yes; I think I remember her.

MR. JENNER: Slightly built, slender, short.

MR. DE MOHRENSCHILDT: Yes; I remember her. She was married to some "cuckoo nut," another "cuckoo nut" who escaped from Soviet Russia—Dymitruk. He came to ask me for a job, her husband. He came to ask me for a job several times, and then he disappeared.

MR. JENNER: Lydia Dymitruk's husband?

MR. DE MOHRENSCHILDT: Yes; her ex-husband. I understand she is a very nice person, very hard working, and is making a living for herself, and that she left him. That is my recollection.

MR. JENNER: You brought the Oswalds to the party?

MR. DE MOHRENSCHILDT: Yes.

MR. JENNER: And—

MR. DE MOHRENSCHILDT: Having asked previously either myself or my wife—having asked Mrs. Ford would she mind having the Oswalds, because they seemed to be bored to death, especially Marina seemed to be bored to death. And she said yes.

MR. JENNER: And after a while you folks left, around midnight?

MR. DE MOHRENSCHILDT: Yes.

MR. JENNER: And did you take the Oswalds with you?

MR. DE MOHRENSCHILDT: I think we did. And this is the reason why—because I think they left the child in our house while they came to the party, and we asked another friend of ours, an elderly lady, Mrs. Frangipanni, to take care of the baby while they were gone, which she did.

MR. JENNER: Did Oswald drink at that party?

MR. DE MOHRENSCHILDT: That I do not recall. I know I drank quite a few glasses.

MR. JENNER: What impression did you have as to how the people at the party reacted to Marina and to Oswald—take them separately.

MR. DE MOHRENSCHILDT: I did not pay any attention. I left them to their own devices. I spoke to various people. I thought I had done my duty by bringing them along. What really impressed me that particular night was an extraordinary interest which developed between this Japanese girl, Yaeko—I don't remember her last name—but I already had given that impression of mine at the American Embassy so they could check on that. She was a Japanese girl, very good looking, who worked, I think, at Neiman-Marcus in Dallas, and was brought into Dallas from Japan by some people in the cotton business to take care of their babies. Now, this girl is a much superior girl as to be just a baby caretaker. She eventually left that couple that is all hearsay, you see, and became sort of a girl friend of a Russian musician who lives in Dallas by the name of Lev Aronson. And I do not recall whether he was at the party or not. But Yaeko was, and they developed an immediate interest in each other—Oswald and Yaeko. They just went on sight and started talking and talking and talking. I thought that was understandable because Oswald had been in Japan, you see. But the interest was so overwhelming that Marina objected, and became very jealous. She told us, either that night or later, that Oswald got her telephone number. She noticed that Oswald got this girl's telephone number. And once or twice later on she told us that she has the impression that Oswald is carrying on something with this girl. Now, this is hearsay again. But—

MR. JENNER: Well, it is not hearsay that Marina told you.

MR. DE MOHRENSCHILDT: Yes; but hearsay that they are carrying something on. That is what she told us. But nothing definite.

MR. JENNER: Did you notice any incidents in which—at that party—in which people—

MR. DE MOHRENSCHILDT: My wife will tell you more about this Yaeko incident, because she knows a little bit better.

MR. JENNER: I will make a note of that so I can talk to her about it.

MR. DE MOHRENSCHILDT: And she is more on the gossipy side. I'm always happy if a girl likes a boy and a boy likes a girl it does not matter who they are.

MR. JENNER: Were there any incidents that you recall in which members at that party were talking with Marina and Oswald interrupted?

MR. DE MOHRENSCHILDT: No; I do not recall, because I did not speak to them. I just left them alone, hoping that they would find some people to talk to.

MR. JENNER: And the contacts you had with Marina and Lee, was there ever any discussion on the subject of whether people in Russia when they were there were chary about talking with Lee because they were afraid he might be an agent of some kind?

MR. DE MOHRENSCHILDT: It is a question I have to try to think a little bit about. I have a vague recollection that either Lee or Marina did tell me the people were afraid of him, and I think that was probably Oswald that told me, that the people were afraid of him, like many foreigners. So I thought that was very understandable, because you know the Communists are scared—not the Communists, but the people in Russia are scared to talk to foreigners. We had an incident ourselves when we went to Mexico, to a Russian exhibit, to a Russian Fair, and tried to speak to an architect there in charge of the architectural exhibit. This was a lady architect, a charming woman. We spoke to her for about 5 minutes, and then she disappeared, and you could not find her any more. She ran away from us. She was scared of us. That is the usual thing. So I did not pay particular attention to that fact. If people were scared of talking to Oswald, it was understandable.

MR. JENNER: Did that ever arise, discussions as to why—possibly affecting his desire to return to the United States?

MR. DE MOHRENSCHILDT: I do not recall that. The most important answer I think I got from Oswald—and that was one of the reasons we liked him and thought that he was rather intelligent in his estimation of Soviet Russia—is the fact that we asked him, both my wife and I, "Why did you leave Soviet Russia," and he said very sincerely, "Because I did not find what I was looking for."

MR. JENNER: And did you ask him what he was looking for?

MR. DE MOHRENSCHILDT: A Utopia. I knew what he was looking for—Utopia. And that does not exist any place.

MR. JENNER: This man could not find what he was looking for anywhere in this world.

MR. DE MOHRENSCHILDT: He could not find it in the States, he could not find it any place.

MR. JENNER: He could find it only in him.

MR. DE MOHRENSCHILDT: Exactly. He could find it in himself, in a false image of grandeur that he built in himself. But at the time that we knew him that was not so obvious. Now you can see that, as a possible murderer of the President of the United States, he must have been unbelievably egotistical, an unbelievably egotistical person.

MR. JENNER: Do you know what paranoia is?

MR. DE MOHRENSCHILDT: Yes.

MR. JENNER: Well—

MR. DE MOHRENSCHILDT: I know it very well.

MR. JENNER: Did you notice—

MR. DE MOHRENSCHILDT: Because I am interested in medicine.

MR. JENNER: Did you notice any tendencies—this may be rationalization, of course, now that you are thinking back.

MR. DE MOHRENSCHILDT: I would call him a stage below definite paranoia, which means a highly neurotic individual. But even an M. D. would not give you a right definition, or a right demarcation between the two.

MR. JENNER: Did you have any feeling, while you knew him, and before this tragic event occurred, that there was any mental aberration of that nature?

MR. DE MOHRENSCHILDT: I did not know anything about his background, you see. I did not know anything about his previous background, except that he had been in the Marine Corps—that he came from a poor family, that he had lived in New Orleans. That is all I knew about him.

MR. JENNER: I wanted to ask you about that. Was your discussion with him as to his background, let us say, if I may use a conclusion myself, superficial?

MR. DE MOHRENSCHILDT: Very superficial, because I was not—I know that type of person, I know his background. I know the people in New Orleans. I lived there. I know people in Texas of the very low category. I know the way they live. I could see clearly what type of background he had. I did not have to ask him questions. And he mentioned that while living in New Orleans, and very poorly, he started going to the public library to read the Marxist books, all by himself. That he was not induced by anybody. I said, "Who told you to read the Marxist books"—that interested me. And he said, "Nobody, I went by myself. I started studying it all by myself."

MR. JENNER: He read those high-level books, but in your opinion he did not understand them?

MR. DE MOHRENSCHILDT: I would not understand them. I would not bother reading them. I never read any Marxist books, because I know what they contain.

MR. JENNER: But you could read them with a critical mind, could you not?

MR. DE MOHRENSCHILDT: Yes; I could read with a critical mind. But that is something that does not interest me. And I know that they are very difficult. I know that they are written in a difficult manner, that they are highly theoretical, and to me very boring.

MR. JENNER: There is some intimation that at this party Oswald had said several times that he liked Russia and he might go back. Did you overhear any of that?

MR. DE MOHRENSCHILDT: No.

MR. JENNER: And from all your contact with him, had he ever expressed that notion to you, that he might go back?

MR. DE MOHRENSCHILDT: I do not recall exactly, but something comes to my mind that he might have mentioned that, that if he does not get a better job, or if he does not become successful, he might as well go back to Russia.

MR. JENNER: Well, this was really something said in despair.

MR. DE MOHRENSCHILDT: More or less—"After all, what is my life in Russia"—I remember he said that, that his life in Russia was actually better than here. But Marina never said that.

MR. JENNER: She didn't?

MR. DE MOHRENSCHILDT: No.

MR. JENNER: Do you remember some people at that party by the name of Mr. and Mrs. Daniel F. Sullivan of Lafayette, Louisiana, a divisional geologist for Continental Oil Co.?

MR. DE MOHRENSCHILDT: No.

MR. JENNER: Was there any discussion at that party about the possibility that Oswald might be a Russian agent?

MR. DE MOHRENSCHILDT: I never heard that.

MR. JENNER: And that this theory was thrown out because Oswald was broke, and that it could not be that way, because Russia would not permit one of its agents to be that penniless?

MR. DE MOHRENSCHILDT: That is an intelligent estimation, but I certainly have not heard that.

MR. JENNER: Any discussion there or speculation that there was something peculiar in the fact that allegedly they had had little trouble in getting Marina out of Russia?

MR. DE MOHRENSCHILDT: That he had trouble getting her out?

MR. JENNER: Relatively little.

MR. DE MOHRENSCHILDT: That is a question that always was sort of a big question mark to me. Not being interested, I did not probe them. But it always remained a question mark in my mind, how is it possible for somebody to take a citizen of Soviet Russia so easily out of the country. But I have known of other examples of it being done.

MR. JENNER: Was there any discussion at any time while you knew the Oswalds about any attempt to commit suicide?

MR. DE MOHRENSCHILDT: When he was in Russia, no; I don't remember anything about that.

MR. JENNER: Did you ever notice he had a scar on his left wrist?

MR. DE MOHRENSCHILDT: No; I didn't notice it.

MR. JENNER: Did you ever note whether he was right or left handed?

MR. DE MOHRENSCHILDT: Something vaguely I remember that he might be left handed but I could not recall.

MR. JENNER: This is pure vagueness on your part?

MR. DE MOHRENSCHILDT: Very, very. My wife may recall that.

MR. JENNER: You wouldn't want to express any opinion one way or the other on it?

MR. DE MOHRENSCHILDT: No.

MR. JENNER: Did you ever discuss with him his experiences in Russia with respect to hunting?

MR. DE MOHRENSCHILDT: Never have.

MR. JENNER: No discussions?

MR. DE MOHRENSCHILDT: [None.]

[MR. JENNER:] Or the use of any weapons or his right to have weapons when he was in Russia?

MR. DE MOHRENSCHILDT: I did not know even that he was interested in weapons 'til the day—which probably you will ask me later on—Easter, I think, when my wife saw his gun. I didn't know he was interested. I didn't know he had the gun. I didn't know he was interested in shooting or hunting. I didn't know he was a good shot or never had any impression.

MR. JENNER: Now that you have mentioned that we might as well cover that fully in the record.

MR. DE MOHRENSCHILDT: Yes.

MR. JENNER: Tell me about that incident.

MR. DE MOHRENSCHILDT: That incident is very clear in my mind.

MR. JENNER: This was in 1963?

MR. DE MOHRENSCHILDT: In 1963, and the last time we saw them.

MR. JENNER: It was the last time?

MR. DE MOHRENSCHILDT: The very last time we saw them.

MR. JENNER: This was around Eastertime?

MR. DE MOHRENSCHILDT: Around Eastertime.

MR. JENNER: In April?

MR. DE MOHRENSCHILDT: In April. It was in the second apartment that they had.

MR. JENNER: That was on Neely Street?

MR. DE MOHRENSCHILDT: On Neely I think, one block from the previous place they used to live.

MR. JENNER: Yes.

MR. DE MOHRENSCHILDT: And Jeanne told me that day, "Let's go and take a rabbit for Oswald's baby."

MR. JENNER: This was on Easter Sunday?

MR. DE MOHRENSCHILDT: Easter day. I don't remember it was Easter Sunday.

MR. JENNER: Easter is always on Sunday.

MR. DE MOHRENSCHILDT: Yes; maybe it was the day before, the day after, but I think it was on the holiday. Maybe my wife will remember the date exactly. And so we drove over quite late in the evening and walked up—I think they were asleep. They were asleep and we knocked at the door and shouted, and Lee Oswald came down undressed, half undressed you see, maybe in shorts, and opened the door and we told him that we have the rabbit for the child. And it was a very short visit, you know. We just gave the rabbit to the baby and I was talking to Lee while Jeanne was talking to Marina about something which is immaterial which I do not recall right now, and all of a sudden—

MR. JENNER: Excuse me. Mr. Reporter, Jeanne is spelled J-e-a-n-n-e.

MR. DE MOHRENSCHILDT: And I think Oswald and I were standing near the window looking outside and I was asking him "How is your job" or "Are you making any money? Are you happy," some question of that type. All of a sudden Jeanne, who was with Marina in the other room told me, "Look, George, they have a gun here." And Marina opened the closet and showed it to Jeanne, a gun that belonged obviously to Oswald.

MR. JENNER: This was a weapon? Did you go in and look?

MR. DE MOHRENSCHILDT: No; I didn't look at the gun. I was still standing.

The closet was open. Jeanne was looking at it, at the gun, and I think she asked Marina "what is that" you see. That was the sight on the gun. "What is that? That looks like a telescopic sight." And Marina said, "That crazy idiot is target shooting all the time." So frankly I thought it was ridiculous to shoot—target shooting in Dallas, you see, right in town. I asked him, "Why do you do that?"

MR. JENNER: What did he say?

MR. DE MOHRENSCHILDT: He said "I go out and do target shooting. I like target shooting." So out of the pure—really jokingly I told him, "Are you then the guy who took a potshot at General Walker?" And he smiled to that, because just a few days before there was an attempt at General Walker's life, and it was very highly publicized in the papers, and I knew that Oswald disliked General Walker, you see. So I took a chance and I asked him this question, you see, and I can clearly see his face, you know. He sort of shriveled, you see, when I asked this question.

MR. JENNER: He became tense?

MR. DE MOHRENSCHILDT: Became tense, you see, and didn't answer anything, smiled, you know, made a sarcastic—not sarcastic, made a peculiar face.

MR. JENNER: The expression on his face?

MR. DE MOHRENSCHILDT: That is right, changed the expression on his face.

MR. JENNER: You saw that your remark to him—

MR. DE MOHRENSCHILDT: Yes.

MR. JENNER: Had an effect on him.

MR. DE MOHRENSCHILDT: Had an effect on him. But naturally he did not say yes or no, but that was it. That is the whole incident. I remember after we were leaving, Marina went in the garden and picked up a large bouquet of roses for us. They have nice roses downstairs and gave us the roses to thank for the gift of the rabbit.

MR. JENNER: Do you recall an occasion when you came to their home—

MR. DE MOHRENSCHILDT: Excuse me, before I forget I wanted to insist on one thing which I meant to tell you before that. What was the main thing that I really liked about Oswald, you see. You asked me that question before.

MR. JENNER: Yes.

MR. DE MOHRENSCHILDT: He was ferociously, maybe too much so, for integration, advocate of integration. He said that it was hurting him, the fact that the colored people did not have the same rights as the white ones, and this is my opinion also, you see. I was very strongly opposed to segregation, and I am sometimes very violent on that subject, because it hurts me that I live in Texas you know and I do not have colored friends, I cannot afford to have colored friends, you see. It annoys me. It hurts me. I am ashamed of myself. And I try to make some friends among the colored people and the situation is such that it is hard to keep their friendship in Texas, you know. So I know what the situation is. On that point Oswald and I agreed. And this is another reason why Oswald and Bouhe fought so bitterly, because Bouhe is a segregationist. He is an old-guard segregationist that he learned from the Texans you know that the colored man is just a flunky. And I had quite a few fights with him about that, with Bouhe. And possibly his animosity, Oswald's animosity to Bouhe and vice versa were based on that, you see, although I am not so sure about it. But I assumed that that was one of the reasons. And I think that was a very sincere attitude on his behalf, very sincere.

MR. JENNER: I would like to return to this gun, this weapon incident, the Walker incident.

MR. DE MOHRENSCHILDT: Yes.

MR. JENNER: Was there ever an occasion after this time, when you and Mrs. De Mohrenschildt came to see the Oswalds, that as soon as you opened the door, you said, "Lee, how is it possible that you missed?"

MR. DE MOHRENSCHILDT: Never. I don't recall that incident.

MR. JENNER: You have now given me your full recollection of that entire rifle incident?

MR. DE MOHRENSCHILDT: Yes.

MR. JENNER: Weapon incident, and what you said to him?

MR. DE MOHRENSCHILDT: Yes, yes, yes, yes; that is right. How could I have—my recollections are vague, of course, but how could I have said that when I didn't know that he had a gun you see. I was standing there and then Jeanne told us or Marina, you know, the incident just as I have described it, that here is a gun, you see. I remember very distinctly saying, "Did you take the potshot at General Walker?" The same meaning you know, "Did you miss him," about the same meaning? I didn't want him to shoot Walker. I don't go to that extent you see.

MR. JENNER: You didn't want him to shoot anybody?

MR. DE MOHRENSCHILDT: Anybody. I didn't want him to shoot anybody. But if somebody has a gun with a telescopic lens you see, and knowing that he hates the man, it is a logical assumption you see.

MR. JENNER: You knew at that time that he had a definite bitterness for General Walker?

MR. DE MOHRENSCHILDT: I definitely knew that, either from some conversations we had on General Walker, you know—this was the period of General Walker's, you know, big showoff, you know.

MR. JENNER: He was quite militant wasn't he.

MR. DE MOHRENSCHILDT: He was, yes—

MR. JENNER: Mr. De Mohrenschildt, up to that moment, is it your testimony that you never knew and had no inkling whatsoever, that the Oswalds had a rifle or other weapon in their home?

MR. DE MOHRENSCHILDT: Absolutely positive that personally I didn't know a damn thing about it, positive, neither did my wife.

MR. JENNER: And as far as you know your wife didn't either?

MR. DE MOHRENSCHILDT: No.

MR. JENNER: Did you see the weapon?

MR. DE MOHRENSCHILDT: I did not see the weapon.

MR. JENNER: I won't show it to you then. Was there any discussion about the weapon thereafter?

MR. DE MOHRENSCHILDT: No, no discussion. That ended the conversation, the remark about Walker, ended the conversation. There was a silence after that, and we changed the subject and left very soon afterwards.

MR. JENNER: Did you have a feeling that he was uncomfortable?

MR. DE MOHRENSCHILDT: Very, very uncomfortable, but I still did not believe that he did it, you see. It was frankly a stupid joke on my part. As the time goes by it shows that sometimes it is not so stupid. But you know my wife will tell you probably that I have a very stupid, bad sense of humor, she says, you know.

MR. JENNER: Some people say you have a sadistic sense of humor.

MR. DE MOHRENSCHILDT: Possibly. She says so also, my wife usually says that I like to tease people.

MR. JENNER: And you do, don't you?

MR. DE MOHRENSCHILDT: She dislikes it. I like to, certainly, and I don't mind if people tease me. I never get mad you know. It is perfectly all right if somebody teases me.

MR. JENNER: Are you a member of a group in Dallas known as the Bohemian Club?

MR. DE MOHRENSCHILDT: Oh, yes, yes.

MR. JENNER: Tell us about the Bohemian Club. Did you organize it?

MR. DE MOHRENSCHILDT: Yes; Mr. Ballen and I organized it together and the occasion arose one day when Mr. Ballen and I were driving back from a well, an oil well we were driving far away from Dallas. It was a long drive and we were discussing our lives in Dallas—and a little bit exchange about the sort of boring people we have around in Dallas you know, nothing but Texans. And then by God, says Ballen, "We should do something about it. We should organize—there are some interesting people in Dallas. We should organize a group for free discussion. And also we should put—we all like to eat well. Let's combine it with good eating." And that is how the idea originated.

MR. JENNER: And you called it what?

MR. DE MOHRENSCHILDT: We called it the Bohemian Club, a little bit based on the Bohemian Club in San Francisco. And we invited—we decided to invite people who are sort of unusual and in different professions, and that no business should be discussed during the meetings, that the member whose turn it is to make a speech should also provide the dinner, and either cook it himself or his wife would cook it or he should invite all of us to a restaurant of his choice. This lasted I guess for a year or two years you know. We had quite a few meetings, very interesting, controversial meetings, because the main point was that you had to express yourself freely on the subject which is very important to you. Then followed a discussion of all the other members.

MR. JENNER: On the subject.

MR. DE MOHRENSCHILDT: On the subject.

MR. JENNER: Was it intended that the discussions be provocative or presented in a provocative fashion?

MR. DE MOHRENSCHILDT: As much as possible, and we had some real lulus there, some very provocative discussions.

MR. JENNER: Was there an occasion when you had this club at your home or restaurant that you supplied the meal?

MR. DE MOHRENSCHILDT: Yes; one day I think I made one particular speech that I made on the subject of Vlasov's Army which are the White Russians and refugees who decided to fight with the Germans against Soviet Russia. They were helped by General Vlasov who was a Soviet General, and then later on became Commander, was made prisoner by the Germans and then decided to fight the Communists, because obviously he was dissatisfied with the Stalinist regime, and it was quite a large group. I never met any people of that type, but Mr. Voshinin provided me the material on that subject, and I made this little speech and I think everybody was very satisfied with the speech except Lev Aronson who is a Jewish friend, a Jewish friend of mine who was in the German concentration camp and he obviously had met some of those Vlasov soldiers, and anyway he criticized me quite a lot on that speech.

MR. JENNER: Did he criticize you during the course of the meeting?

MR. DE MOHRENSCHILDT: During the course of the meal?

MR. JENNER: Yes.

MR. DE MOHRENSCHILDT: Yes, yes.

MR. JENNER: Did you accuse anybody of being a Nazi?

MR. DE MOHRENSCHILDT: Did he accuse?

MR. JENNER: Did you?

MR. DE MOHRENSCHILDT: Did I accuse anybody?

MR. JENNER: In the way of provoking the discussion?

MR. DE MOHRENSCHILDT: Of provoking the discussion? I don't remember that. Possibly I had, but I don't remember that. Actually he accused me more or less of being pro-Nazi by giving that speech you see. He accused me of being, which I am not you know, but that expresses my opinion of the difficulty that sometimes the refugees are in when their opinions, political opinions, differ with their own country you see. Those are the people who are fighting their own country because they were deeply inside anti-Communists, you see. I didn't say that I was all for them you see. I just described this as an interesting incident because I just read a book on that subject or something you know, and I thought that it was an interesting incident of the last war that occurred.

MR. JENNER: Did you ever see Oswald operate an automobile?

MR. DE MOHRENSCHILDT: No; I had the impression that he didn't know how to drive and I was quite surprised—

MR. JENNER: What gave you the impression that he didn't know how to drive?

MR. DE MOHRENSCHILDT: I couldn't swear to that, but I think I asked him, "Do you know how to drive an automobile? Why don't you buy yourself an automobile?" I remember saying.

MR. JENNER: Where would he get the money?

MR. DE MOHRENSCHILDT: Well, you know you can buy a car for $20, or $30, some old wreck, and somebody with any mechanical ability could fix it.

MR. JENNER: What was his response to that?

MR. DE MOHRENSCHILDT: I have the impression that he said that he didn't know how to drive, but I couldn't swear to that. And naturally Marina was needling him all the time to buy an automobile.

MR. JENNER: Oh, she was?

MR. DE MOHRENSCHILDT: Yes; she was.

MR. JENNER: You have a definite impression?

MR. DE MOHRENSCHILDT: A definite impression of that. She was needling him.

MR. JENNER: Apart from an impression, as a matter of fact you were present and knew she was needling him to purchase an automobile.

MR. DE MOHRENSCHILDT: I could almost swear to that, but again it is so vague I could not recall the exact words, you see.

MR. JENNER: But you do have a definite impression of that?

MR. DE MOHRENSCHILDT: Yes, I have a definite impression of that. I might have put it in her mind you know. Either my wife or I might have put it in her mind because it is incomprehensible to live in Texas without an automobile. It is not like New York. They were completely isolated where they were living, you see.

MR. JENNER: And you were suggesting it.

MR. DE MOHRENSCHILDT: I might have suggested it.

MR. JENNER: Because of that.

MR. DE MOHRENSCHILDT: Or my wife.

MR. JENNER: What impression, if you have any, do you have with respect to his sexual habits? Did you ever have any thoughts?

MR. DE MOHRENSCHILDT: Yes.

MR. JENNER: As to whether he was a homosexual?

MR. DE MOHRENSCHILDT: No.

MR. JENNER: He was not in your opinion?

MR. DE MOHRENSCHILDT: I don't think so, I think he was an asexual person, asexual, and as I told you before, Marina was bitterly complaining about her lack of satisfaction. This is really the time that we decided just to drop them you see. One of the reasons you see we decided not to see them again, because we both found it revolting, such a discussion of marital habits in front of relative strangers as we were, see.

MR. JENNER: And this occurred more than once?

MR. DE MOHRENSCHILDT: You see this occurred probably in the first period when we knew Oswald. You know there was a first period when we knew them, until about October. Then we didn't see them anymore, and I think it was caused by many factors you know. We just got tired of them. We didn't like them. We did not like this particular remark about sex life, and other things you know. We just were not interested in them, and then the fact that she returned back to Oswald, see what I mean, after we had taken her away from him, that she went back to him that disgusted us. We told her,

"Now we helped you. We are not going to do anything more about you."
And we didn't see them in October, November, December, see.

MR. JENNER: Except for this party?

MR. DE MOHRENSCHILDT: Except for the party, and then Christmas came and we thought well, the Oswalds all by themselves you know. It is Christmas time, we should take them out. For that period they were completely out of my mind you see. Then we decided to take them out, and I think it was in January after this party that we took them again to meet Everett Glover.

MR. JENNER: I will get to that in a moment.

MR. DE MOHRENSCHILDT: I think actually there were two parties that we took them to. One at Ford's and the other at Everett Glover's. No, pardon me, I made a mistake. We took them also, both of them one afternoon, and I think it was still in the first period of us knowing them, to the house of Admiral Bruton who is a friend of ours, and a retired U.S. Admiral who works in Dallas and has—both he and his wife are good friends of ours. And they are very kind people. Mrs. Bruton loves the children. She is a grandmother, and we told her that here we have that miserable couple with a child, could we bring them to the pool one day? And she said, "fine, bring them along." And we brought them to the pool, and no sooner the admiral saw Oswald you know, and heard a few words from him, he said, "take this guy away from me." This Bruton was quite a hero in the war you know, and he immediately sensed that Oswald was a revolutionary character you see, and no good. He sensed that, being a military man you see. I think he asked him a few questions, "is it true that you were in the Marine Corps?" And Oswald made kind of a sour face about the Marine Corps. So it was very short and very unpleasant interview because the admiral left you know, and his wife, being a kind person, stayed there for a while you know, and then we took the Oswalds back again.

MR. JENNER: You never did use the pool?

MR. DE MOHRENSCHILDT: They never used the pool because I don't think Oswald liked swimming. And just recently I got a letter from Mrs. Bruton in Paris saying, "is that the same man that you brought once to my house?" She has been reading the story of Oswald.

MR. JENNER: When you went over to pick up the Oswalds to take them to that Christmas party did you enter their home?

MR. DE MOHRENSCHILDT: It is just vague to me. I don't remember how we got them. Whether I did or my wife did—I do not recall how it was done.

MR. JENNER: I was going to ask you whether you noticed if they had a Christmas tree or any indication of celebration of Christmas?

MR. DE MOHRENSCHILDT: I have some vague recollection of some kind of celebration but I do not recall.

MR. JENNER: Did you ever have any discussion with him as to whether he did or didn't believe in Christmas?

MR. DE MOHRENSCHILDT: I don't remember. I assumed that he did not. Marina was naturally interested in Christmas.

MR. JENNER: She was?

MR. DE MOHRENSCHILDT: She was.

MR. JENNER: Did the Oswalds, either together or separately, come to your home frequently or several times and spend the day with you?

MR. DE MOHRENSCHILDT: I was trying to pin down how many times we saw them in all, and it is very hard you know. I would say between 10 and 12 times, maybe more. It is very hard to say. Usually they were together.

MR. JENNER: She came alone?

MR. DE MOHRENSCHILDT: Sometimes she came alone; yes. I don't recall his coming all by himself. I don't recall any incident.

MR. JENNER: There was some testimony to the effect—I want you to pause before I ask you another question, exhaust your recollection on this.

MR. DE MOHRENSCHILDT: Yes.

MR. JENNER: Were there occasions when they came in the morning and stayed all day?

MR. DE MOHRENSCHILDT: Marina might have stayed all day you see, or 3 or 4 hours you see. My wife will remember, will have a better recollection of that, because I was at that time busy on three projects, and really my mind was on something else, you see.

MR. JENNER: Having exhausted your recollection, there is testimony to the effect, about Marina, that "we used to come early in the morning, and leave at night. We would spend the entire day with them. We went by bus."

MR. DE MOHRENSCHILDT: By bus? My wife will remember that better. Possibly I was not at home you see. I was running around doing business, my business you know.

MR. JENNER: You came to their home for short visits?

MR. DE MOHRENSCHILDT: I came to their home for short visits, and sometimes would find Marina alone, maybe twice, something like that you see, would find Marina alone, and ask her, "How are you getting along? Goodbye."

MR. JENNER: Did you ever visit them and bring some foodstuffs?

MR. DE MOHRENSCHILDT: I do not recall that. My wife will remember that better than I do.

MR. JENNER: Does this refresh your recollection in any degree, testimony that "the De Mohrenschildts visited us, they usually came for short visits. They brought their own favorite vegetables such as cucumbers. George likes cucumbers."

MR. DE MOHRENSCHILDT: Yes; I like cucumbers, and I am sure that my wife will remember that, because it was her idea, not mine. She was in charge of food you know. If they did spend the whole day with us, it is possible it was at the very beginning when my wife took Marina to the doctor, you know, and then brought her back again, something like that. I don't remember seeing them in the house all day long.

MR. JENNER: But they might have been there all day long when you weren't around.

MR. DE MOHRENSCHILDT: They might have been, might have been. My wife will remember that, you see.

MR. JENNER: Were there occasions when they had meals at your house?

MR. DE MOHRENSCHILDT: Oh, yes; I think so. I think so. I don't remember the exact occasion but I am sure that we fed them quite often, because they were hungry.

MR. JENNER: As a matter of fact you went out of your way to see that they were fed?

MR. DE MOHRENSCHILDT: Yes, yes; I think so. My wife did, not I.

MR. JENNER: Was there any discussion on your part with Oswald with respect to his family, his mother, his brothers?

MR. DE MOHRENSCHILDT: Yes; this is very interesting. I remember distinctly that Marina especially told me that they had lived with the brother, and that he told them to leave the house. Now we assumed that it was—

MR. JENNER: Recapture your recollection a little more about this.

MR. DE MOHRENSCHILDT: It is something to that effect, you know, and it was a little bit surprising to me, and then after seeing her for a little while, I realized why they did, because she was incredibly lazy you see. She wouldn't help anybody.

MR. JENNER: Who was incredibly lazy?

MR. DE MOHRENSCHILDT: Marina, very lazy, wouldn't help anybody with anything. When she stayed for instance with the Mellers, and the baby you see, Mrs. Meller told us that she wouldn't help her at all, you know, around the house.

MR. JENNER: Yes.

MR. DE MOHRENSCHILDT: Would sit there and smoke and do nothing. Now I have a recollection, a vague recollection of Lee telling me that he didn't get along with his mother. Actually it was surprising how little he spoke about his family. It was just something completely that was not discussed you know. He didn't talk about it. But I have a vague recollection that he disliked his mother. He didn't get along with his mother, and Marina disliked the mother.

MR. JENNER: Marina disliked the mother also?

MR. DE MOHRENSCHILDT: Marina disliked the mother also.

MR. JENNER: You have a definite recollection of that?

MR. DE MOHRENSCHILDT: I have a recollection of some kind, not in any exact words, but that is the impression I had.

MR. JENNER: Was there any discussion or did you become aware that they had lived also with the mother as well as the brother?

MR. DE MOHRENSCHILDT: I do not recall that.

MR. JENNER: But you have a definite recollection that Marina had met the mother and had a reaction to her?

MR. DE MOHRENSCHILDT: Yes; Oh, that she met the mother, definitely. I assumed that you knew.

MR. JENNER: And that reaction was an unfavorable one?

MR. DE MOHRENSCHILDT: Unfavorable reaction, and possibly my wife will remember more than I do.

MR. JENNER: Did you get any reaction as to how Oswald felt with respect to his brother?

MR. DE MOHRENSCHILDT: Again a vague idea that he did not get along with his brother.

MR. JENNER: Did you become aware that he had two brothers?

MR. DE MOHRENSCHILDT: I didn't even know he had two brothers.

MR. JENNER: Was there any occasion when it came to your attention that there was any alarm on Marina's part with respect to Lee possibly inflicting some harm on Vice President Nixon, or former Vice President Nixon?

MR. DE MOHRENSCHILDT: No.

MR. JENNER: That doesn't ring a bell at all?

MR. DE MOHRENSCHILDT: It doesn't ring a bell at all. But what I wanted to underline, that was always amazing to me, that as far as I am concerned he was an admirer of President Kennedy.

MR. JENNER: I was going to ask you about that. Tell me the discussions you had in that connection. Did you have some discussions with him?

MR. DE MOHRENSCHILDT: Just occasional sentences, you know. I think once I mentioned to him that I met Mrs. Kennedy when she was a child you know, she was a very strong-willed child, very intelligent and very attractive child you see, and a very attractive family, and I thought that Kennedy was doing a very good job with regard to the racial problem, you know. We never discussed anything else. And he also agreed with me, "Yes, yes, yes; I think it is an excellent President, young, full of energy, full of good ideas."

MR. JENNER: Did he ever indicate any resentment of Mr. Kennedy's wealth?

MR. DE MOHRENSCHILDT: That is definitely a point there, you know. He did not indicate, but he hated wealth, period, you see. Lee Oswald hated wealth, and I do not recall the exact words, but this is something that you could feel in him, you see. And since he was very poor, you know, I could see why he did, you see. I even would tell him sometimes, "That is ridiculous. Wealth doesn't make happiness and you can be poor and be happy, you can be wealthy and be very unhappy; it doesn't matter." I met a lot of wealthy people in my life and found that quite a few of them are very unhappy and I have met quite a few poor people and they are very happy. So it is nothing to be jealous of.

MR. JENNER: Did you ever discuss with him Governor Connally?

MR. DE MOHRENSCHILDT: Never discussed it with him.

MR. JENNER: Did he ever express any opinion with respect to Governor Connally?

MR. DE MOHRENSCHILDT: Never had a word about it. You see, I was not familiar with the fact that he did have a dishonorable discharge.

MR. JENNER: That is another subject.

MR. DE MOHRENSCHILDT: Yes.

MR. JENNER: You were not familiar with that at all? It was never discussed?

MR. DE MOHRENSCHILDT: It was only in the papers that I read after the assassination that I read in the papers that he had a dishonorable discharge. I assumed that he had an honorable discharge. I assumed that.

MR. JENNER: There was never any discussion in the Russian colony on the subject that he had not had an honorable discharge?

MR. DE MOHRENSCHILDT: I do not recall that. I do not recall. But I was again probing in my mind whether I heard anything about this dishonorable discharge or not.

MR. JENNER: As you are sitting there, you are probing your mind?

MR. DE MOHRENSCHILDT: Yes, my mind, thinking about it, now you know, and it is impossible to say because I read in the paper that he had a dishonorable discharge, after the assassination.

MR. JENNER: And you don't want to rationalize?

MR. DE MOHRENSCHILDT: I do not want to.

MR. JENNER: Now let us turn to the party at the Glovers.

MR. DE MOHRENSCHILDT: Yes.

MR. JENNER: You were acquainted with Mr. Glover, were you?

MR. DE MOHRENSCHILDT: Yes.

MR. JENNER: Everett Glover?

MR. DE MOHRENSCHILDT: Everett Glover.

MR. JENNER: Who is Everett Glover?

MR. DE MOHRENSCHILDT: Everett Glover is a chemist at Magnolia Laboratories, Standard Oil of New York Research Laboratories.

MR. JENNER: Now, had Everett Glover met the Oswalds prior to this party at his home?

MR. DE MOHRENSCHILDT: He might have, I don't recall. He might have met them, either Marina or both of them, for a short time.

MR. JENNER: Have you exhausted your recollection on that subject?

MR. DE MOHRENSCHILDT: My wife may remember this more distinctly.

MR. JENNER: But have you exhausted your recollection?

MR. DE MOHRENSCHILDT: Yes; I don't recall.

MR. JENNER: Does this serve to refresh your recollection? Mr. Glover has stated that he had met Marina previously.

MR. DE MOHRENSCHILDT: Yes.

MR. JENNER: At your home several times?

MR. DE MOHRENSCHILDT: It could be; yes.

MR. JENNER: It could be?

MR. DE MOHRENSCHILDT: It could be; yes.

MR. JENNER: And had been invited to your home several times because she was a Russian-speaking person who was having marital difficulties with Lee Oswald?

MR. DE MOHRENSCHILDT: Very possible, very possible. Now I recall even this, since you mention this. I suggested that they might live with Everett Glover, this couple.

MR. JENNER: You made a suggestion?

MR. DE MOHRENSCHILDT: Yes.

MR. JENNER: To whom?

MR. DE MOHRENSCHILDT: To Glover. "You have an empty house. Why don't you let them live with you and pay you so much per month?" And I think he declined that.

MR. JENNER: He did organize this party, however?

MR. DE MOHRENSCHILDT: Who? Everett?

MR. JENNER: Yes.

MR. DE MOHRENSCHILDT: Yes.

MR. JENNER: Now he says it was on February 23, 19—

MR. DE MOHRENSCHILDT: 1963.

MR. JENNER: 1963?

MR. DE MOHRENSCHILDT: That is about it.

MR. JENNER: Does that refresh your recollection?

MR. DE MOHRENSCHILDT: Yes; I was placing it around January or February; at that time.

MR. JENNER: Did you attend that party?

MR. DE MOHRENSCHILDT: Yes; as far as I remember, I did.

MR. JENNER: And Jeanne as well?

MR. DE MOHRENSCHILDT: Yes.

MR. JENNER: Who else was there?

MR. DE MOHRENSCHILDT: At this party was a lot of friends of Everett Glover's whose names I do not recall.

MR. JENNER: Volkmar Schmidt?

MR. DE MOHRENSCHILDT: Yes, yes; definitely. We called him Messer Schmidt. He is a German; very intelligent, young Ph.D. in sociology who also works at the same laboratory as Everett Glover.

MR. JENNER: Magnolia?

MR. DE MOHRENSCHILDT: Magnolia Laboratory.

MR. JENNER: And was living with Glover at that time?

MR. DE MOHRENSCHILDT: Was living with Glover at the time, I think.

MR. JENNER: He was present?

MR. DE MOHRENSCHILDT: Yes.

MR. JENNER: He is a bachelor?

MR. DE MOHRENSCHILDT: A bachelor.

MR. JENNER: And who else?

MR. DE MOHRENSCHILDT: I think we invited our neighbors, Mrs. Fox who lived right next door to us, to that party.

MR. JENNER: Mrs. Fox?

MR. DE MOHRENSCHILDT: Yes.

MR. JENNER: What is her first name?

MR. DE MOHRENSCHILDT: Mary Fox.

MR. JENNER: What is her husband's name?

MR. DE MOHRENSCHILDT: She is a widow. I think, but it might have been a different party, but I have the impression that she was there.

MR. JENNER: Anybody else?

MR. DE MOHRENSCHILDT: I think we invited our landlord also.

MR. JENNER: Who is your landlord?

MR. DE MOHRENSCHILDT: I forgot his name. Anyway he is my landlord. I forgot his name. My wife has a better memory of names.

MR. JENNER: Anybody else that you recall?

MR. DE MOHRENSCHILDT: And Ruth Paine.

MR. JENNER: Ruth Paine?

MR. DE MOHRENSCHILDT: Yes.

MR. JENNER: Had you ever met Ruth Paine before?

MR. DE MOHRENSCHILDT: No; I think that was the first time we met Ruth Paine.

MR. JENNER: You have never been in any singing groups with her?

MR. DE MOHRENSCHILDT: No.

MR. JENNER: Of which she was a member?

MR. DE MOHRENSCHILDT: No, no.

MR. JENNER: You did engage in some singing groups, did you not?

MR. DE MOHRENSCHILDT: Yes; but a different type of singing. I was engaged only in the church choir singing and I think she engaged in some sort of classical music singing.

MR. JENNER: Madrigal?

MR. DE MOHRENSCHILDT: I beg your pardon?

MR. JENNER: Madrigal?

MR. DE MOHRENSCHILDT: Madrigal; that is right. There is a group in Dallas to which Everett Glover belongs, you know, who I think spent some time singing in the madrigal.

MR. JENNER: Have you exhausted your recollection now as to everybody who was present?

MR. DE MOHRENSCHILDT: There were quite a lot of people there, but if you mention the names I will say yes or no.

MR. JENNER: I want you to exhaust your recollection first.

MR. DE MOHRENSCHILDT: I am not so sure. I think my daughter was there.

MR. JENNER: Alex?

MR. DE MOHRENSCHILDT: Alex. I don't remember if Gary was there.

MR. JENNER: That is her husband?

MR. DE MOHRENSCHILDT: Her husband. See, we showed our movie quite a few times.

MR. JENNER: Did you show it that night?

MR. DE MOHRENSCHILDT: I think we showed the movie that night.

MR. JENNER: Were Mr. and Mrs. Norman Fredricksen present?

MR. DE MOHRENSCHILDT: That name is familiar to me but I couldn't identify them.

MR. JENNER: Were these people interested in meeting the Oswalds?

MR. DE MOHRENSCHILDT: I think Oswald mentioned to me—Glover mentioned to me that Mrs. Paine was a student of the Russian language, that she would like to meet somebody with whom she could practice. That is my recollection.

MR. JENNER: Did the people engage in conversation with both of the Oswalds?

MR. DE MOHRENSCHILDT: They were surrounded by the whole group. I do not recall what happened, because I was busy making the description of our trip while the movie was being shown. That movie, by the way, did not interest Oswald at all. He was not interested.

MR. JENNER: The Mexican trip movie?

MR. DE MOHRENSCHILDT: No; he was not interested. Neither Marina nor Oswald were interested.

MR. JENNER: Neither one?

MR. DE MOHRENSCHILDT: No.

MR. JENNER: Why was that, do you think?

MR. DE MOHRENSCHILDT: They were not the outdoor-type people who would appreciate that sort of thing, not. sufficiently outdoor-type people, not sufficiently sophisticated to appreciate that sort of a thing. At least that was my impression.

MR. JENNER: Did any of these people inquire of Oswald as to his life in Russia?

MR. DE MOHRENSCHILDT: I think so. I think after the movie there was quite an animated discussion there asking many questions and many answering. He was there very happy you see, because he loved to be asked questions. He loved to be the center of attention, and he definitely was the center of attention that night.

MR. JENNER: That night. What about Marina?

MR. DE MOHRENSCHILDT: Well, you know that she couldn't speak English.

MR. JENNER: Yes. There were people there who could speak Russian, weren't there?

MR. DE MOHRENSCHILDT: I think she was talking mainly to Mrs. Paine, and I noticed immediately that there was another nice relationship developed there between Mrs. Paine and Marina.

MR. JENNER: Did you have some acquaintance with Mrs. Paine afterward; you and Mrs. De Mohrenschildt?

MR. DE MOHRENSCHILDT: Never saw them again. Never saw them again as far as I remember. That in my recollection was the only time I saw her. I remember her distinctly because she is a very interesting and attractive person.

MR. JENNER: Do you remember a Richard Pierce and a Miss Betty MacDonald attending that party?

MR. DE MOHRENSCHILDT: Yes; I remember now Betty MacDonald. I don't remember whether she was at the party but I think she was the librarian at the Magnolia Research Laboratory. Mr. Pierce is another friend of Everett's who also works at Magnolia, who eventually became his roommate, or maybe he was already a roommate at the time. I think he became a roommate later on.

MR. JENNER: Is there anything that occurred at that meeting that you think might be significant that you would like to tell us about?

MR. DE MOHRENSCHILDT: I really do not remember anything significant.

MR. JENNER: Did you remain throughout the whole evening, or did you leave before the party was over?

MR. DE MOHRENSCHILDT: I do not recall.

MR. JENNER: I take it you did not bring the Oswalds to that meeting?

MR. DE MOHRENSCHILDT: I do not recall either. I think they possibly have come by themselves. Maybe somebody else brought them. Maybe Everett brought them.

MR. JENNER: Either that or Everett?

MR. DE MOHRENSCHILDT: Yes; somebody else might have.

MR. JENNER: It was not your party?

MR. DE MOHRENSCHILDT: No.

MR. JENNER: You assisted him, however, in arranging it?

MR. DE MOHRENSCHILDT: Yes; exactly.

MR. JENNER: Do you recall anything said at that meeting with respect to their eliciting from Oswald his views with respect to Russia, and in particular the former government in Russia?

MR. DE MOHRENSCHILDT: I remember quite a vivid discussion going on, you know, because all those people are highly intelligent, and, very intellectual group of people interested in what goes on in the world, and as far as I know none of them has ever seen a Russian, and it was just like a new specimen of humanity, you see, that appeared in front of them, both Marina and Oswald, an American but who had been to Russia. But I don't remember any particular discussion or disagreement or agreement. I think probably Oswald was talking most of the time.

MR. JENNER: Oswald was pretty proud, was he, of his ability to speak Russian?

MR. DE MOHRENSCHILDT: He was proud of it, yes; because it is quite an achievement for a man with a poor scholastic background to have learned the language. It is surprising to me. It was an extraordinary surprise for my wife and myself that he was able to learn to speak it so well for such a short time as he was supposed to have stayed in Russia. As I understand it, he stayed there some 2 years, I gather.

MR. JENNER: That is all.

MR. DE MOHRENSCHILDT: And it is amazing.

MR. JENNER: In speaking of that, as I recall, you noted he had a conversational command of the language.

MR. DE MOHRENSCHILDT: Yes.

MR. JENNER: But that he did not speak a refined Russian.

MR. DE MOHRENSCHILDT: No, no; not a refined Russian.

MR. JENNER: He had trouble with his grammar?

MR. DE MOHRENSCHILDT: Yes, yes.

MR. JENNER: Were there occasions when you knew them in which Marina would correct his grammar and there would be an altercation between them or something?

MR. DE MOHRENSCHILDT: Oh, yes; there was bickering all the time. There was bickering all the time. I don't remember whether it was especially on the point of grammar, but there was bickering between them all the time. But as I said before, the bickering was mainly because Marina smoked and he didn't approve of it, that she liked to drink and he did not approve of it. I think she liked to put the makeup on and he didn't let her use the makeup. My wife will explain a little bit more in detail what was going on between them, you see, because she was a confidante of Marina's, you see. I was not.

MR. JENNER: Would you elaborate, please?

MR. DE MOHRENSCHILDT: Well, my wife being a woman was interested in a woman's problems, you see, Marina's, in the baby and in her makeup, in the way she dressed and the way she behaved, you see. She tried to correct her manners, correct, teach her how to be a human being, you see, which Marina did not know very well. She was doing her best to learn. She wanted to, but she really had a very poor background, you see.

MR. JENNER: You made a comment that you just said your wife had confidence in Marina, but you didn't. What did you mean by that?

MR. DE MOHRENSCHILDT: Confidence from what point of view?

MR. JENNER: I don't know.

MR. DE MOHRENSCHILDT: Yes; I mentioned that because I don't like a woman who bitches at her husband all the time, and she did, you know. She annoyed him. She bickered. She brought the worst out in him. And she told us after they would get a fight, you know, that he was fighting also. She would scratch him also.

MR. JENNER: She would scratch him?

MR. DE MOHRENSCHILDT: She would scratch him also.

MR. JENNER: Do you recall the time? I will put the question this way in order to draw on your recollection, rather than mine. There was an occasion, was there not, that Marina left Lee by herself?

MR. DE MOHRENSCHILDT: Yes.

MR. JENNER: Without being taken?

MR. DE MOHRENSCHILDT: Yes; I have a recollection of that.

MR. JENNER: Tell us about that. When did it occur?

MR. DE MOHRENSCHILDT: I don't remember when it occurred.

MR. JENNER: Does October 1962 refresh your recollection?

MR. DE MOHRENSCHILDT: Very possible, but that was the period when we were very busy with our cystic fibrosis campaign. I do recall that one day I was in Fort Worth and I decided to come to see Mrs. Hall, with whom Marina was staying.

MR. JENNER: Were you aware of the fact that Marina was at Mrs. Hall's?

MR. DE MOHRENSCHILDT: Yes.

MR. JENNER: Were you aware of how she had gotten there?

MR. DE MOHRENSCHILDT: I do not recall how it happened, but I was aware, somebody told me that, that she was staying at Mrs. Hall's.

MR. JENNER: The Halls were separated at that time, were they not?

MR. DE MOHRENSCHILDT: Yes; and Mrs. Hall had the boyfriend who was a friend of mine.

MR. JENNER: What was his name?

MR. DE MOHRENSCHILDT: A long name, German name, but he was of Polish extraction. He was in the plastic business. Now, his name, Doctor—he worked for some plastic company in Fort Worth. Kleinlerer, Alex Kleinlerer. That is the name. Well, I had a very hard time finding the house where Mrs. Hall lived. I think Mr. Clark told me. That is probably it.

MR. JENNER: Max Clark.

MR. DE MOHRENSCHILDT: Max Clark probably told me that Marina is there.

MR. JENNER: Is that 4760 Trail Lake Drive?

MR. DE MOHRENSCHILDT: Yes; Trail Lake Drive. That is the place. And I drove over and here was Marina, Mrs. Hall, and Alex Kleinlerer. I don't remember what we were talking about, what we discussed at that time. It was a friendly visit to say how are you.

MR. JENNER: What I was getting at, Mr. De Mohrenschildt, was that this was an occasion when Marina had left her husband?

MR. DE MOHRENSCHILDT: Yes.

MR. JENNER: And come to the Halls?

MR. DE MOHRENSCHILDT: Yes.

MR. JENNER: That is, it is an occasion distinct from the one in which you took Marina?

MR. DE MOHRENSCHILDT: Oh, yes.

MR. JENNER: Away from her husband. And this occasion we are now talking about at the Halls occurred subsequently to the time that you had taken her to the Mellers?

MR. DE MOHRENSCHILDT: Yes. I think it was after our taking her away to the Mellers.

MR. JENNER: When you arrived there, what did you discuss in respect to why Marina was there?

MR. DE MOHRENSCHILDT: No; I think I was discussing, I was talking to Alex Kleinlerer and to Mrs. Hall. Yes; something vaguely comes to my mind that Mrs. Hall was saying that Marina should leave their place.

MR. JENNER: Should leave the Halls?

MR. DE MOHRENSCHILDT: Should leave the Halls. The husband is coming back or something like that, something to that effect.

MR. JENNER: Her husband is returning?

MR. DE MOHRENSCHILDT: Yes; something to that effect.

MR. JENNER: And did Marina leave?

MR. DE MOHRENSCHILDT: That I do not recall.

MR. JENNER: You don't recall that she then went somewhere else?

MR. DE MOHRENSCHILDT: I do not recall. If you could refresh my memory I may remember better. Again, I want to underline that all this is history for me, you see.

MR. JENNER: I appreciate that, and I must avoid trying to put things in your mind also.

MR. DE MOHRENSCHILDT: Yes.

MR. JENNER: Which is what I am attempting to do.

MR. DE MOHRENSCHILDT: That is right. As I remember, take Mrs. Hall—yes; I remember what we were talking about. Mrs. Hall had had an accident, and she had either a broken leg or a broken arm, something like that, and she was in a cast. That is it. So we were talking about the accident most of the time, you see, what happened.

MR. JENNER: Well, that is a fact.

MR. DE MOHRENSCHILDT: Yes; she had an accident. I remember now.

MR. JENNER: Did you have any discussion or do you have any opinion with respect to Marina's religious belief, whether she had any, any religious feeling?

MR. DE MOHRENSCHILDT: I had a vague impression—I don't remember because I do not discuss religion too often—that she had religious beliefs of some sort, you see. She was a Greek Orthodox and did have some sort of religious belief.

MR. JENNER: What about Lee, on the other hand?

MR. DE MOHRENSCHILDT: Lee, I think religion did not exist for him.

MR. JENNER: He didn't believe in God?

MR. DE MOHRENSCHILDT: God, I don't know, because I didn't ask him a straight forward question, but I know that he did not believe in any organized religion. That is for sure. But he never was militantly against religion as far as I remember.

MR. JENNER: But you have no recollection of any discussions or any impression on your part about Marina going back to Russia at any time?

MR. DE MOHRENSCHILDT: Something vaguely goes on in my head.

MR. JENNER: Oswald trying to get her to return to Russia?

MR. DE MOHRENSCHILDT: Something vaguely goes on in my mind, but I do not recall. Very possible, you see, that something was mentioned like that. I didn't pay any attention, in other words.

MR. JENNER: Did Oswald express views with respect to individual liberty and freedom of the press?

MR. DE MOHRENSCHILDT: I don't think he understood the freedom of the press, and individual liberties. I think he was too stupid to understand the advantages we have of the free press and the free speech. Not too stupid, I mean, but too uneducated to understand the great advantages we have in free press and free discussion and in individual freedoms. Like many native-born Americans, he did not appreciate the advantages you get in this country, you see. You have to be a foreigner to appreciate it a little bit more. Many Russians, all the Russian refugees appreciate that, you see, but many who are born here don't appreciate it. Not all of them.

MR. JENNER: What about Marina and her politics?

MR. DE MOHRENSCHILDT: Marina was definitely more appreciative of life in the United States.

MR. JENNER: Was she inclined to discuss politics?

MR. DE MOHRENSCHILDT: Not too much; no. That was Lee's main point, you see, to discuss politics.

MR. JENNER: What was her attitude toward Lee's views in that respect?

MR. DE MOHRENSCHILDT: She more or less considered him a crackpot, as far as I remember, you see. A few times she said, "Oh, that crazy lunatic. Again he is talking about politics." This is one of the reasons we liked her, because that was a very intelligent attitude, you see, but it was very annoying to Lee.

MR. JENNER: That was another source of annoyance between them?

MR. DE MOHRENSCHILDT: Yes; there were so many sources of annoyance, as you know, that it was just an unhappy marriage.

MR. JENNER: You have stated at one time Oswald gave you something to read that he had written.

MR. DE MOHRENSCHILDT: Yes; I don't remember at what particular time, but he gave me to read his typewritten memoirs of his stay in Minsk.

MR. JENNER: Was it in the form of a diary?

MR. DE MOHRENSCHILDT: Yes, more or less the form of a diary, not day by day, but just impressions. And as far as I remember, I read through these typewritten pages, I don't remember how many of them there were, and made comments on it, you see. But I don't think they were fit for publication.

MR. JENNER: Were they political in nature?

MR. DE MOHRENSCHILDT: No; not political in nature, but there was nothing particularly interesting to an average person to read. It was just a description of life in a factory in Minsk. Not terribly badly written, not particularly well.

MR. JENNER: Not good, not bad?

MR. DE MOHRENSCHILDT: Not good, not bad. Nothing that I really remember too well. I don't remember too well what was written there.

MR. JENNER: I will show the witness pages 220 through 244, Commission Document No. 206. Would you glance through those pages and tell me if it has the material he showed you?

MR. DE MOHRENSCHILDT: No; I don't remember seeing that beginning.

MR. JENNER: Let's get over to the area in Minsk.

MR. DE MOHRENSCHILDT: No; that is not at all familiar to me.

MR. JENNER: The witness is now looking at page 232.

MR. DE MOHRENSCHILDT: Starting here at the bottom of page 232 it looks familiar to me. How many mistakes he makes here, it is terrible. It does not look familiar to me. I think it was something else that he showed me. I do not recall that. That I definitely do not remember.

MR. JENNER: What?

MR. DE MOHRENSCHILDT: I would have remembered that sentence, you know.

MR. JENNER: You are now on page 235: "I am having a light affair with Nell Korobka."

MR. DE MOHRENSCHILDT: I would have remembered something like that, you see. Again another sentence I do not recall.

MR. JENNER: "My conquest of Anna Tachina, a girl from Riga."

MR. DE MOHRENSCHILDT: Do you want me to glance through that? It does not look like the same document.

MR. JENNER: If it is not the same document.

MR. DE MOHRENSCHILDT: No; I don't think it is the same document.

MR. JENNER: Now I will have the witness look at pages 247 through 301. This is a composition entitled "The Collective" and "Minsk, Russia," with a foreword, an autobiographical sketch of Oswald. I will direct your attention to some of these headings, "Description of Radio Factory," "Quota Conditions," "Description of TV Shop," "Background of Shops," "Individual Workers," "Controls of Collectives," "Demonstrations in Meetings," "Factory Makeup," and "Peoples," "Layout of City of Minsk," "Tourist Permits and Tourist Passports," "Collective Farms and Schools, Vacations."

MR. DE MOHRENSCHILDT: No; I don't remember this document, but I think I remember something, "Layout of City of Minsk," because that would have attracted my attention.

MR. JENNER: All right, let's find that spot.

MR. DE MOHRENSCHILDT: That looks familiar to me.

MR. JENNER: First there is a heading, "About the Author." I call your attention to a statement which says, "Exotic journeys on his part to Japan and the Philippines and the scores of odd islands in the Pacific." Did he ever discuss that with you?

MR. DE MOHRENSCHILDT: No.

MR. JENNER: He was at Subic Bay in the Philippines?

MR. DE MOHRENSCHILDT: No; I don't remember him mentioning that to me.

MR. JENNER: Now the witness is looking at part 1, which is on page 248.

MR. DE MOHRENSCHILDT: Yes; this looks slightly, vaguely familiar, starting from page 248. That looks vaguely familiar. I am not going to read all this because it looks very boring to me. I mean it is something that doesn't interest me. It looks vaguely familiar.

MR. JENNER: Does it also refresh your recollection of discussions you had with him before his life in Russia?

MR. DE MOHRENSCHILDT: That looks familiar to me.

MR. JENNER: This whole division?

MR. DE MOHRENSCHILDT: This whole division looks familiar to me. As I said before, I did not look carefully when I originally saw this document, and I think this is the same one, because it looks familiar to me. I just glanced through. I realized that it is not fit for publication. You can see it right away. Who is interested to read about comrade this and comrade that, you see? But it is a factual, it seems like a factual report on his conditions of life of a worker.

MR. JENNER: It is horrible grammar.

MR. DE MOHRENSCHILDT: Horrible grammar.

MR. JENNER: And horrible spelling.

MR. DE MOHRENSCHILDT: Yes.

MR. JENNER: But it could be reworked by somebody?

MR. DE MOHRENSCHILDT: That is right.

MR. JENNER: Let's get to the next division here.

MR. DE MOHRENSCHILDT: Here is something that I remember we discussed.

MR. JENNER: You are now at page 262.

MR. DE MOHRENSCHILDT: I think here he talks about those meetings.

MR. JENNER: That he did not like?

MR. DE MOHRENSCHILDT: That he did not like. Do I have to read that? Frankly, it is very—

MR. JENNER: No; you don't. We are trying to find out whether this is the paper he showed you.

MR. DE MOHRENSCHILDT: Here is something.

MR. JENNER: I now direct your attention to page 269.

MR. DE MOHRENSCHILDT: This is something that is much more familiar to me because I was interested in the town itself.

MR. JENNER: And this is the paragraph beginning, "The reconstruction of Minsk is an interesting story reflecting the courage of its builders."

MR. DE MOHRENSCHILDT: Yes; that was something that interested me because I lived in my childhood in this town and I remembered some of the buildings. I remember asking Oswald about what happened to this street and that street, you see. But I forgot the names. I just described them. What happened to this street and that street? He gave me some sort of an

answer that now it is full of big buildings, you see, and I remember it as
being full of small provincial houses, you see. And again I cannot swear
to the fact that that is the same paper I saw.

MR. JENNER: But this seems to you more familiar?

MR. DE MOHRENSCHILDT: More familiar maybe because I paid more attention to the city than I paid to something else.

MR. JENNER: This is quite a long diatribe.

MR. DE MOHRENSCHILDT: It couldn't be the same document because that
wasn't as long as that.

MR. JENNER: It was not?

MR. DE MOHRENSCHILDT: No.

MR. JENNER: I now exhibit to the witness a series of five untitled composi-
tions on political subjects appearing in the same exhibit I have already
identified, the first of which is at page 304.

MR. DE MOHRENSCHILDT: This is definitely not familiar to me.

MR. JENNER: And runs through page 309.

MR. DE MOHRENSCHILDT: I am just glancing through but it doesn't look
familiar to me. Maybe I just didn't pay any attention.

MR. JENNER: The next commences on page 310 and runs through to page
312. It is a short one.

MR. DE MOHRENSCHILDT: No; that doesn't look familiar to me.

MR. JENNER: The next commences at page 313 and concludes at page 315.

MR. DE MOHRENSCHILDT: It does not look familiar to me. As I said before,
I have the impression that the pages he showed me were only about the
city of Minsk and the TV factory there, but not about his life.

MR. JENNER: Were they typewritten or in longhand?

MR. DE MOHRENSCHILDT: Typewritten.

MR. JENNER: The balance is on pages 318 through 329. Would you glance
through those, please?

MR. DE MOHRENSCHILDT: Oh, that is definitely nothing that I have seen before, because it has the name of General Walker in it.

MR. JENNER: And you had not seen it?

MR. DE MOHRENSCHILDT: No; I had not seen it. Now, the publication, not
the publication, the document I saw was, as far as I remember, not political, but a very simple account of his life in Minsk, and in the TV factory.

MR. JENNER: I think we had better call Mrs. De Mohrenschildt and tell her—

MR. DE MOHRENSCHILDT: That she is ready for action?

MR. JENNER: No; that we are going to run you well into the afternoon. I have
got a couple more pages of notes here. Maybe around 3:30 will be closer.

MR. JENNER: As I recall, yesterday you testified your recollection was that early in your acquaintance with the Oswalds, you approached Sam Ballen to see if he could undertake or might be able to employ Oswald.

MR. DE MOHRENSCHILDT: Yes.

MR. JENNER: To refresh your recollection in that regard, Mr. Ballen says his recollection is that he first met Lee in December 1962 or January 1963 at your home.

MR. DE MOHRENSCHILDT: It could be.

MR. JENNER: And he was aware that you had approached Mr. Ballen's wife and other people to assist the Oswalds, and also to have them out socially.

MR. DE MOHRENSCHILDT: Yes.

MR. JENNER: You did do that, did you?

MR. DE MOHRENSCHILDT: Yes, I don't remember whether I asked the Ballens to invite them, but I did ask some other people to invite them, because they were so lonesome. And maybe fortunately for them, they refused. I remember I asked a physicist to invite them in Dallas, and they just refused. He said, "I don't know those people. I don't want to have anything to do with them."

MR. JENNER: His recollection is about ten days after he met them at your home, you called him and asked if he might be able to employ him, or might be helpful in his obtaining a job. Does that stimulate your recollection that the events you mentioned yesterday occurred probably in December 1962 or January 1963—that is, the event regarding your effort to induce Mr. Ballen?

MR. DE MOHRENSCHILDT: Yes—it should be probably at that time, because I had the impression that it was earlier than that—when he was moving from Fort Worth to Dallas, at the very beginning. I still have the impression. Because that is where I was interested, to help them, you see. I did not know that he lost his job with the other company. I didn't know that. All this is later, after we had already gone. So I have the impression that maybe he confused the time. It seems to me that I asked him at the very beginning when I met the Oswalds, when he lost his first job in Fort Worth and was trying to move to Dallas—that was the time.

MR. JENNER: He lost his job at Leslie Welding Co.

MR. DE MOHRENSCHILDT: Yes. I don't know the name of that company, but it was some welding outfit.

MR. JENNER: Sheetmetal work.

MR. DE MOHRENSCHILDT: Yes, that is right.

MR. JENNER: Do you recall the period when Marina stayed at the Fords, in November?

MR. DE MOHRENSCHILDT: When she stayed at the Fords?

MR. JENNER: Yes.

MR. DE MOHRENSCHILDT: That was the time when we took Marina and the child away from Lee and put her in the house of Mellers, and then the Mellers asked Mrs. Ford to take her. I think that was the time. And then, later on, the Fords asked Mrs. Ray to take Marina. She moved from one place to another—three times, as far as I remember, she changed domiciles. And finally returned to Lee.

MR. JENNER: You remember this event you related yesterday, when you took Marina from the home?

MR. DE MOHRENSCHILDT: Yes.

MR. JENNER: As having occurred.—

MR. DE MOHRENSCHILDT: In September. I have the impression it was in September. But it is, again, only a recollection, because I remember that it was a very hot day—very sunny, hot day. So it could be in October. And also in October we started working on this campaign, cystic fibrosis campaign, and were very busy. But it might have been in October.

MR. JENNER: Mrs. Ford's recollection is that Marina was at her home—she came there on November 11, and left on November 17.

MR. DE MOHRENSCHILDT: It could be that.

MR. JENNER: And this is while Marina was separated temporarily from her husband?

MR. DE MOHRENSCHILDT: Yes. Unless she had been twice at her home. I think she was only once at her home. There were three homes—once at Mellers, the Fords, and the third at the Rays, one after another, in succession.

MR. JENNER: Now, this is apparently part of that series of changes she made when she left, herself—that is, this was not an occasion when you took her?

MR. DE MOHRENSCHILDT: No; I think that is the occasion we took her—we took her to the Mellers, and then she moved from them by herself—that we had no knowledge of. How she moved or who took her from one house to another, I do not know.

MR. JENNER: You have a recollection there were two periods—one period that you are talking about when you took her from the home, and then, another period when she left the home, herself?

MR. DE MOHRENSCHILDT: That could be, very easily. But then it would fit very well in my schedule that would have been the second time because, at that time, we were not seeing the Oswalds. We were busy on something else, Jeanne was working both in the store and at the foundation, I was preparing my project, and we were very busy, and didn't see anybody, practically, and especially the Oswalds. October, November; I don't think we saw them at all in October, November, December.

MR. JENNER: Did I ask you about Betty MacDonald this morning, as to whether she was at that February 1963 party?

MR. DE MOHRENSCHILDT: Oh, yes; I think that is the librarian. The name MacDonald sounds familiar to me. Is she Pierce's fiancé? That is how I remember her.

MR. JENNER: I am just trying to get these two events. Marina recalls when they lived on Elsbeth Street she had a dispute with Lee, and—about her Russian friends, in which he said, "Well, if you like your friends so much, then go ahead and live with them." And she said that left her no choice, so she got in a cab and went over to Anna Meller's house with the baby.

MR. DE MOHRENSCHILDT: Oh, that is how she described it.

MR. JENNER: She was there a week.

MR. DE MOHRENSCHILDT: That was the second time? What month was it?

MR. JENNER: I don't know.

MR. DE MOHRENSCHILDT: Well, we took her there. But maybe she went there for the second time, you see.

MR. JENNER: Well, she may have forgotten you took her.

MR. DE MOHRENSCHILDT: Yes; maybe she forgot it. You know, we took all the furniture also. I could not forget that—because my car was loaded. You could practically feel the ground. I still have the same car in Haiti today. We had a tremendous load in our car. It took us the whole day to load and unload and carry them.

MR. JENNER: Now, she voiced the opinion that—she said Lee liked you.

MR. DE MOHRENSCHILDT: I am sorry that he did but, obviously, he did.

MR. JENNER: She said because you were a strong person. She is expressing her opinion now, of course. But he only liked you among all this group. He disliked Bouhe, he disliked Anna Meller.

MR. DE MOHRENSCHILDT: That I am surprised, because Bouhe is very—a person that you can like or dislike immediately. As to Mrs. Meller, I am surprised, because she is very kind and a nice person.

MR. JENNER: Well, this is Lee Oswald. That could possibly arise out of the fact that Anna Meller befriended her when she left the household.

MR. DE MOHRENSCHILDT: That is right.

MR. JENNER: I don't know what the reason was. But you have confirmed the fact that he didn't care for the people in the Russian colony.

MR. DE MOHRENSCHILDT: He did not have any friends, you see. Maybe he identified me not as a Russian, because I have not much Russian blood in me anyway. Maybe he identified me as some sort of an internationalist, American.

MR. JENNER: Maybe you are.

MR. DE MOHRENSCHILDT: I am trying to think of other friends that he had. I cannot recall, myself, a friend of his, actually. I could not say that. He could be my son in age, you see. He is just a kid for me, with whom I played around. Sometimes I was curious to see what went on in his head. But I certainly would not call myself a friend of his.

MR. JENNER: Well, that may well be. But Marina, at least, expresses herself that way—that you "were the only one who remained our friend."

MR. DE MOHRENSCHILDT: She said we were the only ones—

MR. JENNER: Who remained their friends—the others sort of removed themselves.

MR. DE MOHRENSCHILDT: Sure, we left, you know. We were no friends, nothing. We just were too busy to be with them—period.

MR. JENNER: I am not talking about you. I am talking about the other people now. As you related this morning, they began to withdraw.

MR. DE MOHRENSCHILDT: Yes; and we were too busy. We saw them—we withdrew also to an extent—you see what I mean. We saw a lot of them at the beginning, and then we stopped seeing them. Then we saw them again for Christmas and invited them to another party, and that is all. Then we saw them the last time for Easter. I am not defending myself for having seen them. But that is a fact.

MR. JENNER: Well, I appreciate that. What was your impression as to whether this was a hospitable man?

MR. DE MOHRENSCHILDT: Who, Oswald?

MR. JENNER: Oswald. Was he a man who was not very hospitable?

MR. DE MOHRENSCHILDT: No; I would not say so. To us, he was always quite hospitable.

MR. JENNER: To you, I appreciate that. I am trying to find out—

MR. DE MOHRENSCHILDT: About the others, I don't know, because I never saw anybody else there in the house. I don't know how he would receive the people. I think he responded by kindness with kindness. He was responsive to kindness.

MR. JENNER: Was there an impression among the people in this—we have talked about, that they came to feel that he didn't care for them?

MR. DE MOHRENSCHILDT: Oh, yes, yes; he didn't care for them because—well, let me put it this way. He didn't care for them because they didn't care for him, and vice versa. But you see most of the colony in Dallas is more emotionally involved in Russian affairs than we are, because they are closer to them. All of them have been relatively recently in Soviet Russia—while my wife has never been in Soviet Russia in her life, and I was 5 or 6 when I left it. So to me it doesn't mean very much. I am curious, but it doesn't mean anything—it is too far removed.

MR. JENNER: Did he ever express any views to you or give you the impression that he thought these people who had left Russia were fools for having left Russia?

MR. DE MOHRENSCHILDT: No; I don't think so. I don't remember that. Possibly he told somebody else. But not in my presence.

MR. JENNER: Did he express any view to you or did you get the impression that these people in this colony or group, they only liked money, and everything was measured by money?

MR. DE MOHRENSCHILDT: Well, naturally—he didn't tell that to me, but you can guess that that would be his opinion, because he was jealous of them. I tried to induce him a few times to get on to some money-making scheme. I said, "Why don't you do something to make money?" But, obviously, it wasn't interesting to him. Would you like me to say what I told you about this Solidarist?

MR. JENNER: Yes.

MR. DE MOHRENSCHILDT: You were interested—you asked me if I belonged to some political party, and I said no. This group of Russian refugees called themselves Solidarists. And Mr. and Mrs. Voshinin in Dallas belonged to that group and tried to make me join it. Not being interested, I refused, but I read some of their publications. And it is a pro-American group of Russian refugees who have an economic doctrine of their own. And they seem to have some people working in the Soviet Union for them, and all that sort of thing. It is a pretty well-known political party that—their headquarters is in Germany. That is about all I know about them.

MR. JENNER: But that group didn't interest you?

MR. DE MOHRENSCHILDT: No, no; nor any other group.

MR. JENNER: I notice in the papers at my disposal some participation on your part in a foreign council discussion group in Dallas.

MR. DE MOHRENSCHILDT: Yes; I belonged to that group—I don't remember during what period—and came quite often to the meetings.

MR. JENNER: What is the name of it?

MR. DE MOHRENSCHILDT: The Dallas Council of World Affairs. I met quite a few people at the meetings. But they were open, public meetings, where international affairs were discussed. I remember several of the Dallas real conservatives called that Dallas council very leftist. But I never noticed anything in particular.

MR. JENNER: Were there people of substance that participated in that group?

MR. DE MOHRENSCHILDT: Yes; very much so. Mr. Marcus was the president of it. Mr. McGee was the president of it. Mr. Mallon was president of that, and actually organized this group. Mr. Mallon is chairman of the board of Dresser Industries. But they invited some people to Dallas who are possibly socialists—I don't remember seeing anyone, but I guess they might have invited them.

MR. JENNER: Did you on any occasion express a view to or say to anybody in Dallas among your friends that Oswald was an idealistic Marxist?

MR. DE MOHRENSCHILDT: Yes; I might have said that.

MR. JENNER: What did you mean by that?

MR. DE MOHRENSCHILDT: That he had read and created some sort of a theory, a Marxist theory, for himself. In other words, he created a doctrine for himself, a Marxist doctrine.

MR. JENNER: Is that what you meant by use of the word "Idealist"?

MR. DE MOHRENSCHILDT: Yes; that it was an idea in his head that he had—not in a very flattering way I meant that. That he was building up a doctrine in his head.

MR. JENNER: Did you ever say anything to anybody on the subject that Oswald was opposed to the United States policy on Castro in Cuba?

MR. DE MOHRENSCHILDT: That I think he mentioned to me a couple of times.

MR. JENNER: What did he say?

MR. DE MOHRENSCHILDT: I do not remember the exact wording, but he said that he had admiration for Castro for opposing such a big power as the United States.

MR. JENNER: Did the Voshinins ever ask you not to bring the Oswalds to their house?

MR. DE MOHRENSCHILDT: Yes. They refused to see and to meet the Oswalds, either one of them. And I was quite surprised, frankly, why they didn't, because we all did and at first helped them—and they usually were very cooperative in helping the other people. In this particular case, they completely refused and looked sort of mysterious—why they didn't want to meet them. I never asked any questions. But that is their privilege, not to see them.

MR. JENNER: Do you remember the days you were in Abilene?

MR. DE MOHRENSCHILDT: Yes, sir.

MR. JENNER: Do you recall having discussed politics there, in which you indicated, whether in provocation or otherwise, some admiration for the Soviet system of government?

MR. DE MOHRENSCHILDT: No; I don't remember saying anything like that. It might have been misinterpreted. But I believe in peaceful coexistence. I think we can all live together without blowing each other to hell—and many other people believe that we couldn't do that. Probably the person with whom I was discussing it believed in immediate atomic retaliation. So, naturally, I told him what the hell.

MR. JENNER: Do you recall having said that if this country is ever invaded by Russia, you would have a very good chance of coming into a top position with the Russians if they invaded the United States?

MR. DE MOHRENSCHILDT: I never said that. That is a purely Texas invention. It must have been a real enemy of mine who said that.

MR. JENNER: You are intellectually opposed to the Communist system?

MR. DE MOHRENSCHILDT: Yes; I am. I am not interested in it—period.

MR. JENNER: You wrote—I don't know whether it was after your 8 or 9 months in Mexico, when you were enamored of Lilia Larin, or whether it was on this previous occasion—when you were at the University of Texas, had you written or were you writing a manuscript entitled *Experiences of a Young Man in Mexico*?

MR. DE MOHRENSCHILDT: Yes, yes; but that is more or less a romantic dissertation, a romantic book based on some of my experiences there.

MR. JENNER: Did you relate some of your romantic experiences?

MR. DE MOHRENSCHILDT: Well, is it absolutely necessary? I don't recall even what I had written there.

MR. JENNER: I just wanted the general nature of it.

MR. DE MOHRENSCHILDT: I don't recall what it is. It is probably based on the travel in Mexico with some girls—that is about all. That is what I would write at that time and that age.

MR. JENNER: You were interested in girls?

MR. DE MOHRENSCHILDT: Yes, at that time.

MR. JENNER: Did you ever have any people refer to you as the Mad Russian?

MR. DE MOHRENSCHILDT: That is an unfortunate term they call me quite often.

MR. JENNER: You mentioned somebody from Brazil that had the sobriquet of King of Bananas. Was that the King of Orchids rather than the King of Bananas?

MR. DE MOHRENSCHILDT: Well, maybe. But we called him the King of Bananas. At least I called him that. I remember his name now—I mentioned it to you. Dr. Decio de Paulo Machado. I still—I think he is still in existence, because I asked about him recently.

MR. JENNER: If I said you were an extrovert, would that agree with your own judgment of yourself?

MR. DE MOHRENSCHILDT: Well, I don't know if it is for others to call me. I would rather be an extrovert than an introvert.

MR. JENNER: Well, for example, I regard myself as an extrovert.

MR. DE MOHRENSCHILDT: Then I am happy to be an extrovert. I don't like to be accused of being too much of an extrovert, because I think if you pass the limit it is too much.

MR. JENNER: Of course. Any extreme is bad. I made a reference yesterday to Professor Zitkoff, in Houston. I thought that might stimulate your recollection. Did you make regular trips to Houston?

MR. DE MOHRENSCHILDT: Yes; quite often.

MR. JENNER: Were they substantially regular—once a month?

MR. DE MOHRENSCHILDT: No, no. Without regularity, but quite often—mainly to see my clients there.

MR. JENNER: And your clients were who?

MR. DE MOHRENSCHILDT: In the oil business—I mainly used to come to see my friend John Jacobs, vice president of Texas Eastern, and the social acquaintances that I had there—Andy Todd, an architect there, a professor at Rice Institute. And maybe somebody else I don't recall the name.

MR. JENNER: But these trips to Houston were strictly business?

MR. DE MOHRENSCHILDT: Yes. Maybe I was trying at the time to push forward my project in Haiti, you see, whereby I was trying to raise some money for the development of small industries in Haiti. And on that occasion I saw quite a few important people. But purely for that purpose—purely for business.

MR. JENNER: All right. Is your daughter, Alexandra, a painter or an artist?

MR. DE MOHRENSCHILDT: No; my wife's daughter is a painter.

MR. JENNER: Christiana?

MR. DE MOHRENSCHILDT: Yes.

MR. JENNER: Was there a time when both Christiana and your daughter were living in Dallas with you?

MR. DE MOHRENSCHILDT: Yes, indeed.

MR. JENNER: In your 1957 venture with the International Cooperation—as an agent of the International Cooperation Administration, in addition to Poland, as I understand it, you visited France?

MR. DE MOHRENSCHILDT: Yes.

MR. JENNER: Switzerland?

MR. DE MOHRENSCHILDT: No. Sweden and Denmark.

MR. JENNER: France, Sweden and Denmark?

MR. DE MOHRENSCHILDT: Yes.

MR. JENNER: Had you in mind, or did you hope during that period, that you would also visit Switzerland, England, Italy, and West Germany?

MR. DE MOHRENSCHILDT: Yes; but I didn't see those countries—I didn't have time to see them. Instead of that, I stayed much longer in Sweden, visiting some distant relatives there.

MR. JENNER: Did you have any political discussions with any so-called true Communists when you were in Yugoslavia?

MR. DE MOHRENSCHILDT: Political discussions?

MR. JENNER: Arguments?

MR. DE MOHRENSCHILDT: Arguments; yes. Discussions, occasionally. The real argument I had—I think maybe I mentioned it yesterday—was with the head of the Communist Party in Slovenia, who attacked me very strongly for being an American and for the fact that we had this Arkansas case, with Governor Faubus. He was very obnoxious, and I told him that he reminded me of an ultraconservative in the United States—they were both of the same type, very illogical and very biased in their opinions.

MR. JENNER: Biased and rigid?

MR. DE MOHRENSCHILDT: Yes; but I think in my stay in Yugoslavia, and without taking too much pride in it, I made more friends for the United States than anybody else, because they could—I could explain to them the opportunities given to foreign born in the United States, and how joyful the life is in the States. For instance, I used to explain to them how an independent can drill an oil well with no money. To them it was beyond comprehension. To them it was a miracle that a man like me was able to promote enough money to drill an oil well. For them, it needed endless bureaucracy and enormous amount of papers and all that, and finally the well was drilled, and at an enormous price when it could have been done very cheaply by purely organizing a small syndicate. And since I had small production of my own, I explained to them how I did that. And it was a fascinating story for them. So I think I did a good job and made a lot of friends, who used to write to me from there.

MR. JENNER: Did you make a trip to Europe in 1960? At that time, did you plan to leave early in March, March 11, and visit France, Yugoslavia, England, and Belgium, for a period of 3 weeks, on geological visits?

MR. DE MOHRENSCHILDT: There might have been some projects to do that, and it did not materialize.

MR. JENNER: Maybe this will stimulate you. You, at that time, were at the Statler Hilton Hotel in Washington, D.C.?

MR. DE MOHRENSCHILDT: In 1960?

MR. JENNER: March 10, as a matter of fact. Do you remember your passport being renewed on March 11?

MR. DE MOHRENSCHILDT: Did I go to Europe or not? I don't remember. Maybe I went to Ghana at that time, in 1960 instead of going to Belgium—I went on this consulting job to Ghana. I don't recall. My wife will recall all that precisely, because she remembers the dates. I did go to Europe in 1960, because I remember I went to see my little boy in Philadelphia at that time before going to Europe. I was planning to. But my wife will remember all that.

MR. JENNER: So we can identify you as far as these papers are concerned, is this a fair description of you? That you are a white male, 6'1" tall, brown hair—dark brown hair, blue eyes—do you have a scar on your face?

MR. DE MOHRENSCHILDT: This scar is an old scar on the right-hand side, I think you can see.

MR. JENNER: Right-hand cheek?

MR. DE MOHRENSCHILDT: On the cheek—it comes from a dog bite in my childhood. And this one is a new one, I got it in Yugoslavia.

MR. JENNER: That is about the center of your forehead, up top, near your hairline?

MR. DE MOHRENSCHILDT: Yes.

MR. JENNER: You suffered that in Yugoslavia?

MR. DE MOHRENSCHILDT: Yes; I fell down on a rock with my head—had a few stitches taken.

MR. JENNER: And your—

MR. DE MOHRENSCHILDT: By the way, I may say—my wife reminded me of it today—regarding the fact that I was taking sketches of so-called Coast Guard in Texas, in 1940 or 1941—of course, which I was not doing, because I was sketching the beach. The same thing happened to me in Yugoslavia, except that this time they were the Communists who thought

I was making sketches of their fortifications. Actually, I was also making drawings of the seashore. And this time they shot at us.

MR. JENNER: Shot?

MR. DE MOHRENSCHILDT: Shot. And they told me to get away—we were in a little boat. And they kept on shooting at me. And the bullets were hitting the water right around us—until we were away out into the sea. So I made a complaint to the U.S. Embassy in Belgrade, and some kind of an investigation was made. But this is an interesting correlation—that I am accused both by the Yugoslavs and here, also, making sketches. I should abandon making sketches in the future. No more painting.

MR. JENNER: You have a ruddy complexion, but also you have a dark skin.

MR. DE MOHRENSCHILDT: Yes.

MR. JENNER: Is that a pigmentation, or from being out in the sun?

MR. DE MOHRENSCHILDT: No; I spend a lot of time in the sun.

MR. JENNER: Your brother Dmitri is a naturalized American citizen, is he not?

MR. DE MOHRENSCHILDT: Yes; much earlier than myself, because I think he came to this country in the early twenties.

MR. JENNER: The records show he was naturalized November 22, 1926, in the U.S. district court at New Haven, which is where Yale University is located.

MR. DE MOHRENSCHILDT: Yes. He went to school at that time, to Yale.

MR. JENNER: Do those facts square with your recollection?

MR. DE MOHRENSCHILDT: Yes; approximately the right period. I remember he went to Yale with Rudy Vallee—they were roommates.

MR. JENNER: You mentioned that your brother came over to Europe and was in Belgium while you were still there, just before you came back to this country.

MR. DE MOHRENSCHILDT: No, no; before I came back for the first time to this country.

MR. JENNER: That is correct.

MR. DE MOHRENSCHILDT: Yes. Because it is my brother who helped me to arrange my passport and my entrance. He didn't help me financially, but arranged my permit.

MR. JENNER: To refresh your recollection, the passport records indicate that your brother applied for a passport for a visit in 1936, to visit Poland and France for 3 months, and for the purpose of visiting his family, and collecting material for magazine articles.

MR. DE MOHRENSCHILDT: Yes.

MR. JENNER: Does that square with your recollection?

MR. DE MOHRENSCHILDT: That is about the right time when I first saw him after many, many years—we took a trip together to see our father in Poland.

MR. JENNER: Now, at that time, he had already completed his work at Yale, had he not?

MR. DE MOHRENSCHILDT: Yes.

MR. JENNER: He obtained his degree at Yale in 1926?

MR. DE MOHRENSCHILDT: Yes. I don't know what year he completed.

MR. JENNER: Did he take some additional—

MR. DE MOHRENSCHILDT: Yes. He took a Ph.D. at Columbia. But I don't know what year he received his Ph.D.

MR. JENNER: Well, I would suggest to you it was 1927.

MR. DE MOHRENSCHILDT: Ph.D. at Columbia? I don't know the year exactly.

MR. JENNER: Your brother travels relatively frequently, does he not?

MR. DE MOHRENSCHILDT: Yes; he travels whenever he had—whenever he can get away from teaching.

MR. JENNER: And he is a Ph.D. and a professor at Dartmouth College?

MR. DE MOHRENSCHILDT: He is a full professor at Dartmouth College.

MR. JENNER: Hanover, New Hampshire?

MR. DE MOHRENSCHILDT: That is right. He also is editor of the *Russian Review*, a magazine.

MR. JENNER: Didn't he found that?

MR. DE MOHRENSCHILDT: Yes; he founded that magazine.

MR. JENNER: And what does he teach at Dartmouth?

MR. DE MOHRENSCHILDT: I think he is a professor of Russian culture, Russian civilization, history.

MR. JENNER: Do you recall—is this a description of him: He is a white male, 5 foot 11 inches tall, gray hair, brown eyes?

MR. DE MOHRENSCHILDT: Yes; very strong brown eyes, very dark brown eyes.

MR. JENNER: Unlike yours that are blue?

MR. DE MOHRENSCHILDT: Yes. He is brown eyed.

MR. JENNER: Did you see your brother when he visited Europe in 1957?

MR. DE MOHRENSCHILDT: Yes; an amazing thing happened. You know, he didn't know that we were in Europe.

MR. JENNER: Neither knew that the other was?

MR. DE MOHRENSCHILDT: Neither knew. And we bumped into each other in the most crowded street in Paris. It is an amazing coincidence.

MR. JENNER: Does your brother have a mustache?

MR. DE MOHRENSCHILDT: He used to. I don't think he has now. He may have grown it lately.

MR. JENNER: Your daughter Alexandra has another given name, hasn't she—Romeyn?

MR. DE MOHRENSCHILDT: Yes. That is a family name of the Piersons.

MR. JENNER: She was born April 17—December 25, 1943. We brought that out yesterday.

MR. DE MOHRENSCHILDT: Yes.

MR. JENNER: Christmas Day.

MR. DE MOHRENSCHILDT: Yes.

MR. JENNER: Did you ever know your wife Phyllis' parents, Simone Fleischer—Simone Fleischer Washington and Jack Stecker?

MR. DE MOHRENSCHILDT: No; I didn't know her real father. But I met her stepfather—Walter Washington Stecker.

MR. JENNER: She was the daughter of Simone Fleischer, and was adopted by Walter Washington?

MR. DE MOHRENSCHILDT: Yes.

MR. JENNER: Did you have any contact with the Dominican Embassy in 1958?

MR. DE MOHRENSCHILDT: In 1958, Dominican Embassy?

MR. JENNER: The month of April.

MR. DE MOHRENSCHILDT: Yes. I think I was invited to—Dominican Embassy. Yes.

MR. JENNER: Here in Washington?

MR. DE MOHRENSCHILDT: Yes. I was trying to work up some kind of concession, I think. I was working on some kind of oil deal, and tried to contact the Dominican Ambassador—purely for business reasons—some kind of an oil project which had to do with the Dominican Republic.

MR. JENNER: All right. Have you been in the Dominican Republic in the last—let's say the last 6 months?

MR. DE MOHRENSCHILDT: Yes; I was there several times. Number one in March 1963 on my way to Haiti to sign a contract with the Haitian Government, but spent only one night at the hotel there, between planes. It was necessary to stop there, because there was no right connection. Pan American arranged so that the passengers to Haiti would stop in the Dominican Republic for the night, and then leave the next morning.

MR. JENNER: Is that the first time you were ever in the Dominican Republic?

MR. DE MOHRENSCHILDT: That is the first time I have ever been there.

MR. JENNER: When next were you there?

MR. DE MOHRENSCHILDT: The next time we were with—let's see—yes; we were—my wife and I when we were coming to Haiti, exactly on the same—in the same, the same occasion, to spend the night.

MR. JENNER: Just spent overnight?

MR. DE MOHRENSCHILDT: Overnight, and take the plane the next morning, on our way to Haiti in June—I think the first or second of June in 1963. And then just recently, about a week ago, when I went to check on some mining possibilities, and get some information from the Bureau of Mines in the Dominican Republic. And again I went to San Juan, and then picked up my wife, and then brought her back into the Dominican Republic, finished getting the information, and returned to Haiti. And then again on the way to the United States now, just stopping there.

MR. JENNER: On this present trip?

MR. DE MOHRENSCHILDT: Yes; just stopping for 20 minutes.

MR. JENNER: Those have been your sole contacts in the Dominican Republic?

MR. DE MOHRENSCHILDT: Yes; to the best of my memory—yes; I remember now why I tried to contact the Dominican Embassy in 1957. Somebody told me I don't remember who—that they needed a consulting geologist in the Dominican Republic, and I tried to contact the ambassador, and never was able to see him.

MR. JENNER: Do you recall commenting, along with Mrs. De Mohrenschildt, that you know of no connection that did or could have existed between Lee Oswald and any organization or government because you thought nobody could stand him, and that you questioned his mental stability?

MR. DE MOHRENSCHILDT: That is right. I remember making that statement. I think it was in Port-au-Prince that I made that statement. Naturally anybody—who would—in our opinion, if he killed the President of the United States, he must have been mentally unstable. I could not find any other explanation. Or somebody might have paid him for it. But this is another speculation that came to me later on. But, again, it is purely speculation on our part.

MR. JENNER: Well, you had no—now that you have made that statement, I have to pursue it.

MR. DE MOHRENSCHILDT: By reading the papers, you know—we had no other information. By reading the papers and putting two and two together we started wondering, maybe there is something behind it, you see—especially I remember reading in one of the papers that—

APPENDIX B

MR. JENNER: Which papers are these—foreign language papers?

MR. DE MOHRENSCHILDT: No; American papers. We haven't read any foreign language papers. We get the *Miami Herald*, *New York Times*, we get Haitian papers, French language papers, of course. And I think in one of those papers it was said that Lee Oswald mentioned to his wife before the assassination that he was going to get some money.

MR. JENNER: So when you read that article—

MR. DE MOHRENSCHILDT: When I read that article, then the idea started coming—arising in my imagination.

MR. JENNER: Assuming the article was correct, that Oswald had said to Marina that he was going to get some money from some source?

MR. DE MOHRENSCHILDT: Yes; that is right.

MR. JENNER: But you knew of no such thing?

MR. DE MOHRENSCHILDT: No.

MR. JENNER: And you had no hint of it while you knew the Oswalds?

MR. DE MOHRENSCHILDT: No; when we knew the Oswalds, they were always in dismal poverty.

MR. JENNER: When you visited Dallas at the end of May 1963, before you went to Haiti, did you see the Oswalds then?

MR. DE MOHRENSCHILDT: No; I don't think so. My wife will tell you exactly. I don't think we had time to see anybody. We were just packing. As I recall it, I did receive a card, a postcard, from Oswald—I don't remember when—before we left the United States, saying, "We are in New Orleans," and giving the address. And I lost that card.

MR. JENNER: Did you write a letter to Mrs. Hugh D. Auchincloss in December of 1963?

MR. DE MOHRENSCHILDT: Yes; I don't remember the date, but I did write a letter to her.

MR. JENNER: From where?

MR. DE MOHRENSCHILDT: From Haiti.

MR. JENNER: You expressed your sympathy to her with respect to the death of her son-in-law, John Fitzgerald Kennedy?

MR. DE MOHRENSCHILDT: Yes.

MR. JENNER: Do you recall making this statement in the letter: "Since we lived in Dallas permanently last year and before, we had the misfortune to have met Oswald, and especially his wife Marina, sometime last fall."

MR. DE MOHRENSCHILDT: Yes.

MR. JENNER: What do you mean by the misfortune to have met Oswald and especially his wife Marina?

MR. DE MOHRENSCHILDT: Well, now, since all this happened, it causes—it is not pleasant to have known the possible assassin of the President of the United States. And since he is dead, it doesn't matter. But we still know Marina. We had the misfortune of knowing her—it caused us no end of difficulty, from every point of view.

MR. JENNER: That is what you meant by misfortune?

MR. DE MOHRENSCHILDT: Yes; and misfortune also now, when you look the situation over, it was just a misfortune that we helped them, that is all. We shouldn't have done it. We should have known better. And, actually—

MR. JENNER: Why should you have known better, Mr. De Mohrenschildt? What was wrong with what you did?

MR. DE MOHRENSCHILDT: Nothing wrong. But it is wrong that we were charitable to a person who turned out to be an assassin, maybe.

MR. JENNER: But you wouldn't have been charitable if you had any notion he might have been. So what you did was a spontaneous, normal thing of an outgoing person who wanted to help somebody. Is that a fair statement?

MR. DE MOHRENSCHILDT: Yes; it is correct. But still I regret that I have known him. I shouldn't have been so extroverted.

MR. JENNER: Do you recall saying in your letter, "Both my wife and I tried to help poor Marina, who could not speak any English, was mistreated by her husband. She and the baby were malnourished and sickly."

MR. DE MOHRENSCHILDT: That is correct.

MR. JENNER: That is all correct?

MR. DE MOHRENSCHILDT: Yes.

MR. JENNER: And you told me all about that in some detail.

MR. DE MOHRENSCHILDT: Yes.

MR. JENNER: You also said, if you will recall—"sometime last fall we heard that Oswald had beaten his wife cruelly, so we drove to their miserable place and forcibly took Marina and the child away from the character."

MR. DE MOHRENSCHILDT: That is right.

MR. JENNER: And you have told me about that?

MR. DE MOHRENSCHILDT: That is right.

MR. JENNER: "Then he threatened me and my wife, but I did not take him seriously."

MR. DE MOHRENSCHILDT: That is exactly right.

MR. JENNER: "Marina stayed with a family of some childless Russian refugees for a while, keeping her baby, but finally decided to return to her husband." You have told me about that course of events.

MR. DE MOHRENSCHILDT: That is right.

MR. JENNER: And that is what you had in mind?

MR. DE MOHRENSCHILDT: That is exactly right.

MR. JENNER: Then you comment, "It is really a shame that such crimes occur in our times and in our country, but there is so much jealousy for success, and the late President was successful in so many domains, and there is so much desire for publicity on the part of all shady characters, that assassinations are bound to occur. Better precautions should have been taken." Now, let me ask you about the first two sentences.

MR. DE MOHRENSCHILDT: In my opinion, if Lee Oswald did kill the President, this might be the reason for it, that he was insanely jealous of an extraordinarily successful man, who was young, attractive, had a beautiful wife, had all the money in the world, and was a world figure. And poor Oswald was just the opposite. He had nothing. He had a bitchy wife, had no money, was a miserable failure in everything he did.

MR. JENNER: Well, do you have a view, perhaps, that this might be a way of this man—of what he thought of raising himself up by his own bootstraps?

MR. DE MOHRENSCHILDT: Exactly. It made him a hero in his own mind—it made him a hero in his own mind. He did not realize possibly that he was doing it at the expense to the whole nation. He might have had a mental blackout.

MR. JENNER: Then you make the comment "better precautions should have been taken."

MR. DE MOHRENSCHILDT: That is my very strong opinion, that better precautions should be taken by whatever authorities were in Dallas at the time to protect the President. Now, I do not consider myself an exceedingly—a genius. But the very first thought after we heard that some character was mixed up in the assassination of the President, when we were listening to the radio in the house of an employee of the American Embassy in Port-au-Prince, and he mentioned that the name of the presumable assassin is something Lee, Lee, Lee—and I said, "Could it be Lee Oswald?" And he said, "I guess that is the name."

MR. JENNER: That occurred to you?

MR. DE MOHRENSCHILDT: That occurred to me.

MR. JENNER: As soon as you heard the name Lee?

MR. DE MOHRENSCHILDT: As soon as I heard the name Lee. Now, why it occurred to me—because he was a crazy lunatic.

MR. JENNER: Did you think about the rifle you had seen?

MR. DE MOHRENSCHILDT: Immediately something occurred in my mind—

the rifle. Actually, my wife and I were driving from a reception at the Syrian Embassy, where we heard the story of the assassination. We were driving to the house of this friend of ours who works at the Embassy and wondering who could it be. And as soon as we heard that name, some association started working in our minds—and the fact that there was a gun there. But my opinion—and again—was influenced naturally by what you read and hear in the papers. We were out of contact with people in Dallas, and out of contact with events. The only thing we could judge is what we read in the papers. Sometimes you read something like he was going to get some money, and naturally you start thinking that possibly somebody bought him. Now, we heard, also, that he was getting some regular checks from somewhere.

MR. JENNER: Where did you hear that?

MR. DE MOHRENSCHILDT: That I read in the papers some place he was getting regular checks.

MR. JENNER: That didn't score with your recollection, did it?

MR. DE MOHRENSCHILDT: No; I just read that in the papers some place. Then you read this and that. I am not a detective. It is not up to me to make any conclusions.

MR. JENNER: This letter was written, I take it—it is dated December 12, 1963. At the time you wrote it you had some of these newspaper articles in mind that were affecting your opinion, were they?

MR. DE MOHRENSCHILDT: Yes; but it contains all the facts—

MR. JENNER: Excuse me. Have you looked at the original of that letter?

MR. DE MOHRENSCHILDT: Well, it looks to me that this is the original.

MR. JENNER: That is your signature on the letter?

MR. DE MOHRENSCHILDT: Yes.

MR. JENNER: You will note it is dated December 12, 1963.

MR. DE MOHRENSCHILDT: December 12, 1963.

MR. JENNER: Would you look at the envelope that is attached to the letter. Is that envelope addressed in your handwriting, or does it have any of your handwriting on it?

MR. DE MOHRENSCHILDT: No; it is printed.

MR. JENNER: Typed?

MR. DE MOHRENSCHILDT: Typed, yes.

MR. JENNER: And is that the envelope in which you dispatched that letter?

MR. DE MOHRENSCHILDT: Yes; it looks like that envelope.

MR. JENNER: What is the date of the stamp cancellation?

MR. DE MOHRENSCHILDT: December 13, 1963.

MR. JENNER: Where?

MR. DE MOHRENSCHILDT: Port-au-Prince, Haiti. It was sent from Haiti, this letter.

MR. JENNER: Yes; that is your letter, and you dispatched it?

MR. DE MOHRENSCHILDT: Yes.

MR. JENNER: Now, you say in that letter, after expressing your sympathies to Mrs. Auchincloss, and your very kind comments about Mrs. Kennedy, "I do hope that Marina and her children (I understand she has two now) will not suffer too badly throughout their lives, and that the stigma will not affect the innocent children. Somehow, I still have a lingering doubt, notwithstanding all the evidence, of Oswald's guilt."

MR. DE MOHRENSCHILDT: Exactly.

MR. JENNER: Now, please explain that remark in that letter.

MR. DE MOHRENSCHILDT: Unless the man is guilty, I will not be his judge unless he is proven to be guilty by the court, I will not be his judge, and there will be always a doubt in my mind, and throughout my testimony I explained sufficiently why I have those doubts. And mainly because he did not have any permanent animosity for President Kennedy. That is why I have the doubts.

MR. JENNER: And that expression in this letter is based on all the things you have told me about in this long examination?

MR. DE MOHRENSCHILDT: Yes.

MR. JENNER: A natural, I would assume, view on the part of any humanitarian person—that you just cannot imagine anybody murdering anybody else?

MR. DE MOHRENSCHILDT: Yes.

MR. JENNER: And he in turn had been murdered.

MR. DE MOHRENSCHILDT: Yes.

MR. JENNER: And his trial would never take place?

MR. DE MOHRENSCHILDT: That is right.

MR. JENNER: And on the basis of what little you knew, you had lingering doubts?

MR. DE MOHRENSCHILDT: Exactly.

MR. JENNER: Not because you felt that anybody else might have been involved?

MR. DE MOHRENSCHILDT: No, no.

MR. JENNER: And you had no notion of anybody else, and no information of anybody else being involved?

MR. DE MOHRENSCHILDT: No information.

MR. JENNER: I want to give you an opportunity to explain that fully.

MR. DE MOHRENSCHILDT: No; I have no information whatsoever, except what you hear now living in Port-au-Prince from the foreigners who read foreign papers. And, of course, they are all of the opinion that Oswald did not kill the President, that there was a plot, that there was—that somebody else was standing on the bridge, there was a car there on the bridge from where they were shooting, that there were four shots—and all those things are discussed all day long in Haiti right now, in the colony of foreigners—Embassy People and businessmen who live in Haiti, most of them Europeans, of course. They discuss it all day long.

MR. JENNER: And they are confining their judgment to what they read in the papers they receive from their homeland?

MR. DE MOHRENSCHILDT: Purely; yes—purely. As you know, there are sensational articles being published right now in Europe on that subject.

MR. JENNER: Mr. De Mohrenschildt, you know of no supposed facts that you have read in these foreign language newspapers, do you?

MR. DE MOHRENSCHILDT: Do I know what?

MR. JENNER: You don't know if there is any merit one way or another?

MR. DE MOHRENSCHILDT: No; I don't know of any merit one way or the other.

MR. JENNER: And this remark of yours in the letter to Mrs. Auchincloss was not intended to imply that?

MR. DE MOHRENSCHILDT: No, no; it was not. It was purely based on whatever was expressed in my testimony. And I think it will be fair to say that I will have that lingering doubt for the rest of my life.

MR. JENNER: You may have an opportunity to read the Commission report, which I assume you will.

MR. DE MOHRENSCHILDT: I wish you the best of luck.

MR. JENNER: You wrote Mrs. Auchincloss again, did you not, in February 2, 1964?

MR. DE MOHRENSCHILDT: Yes.

MR. JENNER: I hand you the envelope and letter. Do you identify those as being the letter you sent to her and the envelope in which the letter was enclosed?

MR. DE MOHRENSCHILDT: Yes; it is exactly the letter I have written.

MR. JENNER: This letter leads me then into your Haiti venture. Tell us about it. How did that arise, when did you first think about it?

MR. DE MOHRENSCHILDT: I started doing geological work in Haiti in 1956, I think, the first time, where I worked for some Haitian people connected with the Sinclair interests in Haiti. I worked up a geological prospect for oil and gas drilling in the northern part of Haiti, and we were able to sell the projects to a company in Tulsa, and finally the deal fell through because of the Cuban situation. In other words, the company did not want to drill in Haiti because of the expropriations going on in the Caribbean area. And the next time then I was in Haiti, as I explained before, after our trip—

MR. JENNER: That is the trip you made down there, Mexico and the Central American countries?

MR. DE MOHRENSCHILDT: Yes—in 1961—and started preparing this project from then on. Finally the project came to fruition in March 1963, and we left for Haiti—at the end of May 1963.

MR. JENNER: You made a trip to New York City before you went to Haiti, did you not?

MR. DE MOHRENSCHILDT: Yes.

MR. JENNER: The first part of May 1963?

MR. DE MOHRENSCHILDT: Yes.

MR. JENNER: About 2 weeks?

MR. DE MOHRENSCHILDT: Yes; New York, Philadelphia, Washington.

MR. JENNER: Visited your daughter?

MR. DE MOHRENSCHILDT: Visited my daughter. And also was in Washington preparing for the eventuality of this project, checking with the people, Bureau of Mines, and so forth.

MR. JENNER: Is there a gentleman by the name of Tardieu whom you were attempting to interest?

MR. DE MOHRENSCHILDT: No, no; he is actually interested, and he is a Frenchman living in Haiti, who was instrumental to an extent in getting this contract.

MR. JENNER: I hand you a document which we will mark "De Mohrenschildt Exhibit No. 1." (The document referred to was marked "De Mohrenschildt Exhibit No. 1" for identification.)

MR. JENNER: It appears to be a piece of promotional literature issued in connection with the Haiti venture. Am I correct about that?

MR. DE MOHRENSCHILDT: Yes, sir.

MR. JENNER: Did you send that to Mr. Raigorodsky?

MR. DE MOHRENSCHILDT: Yes.

MR. JENNER: Now, the upper portion is in French. Would you favor me by reading first that which is on the left, and then that which is on the right?

MR. DE MOHRENSCHILDT: That is a very long article. "A Magnificent Success for the Commercial Bank of Haiti." The result of a trip—

MR. JENNER: That is a headline?

MR. DE MOHRENSCHILDT: Headline.

MR. JENNER: All right.

MR. DE MOHRENSCHILDT: Shall I make a short resume of that?

MR. JENNER: I would prefer—can you translate that literally?

MR. DE MOHRENSCHILDT:

The recent trip to the United States of America by Mr. Clémard Joseph Charles, the active president and manager general of the bank, Commercial Bank of Haiti, has constituted a magnificent success for this banking establishment which is prospering right now.

In reality, during one of the most amicable ceremonies, the assistant mayor of New York, Mr. James O'Brien, has given to Mr. Clémard Joseph Charles the keys of the city of New York in the name of Mayor Wagner, who was at that time in Europe.

The dinners and lunches have been offered in honor of Mr. Clémard Charles, namely, by the American Express, Patent Resources, Inc., and the Hanover Trust Co. A short contact with Mr. Clémard Joseph Charles has permitted us to obtain certain information for the readers. The active president and director general of the Commercial Bank of Haiti has been able to conclude an important contract with one of the largest financial companies in New York which does business in the millions of dollars. This enterprise guaranteed by the Import-Export Bank, the Chase Manhattan Bank, and the Bank of America, will make possible to the Haitian importers of American merchandise through the Commercial Bank of Haiti the credits of unlimited amounts for 6 months and longer periods.

One other financial society which specialized in the real estate business which does business for some $150 million per year, will start through the intermediary of the Commercial Bank of Haiti a program of construction of houses whereby the credit will be given for 10 years.

A system of insurance will cover the construction and a house that will be given as a reward for the clients of the enterprise. Our country will be benefited with important advantages because of the interesting contracts taken by Mr. Clémard J. Charles, in New York. The president and the director general of the bank will take soon the plane for Canada and Mexico in order to follow on these important contracts which will be very favorable to our economy, and will permit the Commercial Bank of Haiti to be of further advantage to the people of Haiti.

MR. JENNER: You have read the two columns appearing under that heading that you described. Now, would you read the column to the right of those two columns?

MR. DE MOHRENSCHILDT:

Mr. C. J. Charles, honorary citizen of the city of New York. Mr. Clémard Joseph Charles, president and director of the Bank Commercial of Haiti, Port-au-Prince, has come back yesterday morning with his charming wife, Sophie, from a trip of 2 weeks in New York, and was accompanied by Mr. James R. Green, vice president of the Manufacturers Hanover Trust Co., which is a large bank of Wall Street, New York.

Mr. Green spent just a few hours in the capital, just sufficient time to visit the Commercial Bank with which Hanover Trust Co. wants to do business. Mr. Charles is very satisfied from the contacts which he has made during this trip, and satisfied with the promotion of his commercial bank. The Haitian banker was honored by Mayor Wagner of the city of New York, and has made his assistant, Mr. O'Brien, give the key of the city as an honorary citizen, to Mr. Charles.

MR. JENNER: Mr. Reporter, would you mark that "George S. De Mohrenschildt Exhibit No. 1"?

MR. DE MOHRENSCHILDT: This is by the way the photograph of a paper.

MR. JENNER: This is a Photostat of two news items, in the Haitian paper in Port-au-Prince, together with a telegram. Now, all those together comprised, did they, some of the promotion literature with respect to your Haitian venture?

MR. DE MOHRENSCHILDT: Yes.

MR. JENNER: In what respect? Can you give us the thrust of that?

MR. DE MOHRENSCHILDT: In the respect that they acquaint the possible investor with the personalities involved.

MR. JENNER: All right. Who is the gentleman who sent the telegram?

MR. DE MOHRENSCHILDT: Mr. Tardieu.

MR. JENNER: What is his first name?

MR. DE MOHRENSCHILDT: Mr. B. Juindine Tardieu, who is the agent and you might say a broker who negotiated the contract with the Haitian Government.

MR. JENNER: Well—

MR. DE MOHRENSCHILDT: He is domiciled in Haiti.

MR. JENNER: All right. Now, you had some correspondence with Clémard Joseph Charles?

MR. DE MOHRENSCHILDT: Yes.

MR. JENNER: Is the letter I now hand you, which we will identify as George S. De Mohrenschildt Exhibit No. 2, a photostatic copy of correspondence between you and that gentleman, a copy of which you transmitted to Paul Raigorodsky?

MR. DE MOHRENSCHILDT: Yes; that is the letter I received. (The document referred to was marked "George S. De Mohrenschildt Exhibit No. 2" for identification.)

MR. JENNER: Now I will show you a series of three documents, the first sheet consisting of a photostat of an envelope addressed, I believe in your handwriting, to Mr. Paul Raigorodsky; is that correct?

MR. DE MOHRENSCHILDT: Yes.

MR. JENNER: In Dallas. The next being a personal note of yours in your longhand to Mr. Raigorodsky; is that correct?

MR. DE MOHRENSCHILDT: Yes, indeed.

MR. JENNER: The next being in the form of a copy of a letter from you, dated July 27, 1962, to Mr. Jean de Menil.

MR. DE MOHRENSCHILDT: Yes.

MR. JENNER: In which you have written in the upper right-hand corner in your handwriting, "Copy for Mr. Raigorodsky." Is what I have said correct?

MR. DE MOHRENSCHILDT: Yes.

MR. JENNER: And lastly, there appears to be promotional literature, one sheet, dated August 1, 1962, signed by you at the bottom?

MR. DE MOHRENSCHILDT: Yes, indeed.

MR. JENNER: And on your letterhead—George De Mohrenschildt, Petroleum Geologist and Engineer, 1639–40 Republican National Bank Building, Dallas, Tex.

MR. DE MOHRENSCHILDT: Yes.

MR. JENNER: Mr. Reporter, would you mark those in the record, I have given them to you, as "De Mohrenschildt Exhibits 3, 4, 5, and 6." (The documents referred to were marked "De Mohrenschildt Exhibits 3, 4, 5, and 6" for identification.)

MR. JENNER: In addition to those materials, did you also transmit to Mr. Raigorodsky two additional documents which I have in my hand—one a photostatic copy of a Western Union telegram, dated August 3, 1963, from Tardieu to you, and the second document a copy of a letter of yours to the gentleman I mentioned a moment ago, Mr. Jean de Menil; dated

August 7, 1962, upon which there appears some handwritten notes of yours to Mr. Raigorodsky?

MR. DE MOHRENSCHILDT: Yes, sir.

MR. JENNER: Is that your handwriting?

MR. DE MOHRENSCHILDT: Yes, sir; that is right.

MR. JENNER: Mr. Reporter, mark those documents, if you will, as "De Mohrenschildt Exhibits 7 and 16." (The documents referred to were marked "De Mohrenschildt Exhibits 7 and 16" for identification.)

MR. JENNER: On September 12, you appear to have transmitted some additional materials to Mr. Raigorodsky. I hold in my hand three documents. The first, a photostatic copy of an envelope, with your letterhead in the upper left-hand corner, your Dallas office, addressed to Mr. Paul Raigorodsky. The second, a letter signed "George and Jeanne" over a typewritten signature, "Jeanne and George De Mohrenschildt." Is the George and Jeanne in handwriting your handwriting?

MR. DE MOHRENSCHILDT: Yes.

MR. JENNER: And this letter is dated September 12, 1963. You transmitted that letter to Mr. Raigorodsky?

MR. DE MOHRENSCHILDT: Yes, indeed.

MR. JENNER: In the envelope we have just identified. And did you also enclose the third document, which is a diagram of—

MR. DE MOHRENSCHILDT: Of the planned development in Haiti.

MR. JENNER: And it has in the lower left-hand corner in longhand "Credits available for these industries—George De M. Dallas, September 11, 1963." Is that your handwriting?

MR. DE MOHRENSCHILDT: Yes, indeed.

MR. JENNER: Did you also send Mr. Raigorodsky a map of Haiti, in which you—excuse me. Mr. Reporter, would you mark the three documents I have just identified as De Mohrenschildt Exhibits 8, 9, and 10. (The documents referred to were marked "De Mohrenschildt Exhibits 8, 9, and 10" for identification.)

MR. JENNER: Mr. Reporter, identify the next document as De Mohrenschildt Exhibit No. 11. (The document referred to was marked "De Mohrenschildt Exhibit No. 11" for identification.)

MR. JENNER: For the purpose of the record, it is the description map of Haiti. This is a map published by the Texaco Co., and it is available to anybody who wants to pick up a map at a gasoline service station, is it not?

MR. DE MOHRENSCHILDT: Yes.

MR. JENNER: It is not a fancy geologist's map, for example?

MR. DE MOHRENSCHILDT: No.

MR. JENNER: Did you send that to Mr. Raigorodsky?

MR. DE MOHRENSCHILDT: Yes, indeed.

MR. JENNER: There is some longhand on it, do you see that?

MR. DE MOHRENSCHILDT: Yes.

MR. JENNER: And is that your longhand?

MR. DE MOHRENSCHILDT: Yes.

MR. JENNER: In the upper right-hand corner—

MR. DE MOHRENSCHILDT: It shows the possibility for—

MR. JENNER: Excuse me. I just want you to read the words, and not elaborate. I am going to have you elaborate on them. There is in the upper right-hand corner first near the letter "A" of "Atlantic," an arrow pointing to the left, to a small island. What are the words there?

MR. DE MOHRENSCHILDT: "New resorts."

MR. JENNER: And then to the right of that inscription, there are three lines of words, and an arrow pointing to an area in which I see the word "Caracol." Read those words.

MR. DE MOHRENSCHILDT: "New resort, Chou-Chou Beach."

MR. JENNER: All right. Now, in the lower left-hand portion of the upper right-hand quadrant there appears an inscription with an arrow pointing to "Mont Rouis." And then below that, over what appears to be a series of islands encircled, there appears more writing.

MR. DE MOHRENSCHILDT: "Oil possibilities on this island."

MR. JENNER: All right. Do the words "on this island" appear?

MR. DE MOHRENSCHILDT: No. Just "oil possibilities."

MR. JENNER: I am just getting the wording first, and then I will have you explain it all later.

MR. DE MOHRENSCHILDT: "Our Shada concession."

MR. JENNER: Now, the words "Our Shada concession" are the words at the lead end of the arrow which points to Mont Rouis, which you have already identified in the record. Now, to the extreme right, and at the margin, opposite the inscriptions we have just described, there is some more writing. Would you read that?

MR. DE MOHRENSCHILDT: "Brown and Root built this dam."

MR. JENNER: All right. Now, there is an encirclement around—between the two we have identified, but above it looks as though the center of this island here—there is an inscription. This appears in the area—there is an X there—an airplane indication Hinche and there is some writing. What is that?

MR. DE MOHRENSCHILDT: "Oil possibilities."

MR. JENNER: All right. Now, Port-au-Prince is encircled. Then at the bottom, which is the lower right-hand quadrant, there is an arrow pointed to Pationville. And that arrow leads to some handwriting.

MR. DE MOHRENSCHILDT: "Ibolele Hotel."

MR. JENNER: Now, to the left of that inscription, and in the center of the map, the lower half, there is an encirclement that encircles an area, the chief town of which appears to be what?

MR. DE MOHRENSCHILDT: Lescayes.

MR. JENNER: And what is written there?

MR. DE MOHRENSCHILDT: "Oil possibilities."

MR. JENNER: Now, I guess we have gotten everything you have written on there. Now, with those papers, would you proceed to tell us now about your Haitian venture, and take those papers, since they seem to be in some order of sequence as to time, and tell us all about it.

MR. DE MOHRENSCHILDT: Well—

MR. JENNER: In other words, this venture is no mite, is it?

MR. DE MOHRENSCHILDT: No. It started—it already started by my previous work there in 1956. It is the result of many trips I took to Haiti in the meantime. And it is a result of an effort which started in 1961. I have in my possession a letter from the minister of mines which—

MR. JENNER: Of what country?

MR. DE MOHRENSCHILDT: Of Haiti. Dated in 1961, giving me an opportunity to present a geological survey of Haiti.

MR. JENNER: What was that to be for?

MR. DE MOHRENSCHILDT: This was to search and study the oil and gas and all the mineralogical points of the whole country.

MR. JENNER: Did this have anything, any purpose or intent, other than a legitimate effort on your part, on behalf of the Haitian Government, to you a petroleum engineer and geologist, to discover in Haiti mineral deposits that might be of economic value to Haiti, and to those who might be willing to risk their capital to develop it?

MR. DE MOHRENSCHILDT: This is the only purpose I have—purely business promotional project.

MR. JENNER: And this is in no way linked, directly, indirectly, or in any remote possibility, with any mapping of this country with great care for the possibility of its being employed by any other nation or group?

MR. DE MOHRENSCHILDT: No; no other nation could use my maps, and no other project, except our own commercial and geological project—

nothing else. Anyway, the whole Island of Haiti has been mapped in complete precision by the U.S. Government already, and the maps are available right here in Washington. And my office in Port-au-Prince, actually they are offices of Inter-American Geodetic Survey. On one side is the American representative of the Geodetic Survey, and on the other side I am doing my geological work in the same building. He helps me with some of his equipment, some of his advice, some of his maps, and we pursue our own work there. I employed in the last 8 months since we have been in Haiti an Italian geologist who came especially to Haiti from South America, with all the equipment, and stayed with us for several months. I employed a Swiss assistant. I employed—I am employing an American geologist right now, recommended by the University of Texas, who is living in Haiti with his family, and whose salary I am paying; I am responsible for him. I have also, in addition to that, employed a prospector from Alaska, an American. And I am employing a group of Haitian engineers and geologists, engineers, not geologists, because they don't have geologists. Engineers. And it is a project which—for which the Haitian Government is supposed to pay me $285,000, out of which they pay $20,000 in cash, and the rest they are paying from the interest in the sisal plantation at Mont Rouis. This plantation started to be operated jointly by Mr. Clémard J. Charles, president of the Commercial Bank of Haiti, and myself; and now Mr. Charles is operating it for me, doing all the administrative work, and I am pursuing my geological work. Up to now, we found some things which were indicated on the map here.

MR. JENNER: I don't want you to reveal any business secret, because I appreciate—all I am getting at is the general description of the project, and its good faith.

MR. DE MOHRENSCHILDT: That is right. I hope that this will be sufficiently justified in good faith.

MR. JENNER: And these documents we have identified are documents which you sent to Mr. Raigorodsky with what thought in mind?

MR. DE MOHRENSCHILDT: With the thought of having him eventually participate in various enterprises which may come out of it.

MR. JENNER: Such as?

MR. DE MOHRENSCHILDT: Such as development of small industries, development of oil production, development of new hotels and new resorts, et cetera. Because the country is open to new business and I think has excellent opportunities for American investments.

MR. JENNER: All right. Now, you have expressed an opinion, have you not, as to the activity or lack of activity on the part of the FBI in connection with the assassination of the President?

MR. DE MOHRENSCHILDT: Well, I think that they should have sent away from Dallas every suspicious person, like any other country would do—when somebody—when an important figure arrives to town, and there are deranged people, or people who have habits of shooting guns at targets or ones who have been traitors to their country to some extent, you know—any controversial people should be not necessarily put to jail, but sent away from the town.

MR. JENNER: And you have Lee Oswald in mind, do you?

MR. DE MOHRENSCHILDT: Yes; I have Lee Oswald in mind.

MR. JENNER: You assume that the FBI was aware that he had this weapon, and he was target practicing with it?

MR. DE MOHRENSCHILDT: That I do not know, whether they had that knowledge of the weapon. But it is not for me to judge them. But I think they should have known. If they didn't know, they should have known.

MR. JENNER: And I take it your opinion, whether they did or did not know of the weapon, they had other information with respect to Oswald's attempted defection and matters of that nature which you feel—

MR. DE MOHRENSCHILDT: They must have had that information.

MR. JENNER: And as an American citizen, it is your view that they should have done what?

MR. DE MOHRENSCHILDT: I think they should have—in my opinion, they shouldn't have let him come back to the United States—number one. And number two, the people like us should have been protected against even knowing people like Oswald. Maybe I am wrong in that respect.

MR. JENNER: Well, it is an opinion. That is all I am asking you for.

MR. DE MOHRENSCHILDT: And thirdly, Oswald was known as a violent character, especially in the last time. He was known, as I read from the papers, that he participated in pro-Castro demonstrations in New Orleans. That is what I read in the papers. And so therefore, he should have been kept away from Dallas when the President was there.

MR. JENNER: Mr. Reporter, would you mark the Auchincloss letter, dated February 2, 1964, and its accompanying envelope as De Mohrenschildt Exhibits 12 and 13, respectively? (The documents referred to were marked "De Mohrenschildt Exhibits 12 and 13," for identification.)

MR. JENNER: And the Auchincloss letter of December 12, 1963, and its accompanying envelope as De Mohrenschildt Exhibits 14 and 15, respectively. (The documents referred to were marked "De Mohrenschildt Exhibits 14 and 15," for identification.)

MR. DE MOHRENSCHILDT: All these contracts in Haiti have been made official by an act of the Congress of Haiti on March 13, 1963, and signed by the president of the country and by all the ministers, stipulating that the price of the geological survey would be $285,000, and the consideration for it will be the concession of the sisal in Haiti, originally an American company called Shada, built by the U.S. Department of Agriculture and developed during the war, and later on sold to the Haitian Government. This concession is given to me for the duration of 10 years, with an extended duration of 10 years more. I think that will explain it.

MR. JENNER: Fine.

MR. DE MOHRENSCHILDT: I could talk for hours about this project, because it was developed through so many years, and so much effort.

MR. JENNER: In order that the correspondence be complete, Mr. De Mohrenschildt has produced for me the response he received to his letter of December 12, 1963, to Mrs. Auchincloss. Mr. De Mohrenschildt, since it is a personal letter, I will ask you to read the letter in evidence. It has a longhand note on it. You might want to keep the original. So just read it. And just for the purpose of the record, and not because I am suspicious of you, I will watch you read it. It is on letterhead, 3044 O Street, Northwest, Washington, D.C.

MR. DE MOHRENSCHILDT: That is correct.

Dear George:

Thank you for your letter and for your sympathy for Jacqueline. Please accept my deepest sympathy in the loss of your son. How tragic for you.

It seems extraordinary to me that you knew Oswald and that you knew Jackie as a child. It is certainly a very strange world.

MR. JENNER: Hold it a minute. The second paragraph begins with the words "it seems."

MR. DE MOHRENSCHILDT:

You did not say why you were in Haiti, so I imagine that you are in our Foreign Service. If you come to Washington again, I would like to talk with you, and I would very much like to meet your wife. When you next write to Dmitri, will you send him my warmest regards, and thank him for his sympathy.

APPENDIX B

MR. JENNER: Dmitri is your brother?

MR. DE MOHRENSCHILDT: Yes.

MR. JENNER: Now, there is a longhand note.

MR. DE MOHRENSCHILDT: Yes.

I live now in Georgetown. Your letter has made me think a good deal. I hope too—that Mrs. Oswald will not suffer.

Very sincerely,
Janet Lee Auchincloss

MR. JENNER: Dated?

MR. DE MOHRENSCHILDT: Wednesday, January 29.

MR. JENNER: All right. You just keep that original.

MR. DE MOHRENSCHILDT: Thank you.

MR. JENNER: I show you what purports to be a transcript of a Christmas card, 1963, allegedly transmitted by you, appearing at page 3, Commission Document 703-F. Would you read it, please?

MR. DE MOHRENSCHILDT: This paragraph?

MR. JENNER: The whole card.

MR. DE MOHRENSCHILDT:

Merry Christmas and Happy New Year. Best wishes for 1964, George and Jeanne De M.

Alex is in New York State, supposedly working at some mental hospital. Gary Taylor takes care of Cousin Lil. Nancy is alive, still kicking. We are happy here. Appalled at the crimes in Dallas.

George

MR. JENNER: You transmitted that Christmas card with that inscription?

MR. DE MOHRENSCHILDT: Yes.

MR. JENNER: Now, would you explain your statement, "appalled at the crimes in Dallas"?

MR. DE MOHRENSCHILDT: Well, I mean the assassination of the President and subsequent assassination of Lee Oswald by Ruby, and the assassination by Oswald of this policeman—three assassinations, one after another.

MR. JENNER: All right. By the way, did you ever see Jack Ruby in the flesh?

MR. DE MOHRENSCHILDT: Never; no. On TV you mean?

MR. JENNER: No. Did you know him when you were in Dallas?

MR. DE MOHRENSCHILDT: No.

MR. JENNER: To the best of your recollection, had you ever seen him when you were in Dallas?

MR. DE MOHRENSCHILDT: Don't recall.

MR. JENNER: Was his name ever mentioned at any conversation that took place in the presence of Lee Oswald while you were present?

MR. DE MOHRENSCHILDT: Never.

MR. JENNER: Was at any time there any conversation, or did anything occur while you were in Dallas to lead you to believe directly or indirectly, or to any degree whatsoever, that Lee Oswald knew Jack Ruby?

MR. DE MOHRENSCHILDT: No, sir; not one indication.

MR. JENNER: Did anything occur in Dallas by way of any statements to you, statements made in your presence, or anything you noticed or saw, that would lead you at any time while you were in Dallas, to lead you to believe that Lee Oswald was ever in the Carousel Club in Dallas?

MR. DE MOHRENSCHILDT: No.

MR. JENNER: Did you try to interest Mr. Kitchel in your Haiti venture?

MR. DE MOHRENSCHILDT: Yes.

MR. JENNER: And he did not join?

MR. DE MOHRENSCHILDT: No.

MR. JENNER: That was a friendly gesture on your part, was it?

MR. DE MOHRENSCHILDT: Yes.

MR. JENNER: I am pleased to say to you that he so regarded it.

MR. DE MOHRENSCHILDT: I am glad to hear that.

MR. JENNER: That he thought you were in good faith, offering him an opportunity to participate, and you were not thinking in terms of any business advantage.

MR. DE MOHRENSCHILDT: No, no.

MR. JENNER: And that is the fact; is it?

MR. DE MOHRENSCHILDT: Yes; of course. I offered this project to quite a few people, and it so happened that at the time they were afraid of Haiti, and I am very happy to say that I am now the sole proprietor of the whole project. It may be all for the best.

MR. JENNER: I will show the witness pages 4, 5 and 6 and 7 of Commission Document No. 542. I wish to direct your attention primarily to the— what purports to be a letter from you to Mr. Kitchel, setting forth the background of information on a holding company that you were developing in Haiti. Would you read the letter?

MR. DE MOHRENSCHILDT: "Haitian Holding Company."

MR. JENNER: Excuse me. It may already be in evidence.

MR. DE MOHRENSCHILDT: "August 1, 1962."

MR. JENNER: I think not—but if you will hold a minute. What I have just shown you is a copy of De Mohrenschildt Exhibit No. 6.

MR. DE MOHRENSCHILDT: Yes, sir; this was followed, of course, by many other letters and correspondence with our prospective investors and people who might be interested in a mining development of Haiti. I am negotiating right now with an aluminum company for the development of bauxite, and with oil companies in regard to development of oil possibilities.

MR. JENNER: Mr. De Mohrenschildt, we have had some discussions off the record, and I had lunch with you a couple of times. Is there anything that we discussed during the course of any off-the-record discussions which I have not already brought out on the record that you think is pertinent and should be brought out?

MR. DE MOHRENSCHILDT: I don't remember any.

MR. JENNER: None occurs to you?

MR. DE MOHRENSCHILDT: No.

MR. JENNER: Now, I don't know everything by any means. I will ask you this general question. Is there anything else, despite all our careful investigation, and my questioning of you at some length, that you think is pertinent and might be helpful to the Commission in its important work, and if you can think of anything, would you please mention it?

MR. DE MOHRENSCHILDT: Frankly, I cannot think of anything else you could do. All the rest—what else can you do except investigate as much as you can?

MR. JENNER: Mr. De Mohrenschildt, you appear here voluntarily and at some inconvenience?

MR. DE MOHRENSCHILDT: Yes, sir.

MR. JENNER: And on behalf of the Commission, and the Commission staff, I want to express our appreciation to you for having come to this country, at some inconvenience, and your answering my questions here for 2 days spontaneously and directly. Some of them have been highly personal. But you have exhibited no discomfiture because they have been personal. We appreciate your assistance and your help.

MR. DE MOHRENSCHILDT: I hope I have been helpful to some extent.

MR. JENNER: Now, as I spoke to you yesterday, you have a right to read your deposition, and to sign it, and you told me I think yesterday that you would like to read it over.

MR. DE MOHRENSCHILDT: If it won't be a very lengthy job and very hurried job to do that, and inconvenience the reporter. I think I have said everything I could know. I don't think I could add or change very much. It is all right as far as I am concerned.

MR. JENNER: As far as you are concerned, you would just as soon waive the necessity of reading and signing?

MR. DE MOHRENSCHILDT: Yes.

MR. JENNER: Fine.

MR. DE MOHRENSCHILDT: If I made a mistake, it was involuntary. I might have missed a date or something. But I did to the best of my ability.

MR. JENNER: We will have your deposition by tomorrow. And Mrs. De Mohrenschildt will be here tomorrow. If you would like to come over and read it, you may. Otherwise, if you don't return to read it, we will consider that you have waived it. I offer in evidence the exhibits I have heretofore marked, being De Mohrenschildt Exhibits 1 through 16, inclusive.

∾

Letter from George
de Mohrenschildt to Richard
Billings at *Life* Magazine

EDITOR'S NOTE: *The vignette "More Unusual Visitors" in Chapter 5 is among the more mysterious in the manuscript. De Mohrenschildt does not tell the reader of his association with* Life *magazine's Richard "Dick" Billings, merely saying that he wrote "one of the editors of* Life *magazine" to discuss his discovery of the photo of Oswald with Lee's dedication on the back. The manuscript describes the two visitors as being named "Fernandez" and "Smith" and indicates that the visitors showed him photographs of "some twenty men, mostly of Latin appearance," that neither de Mohrenschildt nor his wife recognized. After "a few days went by" he became suspicious and decided to "check" with* Life's *office in New York only to learn the two men were imposters, not* Life *employees as they had claimed. In truth it was just two days later that de Mohrenschildt contacted Billings, and the letter he wrote offers a similar yet different account. Most importantly the photos are identified as Cubans who landed in Haiti seeking to overthrow his old employer, the dictator François Duvalier. Perhaps because he still hoped to win a settlement from the Haitian government de Mohrenschildt decided to omit these details from the manuscript. The letter also refers to "HLO" who is presumably Lee Harvey Oswald. Years later, on November 27, 1973, de Mohrenschildt would tell yet another version of the incident to Willem Oltmans and Dr. Cyril Wecht, who were visiting him in Dallas. As recounted by Oltmans in his memoirs, "de Mohrenschildt told Dr. Wecht about how* Life *magazine had come to interview him. Two days later people from* Life *came back and showed him some pictures of Cubans who might possibly have been involved in the assassination of JFK. . . . George became suspicious and telephoned* Life *about this second visit, who said they knew nothing about Cubans or a second visit. George said, 'One of them looked like a real killer.'" In the end we are left with three different versions of the same event, and as many questions as answers.*

August 29, 1967

Dear Dick,

Two days ago a reporter and a photographer from your magazine called me up, referred to you, and came to my house. Their names escape me; one had a Spanish name, another Arthur something. They constantly referred to my conversations with you and then showed me some Cubans involved in the unsuccessful invasion of Haiti. They asked us some questions about HLO but mostly about the situation in Haiti.

Naturally I did not say much, because I have a pending suit against Haiti, nor was I familiar with any of the characters they had mentioned.

Now I am wondering if they were actually people from your magazine; they took some pictures of us and our dogs.

Anyway, I did not say anything of importance and I did insist that nothing should be printed about us.

However, they both did know of our conversations, so I presume that they actually were from *Life* and that my doubts have no foundation.

Please let me know. In the future I shall ask anyone who will come over for their credentials.

Both my wife and I are anxious to see you again in Dallas.

Sincerely yours,
/s/
G[eorge] de Mohrenschildt

APPENDIX D

❦

Letter from George de Mohrenschildt to CIA Director George H. W. Bush

EDITOR'S NOTE: *The extent and degree to which George de Mohren-schildt and future president George H. W. Bush were acquainted with each other remains controversial. That there was a relationship of some kind, one going back decades, is undeniable. See Appendix E.*

This handwritten letter, seen in the larger context of the many letters de Mohrenschildt wrote during the 1960s and 1970s to promote his Haitian venture, and then to attempt to retrieve the money owed under the terms of his March 1963 contract with the Duvalier regime, is not nearly as sinister as the Kennedy assassination literature makes it out to be. It is simply another example of de Mohrenschildt addressing himself to the highest-placed authority he could reach in order to rectify a perceived problem. As indicated in the Editor's Introduction, this approach was de Mohrenschildt's modus operandi when dealing with a great many professional and personal matters. Instead of going through "proper channels," and all the inconvenient paperwork it usually entails, he would seek out the "alpha male" for a one-on-one conversation. Given his great charm, the strategy often worked.

That de Mohrenschildt's prose is awkward and the meaning of his words opaque is, as we have seen repeatedly, also nothing unusual, given his limited command of written English. The ability to communicate effectively may well have been further compromised by the psychological impact of his daughter Nadya's death, which was almost certainly as devastating as Sergei's had been thirteen years earlier. The letter may also reflect the deterioration and ongoing strain of de Mohrenschildt's relationship with his fourth wife, Jeanne. While continuing to live together, they had divorced three years prior. A letter to Willem Oltmans dated January 29, 1973, begins "You are the first to know. I had something close to a heart attack and filed a divorce against Jeanne. Too much is too much." Finally, the letter is notable because of the sentence "I tried to write . . . about Lee H. Oswald." This appears to be an allusion to the manuscript itself and based on internal references it had been completed just a few weeks prior.

Dallas, Sept. 5, 1976

Dear George,

You will excuse this hand-written letter. Maybe you will be able to bring a solution to the hopeless situation I find myself in.

My wife and I find ourselves surrounded by some vigilantes; our phone bugged; and we are being followed everywhere. Either FBI is involved in this or they do not want to accept my complaints. We are driven to insanity by the situation.

I have been behaving like a damn fool ever since my daughter Nadya died from CF [cystic fibrosis] over three years ago. I tried to write, stupidly and unsuccessfully, about Lee H. Oswald and must have angered a lot of people I do not know. But to punish an elderly man like myself and my highly nervous and sick wife is really too much.

Could you do something to remove the net around us? This will be my last request for help and I will not annoy you anymore.

Good luck in your important job. Thank you so much.

Sincerely,

G[eorge] de Mohrenschildt

ᦏᦅᦎᦗᦗ

Reply, CIA Director
George H. W. Bush to
George de Mohrenschildt

EDITOR'S NOTE: *The arrival of de Mohrenschildt's letter written on September 5, 1976, provoked some surprise at CIA headquarters. It was read by a staffer, who inserted the remark "I was going to forward this to DCI security—but since it is a 'Dear George' letter and from Texas, I thought I should run it through you on the off chance it is a friend of the Director's." One can only wonder what was going through DCI Bush's mind that day: after months of deliberation the House had voted on September 17 to pursue a special investigation on assassinations, including that of President Kennedy in 1963. In a poorly typed internal memo dated the same day Bush replied to the staff inquiry:*

I do know this man DeMohrenschildt.

I first men [*sic*] him in the early 40'3 [*sic*]. He was an uncle to my Andover roommate.

Later he surfaced in Dallas— (50's maybe).

He got involved in some controversial dealings in Haiti.

Then he surfaced when Oswald shot to prominence. He knew Oswald before the assassination of Pres. Kennedy.

I don't recall his role in all this.

At one time he had / or spent plenty of money.

I have not heard from him for many years until the attached letter came in.

After a draft reply was prepared by his staff the following revised and final version was mailed to de Mohrenschildt:

CENTRAL INTELLIGENCE AGENCY
Washington, D.C. 20505

28 September 1976

Mr. G. de Mohrenschildt
2737 Kings Road
Apartment 142
Dallas, Texas 75219

Dear George:

Please forgive the delay in my reply to your September 5th letter. It took some time to explore thoroughly the matters you have raised.

Let me say first that I know it must have been difficult for you to seek my help in the situation outlined in your letter. I believe I can appreciate your state of mind in view of your daughter's tragic death a few years ago, and the current poor state of your wife's health. I was extremely sorry to hear of these circumstances.

In your situation I can well imagine how the attentions you described in your letter affect both you and your wife. However, my staff has been unable to find any indication of interest in your activities on the part of Federal authorities in recent years. The flurry of interest that attended your testimony before the Warren Commission has long subsided. I can only speculate that you may have become "newsworthy" again in view of the renewed interest in the Kennedy assassination, and thus may be attracting the attention of people in the media.

I hope this letter has been of some comfort to you, George, although I realize I am unable to answer your question completely. Thank you for your good wishes on my new job. As you can imagine, I'm finding it interesting and challenging.

Very truly yours,

/s/ George Bush

George Bush
Director

In truth Bush's roommate at Andover, Edward G. Hooker, was the stepson of George's brother Dmitri von Mohrenschildt, which would have made George de Mohrenschildt Edward's step-uncle. Hooker and de Mohrenschildt would form an oil exploration business together in 1950, Hooker and de Mohrenschildt. The business rapidly went bust, but George and Edward remained friends. Hooker died in 1967. These are of course trivial matters. As journalist Russ Baker points out on pages 267–268 of his book Family of Secrets, *the internal memo Bush wrote "appears to be a case study in dissembling and obfuscation" by a career intelligence bureaucrat. Bush's reply strains all credulity: if the Director of Central Intelligence wasn't able to recall the important place de Mohrenschildt's friendship with Oswald occupied in the Kennedy assassination narrative, why would he remember something as trivial as de Mohrenschildt being in Haiti, much less having "controversial dealings" there? Or how would he know that de Mohrenschildt had, or spent, "a lot of money" for that matter?*

Bush's conception of "many years" having passed since his last communication with de Mohrenschildt is certainly open to question. Bush was one of several individuals, including Congressman Earle Cabell and National Security Advisor Henry Kissinger, who made inquiries on behalf of de Mohrenschildt during the late 1960s and early 1970s regarding his still-unfulfilled contract with the Haitian government. This matter of de Mohrenschildt's contract with the government of Haiti may be the "controversial dealings" DCI Bush did not care to elaborate on. While serving as Nixon's UN ambassador Bush had, on May 25, 1971, written the State Department asking if they could assist in de Mohrenschildt's continuing efforts to be paid the money owed under the terms of his March 1963 agreement. Bush would be told by David A. Ross, Chief of Haitian Affairs at the Office of Caribbean Affairs the matter was considered a private one and because of that inappropriate for the State Department to involve itself with.

Then, in 1973, at a time Bush was head of the Republican Party, de Mohrenschildt had again written to him saying, "I've been happily teaching at Bishop College for the last four years" while pointing out the small private college was at a distinct competitive disadvantage vis-à-vis the public University of Texas system "with its enormous state resources." Because of this the college needed help (and he was correct—Bishop was in continuous financial trouble from the early 1970s onward, eventually filing for Chapter 11 bankruptcy in 1987 and closing in 1988). This 1973 letter concludes, "we shall vote for you when you run for President" and was signed "Your old friend G. De Mohrenschildt." All of which suggests a level of immediacy much greater than a simple passing acquaintance.

The memory lapses about his friendship with George de Mohrenschildt are bad; worse, for decades Bush has given only the vaguest of answers of where he was on November 22, 1963, stating he was "somewhere in Texas." The Dallas Morning News reported on November 20, 1963, that "George Bush, president, Zapata Off-Shore Co." would be speaking to the American Association of Oil Drilling Contractors (AAODC) at the Sheraton-Dallas Hotel at 6:30 p.m. the following day. This places Bush in Dallas on the night before the assassination. As chronicled on pages 51–66 of Family of Secrets Bush left Dallas the morning of November 22 on a private plane owned by Joe Zeppa (a former president of AAODC who likely attended the Dallas meeting) for Tyler, Texas (about 100 miles east of Dallas), in order to give a luncheon speech to the local Kiwanis Club. Minutes after Kennedy's death was reported by CBS News Bush called FBI Special Agent Graham Kitchel (see Editor's Introduction, note 41). The memo Kitchel filed, declassified in 1993, has Bush calling long-distance from Tyler and indicating he would be "proceeding to Dallas, Texas," and "would remain in the Sheraton-Dallas Hotel" the night of November 22 before returning to his home in Houston the next day. The tip Bush provided to Kitchel—that he had second-hand knowledge a young Republican named James Parrott had been "talking of killing the President"—was a complete fabrication. The entire episode with Parrot gives the appearance of having been deliberately orchestrated to conceal the fact Bush had already stayed at the Sheraton-Dallas Hotel.

As is well known now, the CIA's Bay of Pigs Invasion was code named operation Zapata; Bush, coincidentally as far as we know at any rate, ran an oil exploration company in the Gulf of Mexico called the Zapata Off-Shore Drilling Company. Two of the invasion craft used by the Cuban exiles were called the Houston and the Barbara or possibly the Barbara J.; Zapata's headquarters and Bush's home were, coincidentally again, Houston, and his wife was named Barbara. Bush has also denied being the "Mr. George

Bush of the Central Intelligence Agency" mentioned in an FBI memo dated November 29, 1963, as having briefed FBI director J. Edgar Hoover on the possibilities of anti-Castro Cubans in the Miami area viewing Kennedy's death as presaging a change in US policy towards Cuba. The final chapter of the de Mohrenschildt manuscript would appear to be correct in at least one sense: the full story of the Bay of Pigs remains untold. Bush, naturally, isn't talking.

Notes

Editor's Introduction

1. U.S. Congress, House of Representatives, *Appendix to Hearings before the Select Committee on Assassinations of the House of U.S. Representatives*, Vol. 12 (US Government Printing Office, 1979), 69–315.

2. Samuel B. Ballen, *Without Reservations: From Harlem to the End of the Santa Fe Trail* (Ocean Tree Books, 2001), 162.

3. Useful biographical information may be found in the following books. First, there is the chapter "The New Old Story of George de Mohrenschildt" in Ray and Mary La Fontaine, *Oswald Talked: The New Evidence in the JFK Assassination* (Pelican, 1996), 91–138. Second, there is the chapter "Oswald's Friend" as well as other material scattered throughout Russ Baker's *Family of Secrets: The Bush Dynasty, America's Invisible Government, and the Hidden History of the Last Fifty Years* (Bloomsbury Press, 2009), 67–84, and see also 99–113 and 262–279. Third, there is the chapter "An Adoptive Texan with Some Intelligence Connections" as well as other material scattered throughout Joan Mellen's *Our Man in Haiti: George de Mohrenschildt and the CIA in the Nightmare Republic* (TrineDay, 2012), 1–57. All of these works should be treated with caution, however, as they have agendas larger than the life story of George de Mohrenschildt. One work written by someone who had no larger agenda and who knew George de Mohrenschildt personally is the chapter "Mischka" by longtime friend Sam Ballen in his colorful memoir *Without Reservations*, 161–179. Ballen's account contains some factual errors because it is by his own admission "authored . . . entirely out of memory." Better still are the chapters "George de Mohrenschildt" and "Lee and George" in Priscilla John-

son McMillan's just republished 1977 book *Marina and Lee: The Tormented Love and Fatal Obsession behind Lee Harvey Oswald's Assassination of John F. Kennedy* (Steerforth Press, 2013), 260–275, 288–300.

4. Denis Diderot (1713–1784) was one of the leading figures of the European Enlightenment in the eighteenth century. He was the chief editor, along with Jean Le Rond d'Alembert, of the twenty-eight volume *Encyclopédie* (1751–1772), an ambitious and innovative work "to make people think," that has been cited as having played an important role in creating the intellectual ferment leading to the French Revolution in 1789.

5. Denis Diderot, *Rameau's Nephew / D'Alembert's Dream* (Penguin, 1966), 33–34.

6. Mellen, *Our Man in Haiti* (TrineDay, 2012), 57.

7. Ibid., 43. Ilya A. Mamantov (1914–1991), a research geologist employed by the Sun Oil Company who was contacted on November 22, 1963, by both the Dallas City Police and prominent Texas Republican Jack Crichton to serve as Marina Oswald's interpreter, had met de Mohrenschildt through George Bouhe around the spring of 1956, describing him to the Warren Commission as a "tall, handsome man, well built, very talkative and loud in society," fond of telling off-color jokes and flirting with women "in a way a well brought up person wouldn't do." The very conservative Mamantov also expressed a strong aversion to the left-leaning de Mohrenschildt's political opinions and claimed to avoid him as much as possible.

8. During his early years in the United States, de Mohrenschildt tried his hand at such trades as selling insurance, perfume, and wine. In the early stages of World War II he worked for Film Facts, Inc., a studio run by a distant cousin, on a documentary film about the Polish Resistance, *Poland Forever*. The cousin, Baron Konstantine B. Maydell, wound up being arrested in September 1942, tried for espionage in federal district court, and held in an internment camp in North Dakota until 1946. De Mohrenschildt's watercolor paintings were exhibited at the Newton Gallery on 57th Street in New York as "Water Colors of Mexico by George de Mohrenschildt." Reviews, including in the *New York Times* on December 12, 1943, were favorable. The positive reviews did not translate into substantial sales, however, with only four or five of the roughly seventy paintings sold.

9. Mellen, *Our Man in Haiti*, 17.

10. Ballen, *Without Reservations*, 171. Ballen's account does not provide additional detail but an FBI report compiled with information supplied by Col. Lawrence Orlov (see Chapter 1) mentions the article with this name as having appeared in September 1958. The *Dallas Times Herald* ran an article titled "Dallas Oil Experts to Aid Yugoslavia" on January 17, 1957. De Mohrenschildt is quoted in the article as saying "Yugoslavia now buys both oil and oil machinery from Russia and the Soviet bloc. Our State Department would like to see Marshall Tito's nation become self-sufficient in oil." He would again be interviewed by the *Times Herald* upon his return in a December 4, 1957, article titled "Yugoslavia Oil Program Seen." Warren Commission Document No. 1012, declassified two months after de Mohrenschildt's death in 1977, indicates the CIA first established contact with him that same month.

11. When for inexplicable reasons Warren Commission assistant counsel Albert Jenner asked for more detail about the manuscript, the now middle-aged de Mohrenschildt, clearly uncomfortable, replied, "I don't recall what it is. It is probably based on [my] travel in Mexico with some girls. That is what I would write at that time and that age." The 200-page story, as recounted by an FBI informant known as SA T-1, was told in the first person and "built around the activities of a young man and . . . [a] sort of Mexican 'Mae West type individual'" and other young girls of Mexican nationality but better morals." The manuscript was "in very rough form," and the English "very poor." On the one hand, the manuscript "indicated a rather thorough knowledge of Mexico" but on the other, it was rather too "licentious" to be publishable.

12. Sometimes referred to as *The Son of the Revolution* or *A Son of the Early Revolution*. See Vincent Bugliosi, *Reclaiming History: The Assassination of President John F. Kennedy* (W. W. Norton, 2007), 657. Bugliosi correctly describes the manuscript as a work separate and distinct from *Adventures of a Young Man in Mexico*. Other secondary sources appear to believe, incorrectly, the two manuscripts were the same work simply with a revised title. The stenographer is mentioned in Mellen, *Our Man in Haiti*, 29.

13. A now-declassified CIA "Contact Report" by WUBRINY/1 dated April 29, 1963, indicates the book's title was "something like *Trois et le Mule*." WUBRINY/1 was Thomas J. Divine (b. 1926), an oil-wildcatter who helped George H. W. Bush found the Zapata Off-Shore Drilling Company in 1953. Divine was also an employee of the CIA who served as an "unofficial foreign affairs advisor" to then representative Bush and accompanied him on a fact-finding trip to Vietnam in December 1967. CIA director of operations Gale Allen called Divine "the most discreet and security conscious business contact" he had ever met. Divine's report mistakenly indicates that the participants were de Mohrenschildt, "his wife and child and a donkey." In truth there were no children present; the "child" was none other than Nero, the de Mohrenschildt's Manchester Terrier. George had apparently spoken of Nero in such glowing terms that Divine took him to be talking about his son, rather than his dog!

14. The best description of this year-long adventure, one that included a roughly ninety-minute 8-mm home movie—mentioned in both the manuscript and by virtually every member of the Dallas–Fort Worth White Russian community in their Warren Commission testimony—may be found in the testimony of de Mohrenschildt's wife Jeanne.

15. In his letter to President Kennedy dated February 16, 1963, de Mohrenschildt mentioned having communicated with George McGhee (1912–2005), Under Secretary of State for Political Affairs. The previous October de Mohrenschildt had written to McGhee offering to show him a slide show of his walking trip through Latin America.

16. *Hearings before the President's Commission on the Assassination of President Kennedy (Warren Commission Hearings and Exhibits)*, Vol. 9 (Washington, DC: U.S. Government Printing Office, 1964), 216. [This work is hereafter cited by

its more commonly used title, *Warren Commission Hearings and Exhibits.*] He may also have harbored some hope of a serialization in the then-popular *Look* magazine. In September 1962 the *Department of Geology, The University of Texas [at Austin] Newsletter* (No. 11) reported on page 26: "George de Mohrenschildt (MA '45) . . . and his wife have just completed a one year exploration trip through Central and South America by mule and on foot and say that their feet are still hurting. *Look* magazine will publish their story soon."

17. De Mohrenschildt's dissertation at the Université de Liège, for example, was written in French. Depending on the source, de Mohrenschildt was said to be fluent in anywhere from five to nine languages. He clearly knew English because the manuscript is written in English. He taught French and Russian at the university level. Polish may be assumed given that he lived in Poland for years and was an officer in the Polish cavalry. FBI documents list him as being fluent in Spanish and German. According to Sam Ballen, who visited the de Mohrenschildts for extended periods of time in Haiti, George "was able to pick up Creole in about six weeks, and that reflects his ease with any foreign language." Haitian Creole or Kreyòl is primarily based on eighteenth-century French and West African languages. See Ballen, *Without Reservations*, 162.

18. *Warren Commission Hearings and Exhibits*, Vol. 9, 216.

19. As described by Jeanne: "He is a terrific person, absolutely terrific. He has a soul of gold. I really mean it. And sometimes he drives me so crazy, I can just smash his head, because he is so impatient. He is extremely impatient. He is always in a hurry. You have to be ten times faster than he is to have [any peace]. . . . He is always rushing somewhere, and everything has to be just immediately. Never a second late."

20. The February 2, 1971, entry in Willem Oltmans's memoirs indicate two Parisian friends of de Mohrenschildt, Yolande and Pierre Giraud, were working on one of de Mohrenschildt's manuscripts, presumably *Trois et le Mule*, though this is not certain. Willem Oltmans, *Memoires 1970–1971* (Papieren Tijger, 2003), 205. Sam Ballen went so far as to say it was as a result of this "failure to secure a publisher for his memoirs of his journey through Central America" that de Mohrenschildt suffered a "serious decline and loss of confidence and spontaneity, leading to his ultimate tragedy." See Ballen, *Without Reservations*, 170. This seems to miss the mark, however, given that it was the crisis provoked by the death of de Mohrenschildt's son from cystic fibrosis that instigated the walking trip through Central America in the first place. The decline and loss of confidence more likely trace to his daughter having died of the same disease a decade later. De Mohrenschildt himself admits to having behaved like "a damn fool" after her death in his letter to CIA Director George H. W. Bush. See Appendix D.

21. Willem Oltmans, *Memoires 1968–1970* (Papieren Tijger, 2003), 93–94.

22. Ibid., 99.

23. Ibid., 331.

24. Willem Oltmans, *Memoires 1976* (Papieren Tijger, 2007), 321–322.

25. Oltmans, *Memoires 1968–1970*, 125.

26. Dick Russell, *The Man Who Knew Too Much: Inquest, Counterplot, and*

Legend (Carroll & Graf, 2003), 172. The complete tale of the negotiations for the book manuscript may be found in Willem Oltmans, *Memoires 1976–1977* (Papieren Tijger, 2007), 115–118.

27. Oltmans's entry for February 16, 1969, continues "I did not show my reaction, but I must have talked out of sheer nervousness. From the beginning Gerard Croiset and Carel Enkelaar had been trying to convince me de Mohrenschildt would 'agree' to confess he was involved in the assassination in Dallas." Oltmans, *Memoires 1968–1970*, 118. De Mohrenschildt repeated the outlandish suggestion exactly two years later on February 16, 1971, over breakfast: "Someday I might acknowledge I am the engineer of the Kennedy assassination. Would that not be something! I would become famous!" The quote is in English in the Dutch original. Oltmans indicated *"Dit gaf me te denken."* Oltmans, *Memoires 1970–1971*, 217. While the suggestion may have given Oltmans something to think about, Sam Ballen, I suspect, would have laughed. Just more of George's outlandish sense of humor.

28. Carel Enkelaar (1920–1996) became head of NOS (Nederlandse Omroep Stichting [Netherlands Broadcasting Foundation]) in 1966, retiring in 1985.

29. In contrast to Enkelaar and the psychic Gerard Croiset, journalist Oltmans appears to have vacillated on the question of de Mohrenschildt's involvement in Kennedy's assassination, unsure what to make of the hints his friend was dropping. On November 27, 1972, he recorded "I still cannot make heads or tails of the real situation . . . and do not know what to believe and what is imaginary or untrue. It remains a puzzle." Departing two days later he wrote it "was the first time I left Dallas with the feeling that George is less guilty than we ever thought" but still believed de Mohrenschildt was connected, somehow, to the assassination. Willem Oltmans, *Memoires 1972–1973* (Papieren Tijger, 2004), 246.

30. Nancy Wertz Weiford, "A Last Wild Ride for George de Mohrenschildt," *Dealey Plaza Echo* 15, no. 1 (March 2011): 49.

31. Ibid., 50–51.

32. Willem Oltmans, "New Mysteries in the Kennedy Assassination?" *Nieuwe Revu*, May 1977, 15. The Strengholt representative was named Guus Janssen.

33. Or at least that is what de Mohrenschildt, in his by-then quite precarious mental state, thought. A two-page affidavit written in Belgium and found in his possession when he died indicated Oltmans wanted "to bully" de Mohrenschildt "into admitting things I did not do." When de Mohrenschildt stopped in Dallas briefly after returning from Europe he told his friend Sam Ballen in their final meeting that Oltmans "was prepared to pay [him] $25,000 if he signed an affidavit connecting the CIA to Oswald." See Ballen, *Without Reservations*, 178.

34. One example is the conclusion to an article that appeared in the *Washington Star* just two days after de Mohrenschildt's death: "If there is an answer to George de Mohrenschildt's troubled life, it may lie in the book he has written and that [his] lawyer [Patrick S.] Russell purportedly has filed away in Dallas." See Jeremiah O'Leary, "The de Mohrenschildt–JFK Enigma," *Washington Star* (March 31, 1977). Another is Howard Swindle and Hugh Aynesworth, "Photo and Manuscript Given to Investigators," *Dallas Times Herald* (April 2, 1977).

35. "Assassination: Now a Suicide Talks," *Time* 109 (April 11, 1977), 20. The article's primary source: Willem Oltmans, who had brought de Mohrenschildt to Europe hoping for a sensationalistic admission regarding Oswald. If de Mohrenschildt was truly an opportunist seeking to cash in on the notoriety of having known Oswald one would think he'd have tried to publish a tell-all book in 1964, not 1977. His motives were clearly more complex and lie elsewhere.

36. William Penn Jones Jr. (1914–1998) purchased the paper in 1946 and sold it in 1974. He was one of the early critics of the Warren Commission's conclusions and also publicized the many mysterious deaths suffered by those connected to the assassination.

37. See Chapter 6.

38. It goes without saying that de Mohrenschildt was using a typewriter; personal computers were very much a thing of the future in the mid-1970s.

39. For example, he says "let me translate a chapter" when he clearly means simply a short passage, as when quoting from the book *L'Amérique Brûle* near the end of the manuscript.

40. This final material, of all the material in the manuscript, was in the roughest condition and needed the most correction and polishing.

41. And not just anyone. De Mohrenschildt was a member of the very elite Dallas Petroleum Club, the left-leaning Dallas Council on World Affairs, and the definitely conservative Texas Crusade for Freedom. His friend, the offshore oil engineer George Kitchel (mentioned in Appendix B), included among de Mohrenschildt's acquaintances the oil barons Clint Murchison, H. L. Hunt, John Mecom, and Sid Richardson. Kitchel himself was an old friend of George H. W. Bush and brother of Graham W. Kitchel, one of J. Edgar Hoover's most trusted associates. Bush would call Special Agent Kitchel long distance from Tyler, Texas, less than ninety minutes after Kennedy's assassination to report a member of the Harris County Republican Party named James Parrott had "been talking of killing the President," a claim that proved to be a complete fabrication. See Appendix E.

42. This is in keeping with de Mohrenschildt's conviction that one must use great discretion regarding reputable people when discussing delicate matters, a practice he identifies, rightly or wrongly, with European investigative agencies. In contrast to this view the manuscript depicts America investigators, especially the FBI, as clumsy, callous, and brutally insensitive with regard to the damage they inflict on the lives of private individuals.

43. Superficially *Ecce Homo* appears a work of impending madness, with such hyperbolic chapter titles as "Why I Am So Wise," "Why I Am So Clever," "Why I Write Such Good Books," and "Why I Am a Destiny," but the work is better understood when viewed alongside Plato's *Apology*. The Socrates of the *Apology* defends the philosophic life based on dialogue and reason and launches the philosophic project; the Nietzsche of *Ecce Homo* dynamites the philosophic project as both an idealistic fraud and the precursor to life-denying Christian morality. The new philosopher, and the philosophy of the future, embraces the life-affirming morality, the *amor fati* of the Greek tragic poets and pre-Socratic philosophers—they are, in a

word, Dionysian. Anyone familiar with Van Gogh will understand the eerie beauty of *Ecce Homo*.

44. The full line reads *"Have I been understood?* Dionysus vs. the Crucified."

45. Recalling Aphorism 146 of his masterpiece *Beyond Good and Evil: Prelude to a Philosophy of the Future*: "When you gaze long into an abyss, the abyss also gazes into you." (New York: Vintage Books, 1989.)

46. On October 28, 1976, a little more than a month after receiving his reply from CIA Director George H. W. Bush (see Appendix E), de Mohrenschildt had attempted to drown himself in his bathtub. It was not his first suicide attempt that year. The next day, complaining "I am depressed, I am killing myself," he told a psychiatrist at the Terrell State Hospital that he wished to be committed as a patient. When the paperwork was ready on November 2, he changed his mind. He entered treatment at Parkland Hospital willingly. There he received both drug treatment and electroconvulsive therapy (ECT), known at the time as electroshock treatment. On its own, ECT does not usually have long-term benefits for the patient and can produce adverse effects such as long-term memory loss. Once again, it should be emphasized the manuscript was complete and finished before ECT was administered.

47. The "summer of 1976" is mentioned twice in Chapter 6, once in the vignette "A New Friend: Willem Oltmans" and once in the vignette "Lee: One Last Assessment." There is also a reference within the manuscript to "President Ford," which at least suggests that no work was performed on the manuscript after the inauguration of Jimmy Carter on January 20, 1977. Carter, despite having become a national figure by the summer of 1976, is never mentioned in the manuscript. In an article published just two months after de Mohrenschildt's death, Oltmans would quote his friend as saying "I wrote a book. In June, 1976, I completed a manuscript. That's when disaster struck." Oltmans, "New Mysteries in the Kennedy Assassination?" 13. De Mohrenschildt's letter to Oltmans dated May 10, 1976, contradicts Oltmans's article, however. It concludes with de Mohrenschildt saying he is too busy with his black students at Bishop College and indicates he "will start [writing] again in July." Moreover his draft of the material that would become the vignette titled "Willem Oltmans and His Clairvoyant" in the original manuscript is dated June 24. It would have taken some time for the draft pages to reach Oltmans, for the Dutchman to edit them, and then for the edits to be mailed back to de Mohrenschildt and incorporated into the manuscript.

48. They are included in the Selected Bibliography, if the reader is so inclined.

49. The two most commonly repeated arguments are the following. The first casts de Mohrenschildt in the role of Oswald's intelligence-appointed "babysitter" or "handler" or "shepherd," purportedly with the idea of setting up Oswald as a "patsy" for the conspiracy that assassinated President Kennedy. Any sober examination of the timeline (and the manuscript itself)—where Oswald was and what he was doing, where de Mohrenschildt was and what he was doing—renders this thesis ridiculous. The de Mohrenschildts and the Oswalds met with each other perhaps fifteen to twenty times, most of them in the fall of 1962. The second portrays de Mohrenschildt's problems in late 1976 and death in early 1977 as either an abrupt

reversal in his mental health, arising out of "guilt" from his role in the earlier conspiracy, or perhaps something actively brought on by the conspirators themselves to discredit and ultimately silence him, and this thesis is equally ridiculous once one has acquired a modicum of understanding about de Mohrenschildt's psychiatric history. There is clear evidence of an emergent paranoia and persecution complex long before the mid-1970s. Sam Ballen would tell FBI special agents W. James Woods and Raymond Yelchak on March 3, 1964, that his friend "had developed something of a persecution complex in recent years and believes the FBI and the John Birch Society are watching him and may have broken into his house." George's 1964 Warren Commission testimony contains a description of a "very peculiar incident" wherein he returned home to find indications someone had read and marked his travelogue manuscript. He and Jeanne went to see their acquaintance in the CIA Domestic Contacts Division, J. Walton Moore. De Mohrenschildt asked, "[Did] you government people . . . look through my book?" The incredulous Moore is quoted as having replied, "Do you consider us such fools as to leave marks on your book if we had? But we haven't." Alongside of this there was the profound despair arising from the diagnosis/death of two of his children from cystic fibrosis. Both deaths, the first in 1960 and the second in 1973, were emotionally devastating. His "walking trip" through Central America enabled him to rebound more or less fully from the first death but the second was something he apparently never fully recovered from.

50. See "Marina and the Walker Incident" in Chapter 5.

51. Fernand Braudel, *Civilization and Capitalism, 15th–18th Century, Volume 1: The Structures of Everyday Life—The Limits of the Possible* (Harper and Row, 1981). On the *longue durée* see Immanuel Wallerstein's translation of Braudel's essay "History and the Social Sciences: The *Longue Durée*," in *The* Longue Durée *and World Systems Analysis* (State University of New York Press, 2012).

52. This is not to say George de Mohrenschildt wrote in the manner of the French *Annales* School. It simply means that different interpretive frameworks view the world differently, and that what counts as fact or as being valid within one paradigmatic milieu may count for little or nothing in another.

53. Jean Richardot, *Journeys for a Better World: An Inside Story of the United Nations by One of Its First Senior Officials* (University Press of America, 1994). Richardot would be expelled by the government of Haiti on May 17, 1963, leaving the country just sixteen days before the arrival of the de Mohrenschildts.

54. A report filed by FBI special agent James E. Freaney on March 25, 1964, gets to the crux of the matter. As explained to him by Serge Obolensky, a manager at the Saint Regis Hotel where de Mohrenschildt lived in the late 1940s:

OBOLENSKY advised . . . that DE MOHRENSCHILDT was a White Russian and that during his formative years he was brought up in the Soviet Union. OBOLENSKY declared that he had known several other Russians with that background. The necessity for survival in the Soviet Union for Russians whose parents had been members of the Czarist Army developed in them a lack of moral standards. He stated that the atmosphere of anxiety and want developed in these young people a self-dependency but no feeling of responsibility towards themselves or their associates. OBOLENSKY said that it was his impression that DE MOHRENSCHILDT was in this category.

This report is Commission Document 777, FBI Letter from Director of 10 April 1964 with Attached Reports. George's father, Sergius, had been an officer in the Czar's army for twenty years until resigning his commission in 1916.

55. Thus the importance of shaking Oswald's hand in the vignette "Brokering a Separation" in Chapter 2, and refusing to shake the hand of FBI Agent Wood in the vignette "Our Move to Haiti" in Chapter 4. When he became angry with author Dick Russell, and Jeanne showed the writer out (see note 61), de Mohrenschildt made the point of rushing to the door and saying "It's been a pleasure," while shaking Russell's hand. See Russell, *The Man Who Knew Too Much*, 171.

56. In the words of Sam Ballen, who knew him as well as anyone: "When George walked into a room, his hauteur and dark good looks brought all discussion to a close. All eyes would concentrate on his arrogant steps. There were many women in Dallas who found him irresistible, and his infidelities became too flagrant for Dede [Sharples] to tolerate. Their marriage came to a close." See Ballen, *Without Reservations*, 165. Sharples would tell the FBI, however, that her husband was faithful throughout their marriage and the divorce had been for other reasons.

57. See Bill Minutaglio and Steven L. Davis, *Dallas 1963* (Grand Central, 2013).

58. The manuscript strongly suggests that the "real criminals" were anti-Castro Cubans who had been captured after the failed Bay of Pigs invasion and later released by the Castro regime in late December 1962. Willem Oltmans's memoirs indicate it was a position de Mohrenschildt maintained throughout the ten years the two were acquainted. For example on February 16, 1971, Oltmans quotes de Mohrenschildt as saying, "Naturally I can say why the Kennedy family is silent about Dallas. What could they do? Those Cubans were potential killers, while they themselves, John and Robert Kennedy, had brought them back from Cuba after the Bay of Pigs. The Kennedy family wanted JFK to be the martyr and hero killed by a Marxist loafer." Oltmans, *Memoires 1970–1971*, 219.

59. Oswald's rifle was of 1940 manufacture. Italy declared war on Britain and France in June 1940 out of sheer opportunism, not careful preparation. The Italian army was ill-equipped for the task on just about every conceivable level: underpowered and thinly armored tanks, artillery dating to World War I, insufficient support weapons, "and even its rifles and machine guns were of obsolete pattern or otherwise unsuitable for modern warfare." See Erwin Rommel, *The Rommel Papers* (Da Capo Press, 1953), 91.

60. As reported by Richard Helms, CIA's deputy director for plans in a secret memorandum to Warren Commission General Counsel J. Lee Rankin (and shared with the FBI):

At a social gathering in Haiti early June 1964 the De MOHRENSCHIDLTS . . . were asked if there was any substance to the view expressed in certain foreign periodicals such as *L'Express*, a left-wing Parisian weekly newspaper, that the Kennedy assassination was a plot organized by Dallas millionaires. George De MOHRENSCHLIDT said that President Kennedy was hated by the Dallas elite, and he felt that it was very likely that certain reactionary elements in Dallas had organized a plot to get rid of Kennedy and used a disturbed individual such as OSWALD to achieve their ends. Mrs. De MORHENSCHILDT agreed fully with this thesis.

Little wonder then that there was such intense interest in the de Mohrenschildts on the part of the US government.

61. Even as late as July 1976 de Mohrenschildt would essentially throw author Dick Russell out of his house, saying disgustedly, "It is defiling a corpse! Defiling a corpse! I don't want to talk about it, it makes me sick!" See Russell, *The Man Who Knew Too Much*, 172. As far as corpses go, de Mohrenschildt's hasn't fared much better than Oswald's.

62. Jeanne comes close to expressing this view in her Warren Commission testimony, which may be why de Mohrenschildt includes it at all:

> MR. JENNER: Did you have any impression that [Oswald] was envious at any time?
>
> MRS. DE MOHRENSCHILDT: No, and in fact that is what doesn't make any sense, because I don't think he ever said anything against [President Kennedy], and whatever the president was doing . . . Lee was completely exactly with the same ideas, exactly. If he would shoot [General] Walker that would be understandable. Even if he would be shooting at [Texas Governor] Connally that is understandable too. We learned that Connally refused him honorable discharge [from the Marine Corps], so he had a grudge against Connally, but President Kennedy, no.

Jenner seems to misunderstand her final sentence, thinking that because she acquired the knowledge about *the discharge* after the assassination, Oswald himself never said anything negative *about Connally* before the assassination. That was not what Jeanne was telling him with her limited command of English: *the grudge existed independently of the question of the discharge.* The manuscript does mention the discharge but only after the intense dislike of Connally has already been established. Whether Jenner chose to deliberately distort the meaning of her words or simply misunderstood them is impossible to know, but the net effect was to allow the questioning to continue to follow down the already well-worn grooves of the "jealous little Marxist" assassination narrative. Interviewing the de Mohrenschildts on October 15, 1967, Willem Oltmans quotes Jeanne as saying "Maybe he shot at Governor John Connally, because apparently he had a dispute with the authorities and the Texas governor about his dishonorable discharge from military service because of his travel and stay in the Soviet Union." Willem Oltmans, *Memoires 1967–1968* (Papieren Tijger, 2002), 131.

63. While this hypothesis is by no means new it has rarely been the subject of prolonged analysis. One exception is James Reston Jr., *The Accidental Victim: JKF, Lee Harvey Oswald, and the Real Target in Dallas* (Zola Books, 2013). Reston's portrait of de Mohrenschildt as a "pompous, flamboyant dandy" (p. 29) who "patronized Oswald mercilessly" (p. 34) is, however, shallow and superficial.

64. In her third and final appearance before the Warren Commission in September 1964, Marina "threw the commission into confusion by testifying that Lee liked the president so much, she thought it must have been Connally he was aiming at." McMillan, *Marina and Lee*, 571.

65. See "We Scholars," aphorism 212, in Nietzsche, *Beyond Good and Evil:* "So far all these extraordinary furtherers of man . . . though they themselves have rarely felt like friends of wisdom but rather like disagreeable fools and dangerous question marks, have found their task . . . in being the bad consciousness of their age."

66. Bertrand Russell, "Sixteen Questions on the Assassination," *Minority of One* 6, no. 9 (September 1964): 6–8.

67. See the vignette "Lee: One Last Assessment," in Chapter 6.

68. Books on de Mohrenschildt rarely even mention Nadya yet it is she who is probably the key to understanding what triggered the decline in his mental health. Shortly after his appearance before the Warren Commission in 1964 de Mohrenschildt wrote from Port-au-Prince to his inquisitor, Albert E. Jenner, "I was happy to have been able to see both my daughters on this trip [back to the U.S.]. Unfortunately my little girl Nadya is not doing well at all. That horrible illness Cystic Fibrosis, is frightening. She is emaciated and already one of her lungs has been damaged." A large photo of her is visible on a desk next to de Mohrenschildt in a photo of Willem Oltmans interviewing him in 1968. Oltmans's entry in his memoirs for January 26, 1969, reads "Nadya de Mohrenschildt (15) was present. She was a child from a previous marriage. . . . She suffers from cystic fibrosis, of which George's only son is deceased. She sleeps in a tent because of her breathing problems. It's very sad to see the powerlessness to help or cheer her up. She's a nice kid. They do not know how long she will live." Oltmans, *Memoires 1968–1970*, 94. A holiday postcard sent by the de Mohrenschildts to Oltmans in late 1972, purchased with a contribution to the Cystic Fibrosis Foundation, reads "Nadya is sending her love" and mentions forthcoming plans for her to attend the University of Miami. Shortly before her death in 1973 Oltmans would observe: "Whenever I come back [to Dallas] the first thing George starts about is his sick daughter Nadya. . . . She was again in critical condition including five days in a hospital in Florida. George went and had stayed with her immediately after she was admitted. He asked me to write to her. I did so, on the spot. He addressed the envelope." Oltmans, *Memoires 1972–1973*, 245.

69. Ballen, *Without Reservations*, 178. Ballen was quite perspicacious comparing de Mohrenschildt's decline and suicide to Hemingway's. Both men became paranoid and believed the FBI was tracing their movements, both had exhibited prior suicidal behavior, both were hospitalized and given drug and electroconvulsive therapies that quite likely only worsened their conditions, and both committed suicide with a shotgun. Hemingway had also been diagnosed with hereditary hemochromatosis (an

inability to metabolize iron that culminates in mental and physical deterioration) a few months before his death. The disease is most common in people of Celtic, British, and Scandinavian origin (10 percent are carriers of the gene, 1 percent suffer from the condition). De Mohrenschildt claimed his ancestral roots traced back to Sweden, specifically aristocratic nobility named von Morenskölde dating back to the reign of Queen Christina (1626–1689). An FBI document dated March 9, 1964, indicates the Swedish von Morenskölde family "can trace its lineage to the Douglas clan in Scotland." Unfortunately de Mohrenschildt's body was cremated after his death, precluding any testing to confirm if he may have been suffering from the same affliction.

Preface: "I'm Just a Patsy!"

1. The opening vignette of de Mohrenschildt's manuscript is titled "Preface in Haiti" but the reader should be aware that no portion of the manuscript was written during the 1963–1966 time period when the de Mohrenschildts were living in Haiti. The first sentence of text immediately echoes the manuscript's misleading title with the twice repeated exclamation "I am a patsy! I am a patsy!" This now (in) famous self-reference was uttered by Oswald on the evening of November 22, 1963, in response to a reporter's question while in Dallas police custody. As discussed in the Editor's Introduction, this was a misunderstanding de Mohrenschildt apparently acquired via a conversation with the owner/editor of the *Midlothian Mirror*, William Penn Jones Jr. Still, given that the manuscript's primary goal is to humanize our view of Oswald, and to keep the now almost comically cliché claim of being a patsy *somewhere* in the manuscript, the quote now becomes the name of the preface.

2. Born October 18, 1939, in New Orleans, Louisiana, and died November 24, 1963, in Dallas, Texas.

3. Boyd was, in fact, still a student. For this reason the word "assistant" has been inserted into the text. The University of Texas at Austin lists Alston Boyd as having received an MA in geology in August 1966. His thesis was titled "Geology of the Western Third of *La Democracia* Quadrangle, Guatemala." His supervisor was R. E. Boyer. The university's *Department of Geological Sciences Newsletter* no. 30 (September 1981) indicates on page 51 that "Alston Boyd (MA '66) is a real estate developer in Austin." Apparently de Mohrenschildt ran short of funds, and both Boyd and his wife returned to the United States in June 1964; their farewell party was June 8. See Joan Mellen, *Our Man in Haiti: George de Mohrenschildt and the Nightmare Republic* (TrineDay, 2012), 179.

4. Replacing "Avenue Truman" in the original manuscript with the correct name.

5. Also called a Quonset hut, the structure is a lightweight prefabricated structure of corrugated galvanized steel having a semicircular cross-section. They were exceptionally popular during World War II with approximately 150,000 to 170,000 constructed between 1941 and 1945. The interior space was highly configurable and could be arranged for many purposes, such as barracks, latrines, offices, and bakeries.

6. A contemporary satellite image of Port-au-Prince at Google Maps reveals three Quonset huts on Boulevard Harry Truman, one of which is identified as Service de

Geodesie et de Cartographie (Cartographic and Geodetic Services). The hut to the immediate north of it is the Institute Haitien de Statistiques (Haitian Institute of Statistics). The location is less than 1,000 feet from Bai de Port-au-Prince (Port-au-Prince Bay), right in the heart of the city as de Mohrenschildt describes.

7. While de Mohrenschildt's manuscript speaks of an *area* called "Tonton Lyle," a UN representative from France living in Haiti in early 1963, Jean Richardot, describes a *single home* with that name. "Tonton Lyle's house, as it was called, had a most interesting history. It had been designed at the turn of the century by a Haitian architect, Leon Mathon." See Jean Richardot, *Journeys for a Better World: An Inside Story of the United Nations by One of Its First Senior Officials* (University Press of America, 1994), 218. Sam Ballen, who was a guest in the de Mohrenschildts' home in Haiti on more than one occasion, calls it the Lyle Estates. Sam Ballen, *Without Reservations: From Harlem to the End of the Santa Fe Trail* (Ocean Tree Books), 171. Both "Villa Valbrune" and "Lyle Estates" are mentioned in Warren Commission Exhibit 3100 and several now declassified CIA documents and for that reason have been inserted here and elsewhere in the manuscript.

8. As described by George McMillan and others the de Mohrenschildts' home in Haiti was evidently built into the side of a hill and was within the presidential compound itself. George McMillan, "The Man Who Knew Oswald," *Washington Post*, April 3, 1977, 31. Ballen described its location as being "about 800 yards from Papa Doc's residence" and mentions it was staffed by three servants. The de Mohrenschildts also had at their disposal an "off-the-road Land Rover" in addition to their convertible that they had shipped from Miami to Port-au-Prince. See Ballen, *Without Reservations*, 171–172. The presidential compound the de Mohrenschildts lived in could only be entered by passing through heavily armed gates. When Duvalier cut power to parts of the island, as an intimidation tactic, it is probably safe to assume the lights in the de Mohrenschildt home remained on.

9. In his Warren Commission testimony de Mohrenschildt says it was the *Syrian* Embassy rather than the Lebanese Embassy. This is not to imply that he is giving a deliberately false account here. His continental conversational style of recollection values the general over the particular, so his having been *in an embassy* that day is what he believes is valuable and worth communicating, while the question of *which* embassy is far less important to him.

10. A Haitian paramilitary force initially created in 1959 in the wake of a failed army coup d'état the year before. Their official name at the time of creation was the National Security Volunteer Militia or MVSN. By 1961 the Macoutes outnumbered the regular army by a ratio of two to one. De Mohrenschildt displays a remarkably cavalier attitude toward them on more than one occasion in the manuscript, seeming to consider them little more than a kind of populist police force. In reality they were utilized by Duvalier to terrorize any and all opponents, committed systematic violence and human rights abuses; they murdered more than 60,000 Haitians. An excellent early account, originally published in 1970, may be found in Bernard Diederich and Al Burt, *Papa Doc and the Tontons Macoutes* (Markus Wiener, 2005).

11. The original manuscript mentions that the reason November 1963 was un-

eventful was the absence of any "shootings" or "invasions" but does not elaborate until the vignette I have titled "Appearing on NBC" in Chapter 4. Haiti had been wracked with political violence all through the spring and summer of 1963. An internal plot initiated by the former head of the Tontons Macoutes, Clément Barbot, and his brother in April had been foiled, and both men were killed while carrying out another plot in July. Several armed incursions by Haitian rebels based in the Dominican Republic and led by former General Léon Cantave had been beaten back by the Macoutes and the Haitian army in August and September.

12. Pan American World Airways, commonly known as Pan Am, was the principal and largest international air carrier in the United States from 1927 until December 4, 1991, when it ceased operations. An inquiry made to the Pan Am Historical Foundation in June 2013 could turn up no further information about anyone named George Morel in Haiti on November 22, 1963.

13. François "Papa Doc" Duvalier (1907–1971) was a doctor by training, receiving a medical degree from the University of Haiti in 1934. In 1946 President Dumarsais Estimé appointed him director general of the National Public Health Service, but when the military initiated a coup Duvalier went into hiding where he remained until 1956, when an amnesty was declared. In the 1957 presidential elections he ran as a military-backed populist candidate, defeating mulatto land-owner and industrialist Louis Dejoie. He promptly exiled Dejoie's major supporters and drew up a new constitution. After the military attempted to oust him in mid-1958 he replaced his chief-of-staff and soon thereafter the entire general staff with officers owing their positions and loyalty to him. He also suffered a massive heart attack in 1959 that left him in a coma for nine hours and may have affected his mental health thereafter. He lost credibility internationally, including with President Kennedy, after holding fraudulent elections in 1961. Two years later, when he was told political rival Clément Barbot had transformed himself into a black dog, Duvalier ordered all black dogs in Haiti to be executed. He also began to tamper with the 1957 constitution, allowing himself to remain in power past the end of his 1963 term. A June 14, 1964, referendum made him "President for Life" with absolute powers; the completely lopsided vote was a farce even by Latin American standards. A good popular account of Haiti in 1963 that de Mohrenschildt himself may have read is "Voodoo Land in Ferment," *Life* 54, no. 10 (March 8, 1963), 28–35. The American government's view of Duvalier may be gleaned from a June 26, 1967, intelligence information cable generated by the CIA: "Situation Appraisal—President Duvalier's Present Strength and Capabilities" in *Foreign Relations of the United States, 1964–1968*, Volume 32, *Dominican Republic; Cuba; Haiti; Guyana*, Document 363, 841–842. In sum: "There has been no doubt for some years that Duvalier is not normal." For a more recent peek behind the curtain that was Haiti in the early 1960s with its many eccentric characters and intrigues, see Mellen, *Our Man in Haiti*. The legacy of Duvalierism for today's Haiti may be seen in Neil A. Burron, "Michel Martelly: Haiti's New Caesar and the Prospects for Democracy," *New Political Science* 35, no. 2 (June 2013): 131–161.

14. Today's American Embassy in Haiti is located in Tabarre, a suburb outside

of Port-au-Prince. According to the embassy's website, prior to relocating to this new location in 2008, "government agencies occupied several different facilities, including the old embassy site [on] Boulevard Harry Truman, in downtown Port-au-Prince." Boulevard Harry Truman is roughly two miles long. The description de Mohrenschildt provides here would appear to be accurate.

15. The 902nd Military Intelligence Group—whose present-day website describes its mission as "counterintelligence activities to protect the U.S. Army, selected Department of Defense forces and agencies, [and] classified information and technologies by detecting, identifying, neutralizing and exploiting foreign intelligence services and transnational terrorist threats"—had interviewed Blaque in the spring of 1963. A declassified memo sent from Port-au-Prince to Dorothe Matlack (Army Intelligence's chief liaison with the CIA) dated May 1, 1963, reads:

> De Mohrenschildt spent only short time Haiti arranging oil business deal therefore not well known. Interview with Embassy officer Blaque revals [sic] he knew De M in New York prior WWII. . . . Blaque out of contact with De M since before WWII and until recently when De M arrived in Haiti. Blaque can not repeat not vouch for character, etc., but states no repeat no reason to suspect him of dishonesty.

Blaque and his wife later turn up in the memoir of American Ambassador Frank V. Ortiz Jr. (1926–2005) while the latter was serving as a political counselor in Lima, Peru, between 1967 and 1970. See Frank V. Ortiz, *Ambassador Ortiz: Lessons from a Life of Service* (University of New Mexico Press, 2005), 100.

16. According to Joan Mellen, Blaque was "for a time the commercial officer at the U.S. Embassy." It would therefore make sense for de Mohrenschildt to have close contact with him, and the fact their acquaintance went back more than two decades may well have worked to de Mohrenschildt's advantage. See Mellen, *Our Man in Haiti*, 95.

17. Port-au-Prince is famous for its picturesque "gingerbread" houses. One is described in loving detail by Richardot who, as a UN representative, may have lived close to Americans such as Blaque and/or de Mohrenschildt:

> It was a two story house, each with gingerbread balustrade, the gingerbread repeated symmetrically under the roof, giving the house much elegance. . . . On the second floor there were a number of bedrooms each with tall French doors opening on the verandah. Lying on the bed of the master bedroom one could see the entire bay and the mountains toward Montrouis and St-Marc, a breathtaking view. The house was topped by turrets on each side and each had a panoramic view of the Cul-de-Sac Plain, its sugar plantations, and the airport beyond the top of the royal palm trees, the bougainvilleas, the oleanders and the hibiscus in profusion in the garden below. The whole property was enchanting.

Richardot, *Journeys for a Better World*, 217–218.

18. Dallas of the early 1960s "was not the shining example of administrative efficiency its boosters sought to project. It was more like New Orleans—spectacularly corrupt." At the same time the city was also "a growing bastion of new money and corporate clout, a center of the domestic oil industry, along with a heavy cluster of defense contractors and military bases." See Russ Baker, *Family of Secrets: The Bush Dynasty, America's Invisible Government, and the Hidden History of the Last Fifty Years* (Bloomsbury, 2009), 89. For additional background information on the city during this time period, see also Bill Minutaglio and Steven L. Davis, *Dallas 1963* (Grand Central, 2013).

19. The original manuscript simply has "the mayor" without any name. Earle Cabell (1906–1975) was the mayor of Dallas from 1961 to 1964 and then a member of the House of Representatives from 1965 to 1973. Both he and de Mohrenschildt were members of the conservative Texas Crusade for Freedom. This organization included other "city fathers" such as Harold Byrd, owner of the Texas School Book Depository, and Ted Dealey, for whom Dealey Plaza was named. It also included Everett L. DeGolyer (1886–1956), a prominent petroleum geologist and geophysicist who had worked for the OSS, the forerunner to the CIA. Cabell's brother was General Charles Cabell (1903–1971), who was deputy director of the CIA under Allen Dulles at the time of the Bay of Pigs disaster and, like Dulles, was forced to resign by President Kennedy in January 1962. New Orleans district attorney Jim Garrison suspected Charles Cabell was linked to the Kennedy assassination. See Iris Kelso, "Garrison Planned to Link General to JFK Slaying," *Washington Post*, September 16, 1973, E10.

20. Probably referring to their interview with Norman E. Warner, first secretary of the American Embassy in Port-au-Prince, on December 4, 1963, that is, barely a week after the assassination. A second interview with Warner was held on December 19. All of this sounds perfectly innocuous, but at the same time the de Mohrenschildts seemingly could not refrain from telling everyone within earshot that they had known the Oswalds, and to make matters worse imprudently accusing de Mohrenschildt's old enemy, the FBI, of being behind the assassination. See the vignette "Why Lee and I Disliked the FBI" in Chapter 1.

21. Marina Nikolayevna Prusakova (1941–present), Oswald's wife from April 30, 1961, until his death on November 24, 1963. See chapters 1, 2, and 3, below, for many additional biographical details.

22. In Haiti it would be a strange day where something unusual *didn't* transpire. According to the novelist Herbert Gold (1924–2011) he was present at the de Mohrenschildts' "luxurious hillside villa" the day after the assassination. Enjoying the food and drink provided by this "suave stranger who was making his fortune in Haiti," Gold would learn that his host not only knew Jacqueline Kennedy, he also knew "that little fellow Lee Harvey" who turned out to be "rather disturbed." Gold observed that de Mohrenschildt (whom he misspells "de Morenschildt") "seemed rather proud of his particular place in history." De Mohrenschildt appeared to be enjoying the party more, recommending ample consumption of the rum and soda being served as the "best thing for the heat and the bites; you forget about them."

See Herbert Gold, *Haiti: Best Nightmare on Earth* (Transaction Publishers, 2004), 131–132.

23. Apparently the letter accused de Mohrenschildt of being a "Polish Communist." On April 24, 1964, while Jeanne was in her second day of testimony before the Warren Commission (his own testimony had preceded hers), de Mohrenschildt visited the State Department and requested a letter exonerating him be sent, presumably to the Haitian ambassador in Washington. According to a CIA internal memo dated April 21 de Mohrenschildt had recently been to the US Embassy in Haiti complaining of someone in the United States trying to sabotage his relationship with Duvalier. Timmons, the recently appointed American ambassador to Haiti, would advise de Mohrenschildt the letter was probably sent by a business rival. Whether or not the letter was truly real is unclear. See Mellen, *Our Man in Haiti*, 173–174. It is true that de Mohrenschildt spent considerable time with the Polish commercial *chargé d'affaires*, Wlodzimierz Galicki. Sam Ballen, who played tennis and went snorkeling with Galicki, observed, "I am sure he was an intelligence agent because of his great shrewdness, and he was always accompanied by a tough-looking Polish security guard who claimed he was his secretary." Galicki, who said he had been to Vietnam, also possessed information about American combat losses there that Ballen did not believe to be factual at the time, but that later turned out to be true. It was the US government and media who had not been factual about the losses. See Ballen, *Without Reservations*, 172.

24. Benson E. L. Timmons III (1916–1997) was US ambassador to Haiti from November 30, 1963, to May 28, 1967. A Rhodes Scholar, he graduated from Oxford in 1941. After working as an executive assistant to the assistant secretary of the treasury from 1946 to 1948, he relocated to the State Department and accompanied Ambassador David Bruce to Paris, serving in several positions between 1948 and 1955. He was involved with American aid to French forces in Indochina during the 1950s. See Theodore Wilson, "Oral History Interview with Benson E. L. Timmons III" (Harry Truman Library, 1970). He replaced Ambassador Thurston, who had been recalled on May 26. On his arrival Duvalier, still angry with the just-assassinated Kennedy's Haitian policies, refused to meet him for five weeks. President Johnson's policies, including aid from the Inter-American Development Bank, were more to the Haitian tyrant's liking. See Alex von Tunzelmann, *Red Heat: Conspiracy, Murder, and the Cold War in the Caribbean* (Henry Holt, 2011), 325. De Mohrenschildt's portrait of Timmons in the manuscript is uniformly negative. See "Our Return to the United States" in chapter 4.

25. The incident with Wood is recalled in greater detail in the vignette titled "Our Move to Haiti" in Chapter 4. Wood arrived in March, after the February letter de Mohrenschildt mentions in the next sentence.

26. See "The Warren Commission" in chapter 4, below. The invitation may well have arrived in February, but the de Mohrenschildts did not give their testimony in Washington, DC, until late April. During the interval the US government, particularly the FBI, was frantically gathering up every scrap of information it could.

27. Elsewhere in the manuscript de Mohrenschildt claims he and his wife had sim-

ply *assumed* their testimony was being gathered for purely informational purposes and would not be published.

28. Marguerite F. Oswald (1907–1981), biological mother of Lee Harvey Oswald.

29. This sentence has been added to help transition from the preface to the main narrative. It also helps to foreshadow the contents of the manuscript's concluding vignette "A Final Word."

30. This would appear to be a summation of de Mohrenschildt's view of how Oswald viewed him, perhaps drawing on his own Warren Commission testimony, rather than being an actual quote made by Oswald while in police custody or at any other time. See Appendix B. He may have been drawing on Marina's testimony as well. It is also possible de Mohrenschildt is thinking of the inscription by Oswald on the back of the "hunter of fascists" photo the de Mohrenschildts discovered in 1967 (see Chapter 5): "For my friend George from Lee Oswald."

Chapter 1: First Conversations with Lee

1. Oswald enlisted in the US Marine Corps on October 24, 1956, shortly after his seventeenth birthday. His primary training was radar operation, a position that required security clearance. From July 9 to August 22, 1957, he was stationed at the Marine Corps Air Station El Toro in Irvine, California. On August 22 he departed for the Naval Air Facility Atsugi in Japan, the largest US Navy air base in the Pacific Ocean, arriving on September 12. On November 20 his unit moved to the Philippines, returning to Atsugi the following March. He was then court-martialed twice, the first time for possessing an illegal firearm and the second for assaulting a superior officer in an incident related to the first. His unit then sailed for Taiwan where, in September 1958, he suffered a nervous breakdown and was transferred back to Atsugi, where he returned to duty after a short time. On November 2 he left Japan, arriving in San Francisco on November 15. After taking a thirty-day leave, Oswald reported back to duty at El Toro on December 22. He received an honorary hardship discharge on September 11, 1959, but after his defection the discharge was downgraded by the marines to undesirable on August 13, 1960.

2. In his Warren Commission testimony de Mohrenschildt indicated he was born in the town of Mozyr (present-day Belarus) on April 17, 1911.

3. George Alexandrovitch Bouhe (1904–1980) was a member of the Dallas White Russian community. He arrived in the United States in April 1924, having left the Soviet Union via Finland. An accountant by trade, he worked for the Chase Manhattan Bank for thirteen years before moving to Dallas in July 1939. For nearly a decade he was the personal accountant of Lewis W. MacNaughton, senior chairman of the board at the geological and engineering firm of DeGolyer and MacNaughton. De Mohrenschildt's calling Bouhe "father superior" may be an allusion to Bouhe's organizing a Greek Orthodox Church congregation when Dallas experienced an influx of Russian-speaking refugees after World War II. In his Warren Commission testimony de Mohrenschildt says he cannot recall whether it was "George Bouhe or . . . Max and Gali Clark" who gave him the Oswalds' address.

4. Inserting the word "September" here. The answer to the question of precisely when and how de Mohrenschildt first became acquainted with Lee Harvey Oswald remains controversial. The following conjecture, however, seems plausible. Bouhe, in his Warren Commission deposition taken in Dallas, claimed to have first met the Oswalds "on Saturday, August 25, 1962." The meeting occurred at a dinner held in the home of Dorothy Lane; Bouhe had escorted Anna Meller, whose husband could not attend. He later mentions de Mohrenschildt "met Oswald somewhere in October or November," but this appears to be a mistake. We know that Marina, while staying with de Mohrenschildt's daughter Alexandra, was taken to the Baylor Dental Clinic on three occasions, the earliest being on Monday, October 8, and that she was accompanied by a woman who could serve as her interpreter. This was almost without question de Mohrenschildt's wife, Jeanne (see note 73). Alexandra in her own Warren Commission testimony said her parents "had called me the night before," which would have been Sunday, October 7. The de Mohrenschildt manuscript refers to two meetings with the Oswalds after the initial encounter with Colonel Orlov. In his own Warren Commission testimony de Mohrenschildt mentions he and Orlov drove to Fort Worth "on some business" and visited the Oswald residence late in the afternoon. In her own testimony before the Warren Commission, Jeanne indicates she first met the Oswalds in "the late summer." This would seem to point to George de Mohrenschildt's first meeting with Oswald as having happened at the end of a business day toward the end of September 1962, give or take a week.

5. The manuscript with one exception uses the phonetic (mis)spelling "Orloff." Orlov (1899–1989), himself a Texas oil speculator, had known de Mohrenschildt since at least the late 1950s. On March 4, 1964, Orlov supplied the FBI with a resume de Mohrenschildt had prepared for him in 1958; the resume was not declassified until 1998. Orlov said in an interview that contrary to this being a first meeting, it was obvious to him that Lee, Marina, and de Mohrenschildt had met before. Given de Mohrenschildt's penchant for conflating closely occurring events the error is not surprising. It is important to note that the Dallas CIA Agent J. Walton Moore, who vigorously denied ever having discussed Oswald with de Mohrenschildt, admitted he and Orlov played handball together. See Joan Mellen, *Our Man in Haiti* (TrineDay, 2012), 52. This at least suggests the possibility the visit may have been at Moore's direct request though it is also possible Moore suggested the idea to Orlov, who then suggested it to de Mohrenschildt. This might explain de Mohrenschildt's claim that he approached Moore shortly after meeting Oswald to ask him if it was all right to associate with a known defector.

6. After returning from the Soviet Union on June 2, 1962, the Oswalds initially stayed with Lee's brother Robert for a month before moving in with his mother, Marguerite. The couple and their baby then moved to the Mercedes Street address on August 10, 1962. The initial deposit was $59.50. The shack is described by de Mohrenschildt in his Warren Commission testimony as having "only two rooms" and being "on a dusty road" that was not paved. It remained the Oswalds' primary residence until November 4 when they would complete a move to their new Dallas residence at 604 Elsbeth Street.

7. Founded in 1872 by Aaron Montgomery Ward as a mail-order company, Montgomery Ward had, by the 1930s, grown into a network of large distribution centers across the country. The company was slow to react to middle-class flight to the suburbs in the 1950s and by the 1960s had begun to lose significant market share to its rivals. The company closed its catalog business in 1985 and in 1997 filed for Chapter 11 bankruptcy. Oswald purchased a television from the Fort Worth store on West 7th Street; because the sale was by credit, his brother Robert co-signed as a reference. In his Warren Commission testimony, however, de Mohrenschildt says, "near Sears [and] Roebuck, as far as I can remember."

8. Full name June Lee Oswald. The baby had been born in the Soviet Union on February 15, 1962. Marina would give birth to a second daughter, Audrey Marina Rachel, on October 20, 1963—just four days after Lee began working at the Texas School Book Depository.

9. Oswald began work at the company on July 17, 1962. His appearance would seem to be an accurate recollection. In de Mohrenschildt's Warren Commission testimony, he mentions arriving at the home with Orlov late "in the afternoon, after business hours, 5 o'clock."

10. On the one hand, this portion of the manuscript says Oswald had no distinguishing physical features, but on the other a later portion of the manuscript mentions that "he had rather attractive gray eyes." The later information has been relocated here where it helps to define his appearance for the reader.

11. De Mohrenschildt was probably thinking of the five years (1934–1938) he spent at the University of Liège in Belgium. To support himself during these years he invested in and worked for a firm that produced ski clothing. During the late 1920s he had been a member of the ski team of Poland; some of its members had participated in the 1928 Winter Olympics but had failed to win a single meet in preliminary trials. See Mellen, *Our Man in Haiti*, 16. Nordic skiing during this era was a sport dominated by, unsurprisingly, Finland, Norway, and Sweden, while Alpine skiing was dominated by Germany. As late as 1948, an acquaintance in Colorado, Mrs. Fern Biddy, would describe de Mohrenschildt as "an excellent skier" who, unfortunately, "preferred the skiing facilities in Aspen to the desert scenery of Rangely" where his work was located.

12. Bouhe, too, described Oswald's Russian as "very good" in his testimony to an assistant counsel to the Warren Commission held in Dallas on March 23, 1964. Oswald's marine proficiency exam taken on February 25, 1959, rated his Russian as "poor." The discrepancy may be explained by the fact that the proficiency exam tested both spoken and written aptitude. Bouhe's testimony expressed doubts as to Oswald's ability to write Russian. Oswald had plenty of time to improve his Russian while living in the Soviet Union. In Warren Commission Exhibit 93, *Notes on His Background*, Oswald indicates, "I studied Russian elementary and advanced grammar from text books with an English-speaking Russian Intourist teacher by the name of Rosa Agafonava, Minsk, January–May 1960. I am totally proficient in speaking conversational Russian, I can read non-technical Russian text without difficulty, and can to a less[er] extent write in the Russian language." According to

Priscilla Johnson McMillan, one "of the chief aims of Intourist, the Soviet travel agency, is to impress foreigners." McMillan, *Marina and Lee: The Tormented Love and Fatal Obsession behind Lee Harvey Oswald's Assassination of John F. Kennedy* (Steerforth Press, 2013), 338. It is also quite likely Oswald received additional language training from his Minsk employer, the Gorizont Electronics Factory.

13. Given Oswald's marine record and the opinions expressed by him later in the manuscript, he was either being polite here, because it was a first meeting, or he was simply lying about his views.

14. A private research university in Dallas, Texas, founded in 1911. In 2008 *The Princeton Review* ranked SMU seventeenth among all US colleges for "Most Conservative Students," and the campus is the site of the George W. Bush Presidential Center, which opened on April 25, 2013. Bush's wife, Laura, is an SMU alumna.

15. This paragraph appears much later in the manuscript, long after de Mohrenschildt has referred to his present wife many times. The original prose is also exceptionally poor and had to be cleaned up more than usual.

16. Eugenia Fomenko (1914–1993) was born in Harbin, China, to Russian parents. The de Mohrenschildts' good friend Sam Ballen described her as "a most handsome woman, a fine ice skater, a great cook, and quite charming—but as outspoken as anyone could be." See Samuel B. Ballen, *Without Reservations* (Ocean Tree Books, 2001), 166. Although well into her forties by the late 1950s she frequently dressed like a teenager, would play tennis in a bikini, and was "so wildly unconventional" she made her husband "seem staid by comparison." See McMillan, *Marina and Lee*, 271. A business acquaintance would say that if you pushed her out the front door she would reappear through a window. FBI informants described her as "strong-willed," "non-conformist," "Bohemian," "extremely bitter," and a "hater."

17. Fomenko met and married Valentin Bogoiavlensky at the age of eighteen, then relocated to Shanghai, where the couple became a dance team and changed their names to Robert and Jeanne LeGon. They immigrated to the United States in 1938, settled in California, and had one daughter, Christina. Robert was institutionalized with an apparently incurable mental illness, and the couple divorced in the spring of 1957. Jeanne had become a successful fashion designer, first in New York and then in Dallas. By her own account she was making $20,000 a year in 1954 and traveling regularly to Europe on paid business trips. She moved to California that year but returned to Dallas in 1955. She met George de Mohrenschildt in 1956, and the two were married on June 23, 1959. Several accounts point to changes in George's behavior as being a result of her influence.

18. Her father was director of the Chinese Eastern Railroad. He resigned in 1925 when the company was sold to the Soviet Union. According to Jeanne's Warren Commission testimony, he was killed by Communist rebels in 1941.

19. A reference to Mǎnzhōuguó (state of Manchuria). Japan seized the region in 1931 following a poorly executed bombing of a Japanese-owned railway staged by the Japanese military, the so-called Mukden Incident. Japan responded with a full invasion, occupying all of Manchuria and installing a puppet state headed by former Chinese emperor Puyi (title character of the film *The Last Emperor*) six months later.

The original de Mohrenschildt manuscript has the historical sequence out of order, with the formation of the puppet state preceding the invasion.

20. To give just one example, Japanese military units conducted experiments on Chinese and Russian civilians and Allied POWs in Mǎnzhōuguó. The infamous Unit 731, a biological and chemical warfare research unit, carried out some of the most horrific atrocities of the World War II, including live vivisection, conventional and biological warfare weapons testing on live human subjects, and lethal experiments involving starvation, pressure chambers, centrifuges, and X-rays. Incredibly, Douglas MacArthur granted members of Unit 731 immunity in exchange for providing the United States, but not its wartime allies, information about their biological warfare research. Some members of Unit 731 continued their activities within Japan during the 1950s.

21. Replacing "movement" in the original manuscript. The context strongly suggests a contrast between prewar Japanese militarism and postwar democratic Japan, not a particular movement *within* democratic Japan.

22. Remainder of the paragraph introducing Nero and Poppaea has been moved here from a later portion of the manuscript. This is done due to repeated references to both dogs before this introductory information is supplied to the reader. As the manuscript will hint on a number of occasions, Jeanne was an even more ardent dog lover than George was. According to one of the de Mohrenschildts' best friends, Sam Ballen, when she saw some Haitian Tontons Macoutes kick a stray dog on a street in Port-au-Prince, Jeanne jumped out of the car and cursed them out "in the crudest Creole" while traffic backed up behind them. See Ballen, *Without Reservations*, 174.

23. Replacing "deprived" in the original manuscript as "devoid" is clearly meant.

24. As in most of the manuscript, de Mohrenschildt here is drawing on notes and tapes he made well after the assassination, and not verbatim transcripts.

25. The discussion that begins with Oswald's lack of a Southern accent is relocated here from much later in the manuscript, the vignette I have titled "Lee: One Last Assessment" in Chapter 6. It makes better sense to describe Oswald's "voice" at the manuscript's beginning given how liberally he is quoted by de Mohrenschildt in the pages to come.

26. The manuscript refers to de Mohrenschildt's college teaching a handful of times but never mentions any of the institutions by name. Given that he taught at Bishop College in Dallas for several years beginning in 1969, and Willem Oltmans's memoirs pinpoint the genesis of the manuscript to that same year, the name of the college is inserted here for the reader's information.

27. In Warren Commission Exhibit 93, *Notes on His Background*, Oswald indicates he read both the *Manifesto of the Communist Party* and *Das Kapital* at the age of fifteen and, after age nineteen, eighteenth-century philosophers and works by Lenin. In her Warren Commission testimony Anna Meller mentions becoming mad at seeing a copy of *Das Capital* and other Communist literature at the Oswalds' Mercedes Avenue home. Marx's *Das Capital: Critique of Political Economy* is a massive and exceedingly complex work requiring a deep understanding of several disciplines to fathom. In both de Mohrenschildt's Warren Commission testimony and the book

manuscript he mentions Oswald having read texts that he clearly did not fully comprehend but would nevertheless use impressive-sounding jargon drawn from these works, for example, "dialectical materialism," which de Mohrenschildt particularly disliked. See Appendix B. In his Warren Commission testimony de Mohrenschildt denigrates this practice as pseudo-intellectual, while in the manuscript he treats it as being more of a humorous quirk. The Marxism of someone of Oswald's educational level was more akin to the shorter and more introductory *Manifesto*. The simple language of rich and poor, exploiter and exploited, that de Mohrenschildt recalls Oswald speaking in certainly points in this direction. The most serious and detailed study of Oswald's Marxism is probably Gary W. O'Brien, *Oswald's Politics* (Trafford, 2010).

28. This sentence is moved here from much later in the manuscript. Oswald's sense of humor is one of the major facets of de Mohrenschildt's attempt to humanize him and needs to be explained to the reader earlier rather than later.

29. The first two jokes are relocated here from another portion of the manuscript, where they are unrelated to the surrounding material.

30. A variant spelling of *muzhik*, a colloquial term for a male Russian peasant.

31. As if in sad confirmation of Oswald's then dim assessment of America, a US Army document produced in 2010 and leaked in 2012, "FM 3–39.40 Internment and Resettlement Options," outlines plans to detain domestic "political activists" in internment camps, where they will be "reeducated" by "PSYOP officers" whose mission is "to pacify and acclimate detainees or DCs to accept U.S.I/R facility authority and regulations." Halliburton subsidiary KBR has been tapped to subcontract regional "emergency environment camps" for FEMA and the US Army Corps of Engineers. In addition, the indefinite detention provision of the National Defense Authorization Act signed by President Barack Obama on December 31, 2011, allows even American citizens to be kidnapped and detained indefinitely without trial.

32. Evidently, Marina's teeth were so bad as to be easily visible to both de Mohrenschildt and Orlov, as the subject is mentioned during their return trip to Dallas and then by Jeanne de Mohrenschildt during her first meeting with the Oswalds. Bouhe's Warren Commission testimony also mentions Marina having "a lot of teeth rotted to the roots." Bouhe goes on to state that after the Oswalds moved to Dallas he gave de Mohrenschildt twenty dollars to take Marina to the Baylor School of Dentistry where four (in truth, five) teeth were extracted.

33. In his Warren Commission testimony de Mohrenschildt quotes Oswald as saying, "I met some Communists in Japan and they got me excited and interested, and that was one of my inducements in going to the Soviet Union, to see what goes on there."

34. Oswald had been due to be released from active duty on December 7, 1959, but on August 17 he filed a request for a dependency discharge, on the grounds his mother had been injured working at her job in December 1958. He was formally released from active duty on September 11 and transferred to the Marine Corps Reserve. While he did register his dependency discharge and enter into the Marine Corps Reserve at the Fort Worth Selective Service Board, he was obligated to serve in

the reserve until December 8, 1962. He would, as we now know, defect to the Soviet Union barely a month later.

35. Essentially correct. After spending two days with his mother in Fort Worth Oswald traveled to New Orleans where on September 20, 1959, he embarked on a boat bound for Europe. Disembarking in the port of Le Havre, France, he then traveled to the English town of Southampton and from there, on October 10, flew to Helsinki. There he obtained a one-week visa to visit the Soviet Union and, on October 15, crossed the border at Vainikkala, proceeding to Moscow.

36. As previously noted the Marine Corps had altered Oswald's discharge to "undesirable," citing his defection as the cause. The change greatly angered Oswald and would explain his agitation when de Mohrenschildt brought the subject up.

37. John Connally (1917–1993) was secretary of the navy from January to December 1961 before becoming governor of Texas on January 15, 1963. After learning his honorable discharge had been downgraded—from his mother who mistakenly reported the wording read "dishonorable" rather than "undesirable"—Oswald wrote a letter to Connally from Minsk appealing his status. The letter, dated January 30, 1961 (actually 1962), arrived after Connally's departure. Oswald received a reply that merely stated his letter had been forwarded to the new secretary of the navy, Fred Korth. Korth, oddly enough, was originally a Forth Worth attorney who in 1948 had represented Oswald's stepfather in his divorce from Lee's mother, Marguerite.

38. Oswald cut his left wrist on October 21, 1959, the day his temporary one-week visa was set to expire.

39. Specifically, as a lathe operator at the Gorizont Electronics Factory, which produced radios as well as military and space electronics in addition to televisions.

40. A tributary of the Biarezina River, 203 miles in length. It flows through the city of Minsk.

41. Correcting "EGB," which appears to be a typo in the original manuscript. The GPU, NKVD, and MGB were all incarnations of the Soviet secret police. In 1922 the GPU (State Political Directorate) had replaced the Cheka, which was in power during the Russian Civil War. In 1934 the GPU was replaced by the NKVD (People's Commissariat for Internal Affairs), and it in turn was replaced by the MGB (Ministry for State Security). The more familiar KGB (Committee for State Security) was created in 1954 and continued to operate until the collapse of the Soviet Union in 1991.

42. Sergius Alexandrovitch von Mohrenschildt (ca. 1870–ca.1944), George's father. His mother, Alexandra Zapolski von Mohrenschildt (ca. 1880–ca. 1920), died of typhus shortly after the family fled the Soviet Union and settled in Poland.

43. This is one of two places in the manuscript where de Mohrenschildt identifies Marina as being from Smolensk, but this appears to be a mistake. Marina lived in Leningrad, not Smolensk, before moving to Minsk.

44. Oswald simply stopped showing up for work at the Leslie Welding Company, last appearing on October 8. He falsely told Marina he had been laid off, and told Bouhe the job had only been temporary. He wrote the company later telling them he had moved to Dallas and requested that unpaid wages be forwarded to him.

45. This entire section on the FBI appears near the end of the manuscript, in the middle of what is now Chapter 6, where it was noticeably out of place with the surrounding material. As it relates a commonality shared by both men it ought to be included much earlier in the text to help establish why such seeming opposites could form a friendship. Interestingly, the material does not really discuss Oswald's views of the FBI in any depth, but other parts of the manuscript make quite clear that Oswald had no love for the organization. Oswald is quoted as saying "Those SOB's annoy me and Marina constantly. They keep on inquiring about me and her. They intimate that I am a suspicious character and that she is a Communist. And so I cannot hold a decent job." And it was true: the FBI had been on Lee's heels almost from the moment he returned from the Soviet Union. A report prepared for President Johnson, declassified in 2000, states "Oswald was interviewed by special agents of this Bureau at Fort Worth, Texas, on June 23, 1962 at which time he was curt, sullen and arrogant. He declined to answer questions as to why he made the trip to Russia or his experiences there."

46. The text implies Oswald wrote a letter and placed it in the mail. In actuality, he visited the Dallas FBI office on November 12, 1963, attempting to find Agent James P. Hosty (1924–2011), who had visited Marina (living then at Ruth Paine's home) on both November 1 and 5. After being informed by a receptionist that Hosty was unavailable, he wrote a note and departed. After the Kennedy assassination and Oswald's murder, Hosty's superior ordered him to destroy the note, whose existence remained unknown until 1975.

47. The text of the letter was supposedly: "If you have anything you want to learn about me, come talk to me directly. If you don't cease bothering my wife, I will take appropriate action and report this to the proper authorities." Hosty's name was in the news in the mid-1970s, for example, in the April 28, 1975, issue of *Newsweek* magazine, which contained a long article titled "Dallas: New Questions and Answers." The article does not mention the letter but merely the well-known fact that Hosty's name and number were found in Oswald's pocket notebook. The content of Oswald's note to Hosty has been the subject of vivid speculation, especially by those who have argued Oswald was an FBI informant. Hosty told the House Select Committee on Assassinations (HSCA) that the letter was not threatening and speculated that Oswald's request to cease harassing his wife arose out of a concern Marina might under questioning reveal the existence of his recent trip to Mexico or his attempt to shoot General Edwin Walker earlier in the year. On the latter, see the vignette "Easter of 1963" in Chapter 3.

48. J. Edgar Hoover (1895–1972) was the first director of the Federal Bureau of Investigation. Fresh out of college, he was hired by the Justice Department to work in the War Emergency Division and became head of the division's Alien Enemy Bureau after US entry into World War I. Immediately after the war he became part of the Bureau of Investigation's Radical Division and was a participant in the Palmer Raids, aimed at arresting and deporting radical leftist elements. In 1924 President Coolidge appointed him director of the BOI. Under his leadership the bureau was reorganized and expanded, as well as renamed the FBI in 1935. For decades Hoover's

zeal was for the investigation of subversives and radicals (and hence the FBI's intense interest in an individual like de Mohrenschildt) while showing little interest in combating the vice rackets typical of organized crime. In 1946 US Attorney General Tom C. Clark tasked Hoover with compiling a list of potentially disloyal Americans who might be detained during a wartime national emergency. When war broke out in Korea in 1950, Hoover submitted a plan to President Truman to suspend habeas corpus protections and detain some 12,000 allegedly disloyal American citizens; Truman declined to carry out the plan. By the time Kennedy assumed office in 1961, Hoover's COINTELPRO program, ostensibly created to combat communism, was widely engaged in infiltration, illegal wiretapping, planting forged documents, and spreading false rumors. Kennedy considered replacing Hoover but concluded the political costs of doing so during his first term were too high. After Kennedy's assassination President Johnson waived the then-mandatory retirement age for government employees, effectively making Hoover FBI director indefinitely. Hoover remained FBI Director until his death in 1972. In 1979 the report of the HSCA would criticize Hoover's reluctance to investigate the possibility of a conspiracy to assassinate Kennedy.

49. A seaside town less than fifteen miles north of San Diego. It has been the home of many prominent scientists, business people, artists, writers, and performers.

50. De Mohrenschildt and Edward J. Walz, an uncle of his third wife, Wynne Sharples, had formed the Waldem Oil Company in 1954. The company name (with slight variations in spelling, yet another instance of de Mohrenschildt's limited command of written English) is mentioned in the alumni news section of the June 1954, June 1955, July 1957, July 1958, July 1960 and July 1962 issues of the *Department of Geology, The University of Texas [at Austin] Newsletter*. A report prepared by the Administrative Services Bureau of the Dallas Police Department on February 27, 1967, recorded that Walz resided in Rancho Santa Fe, California, which is just 18.3 miles north of La Jolla. For these reasons Walz's name is inserted here.

51. The identity of the motel or hotel de Mohrenschildt refers to would appear to be the high-priced and famous Hotel del Charro, which had opened for business in the early 1950s. A *New York Times* article dated January 17, 1954, reported that "a syndicate of well-heeled Texans has spent a reported $1 million on a fabulous hostelry dubbed the Hotel del Charro." The behind-the-scenes owners were Texas oilmen Clint Murchison and Sid Richardson, both acquaintances of de Mohrenschildt in the 1950s. Since de Mohrenschildt and Murchison were members of such elite organizations as the Dallas Petroleum Club, and Jeanne had family ties to Southern California, it is quite possible the event described here actually happened. The manuscript's penchant for discretely omitting names in favor of using an individual's occupation leaves open the possibility Murchison and/or Richardson were among the "oil magnates" present at the table with the FBI director. Hoover stayed at the Hotel del Charro for two weeks every summer, free of charge, from 1952 until his death. See Bryan Burrough, *The Big Rich: The Rise and Fall of the Greatest Texas Oil Fortunes* (Penguin, 2009), 226–230. See also Matt Potter, "Oil and Politics in La Jolla," *San Diego Reader*, January 5, 2011.

52. The year 1941 would have been three years after de Mohrenschildt's arrival. The month and day have been added using declassified FBI documents.

53. While it is true the Selective Training and Service Act was enacted on September 16, 1940, requiring all men between the ages of twenty-one and thirty-five to register with their local draft boards, it seems rather odd that the twenty-nine-year-old de Mohrenschildt, who did not become an American citizen until after the war's end, would have been *required* to do so. He was still a Polish citizen. Yet his Warren Commission testimony says much the same thing, only this time he claims that in 1941 he *volunteered* to enlist in the US Army but was turned down and classified 4F due to his elevated blood pressure.

54. After Germany and the Soviet Union divided Poland between themselves in the fall of 1939, people of Germanic origin, or *Volksdeutsche*, were allowed to cross from Soviet-occupied Poland to German-occupied Poland if they appeared before a commission and declared their allegiance to Germany. As de Mohrenschildt explains in his Warren Commission testimony, this is precisely what his father did; it was far more prudent, given his father Sergius's prior experiences with the Bolsheviks, to be "with the Germans than with the Communists." Sergius would die in an Allied bombing attack near the end of the war.

55. His family name was *von* Mohrenschildt, but he had changed it to *de* Mohrenschildt when he moved to the United States in 1938. His brother Dimitri kept the family name.

56. Actual name Lilia Pardo de Larin (1906–unknown). De Mohrenschildt refers to her as the love of his life in his Warren Commission testimony. As is often the case, de Mohrenschildt is half-correct. The thrice-married de Larin *was* a widow, but that had been an earlier husband; her *current* husband, Jorge Guasco, was very much alive. When Guasco showed up in New York, threatening to shoot them both on sight, de Mohrenschildt and his lawyer "managed to have [him] thrown into jail for six months." See Mellen, *Our Man in Haiti*, 24–25.

57. Lilia was introduced to de Mohrenschildt, at least according to his Warren Commission testimony, by a very wealthy Brazilian named Dr. Palo Muchado (nickname "The King of Bananas"), who also had a romantic interest in her.

58. An FBI report filed in Houston on June 10, 1941, indicates:

Subjects arrived Corpus Christi, Texas, 5/14/41 in 1941 Chrysler Convertible Coupe bearing current New York tags #[illegible], and registered Nueces Hotel in separate rooms. On 5/29/41, they registered as man and wife at Tarpon Inn, Port Aransas, Texas, where they remained until 6/2/41 when they returned to Nueces Hotel. VON MOHRENSCHILDT is reported to have photographed and sketched Coast Guard Station and Ship Channel near Port Aransas.

59. Replacing "We left the hotel early to go to the beach at Arkansas Pass and spent a delightful day there." The manuscript exhibits confusion here, because *Arkansas* Pass is a town well inland and roughly sixty miles due west of Corpus Christi Beach. His Warren Commission testimony correctly indicates the location was *Aran-*

sas Pass, which is just northwest of Corpus Christi and is itself situated on Corpus Christi Bay.

60. De Mohrenschildt was found to have $2,000 in cash in his possession, which may have not been much money by *his* standards, but, adjusted for inflation, it would be the equivalent of carrying $31,769 today.

61. The Mann Act was congressional legislation passed on June 25, 1910, popularly named after its sponsor, Republican James Robert Mann (1856–1922). The act was a response to a wave of "white slavery" hysteria then gripping the country and, in theory, sought to address prostitution, human trafficking, "debauchery," and "any other immoral purpose." In practice "immoral" was liberally interpreted and was used to criminalize forms of *consensual* sexual behavior, most commonly to prosecute men for having sex with under-age females or simply to harass anyone who might incur the wrath of power. The legislation was not updated until 1978, and then again in 1986. Mann would become House Minority Leader from 1911 to 1919.

62. After several months of living with Lilia in Mexico, de Mohrenschildt was informed by the Mexican government that he was *persona non grata* and must immediately leave the country. According to de Mohrenschildt it was because the brother of the president of Mexico, a high-ranking general named Maximino Avila Camacho (1891–1945), who was famous for his womanizing, had taken an interest in Lilia. De Larin and de Mohrenschildt were unsuccessful in their efforts to reunite, she because of her connections with Camacho, whose fascist views made her entry into the US undesirable, and he because of the incident at Corpus Christi. At a hearing held in Washington, DC, on February 12, 1943, de Mohrenschildt's appeal to be issued a permit to reenter Mexico was denied. Just four months later he would marry the first of his four wives, wealthy eighteen-year-old Dorothy Pierson, in a marriage announced in the *New York Times*. They were divorced in June, 1944.

63. The events at Corpus Christi Beach/Aransas Pass took place in 1941; five years later would have been the year 1946. Many accounts indicate the year de Mohrenschildt became a naturalized American citizen was 1947. Some sources say 1948 while Commission Exhibit 3100 indicates July 11, 1949, Certificate of Naturalization #6057081. He may be rounding off the amount of time but in any case the number of years is not totally correct. Apparently he was also never aware that the love of his life, now remarried, had told the FBI: "He is a man capable of anything and for his useless and vicious life he needs large sums of money and so naturally he sells himself to the highest bidder. . . . I am so amazed to know that citizenship has just been granted to that traitor to the country in which he is living."

64. The largest oil field in America in the late 1940s was in Rangely, Colorado, and de Mohrenschildt was employed by "the Rangely Field Engineering Committee, a joint operation of all the oil companies charged with compiling statistics and engineering data for the whole field." See Vincent Bugliosi, *Reclaiming History: The Assassination of President John F. Kennedy* (W. W. Norton, 2007), 657. While living in Colorado de Mohrenschildt married his second wife, Phyllis Washington, on July 11, 1948. She was the adopted daughter of Samuel Walter Washington, a member of the US Diplomatic Service assigned to the American consulate in Madrid, Spain.

Samuel Washington would later do work for the CIA, including in Guatemala before the 1954 coup there. De Mohrenschildt's second marriage, like his first, was announced in the *New York Times*. It, too, ended rather quickly in divorce on December 29 of the following year.

65. Misspelled as "heimatloss" in the original manuscript. The word means a person forced to flee their home country, an exile or refugee. With Poland behind the Iron Curtain after 1945 de Mohrenschildt would in theory have found it difficult to return. According to FBI records de Mohrenschildt entered the United States on May 13, 1938, using a Polish passport issued by the Polish Consulate in Antwerp, Belgium, the previous fall. He did return to Poland on at least two occasions, however. The first was in 1957, visiting relatives briefly while he was working in Yugoslavia. The second was around 1960 when, according to Sam Ballen, he "secured a little commission to go to Poland and make a geologic overview, which essentially consisted of translating Polish professional papers. He came back saying that the country was so dismal and depressed you couldn't even get an erection." Ballen, *Without Reservations*, 171.

66. A January 8, 1958, report de Mohrenschildt provided to the CIA after his return from Yugoslavia has as its subject "Humor in Common Usage." The third of the five jokes reads "The difference between Socialism and Capitalism: Capitalism makes social mistakes, but Socialism makes capital mistakes." It is not impossible, of course, that he told this same joke to Oswald.

67. A substantially longer version of this joke is the first of the five jokes in the same CIA report mentioned in the previous note. While not completely impossible it is doubtful that Oswald would have known a version of the exact same joke.

68. The manuscript mistakenly says "Taggart's." Jaggars-Chiles-Stovall, a Dallas typographic service serving advertisers, the graphic arts industry, and newspapers. The firm also did business with the US Army Map Service, including U-2 spy plane photography. Robert L. Stovall, the president of Jaggars-Chiles-Stovall, told the Warren Commission that Oswald had no part in or access to any confidential or classified work. Several sources dispute this version of the story, claiming de Mohrenschildt secured the position for Oswald himself, and that Oswald was doing more than menial jobs.

69. This is one of several indications that Oswald owned more than the cheap Imperial REFLEX camera that Marina allegedly used to take the now infamous "backyard" photos of him holding the rifle that allegedly killed President Kennedy. The Dallas police discovered several cameras in Oswald's possession but *not* the Imperial REFLEX, which was "found" in Ruth Paine's garage a month and a half after the assassination by Oswald's brother Robert—after the police had already scoured the garage *three* times. An expensive Minox "spy" camera was discovered by Dallas police detective Gus Rose in Oswald's sea bag. Assistant District Attorney William J. Alexander also saw the camera. The Minox was listed with Oswald's other confiscated possessions and turned over to the FBI on November 26, 1963. Two months later the FBI denied the existence of the camera and insisted the Dallas police change their invoice records. The Dallas police refused.

70. By his own recollection Ballen had known de Mohrenschildt since "the summer of 1952" and would last speak to him just weeks before de Mohrenschildt's death in 1977. See Ballen, *Without Reservations*, 162. He was, in addition to being a self-employed financial consultant, chairman of the board at the High Plains Natural Gas Company and Electrical Log Services, Inc.

71. This description of the meeting between Oswald and Ballen does not match Ballen's own testimony in Volume 9 of the *Warren Commission Hearings and Exhibits*. Ballen described his overall impression of Oswald as being "fairly good" and went so far as to say he had the feeling Oswald was "an individual who felt warmly towards President Kennedy." The major impediment to finding Lee employment was, Ballen indicated, Oswald's "lack of any useable training." Secondarily, Ballen also felt Oswald "was too much of a rugged individualist and would not fit in with the team down there [at Electrical Log Services]."

72. Alexandra de Mohrenschildt (1943–present). George was her biological father and Jeanne her step-mother. She had been raised by Nancy Tilton, a relative of her biological mother. At the age of sixteen she eloped, marrying Gary E. Taylor, a decision both George and Jeanne disapproved of. By the time of the Warren Commission the Taylors had divorced.

73. Replacing "daughter" with "my wife Jeanne" for two reasons. First, in another portion of the manuscript de Mohrenschildt indicates that, in addition to handling the move, de Mohrenschildt's wife, Jeanne, "would drive [Marina] to Baylor dental clinic or to the child care center," and it was due "to my wife's help" that "Marina's four spoiled teeth were removed." Second, because the statement by the members of the clinic given to the Warren Commission indicated Marina was accompanied by an unidentified woman who acted as interpreter. This had to be Jeanne because Alexandra, according to her own Warren Commission testimony, could speak just a few words of Russian. There were three visits, all in October, with a cleaning and X-rays on October 8, three teeth extracted on October 10, and two more teeth extracted on October 15, for a total of five, not four.

74. This statement, if it ever was truly made, does not match what we now know of the historical Oswald, whose excessively fragile self-constructed identity was founded on a habitual telling of lies.

75. It is somewhat amusing that de Mohrenschildt would make such a claim. The Warren Commission testimony of his former son-in-law Gary E. Taylor indicates the de Mohrenschildts "have always owned convertibles and they would ride in them in all kinds of weather with the top down." See the *Warren Commission Hearings and Exhibits*, Vol. 9, 99. The manuscript itself mentions the de Mohrenschildts' 1962 Galaxie V-8 convertible. In FBI documents Taylor describes the vehicle as a "white Ford convertible, two tone blue interior with a blue stripe inside the chrome molding on the outside of the car." The Galaxie model produced from 1960 to 1964 was a radical departure from the look of the 1950s with a sleek futuristic appearance.

76. Regarding Diderot, see note 4 in the Editor's Introduction.

77. Diderot spent the last thirty years of his life living in an apartment in Paris, Rue Taranne, though he also spent at great deal of time at Grandval, a rural estate

owned by the Baron d'Holbach. Shortly before his death he was moved to the Rue de Richelieu, to a palatial room provided by his benefactor the tsaritsa of Russia, Catherine the Great. This may be what de Mohrenschildt is speaking of. The text could also be a mistaken allusion to Diderot's famous 1772 essay, "Regrets on Parting with My Old Dressing Gown. Or, A Warning to Those Who Have More Taste Than Money." In this essay Diderot writes, for example, "Beware the contamination of sudden wealth. The poor man may take his ease without thinking of appearances, but the rich man is always under a strain."

78. The death of his son Sergei due to cystic fibrosis had a profound and lasting psychological impact on de Mohrenschildt. Arguably, he never fully recovered from it. See the postscript of his letter to long-time friend Janet Auchincloss in Appendix A.

79. The manuscript merely says "Cubans" here but identifies them as students shortly thereafter.

80. As he apparently did for Alexander Ziger, his boss at the factory in Minsk. Ziger "seems to have taken [Oswald] under his wing and treated him like a son, inviting him to his house and on Sunday rides with his family into the country." Quoted in O'Brien, *Oswald's Politics*, 22. As has been frequently observed Oswald often seemed attracted to or was reaching out toward individuals who from the outside might appear to be father figures. Was he simply replicating an already established pattern with de Mohrenschildt? The manuscript suggests this is a credible assertion.

81. Marina had been trained in pharmacy in the Soviet Union. See Chapter 2.

82. An FBI report filed by James C. Kennedy on March 1, 1964, indicates de Mohrenschildt had presented the following credentials when enrolling in the College of Arts and Sciences, University of Texas at Austin, on March 6, 1944: (1) a diploma in Commercial and Financial Sciences stating "more than satisfactory work," granted in 1933 by the Institute for Higher Studies, Antwerp; (2) a diploma in Common Law and Diplomatic History stating "very great distinction on Moral Philosophy and Psychology," granted in 1935 by the University of Liège; (3) a doctoral equivalent diploma in Commercial Sciences stating "done with distinction," granted in 1936 from the University of Liège. His dissertation was titled "The Economic Influence of the United States on Latin America." At the University of Texas at Austin his grades were excellent, and he received a master's degree in petroleum geology on October 29, 1945. His master's thesis was titled "A Review of the Principles of Reservoir Performance for Petroleum Geologists." While a student at Austin he was employed as a French tutor in the Romance Languages Department.

83. The Warren Commission testimony given by other members of the Dallas–Fort Worth Russian community parallels this self-portrait. George Bouhe, for example, said: "There is something in him . . . [he] is something of a nonconformist, meaning if you invited him to dinner, formally, he might arrive there in a bathing suit, and bring a girlfriend which is not accepted."

84. Pantepec Oil was founded in 1913 by William F. Buckley Sr. (1881–1958), a Texas oil millionaire. Originally based in Mexico, the company relocated to Venezuela in 1924. His son, William F. Buckley Jr. (1925–2008), was a member of the CIA in the early 1950s (working in Mexico alongside later Watergate conspirator

E. Howard Hunt) and went on to start the right-wing magazine *National Review* in 1955 as well as becoming a nationally syndicated columnist and author of numerous conservatively slanted books. The August 1945 issue of *Oil Weekly* published an article by de Mohrenschildt titled "Performance of the Gathering System in Mulata Field, Venezuela."

85. The name of the Soviet ambassador to Venezuela has been inserted using an FBI report dated February 28, 1964: "According to WF T-2, [de Mohrenschildt] described himself as a petroleum engineer who had worked in the Texas oil fields and in Venezuela and while in the latter country became very well acquainted with the Soviet Ambassador FOMA TREBIN." Foma A. Trebin arrived in Venezuela on October 16, 1945, and during formal dinners with prominent Venezuelans criticized the methods employed by US oil companies as inefficient. See Leonard M. Fanning, *Foreign Oil and the Free World* (McGraw-Hill, 1954), 87, and John Burt Mathews, *The Bases of United States–Venezuela Relations, 1900–1950* (University of Wisconsin, 1953), 97.

86. The Branobel Oil Company had been originally established by the brother of Alfred Nobel (1833–1896, founder of the Nobel Peace Prize), Robert Nobel (1829–1896), and others and had by the late nineteenth century become one of the largest oil companies in the world.

87. De Mohrenschildt's father, Sergius, and an uncle had both held directorial positions within Branobel before it was nationalized by the Bolsheviks in 1920.

88. The original manuscript uses the word "instability" here, which appears to be an unfortunate lapse in de Mohrenschildt's English. The surrounding context strongly indicates he is not referring to mental instability such as an inability to maintain a grip on objective reality but rather cognitive uncertainty, an unwillingness to come to a final, fixed, conclusion.

89. On numerous occasions de Mohrenschildt uses a narrow example when speaking of an individual's broad overall traits. At this juncture of the manuscript he only mentions Oswald's job at Jaggars-Chiles-Stovall, but in the manuscript as a whole he indicates that Oswald was happy with more than just that one job.

90. Probably paraphrasing the Warren Commission testimony of good friend Sam Ballen:

> MR. LIEBELER: Was the time that Oswald came to your office the first time that you had met him, or had you met him previous to that?
> MR. BALLEN: If I had met him previously, it would have been on a Sunday morning in the de Mohrenschildts' household for a period of time of about 40 minutes, but I am about satisfied, in talking to other people, that the individual I met on that Sunday morning was not Oswald, but some other stray dog.

91. Certainly this is George Bouhe, who became so afraid of Oswald that he began avoiding him, even as he continued to try to assist Marina.

92. In his Warren Commission testimony George Bouhe indicated he has spent

approximately $75 on the Oswalds, for things such as groceries, bus fares, and items of clothing for Marina and mentions he had spent eleven dollars to buy a playpen for June. He also said he had paid for the dental work performed on Marina's teeth at the Baylor School of Dentistry. See note 32 in this chapter.

93. On June 18, 1962, just four days after arriving in Fort Worth, Oswald asked a stenographer, Pauline Virginia Bates, to type a manuscript he had written in Russia. Over the course of three days she produced ten single-spaced pages. In Bates's Warren Commission testimony she indicates that when she finished the tenth page he paid her $10 and, claiming lack of funds, refused to allow her to continue—despite Bates's offer to work for free or on credit.

94. Apparently it was "one minor article . . . about the potential of the motion picture industry in Europe." See Mellen, *Our Man in Haiti*, 17.

95. Given the deplorable condition of de Mohrenschildt's draft manuscript his statement here is certainly ironic.

96. The February 15, 1969, entry in Willem Oltmans's memoirs quotes Oswald as having told de Mohrenschildt he learned "the method of dialectical materialism" from the copy of *Das Capital* he borrowed from the Loyola University Library. Willem Oltmans, *Memoires 1968–1970* (Papieren Tijger, 2003), 104. In his Warren Commission testimony de Mohrenschildt says, "when it comes to dialectic materialism, I do not want to hear that word again." See Appendix B.

97. By the age of seventeen Oswald had resided at twenty-two different locations and attended twelve different schools. He dropped out of the tenth grade in the fall of 1955 in New Orleans, later reenrolled in Fort Worth in September of 1957 but quit to join the Marines just a month later. He never received a high school diploma.

98. The original manuscript has "depraved masochistic policemen," which, given the context, seems an error on the part of de Mohrenschildt, who probably would have intended Oswald to depict the police of Minsk as sadistic brutes to both scandalize and confirm the worst fears of an American audience.

99. The recollection that Oswald was working on a book manuscript, a sort of memoir of his life in the Soviet Union, is correct. One such work was a four-part document called *The Collective*, which is largely devoted to his time in Minsk.

100. On de Mohrenschildt's Warren Commission testimony, see Chapter 4.

101. As he does on more than one occasion de Mohrenschildt refers to the single-volume *Warren Commission Report* when he actually means the much larger twenty-six-volume *Warren Commission Hearings and Exhibits*. Oswald's manuscript *The Collective* appears as Exhibit 92 in Vol. 16, pages 287–336, of the latter.

102. Oswald's writings, reproduced in their original state within the *Warren Commission Hearings and Exhibits*, are now widely available in more accessible form. Rarely however have they been the subject of serious analysis. For this, see O'Brien, *Oswald's Politics*.

Chapter 2: Lee's Troubled Marriage to Marina

1. Correcting the phonetically spelled "tharist" in the original manuscript.

2. Marina's biological father had been killed in the Great Patriotic War with Nazi

Germany and its allies. Her mother remarried, and Marina lived with her mother and stepfather, first in Severodvinsk (on the White Sea less than thirty miles northeast of Arkhangelsk), followed by Moldavia and then at age twelve Leningrad. After receiving her degree in pharmacy (see note 5) she was assigned to a job in a drug warehouse, which she quit after just a few days. Two months later she moved to Minsk to live with her uncle (see note 10). She found a job in a hospital pharmacy, joined the *Komsomol* (a Communist youth organization), and was apparently quite popular prior to meeting Oswald.

3. Though he had access to Marina's Warren Commission testimony, de Mohrenschildt makes a number of errors with regard to Marina's family history and fails to mention the names of her mother and stepfather. The errors have been corrected and the names have been included given that all this information was clearly available to him, as well as for the benefit of the reader.

4. Compare this portion of the manuscript with the following extract of Marina's Warren Commission testimony:

MR. RANKIN: What was your relationship with your half-brother? Did you get along with him?
MRS. OSWALD: I loved them very much, and they loved me.
MR. RANKIN: And your half-sister too?
MRS. OSWALD: Yes. They are very good children. Not like me.

It could just be coincidental, or he may have actually had the conversation he describes, but one would be justified in at least suspecting that de Mohrenschildt was drawing on Marina's Warren Commission testimony here and refashioning it as remembered dialogue.

5. Her diploma from the Leningrad Pharmaceutical School, granted on June 30, 1959, is Warren Commission Exhibit No. 20. The de Mohrenschildt manuscript incorrectly has her receiving the degree in Minsk. This is yet another instance where two separate events are conflated together in de Mohrenschildt's memory, this time Marina earning her pharmacy *degree* in Leningrad and then finding the hospital pharmacy *job* in Minsk.

6. The manuscript refers to what would appear to be a *second* suicide attempt by Oswald while in the Soviet Union, but the claim appears to be in error.

7. Lee met Marina at a trade dance on March 17, 1961; he was hospitalized with an ear infection from March 30 to April 11. Marina's visits were during this time. De Mohrenschildt has the sequence of events backward. As with his many other gaffes recalling occurrences and reconstructing event chronology there is no deliberate intent to deceive the reader. From his perspective these kinds of details are inconsequential in the relating of the larger truth: Lee and Marina *did* meet, they *did* fall in love, and they *did* marry, on April 30. Editors exist to remind their authors of the minor details.

8. The word "apparently" is inserted here as de Mohrenschildt could not know with absolute certainty Lee's motivation for leaving the Soviet Union. The manu-

script itself points to a disappointment with the Soviet brand of communism, and there is certainly evidence to support this in Oswald's own writings. See Gary W. O'Brien, *Oswald's Politics* (Trafford, 2010).

9. The actual sequence of events leading up to Oswald's departure from the Soviet Union is considerably more complex and convoluted, yet at the same time more banal and pedestrian, than the simple account given by de Mohrenschildt, who may or may not have been relying on Lee and/or Marina for his information. On May 25, less than a month after his marriage to Marina, Lee notified the American Embassy he had wed and his new wife would like to accompany him to the United States. He traveled to Moscow on July 8, his passport was returned on July 10, and Marina filled out paperwork in the embassy on July 11. On August 20 he filed the paperwork to leave the country with Soviet officials. Impatient, perhaps, with the pace of Soviet bureaucracy, he wrote the American Embassy on October 4 requesting that they intervene in his case. The embassy replied on October 12 that there could be little hope of a speedy exit. In December he wrote to Texas senator John Tower asking for help obtaining exit visas. On December 25 Marina was called to the passport office and informed she and Lee would be granted exit visas. A delay ensued when on January 15, 1962, the American Embassy informed Lee he would have to produce an affidavit demonstrating that Marina would not become a "ward of the state." He wrote to his mother, Marguerite, on January 23 requesting her assistance and then on January 26 sent a letter to the International Rescue Commission requesting $1,000 in aid; the embassy replied on February 6 asking him to file a formal application for a loan, which they received on March 3. During March Marina's visa was formally granted and an affidavit for Marina signed by Marguerite's employer arrived. The Oswalds were apparently not in a great hurry to leave the country as an April 12 letter to Lee's brother, Robert, indicates good weather had arrived and the couple was not in any rush to depart. On May 10 the American Embassy in Moscow requested Lee travel there to sign the final paperwork. He picked up his exit visa in Minsk on May 22 and visited the embassy in Moscow two days later. On June 1 he signed a promissory note for the amount of $435.71. The Oswalds then embarked on their return to the United States. The loan would be repaid in full on January 25, 1963.

10. Marina's aunt and uncle were Valya Pruskova and Illya Proskov. Proskov was a colonel in the MVD, the Russian Interior Ministry security service. This agency was something akin to a national police force mixed with something like the FBI.

11. For example, if Oswald had been recruited and trained by Soviet intelligence, who now wished to insert him back into the United States. Though why they would choose to place him in an out-of-the way location like Fort Worth and allow him to spend most of his time trying to find work or employed in menial jobs—all of it done by bus or hitched rides since he couldn't drive—is certainly curious.

12. That "something else" has been the subject of endless speculation in innumerable books. It is worth pointing out that the prose here does slightly recall a portion of the Warren Commission testimony of an acquaintance of de Mohrenschildt, Max Clark. Clark noted that the most "recent arrivals from the Soviet bloc . . . just couldn't understand how the Oswalds got out of Russia so easily," while those who

had "lived in the States the longest period of time" assumed "that they were of no value to the Russians and [Russian authorities] felt it was good riddance."

13. As written in the manuscript: "Personally, I know of one case, a reporter for the *Christian Science Monitor* successfully extracted his wife from Russia during the time of Stalin." The *Monitor* in fact covered the subject of American citizens with Soviet spouses closely for decades, from the 1940s right up until the time de Mohrenschildt finished the manuscript in the summer of 1976. For example, an article titled "This Is Russia Uncensored," written by Edmund Stevens and appearing in the *Monitor* on November 12, 1949, says, "Soviet wives of American citizens are only a small fraction of those who have made efforts to leave the Soviet Union and get to America. Approximately 5,500 applicants have contacted the American Embassy over the past nine years." Another article, titled "Soviet Wife of U.S. Citizen Not Allowed to Join Husband," appeared on July 14, 1976, which would date to precisely when de Mohrenschildt was completing the manuscript. Assuming de Mohrenschildt read the *Monitor* more than once in his lifetime he probably would have been familiar with *many* cases like that of Lee and Marina, not simply the one he mentions here.

14. Oswald's major manuscripts were two works titled *Historic Diary* and *The Collective: Typed Narrative Concerning Russia*.

15. It is not clear why de Mohrenschildt says whatever bonded Lee and Marina was not noticed at that time.

16. Another portion of the manuscript contains the following anecdote:

An amusing incident happened on the way to Baylor, recalls my wife. [She and Marina] had to drive by the predominantly [black] section of town, gaudy but cheerful Hall and Washington streets, almost every decrepit [building] either a night-club, strip-tease joint or a dance hall. Hookers and flashy pimps were strolling along . . . . Suddenly Marina excitedly attracted my wife's attention shouting in Russian to slow down. She looked at the tall, muscled, black youngster standing proudly at the corner and surveying the situation.

"Look at him! Look!" She pulled at my wife's sleeve in a frenzy. "What a handsome man!"

"Oh yes," agreed Jeanne, "he is very handsome."

"No, he is fantastic, fantastic!" exulted Marina.

Such an enthusiasm surprised my wife.

"He is so big and strong! What muscles he must have."

As my wife related this incident, she observed that [it] was not a question of an attraction of a Nordic woman to an exotic man of a dark race, but addressing [the] fact that a young married woman with a child would show such an uninhibited adm[i]ration for a sexy male.

I drove her myself on the same street and teased her myself about her attraction to black men. "Marina," I guessed, "you did not see in Russia such uninhibited, natural men."

She laughed. "Neither Russians nor American whites can compare to such beautiful men," she said candidly. "Maybe the Cubans I met in Minsk were just as attractive."

17. Robert Edwin Oswald Jr. (1934–present). Robert and his family lived at 7313 Davenport Street in Fort Worth. It was Robert who met Lee and Marina at the Dallas Love Field airport on June 14, 1962, after their return from the Soviet Union. The Oswalds stayed with Robert and his family in "June–July of 1962" according to Robert's Warren Commission testimony.

18. Marina Oswald briefly stayed with de Mohrenschildt's daughter Alexandra and her husband. In her Warren Commission testimony Alexandra says her parents asked "if I would please take care of Marina Oswald's child while she went to the dentist, and could she stay overnight with me because she had two appointments in a row." This would seem to point to Marina's dental work of October but then, unable to recall the dates she insisted it was during a period of hot weather, most probably in "the later part of August." Assistant counsel Jenner did not point out the error in recollection. She does however confirm the portrait of Marina as being "exceedingly lazy," mentioning her guest "wouldn't help with the dishes or clearing the table or preparing the meal, cleaning the apartment, anything pertaining to the extra work I had to do because she was there."

19. The original manuscript has "deprived of energy" which would appear to be a slip in de Mohrenschildt's English.

20. Along with Tolstoy, Dostoyevsky is usually regarded as one of the greatest and most influential novelists of the Golden Age of Russian Literature. *The Idiot* was first published in 1869. The plot centers on a young prince who returns to Russia after spending several years at a Swiss sanatorium. He is portrayed as good, but overly trusting and naïve. He is caught in a struggle between two women, leading to disaster. The prince goes mad again and returns to the sanatorium. The reader is left with a strong impression that in a world obsessed with money, power, and sexual conquest a mental asylum may be the only place for a saint. The German philosopher Friedrich Nietzsche, in *The Twilight of the Idols*, wrote that Dostoyevsky was "the only psychologist . . . from whom I had something to learn; he ranks among the most beautiful strokes of fortune in my life." When Nietzsche described Jesus as an "idiot" he may have been thinking of Dostoyevsky's novel, rather than simply using the term abusively.

21. Although they appear elsewhere in the manuscript the second and third sentences of this paragraph fit seamlessly here.

22. Probably a reference to Russia's serfs, who were only freed in 1861. Serfdom was a condition of bondage or modified slavery developed primarily during the High Middle Ages. The basic unit of feudal society was the manor, and the Lord of the Manor and his serfs were bound legally, economically, and socially. Serfs who occupied a plot of land were required to work for the Lord of the Manor who owned the land and, in return, were entitled to protection, justice, and the right to exploit certain fields within the manor to maintain their own subsistence. In a letter to Willem Oltmans announcing his divorce from Jeanne, dated January 24, 1973,

de Mohrenschildt would quip: "Feel like a liberated Russian slave. *Viva la liberte!*" Willem Oltmans, *Memoires 1973* (Papieren Tijger, 2004), 308.

23. The manuscript has "temporal strength" here, which is certainly awkward.

24. Oswald had just begun to learn how to operate a car at the time of his being arrested and charged with killing President Kennedy and policeman J. D. Tippit. Ruth Paine gave him driving lessons in mid-October and on November 3.

25. When asked if Oswald drank alcohol, Bouhe, in his Warren Commission testimony, responded, "He took one vodka in my home, and he probably took a couple of drinks at Katya Ford's house. I think I saw him with a glass [at the Ford house], but I do not know if it was ginger ale."

26. Slang for having cheated by using notes smuggled into class.

27. Franklin, Jefferson, and other leaders of the American Revolution would more accurately be characterized as believers in deism rather than agnostics. The former is the belief that reason, and observation of the natural world, rather than revelation is sufficient to determine the existence of god, while the latter is the belief that the existence or nonexistence of any deity is unknown and possibly unknowable. The word "agnostic" was not coined until 1869, during a speech by the English biologist Thomas Henry Huxley at a meeting of the Metaphysical Society in London.

28. Arnold J. Toynbee (1889–1975), the British historian. During World War I Toynbee worked for the Political Intelligence Department of the British Foreign Office and participated in the Paris Peace Conference of 1919. He was troubled by the 1917 Russian Revolution, viewing Russian society as non-Western and a potential threat to the West.

29. Bertrand Russell (1872–1970), the British philosopher, logician, mathematician, and historian. Russell was also an outspoken social critic. He went to prison for his pacifist opposition to World War I and during the 1950s and 1960s was both a leading proponent of nuclear disarmament and a vocal opponent of American involvement in Vietnam. Greatly dissatisfied with the Warren Commission Report, he wrote "16 Questions on the Assassination," which was published on September 6, 1964, and also formed a "Who Killed Kennedy Committee."

30. Where Lee may have read this is unclear.

31. The baptism occurred at St. Seraphim Eastern Orthodox Church on October 16, 1962. Elena Hall is listed as June's god-parent. See Warren Commission Exhibit No. 1957. The fact that a document as trivial as a baptismal record would have been sent to J. Lee Rankin with a cover letter by none other than J. Edgar Hoover himself would certainly have amused de Mohrenschildt.

32. The South's system of state and local "Jim Crow" laws, which had been in place since 1876, would not be broken until the passage of the Civil Rights Act of 1964 and the Voting Rights Act of 1965.

33. At the predominantly black Bishop College.

34. The Oswalds' primary residence from November 4, 1962, until their move to Neely Street on March 2, 1963.

35. The original manuscript has "conducive to suicide," which is very awkward, but the overall meaning is clear enough.

36. The Oswalds continued to receive mail from people they had known in the Soviet Union before coming to the United States.

37. The Neva River flows west from Lake Ladoga to the Neva Bay of the Gulf of Finland. It was a major line of defense for Soviet forces defending the southern approaches to Leningrad in the summer of 1941. It was, however, breached and Leningrad surrounded; the city would be under siege until early 1944.

38. Based on de Mohrenschildt's description it is doubtful pictures of such quality were taken with the cheap Imperial Reflex camera Oswald supposedly owned.

39. Replacing "infected spot" in the original manuscript.

40. Nikita Khrushchev (1894–1971), premier of the Soviet Union between 1953 and 1964.

41. A reference to Kenneth J. Porter, whom Marina married in 1965.

42. Replacing "rending" which seems out of place here.

43. The text is ambiguous regarding who might be giving Oswald Russian-language literature. Oswald had precious few friends in the United States. Either he was receiving the literature from friends he left behind in the Soviet Union, which seems unlikely given the cost, or de Mohrenschildt is referring to the Russian community in Dallas, who donated to the Oswalds but who were scarcely individuals who would have referred to Lee as a friend or whom Lee would have called his friends.

44. De Mohrenschildt is mistaken here. In early January 1963 Marina wrote a single letter to Anatoly Shpanko, a "medical student whose offers of marriage she had refused both before and after meeting Lee." Priscilla Johnson McMillan, *Marina and Lee* (Steerforth Press, 2013), 303. The letter was returned due to insufficient postage and, after Lee discovered it, Marina never wrote Shpanko again. It is true however that she continued to write friends as well as relatives in the Soviet Union.

45. A series of letters by Marina, which were written in Russian to her aunt and uncle inside the Soviet Union, surfaced in the early 1990s. Oswald seems to have grown dissatisfied with his return to the United States very quickly, as they indicate a desire to return to the USSR as soon as October 1962, much sooner than the end of January 1963 when Marina wrote letters to the Soviet Embassy requesting permission to do so. The embassy requested so much paperwork that Marina soon realized—to her relief as she had no wish to leave the United States—it might be months or even years before a return could be worked out.

46. With attention, presumably, not material things. Lee's distaste for materialism is mentioned on numerous occasions throughout the manuscript.

47. This comment, shocking by contemporary values, should be understood in its historical context. Even the phrase "domestic violence" was relatively new in the 1970s, and it is doubtful de Mohrenschildt, living in a place as conservative as Dallas, was hearing much if anything enlightening on the subject. See note 53.

48. Bouhe, however, by his own account made several efforts to help Marina learn English. First he put her in contact with a student from the University of Oklahoma, Paul Roderick Gregory, who was studying Russian. Then he gave her an English/Russian dictionary "published by the U.S. Government Printing Office in Washington during World War II" and a text written in Russian that she would have

to translate into English. She did so four or five times before stopping. Her letters to her aunt and uncle in Minsk (translated here, see note 45) indicate a desire to learn English: "I am slowly learning English. . . . I already am beginning to understand much" (December 26, 1962); "I am beginning to speak English and Ruth [Paine] helps me much" (April 27, 1963).

49. The date is inserted. The substantial amount of money donated to Marina is mentioned later in the vignettes "Visiting the Auchincloss Home" in Chapter 4 and "Marina after Lee" in Chapter 5.

50. The vignette that follows contains a number of inaccuracies, which may be attributed to both the passage of time, faulty memory, and the complexity of the sequence of events. The correct version is told on pages 276–281 of McMillan, *Marina and Lee*. Marina had fled her husband in the middle of the night in early November with little more than the clothes she was wearing, found her way to a phone, and called the Mellers, who paid for her cab fare and took her and the baby in. She stayed with the Mellers in their very small apartment for a few days and then a meeting was arranged at the de Mohrenschildts' apartment on November 11. George Bouhe drove Marina to the meeting, but as he feared Oswald left immediately. Marina refused to move back in with Lee, so the de Mohrenschildts drove both of the Oswalds back to their home on Elsbeth Street to retrieve her clothes and baby June's things. The de Mohrenschildts then dropped Marina off with the Mellers, where she stayed for only a few hours before George Bouhe showed up and helped her move in with the Fords, who owned a comfortable four-bedroom home.

51. Teofil and Anna Meller. Their first names are inserted into the next sentence to better identify them.

52. Lee's becoming enraged here is significant and points to a growing fear of abandonment and isolation. The de Mohrenschildts had plans to move to Haiti, something they had made abundantly clear, and now Marina was separating from him. These were the three individuals Oswald could most readily identify with and, now, it appeared as if all three were going to abandon him.

53. Given what we now know of de Mohrenschildt's three failed marriages and sex life in general before marrying Jeanne, mentioning the Marquis de Sade (1740–1814) was probably more than a casual reference to French literature. It is very clear that both in and out of the bedroom de Mohrenschildt did not mind making others uncomfortable. Some hated him for it, others were perfectly happy to overlook it.

54. Oswald may have taken de Mohrenschildt's suggestion, at least if Judyth Vary Baker is to be believed. In her book *Lee and Me* she claims to have been romantic with Oswald in New Orleans during the summer of 1963, by which time the de Mohrenschildts were in Haiti. See Judyth Vary Baker, *Lee and Me: How I Came to Know, Love, and Lose Lee Harvey Oswald* (TrineDay, 2011).

55. Referring to de Mohrenschildt's third marriage to Dr. Wynne Sharples (1923–2008). Sharples was a wealthy Philadelphian socialite with a medical degree from Columbia University. They were married on April 7, 1951, and had two children, a son, Sergei, born on September 15, 1952, and a daughter, Nadya (spelled Nadia, Nadejda, or Madejda in some sources), born on November 23, 1953. According to

de Mohrenschildt's Warren Commission testimony they were divorced in 1957 (in truth April 16, 1956), in part because of the strain of having both children diagnosed with cystic fibrosis. Sharples relocated from Dallas to the northeast after the divorce. There were a series of disagreements about a trust fund connected to Sergei after his death and disputes over de Mohrenschildt's visitation rights with Nadya; de Mohrenschildt hints at these protracted legal battles in his Warren Commission testimony when he says he "encountered constant difficulties in regard to my visitation rights [with] the children." Although some describe Sharples as detesting her ex-husband, her comments regarding him in an FBI report dated February 27, 1964, are surprisingly balanced.

56. Replacing "enforcing" in the original manuscript. The de Mohrenschildts had helped bring the separation about, but were not responsible for maintaining it. In fact, they would anger many in the White Russian community when they so quickly provided Lee with Marina's whereabouts.

57. Originally "In the meantime our big convertible Galaxie—which we kept for years in memory of the Oswalds—was filling up high." This sentence has been rewritten to improve clarity. A criminal intelligence report file forwarded to Captain W. F. Dyson of the Administrative Services Bureau, Dallas Police Department, on May 17, 1967, identifies the de Mohrenschildts as owning "a 1962 Ford Convertible, color white, 1967 license LML-222." Priscilla Johnson McMillan, probably relying on information provided by Marina, incorrectly describes the convertible as gray (McMillan, *Marina and Lee*, 278). The de Mohrenschildts apparently held on to their Galaxie until the end of 1968. A letter to Willem Oltmans dated January 29, 1969, and reprinted in his memoirs concludes with the sentence "Have a new marvelous CAR!" Willem Oltmans, *Memoires 1968–1970* (Papieren Tijger, 2003), 331.

58. At this point the manuscript omits a dramatic moment described in de Mohrenschildt's Warren Commission testimony. Oswald is quoted as saying he "will get even" with de Mohrenschildt for taking his wife and child away, and the angry de Mohrenschidlt replied, "You will get even with me?" Physical violence was averted only because Oswald, "a rather puny individual," backed down. He stood no chance in a fight with the larger and physically fit de Mohrenschildt. See Appendix B.

59. As just noted Marina would stay at the Mellers' small apartment for only a few hours. George Bouhe helped transfer her to the home of Declan and Katya Ford, whose four-bedroom house was much more comfortable.

60. Replacing the awkward "practically forgot" with "realized" in the original manuscript, as well as completing a sentence fragment.

61. Arthur Koestler (1905–1983) was a Hungarian-British author and journalist. He was a member of the Communist Party of Germany during the 1930s, traveled widely including to the Soviet Union, but grew disillusioned and left the party in 1938. He is known for several works, perhaps most notably the novel *Darkness at Noon* first published in English in 1941. It is most likely this work that de Mohrenschildt is referring to, but that is by no means certain.

62. "Balsam" is a term used for a variety of pleasant-smelling plant products and the plants that produce them. Some are used in botanical medicines. There is also the

possibility de Mohrenschildt is referring to Balsam, the brand name of a variety of traditional Eastern European herbal liqueurs originally used for medicinal purposes.

63. President Kennedy appeared on the cover of *Time* on January 27, 1961; June 9, 1961; and—as Man of the Year for 1961—on January 5, 1962.

64. Joseph P. Kennedy Sr. (1888–1969). President Roosevelt's oldest son James Roosevelt (1907–1991), was his protégé; the two of them traveled together to Scotland in 1934 to purchase distribution rights to Scotch Whiskey. Somerset Importers, Kennedy's company, became the exclusive American agent for Gordon's Gin and Dewar's Scotch.

65. The Warren Commission testimony of Marina Oswald corroborates this. When asked if Lee ever had anything good to say about President Kennedy, she replied, "I just remember he talked about Kennedy's father, who made his fortune in a not very—in a not very good manner . . . . [Lee] said that he had speculated in wine." She may have misunderstood what was said during the conversation between Lee and de Mohrenschildt, conflating the two examples or the Warren Commission translator conflated her Russian.

66. This is the manuscript's first mention of the Bay of Pigs, the failed American-sponsored invasion of Cuba that took place on April 17, 1961. The event grows in importance as the manuscript progresses. See especially Chapter 6.

67. Racist, possibly, but the American military was not segregated in the early 1960s. Truman's Executive Order 9981 had ended segregation in the armed forces on July 26, 1948.

68. The words spoken by Oswald and the material that immediately follows sound distinctly reminiscent of Commission Exhibit 102 (*Speech Before*):

> Americans are apt to scoff at the idea that a military coup in the US, as so often happens in Latin American countries, could ever replace our government but is an idea that has grounds for consideration. Which military organization has the potentialities of executing such action? . . . Only one outfit . . . the USMC.
> . . . I agree with former President Truman when he said that "The Marine Corps should be abolished."

This is one of several indications that portions of de Mohrenschildt's manuscript are a pastiche of material pulled directly from the *Warren Commission Hearings and Exhibits*.

69. At this juncture in the Cold War the idea of a military coup in the United States was by no means eccentric. The novel *Seven Days in May* had been published in 1962, influenced by such rabid right-wing anti-Communists as General Curtis E. LeMay (1906–1990) and Major General Edwin A. Walker, both of whom had clashed with President Kennedy. Kennedy had read the novel, knew of plans for the film, and even went so far as to schedule a weekend trip to Hyannis Port when scenes with exterior shots of the White House were being filmed. The Pentagon, in contrast, refused to cooperate with the filmmakers. The movie premiered on February 12, 1964. For additional details on Walker and Oswald's apparent

attempt to assassinate him in the spring of 1963, see the vignette "Easter of 1963" in Chapter 3.

70. Another indication of Oswald's intense dislike of Connally.

71. The text mistakenly has 1967, which is clearly a typo. The surrounding material makes it clear that de Mohrenschildt is referring to his trip to Yugoslavia in 1957.

72. One would assume this is a reference to George I. Bloom (1898–1991), though it is unclear if Bloom was ever an in-law of de Mohrenschildt. After receiving a degree from the University of Pittsburgh Law School in 1922 Bloom enjoyed a long career in politics including a stint as chairman of the Republican State Committee of Pennsylvania between 1956 and 1963. In 1963 the State Republican Committee published a sixty-two page document titled *Mr. Chairman: George I. Bloom, 1956–1963*. The website of the Pennsylvania Republic Party indicates that in 1959 "Bloom turned the Republican Party into a statewide organization with new permanent headquarters in Harrisburg." The manuscript collection for Bloom at the Pennsylvania State Archives includes photos of him with Pennsylvania governors Edward Martine, William Scranton, Raymond Shafter, Milton Sharp, and Richard Thornburg, along with US Senators Hugh Scott and John Heinz, as well as Presidents Eisenhower, Nixon, Ford, Reagan, and Bush. In other words, just the sort of man a perpetual name-dropper like de Mohrenschildt would enjoy telling others he was acquainted with.

73. A dubious assertion, unless one wants to start arguing that fingernail scratches produce a more prolonged pain than a black eye or a cigarette extinguished on the skin. Maybe de Mohrenschildt would, given his contrarian ways.

74. Replacing "country of the brave and the free" in the original manuscript. This short paragraph has been relocated here from the vignette "Contrasts between Lee and Marina," earlier in this chapter, given that it has nothing to do with that subject matter.

75. The manuscript does not give the actual date. It is inserted here for clarity. The priest's last name is also not present in de Mohrenschildt's manuscript but is mentioned in the Warren Commission testimony of Igor Vladimir Voshinin and other members of the Dallas–Fort Worth White Russian community. Royster (1923–2011) would also baptize Marina's second daughter, Audrey—a photo of the event was published in the May 1, 1964, issue of *Life* magazine on page 36B. In 1978 he was appointed the first ruling bishop of the newly created Diocese of the South and was elevated to the rank of archbishop in 1993.

76. This version of events is incorrect. Oswald had Marina rip the letter up before his eyes. See McMillan, *Marina and Lee*, 305.

77. On October 15, 1967, during a conversation with Willem Oltmans, de Mohrenschildt told the Dutch journalist Oswald "loved the opera of Tchaikovsky. He talked intelligently about the *Queen of Spades*. Oswald loved Tolstoy and Dostoyevsky. I've . . . never understood why he was later depicted as a failure in the media." Quoted in Willem Oltmans, *Memoires 1967–1968* (Papieren Tijger, 2002), 133.

78. Eugene McCarthy (1915–2005) would have been in the middle of his first term as senator from the state of Minnesota. He had supported twice-defeated presidential candidate Adlai Stevenson, rather than Kennedy, in the 1960 Democratic primaries. Why de Mohrenschildt would have been this enthusiastic about McCarthy in the early 1960s remains unexplained in the manuscript.

79. The original manuscript has "bust into" here, but the context of American military intervention is explicit.

80. A fairly accurate statement on both ends: the FBI, especially, never lost its interest in de Mohrenschildt, and he for his part never stopped being annoyed about the FBI being so interested in him.

81. Mao Tse Tung (1893–1976), the Communist leader of China. In the Cold War paranoia of the time this wasn't a trivial accusation.

82. See Chapter 6, note 117. It refers to an unnamed book published in New York that asserted de Mohrenschildt and Haitian president Duvalier controlled Oswald "via long distance, from Haiti to Dallas."

83. See Chapter 4.

84. The manuscript never mentions Sergei by name, but Sergei de Mohrenschildt, George's son from his third marriage, is mentioned as having passed away of cystic fibrosis in 1960 by de Mohrenschildt in his Warren Commission testimony.

85. Phrasing this sentence as "Mexico and South America" may reflect the de Mohrenschildts' original intention to walk all the way to the tip of South America. See Graydon Heartsill, "Pan American Walking Tour," *Dallas Times Herald*, November 6, 1960. The trip was cut short after they had traversed Mexico and the rest of Central America as far as Panama.

86. This is yet another indication of how deeply the loss of Sergei impacted de Mohrenschildt. For another indication one simply has to look at what Jeanne said regarding their walking trip through Central America: "He almost lost his mind. We had to go on that trip." *Warren Commission Hearings and Exhibits*, Vol. 9, 308.

87. Oswald had turned twenty-three on October 18, 1962; de Mohrenschildt had turned fifty-one a half year earlier on April 17.

88. Marina's stay at the Mellers' cramped residence lasted just a short time. She moved in with the Fords, as described above, on Sunday, November 11. This would seem to indicate the de Mohrenschildts gave Lee the Mellers' phone number almost immediately. According to McMillan, "Marina had been at the Fords' for two days when Lee went to George de Mohrenschildt and found out where she was staying." See McMillan, *Marina and Lee*, 279. Two days would have been November 13.

89. The name of Katya's husband is moved here from later in the manuscript. As mentioned in note 59, Marina had left the Mellers' apartment after just a few hours after being dropped off by the de Mohrenschildts and then moved in with the Fords. See Chapter 3 regarding the holiday party given by the Fords at the end of 1962. Katya Ford appears in the same May 1, 1964, *Life* magazine photo depicting Reverend Royster baptizing Marina's second daughter. She is identified as "Mrs. Declan Ford" and was apparently serving as Audrey's godmother. See note 75.

90. The name of Valentina Ray and her husband, Frank, have been inserted here.

George Bouhe had taken Marina to lunch with Valentina, who had not only invited Marina and June to come live in her home indefinitely, she also had promised to teach Marina English and assist her in going to night school. Marina accepted, and Bouhe thought he had finally achieved his goal of helping Marina.

91. The comment is too casual. Marina's return to Lee so angered Bouhe, who had been angling to separate her permanently from her abusive husband, that it led to the Oswalds being ostracized by nearly the entire Dallas–Fort Worth Russian émigré community. Apparently Bouhe was angry with de Mohrenschildt as well for giving Lee Marina's number. The de Mohrenschildts also distanced themselves from the Oswalds after their November 17 reconciliation, further intensifying Lee and Marina's isolation. This is hinted at a few lines further down in the manuscript's discussion of de Mohrenschildt's fund-raising work to find a cure for cystic fibrosis. Saying things like life was speeding up, that the move to Haiti was looming, and so on, is largely a rationalization. On the other hand, all of these pedestrian and petty intrigues should serve to dispel the idea of de Mohrenschildt being Oswald's CIA-appointed "handler" who then "passed him off" to his new "handler," Ruth Paine, in early 1963. Any careful examination of the timeline between roughly mid-November 1962 and the final meeting between the de Mohrenschildts and the Oswalds (see "Easter of 1963" in Chapter 3) reveals a bare minimum of contact. By the time Ruth Paine met the Oswalds, the de Mohrenschildts had virtually stopped interacting with Lee and Marina, a fact truthfully told by George in his Warren Commission testimony.

92. Valentina Ray, who was actually present, remembered the event somewhat differently: "She said he practically went on his knees and begged her to come back; he was very—and she left. She mostly mentioned he cried and begged her and [she] said 'I think I go back.' I said, 'After all, he is your husband,' you know, 'better of course you go back.'" See *Warren Commission Hearings and Exhibits*, Vol. 8, 423.

93. The de Mohrenschildts also visited Jeanne's brother Sergei Michael Fomenko (1909–unknown) in Los Angeles during the fall of 1962. During their visit, which Fomenko described to the FBI as "brief," they "showed him the film which they had taken during [their] walking tour" through Central America.

94. In 1964 de Mohrenschildt told the Warren Commission that during the previous year he had been "chairman of this foundation in Dallas for the first public subscription to our Cystic Fibrosis Fund for the Dallas children," raising $25,000.

95. In his Warren Commission testimony de Mohrenschildt locates the cystic fibrosis foundation's headquarters in New York rather than Atlanta. He also claims his ex-wife Wynne later denied he had a significant role in co-creating what later became the national organization, even though he had raised the seed money with which to launch the organization in Dallas in 1955. She later resigned, either forced out by the other trustees or on her own, and then started her own foundation in her home town of Philadelphia with the help of her prosperous father. In her memoir Doris F. Tulcin would write: "The National Cystic Fibrosis Foundation was born in Philadelphia at the end of 1955. My father had contacted a Dr. Wynne Sharples, a pediatrician who had two children Nadia & Sergei both born with CF. Her father

was a very wealthy gentleman, Phillip Sharples, and Dad thought it a good connection to start the foundation. The new Foundation was incorporated as a not-for-profit voluntary health agency in the state of Delaware. A charter was drawn up and chapters were organized." See Doris F. Tulcin, *Memoirs of a Monarch: A Chronicle of My Life* (iUniverse, 2008), 34. Tulcin appears unaware of the national organization's origins in Dallas, de Mohrenschildt's role, or even his being the father of the two children she mentions.

96. Replacing "At the end of our relationship with the Oswalds" because Jacqueline Kennedy assumed the position in October of 1962, many months *before* the final meeting between the de Mohrenschildts and the Oswalds in April 1963. The chapter's final sentence suggests the use of "end" may have been a typographical error on de Mohrenschildt's part. Most likely what is meant is the end of *frequent* contact, as the de Mohrenschildts and the Oswalds saw each other far less often after helping Marina move to the Mellers' in early November. Another indication of his bifurcated view of his contact with the Oswalds is the fact that de Mohrenschildt titles another vignette "Rare Meetings in 1963" (see Chapter 3). The rare meetings are meant to contrast with the earlier, more frequent meetings.

97. This sentence is relocated here from the vignette "Further Conversations with Lee, 1962." The original text also continues, "I especially liked 'Black Jack' Bouvier, Jacquie's father, a delightful Casanova of the Wall Street."

Chapter 3: Final Conversations with Lee

1. A character in the novel *Trilby*, written by George du Maurier and first published in 1894. The character Svengali is a rogue and hypnotist who transforms the novel's title character and heroine into a famous singer. It was one of the best-selling works of its time, and the word "Svengali" entered the popular lexicon as a person who, with evil intent, manipulates other persons through both persuasion and deceit to do their bidding.

2. The original manuscript has "living up to Joneses" but the surrounding context makes the meaning clear enough. The idiom "keeping up with the Joneses" refers to the constant comparison of oneself to one's neighbor as a determining benchmark for social caste or the accumulation of material goods. Whereas in the past social status depended on one's family name, capitalist economies, with their conspicuous consumption and materialism, fostered a shift in the definition of social status: people became more inclined to define themselves by the consumer goods they possessed. According to data gathered by the Board of Governors of the Federal Reserve System, household debt in the United States rose from practically nothing in 1950 to $13.8 *trillion* in 2008, before declining to $12.8 trillion in the first quarter of 2013.

3. The manuscript simply says "company," but in his Warren Commission testimony and personal correspondence de Mohrenschildt calls it the "Haitian Holding Company." There were plans to incorporate in the state of Texas. Paul M. Raigorodsky, one of the potential investors approached by de Mohrenschildt, described it as "a $100,000 corporation set up here to do business with Duvalier, the head of the Haitian Government in the making of hemp [rope] and they were giving him

concessions and lots of acreage which you could pick up for drilling and everything else, and he was trying to get people to come here and subscribe to stock but he didn't do anything." In his own testimony de Mohrenschildt goes on to state, "I am negotiating right now with an aluminum company for the development of bauxite, and with oil companies in regard to development of oil possibilities."

4. Tolstoy's exact words were "Man must be happy. If he is not, he is himself to blame. And he must work assiduously until this discomfort or misunderstanding is removed." See Vladimir Vorontsov, ed., *Words of the Wise: A Book of Russian Quotations* (Moscow: Progress Publishers, 1979), 137.

5. Origin of quote unknown.

6. Inserting "to myself" and combining with the material that begins "Here is a good fellow" into a single sentence. Quotation marks have also been inserted because the material is clearly being represented as an interior dialogue de Mohrenschildt is having with himself.

7. Declan P. Ford was a self-employed consulting geologist much like de Mohrenschildt. He had moved to Dallas in January 1960 and worked at DeGolyer & MacNaughton, a consulting firm, until October of 1962. He then went into business for himself, as told to the Warren Commission "in exploration [and the] development of oil and gas fields in the United States and foreign countries." He had married his wife Katherine in July 1960.

8. June's baby-sitter is identified as a Mrs. Frangipanni (almost certainly a phonetic spelling never verified by the Warren Commission) in de Mohrenschildt's Warren Commission testimony. A report filed by FBI Special Agent W. James Wood on March 13, 1964, mentions Jeanne starting "her own sportswear firm" in 1959 using money furnished by a Joe Frangipane; the business had failed after one season and Frangipane had passed away. Anita may well have been Joe's widow.

9. Christmas Eve in 1962 took place on a Monday. The party at the Fords' home by all reports began on Friday, December 28, and continued until the next day. In his Warren Commission testimony de Mohrenschildt says, "right at Christmas or New Year's Eve." Those inclined to see the worst in everything he says consider answers such as this reflective of a career dissembler. He must have been thinking of the Russian Orthodox Christmas, which occurs a week later because it is based on the Gregorian calendar rather than the Julian calendar.

10. The de Mohrenschildt manuscript does not include her last name. On page 722 of Appendix 13 of the single-volume *Warren Commission Report*, the text indicates Yaeko Okui "had been brought to the party by Lev Aronson," a Jewish Latvian émigré and first cellist of the Dallas Symphony Orchestra. She was the southwestern public relations representative for a chain of department stores, Nippon Services, New York. Aronson and de Mohrenschildt knew each other from the Bohemian Club discussion group. They had argued heatedly when de Mohrenschildt praised Heinrich Himmler for convincing Hitler to permit captured Red Army general Andrey Vlasov to organize anti-Communist prisoners of war to fight alongside Nazi Germany. Aronson was a survivor of the Buchenwald concentration camp.

11. By her own account Marina "moved happily from friend to friend, ate heart-

ily, and ended up with a group singing Russian songs at the piano." See Priscilla Johnson McMillan, *Marina and Lee* (Steerforth Press, 2013), 302.

12. In his Warren Commission testimony de Mohrenschildt says something quite different: "I did not pay attention [to the Oswalds]. I left them to their own devices. I spoke to various people. I thought I had done my duty bringing them along."

13. Changing "engrossed" to "engaged" here as the word "engrossed" is repeated again just a few lines later. When interviewed by the FBI in 1964 Okui stated her conversation with Oswald had been about "flower arrangements." While some Kennedy assassination researchers scoff at this and wish to brand her yet another intelligence operative, there is evidence to corroborate her story. Okui had come to the United States in 1959 to, in part, teach *ikebana* (professional flower arrangement). She is mentioned as giving a demonstration of *ikebana* in volume 76 (issues 27–39) of the 1963 issue of the *Southern Florist and Nurseryman*, 72.

14. A quite different account was given by Marina, who noticed Okui "spoke Russian and was drinking only Coca-Cola, nothing stronger." Thinking Okui might be "a spy," she warned Lee not to be "too frank" with her about political subjects. As for de Mohrenschildt he supposedly remarked to Marina, "That Japanese girl—I don't trust her. I think she works for some government or other, but which one I don't know." Quotes found in McMillan, *Marina and Lee*, 302.

15. A letter Marina wrote in Russian to her aunt and uncle just two days before the party at the Fords' (translated into English here) sheds some light on how she saw de Mohrenschildt at this time:

> In Dallas there are a few good Russians—good and bad—different ones in general. We meet with one family, they are Russians but have never been to Russia and were born in China. They are charming and good and travel a lot on foot. He himself is a geologist, loves Negroes and Russia. Soon he will be leaving to go to work in Haiti. His name is George de Mohrenschildt. Just a count's name remains, but otherwise he is a typical Russian guy by nature.

16. By all accounts the de Mohrenschildts and Oswalds left around midnight; the party lasted considerably longer than that.

17. Contradicted by Okui, who told the FBI she never saw Oswald again after the party.

18. That Marina might have found Okui's number in Lee's pocket and assumed the worst is, of course, quite possible.

19. An indication of this distancing in the opening months of 1963 may be found in the Warren Commission testimony of Max Clark: "I have heard that George de Mohrenschildt is the one who took the Oswalds to the Fords' party and that he saw them off and on after that and that during that period of time he would hear in Fort Worth that Oswald had beat Marina up and that she had run off . . . and that George had finally got a hold of Oswald and threatened him—picked him up by his shirt and shook him like a dog and told him that he would really work him over if he ever laid another hand on her." See *Warren Commission Hearings and Exhibits*, Vol. 9,

353. This again rather deflates the notion of de Mohrenschildt as Oswald's constant companion and "handler."

20. Many philosophers might fit the quote in question but it is at least faintly reminiscent of Boethius (c. 480–524) whose great Neoplatonic meditation on fortune, death, and other issues, titled *The Consolation of Philosophy*, was the single most popular text in Europe (after the Bible) during the Middle Ages. Boethius had been imprisoned by the Ostrogothic king Theodoric the Great. Philosophy appears in the allegorical guise of Lady Philosophy, to console him during the year he was imprisoned leading up to his execution. She tells Boethius, "no man can ever truly be happy until he has been forsaken by Fortune"—fame and wealth are transitory, while things of the mind, the "one true good," are superior.

21. The manuscript titles this vignette "Peace for a While with the Oswald Family," yet little of the material that follows is in any way devoted to that subject. The focus is instead a January screening of the film made by the de Mohrenschildts while they were walking through Central America. It is difficult to determine what incident or incidents de Mohrenschildt is referring to here. The text describing the film screening does not appear to contain anything that might portend future events except perhaps the introduction of Marina to Ruth Paine, with Marina's later refusal to leave the Paine residence on November 21, 1963—as well as the de Mohrenschildts' departure for Haiti—leaving Oswald emotionally isolated and unmoored from anyone who might have held his behavior in check. In any event there are two additional problems here. The film screening was on February 13, 1963, in the de Mohrenschildts' home, while the introduction of Ruth Paine was on February 22, 1963, in Glover's home. Once again de Mohrenschildt's memory appears to conflate two (or even three given the January reference) closely occurring events.

22. Warren Commission Document No. 1012 was classified until May 31, 1977; the subject of the document is George de Mohrenschildt. Dated June 3, 1964, the memo was prepared for J. Lee Rankin, general counsel of the Assassination of President Kennedy, by deputy director of the CIA Richard Helms. It consists of nine numbered paragraphs, the third of which is of interest here and will be reproduced as it appears in full:

On the 23rd or 24th of November 1963, after the assassination, our representative in Dallas received a telephone call from one of his contacts who told him that several members of his firm had attended a social or a discussion group in January 1963 and that Lee Harvey OSWALD had also been there. Our representative immediately arranged for the FBI to contact the executive. It was later ascertained from the FBI, and from one of our own sources, that George De MOHRENSCHILDT was present at the meeting and introduced OSWALD to the group.

This document is significant for three reasons. First, it demonstrates that a CIA informant was present at the screening of de Mohrenschildt's film. There can be little doubt that the Helms memo is describing the same event: it takes place in January, there are business executives present, and the event had been both a social event and a group discussion. Second, because the memo again shows the agency viewing de Mohrenschildt as an outsider. Third, the "representative in Dallas" could be none other than J. Walton Moore, who would insist he had no contact or knowledge of de Mohrenschildt after 1961.

23. Everett D. Glover (1917–present) initially became casually acquainted with Jeanne through their mutual love of ice skating. Slightly later, when Jeanne brought her husband to the rink, Glover began to associate with both more regularly. He became—along with Sam Ballen, who had a membership at the Dallas Athletic Country Club—yet another tennis opponent for George, whom Glover described in his Warren Commission testimony as wanting to "play tennis morning, noon, and night." *Warren Commission Hearings and Exhibits*, Vol. 10, 13–14. Glover worked for Magnolia Laboratories, Standard Oil of New York (now Exxon/Mobil).

24. In his Warren Commission testimony Glover describes the following individuals in addition to the Oswalds, the de Mohrenschildts, and himself as being present on February 22, 1963: his roommates Volkmar Schmidt and Dick Pierce; Betty MacDonald, Pierce's girlfriend; Norm Fredrickson and his wife; and Ruth Paine. He also mentions the de Mohrenschildts stayed only a short time, which would be odd given both the considerable length of de Mohrenschildt's film and the fact George describes it as irreplaceable. This, too, indicates the film screening and the party where Glover describes the Oswalds as meeting Ruth Paine were two separate events.

25. Described in his Warren Commission testimony as "an eight millimeter movie which has about 1,200 feet—three big reels." By way of comparison, the famous 8-mm film of the Kennedy assassination taken by Abraham Zapruder was just six feet in length and lasted 26.6 seconds. This would suggest de Mohrenschildt's film was slightly less than an hour and a half long and, assuming the amount of film on each reel was about the same, there would have been just less than a half hour of film on each reel. Given the capacity of most home movie projectors of the time, this, too, appears reasonably accurate.

26. The manuscript does not mention the precise starting point of the walking trip. De Mohrenschildt's Warren Commission testimony gives the location as "Piedras Negras . . . on the Mexican side of the U.S. border." He had been visiting Harper and Harper's wife, Conchita, a few months prior "when there was a long distance call . . . that my boy had died." *Warren Commission Hearings and Exhibits*, Vol. 9, 213. Tito's brother Richard, who lived just nine miles away in Eagle Pass, Texas, would be indicted in 1972 on arms and drug-related charges and was reported to have had ties to the Nixon White House. Myles Ambrose, one of the individuals responsible for creating the DEA under Nixon, would resign after apparently visiting the Harper ranches. Peter Dale Scott, *Deep Politics and the Death of JFK* (University of California Press, 1996), 133–134. Laredo, Texas, is mentioned as the starting point by Gary E. Taylor, the ex-husband of de Mohrenschildt's daughter Alexandra, in his Warren Commission testimony. See the *Warren Commission Hearings and Exhibits*, Vol. 9, 100. Torreon is mentioned in the Warren Commission testimony of Igor Voshinin, but does not appear to be accurate given Torreon is located in central

Mexico, not on the US-Mexico border. See the *Warren Commission Hearings and Exhibits*, Vol. 8, 461. It is possible the de Mohrenschildts, who stuck to old mountain trails, passed through Torreon and mentioned this to Voshinin.

27. In her Warren Commission testimony Jeanne remembered the starting date as either October 5 or 6, 1960. The de Mohrenschildt manuscript continues: "Incidentally, now the situation [has] changed somewhat, possibly because of President Kennedy's assassination, which put in sharp prospective [*sic*] racial discrimination in this country."

28. The term "hegira" is derived from the Arabic *híjra*, meaning "departure" or "exodus" (from the verb *hájara*, meaning "to emigrate" or "to abandon") and is associated with Muhammad and his followers journeying from Mecca to Medina in 622 CE to escape persecution. Sam Ballen observed that "something deep and basic happened in their Hegira. George was now completely under the domination of Jeanne. . . . George, who had spent a lifetime bowling over women, now was caught in the web of the one he really loved." The two of them began alienating old friends and de Mohrenschildt's oil industry contacts because of Jeanne's "outspoken leftist expressions" and the couple's mutual "intolerant atheism" that "knew no limits." See Samuel B. Ballen, *Without Reservations* (Ocean Tree Books, 2001), 167.

29. The manuscript is somewhat contradictory on the matter of how the de Mohrenschildts paid for their walk through Latin America, containing just the following vague and somewhat confused sentence: "We spent quite a lot of money on our trip, but some American lunatic who pretended that he was a saint had done part of our itinerary by himself, without spending a cent, people fed and clothed him out of charity." This seems to say that de Mohrenschildt greatly underestimated the cost, the de Mohrenschildts' resources were drained and/or exhausted, and the couple survived on charity.

30. The de Mohrenschildts wound up at the Panama ranch of Roberto Emilio "Tito" Arias (1918–1989), the lawyer of Aristotle Onassis who was also serving as ambassador to the Court of St. James. According to Peter Evans, de Mohrenschildt and Onassis met at this time, leading to discussions of a partnership in Haiti to search for oil and natural gas reserves. See Peter Evans, *Nemesis: Aristotle Onassis, Jackie, and the Love Triangle That Brought Down the Kennedys* (Harper Collins, 2004), 93. De Mohrenschildt asked Arias's wife, the famed dancer Margot Fonteyn (1919–1991), to do a charity performance to raise funds for cystic fibrosis research. She tentatively agreed, pending her schedule, but he never followed up.

31. During the first day of his Warren Commission testimony, de Mohrenschildt indicates he and his wife spent a good two months recuperating in Haiti. The reference to Michael Breitman is inserted here using the following from de Mohrenschildt's Warren Commission testimony:

Michael Breitman. . . . used to be a very wealthy man in Russia—also involved in the oil industry in Russia, and in Czarist Russia—a friend of my father's. And I discovered that he lived in Haiti sometime in 1946 and 1947 when I went as a tourist there. And we became very close. He considered me almost like his son.

We went to visit him—I was worried that he might die, and he died very soon after our trip.

The de Mohrenschildts would sponsor a religious service in his honor, something that struck their Dallas acquaintances as doubly remarkable: first for giving money to the church (they were considered especially stingy in this regard), and second because it was the first and only time they could remember the radically atheistic Jeanne attending a service. Sam Ballen in his memoir would write, "Breitman . . . lived in the Russian émigré community of Kenskof [Kenscoff], situated at 5,000 feet overlooking Port-au-Prince." See Ballen, *Without Reservations*, 171. While enjoying Breitman's hospitality de Mohrenschildt worked on the manuscript that would become *Trois et le Mule*. Breitman would also introduce de Mohrenschildt to senior-level officials in the Haitian government, to whom he pitched the idea of a geological survey and mapping project.

32. Apparently one such individual was a CIA informant. See note 22.

33. Fidel Castro (1926–present) was one of the leading figures of the Cuban Revolution that succeeded in overthrowing the US-backed military dictatorship of Fulgencio Batista on January 1, 1959 (on Batista see note 47). A Marxist-Leninist, he soon proclaimed Cuba a one-party state and began introducing reforms such as central economic planning and expanding education and welfare. During his visit to the UN in September 1960, Castro attended a reception organized by the Fair Play for Cuba Committee, the same organization Oswald would attempt to create a local chapter for in New Orleans during the summer of 1963. The Eisenhower and Kennedy administrations waged an aggressive campaign to topple the new regime, including an economic embargo, arming and supporting counter-revolutionary groups who staged raids on the island (most notably the failed incursion at the Bay of Pigs in April 1961), while the CIA recruited the Mafia in multiple plots to kill Castro himself. Castro was left out of the US-Soviet negotiations during the October 1962 Cuban Missile Crisis, which nonetheless extracted a US commitment not to invade Cuba in the future. When informed of the assassination of Kennedy during an interview on November 22, Castro labeled it a disaster for Cuba, a view he repeated the next day in a speech delivered on Cuban radio and television (released in English by the Cuban UN delegation as "Concerning the Facts and Consequences of the Tragic Death of President John F. Kennedy"). Castro's regime survived, however, outlasting ten American presidencies as of 2013. Castro himself retired from politics in July 2006, ceding all his duties to his brother Raúl.

34. Ernesto "Che" Guevara (1928–1967) was also one of the pivotal figures of the Cuban Revolution. A native of Argentina, he was present in Guatemala when democratically elected president Jacobo Arbenz, who was attempting to enact land and other reforms, was overthrown by a coup orchestrated by the CIA at the behest of the United Fruit Company, whose board of directors just happened to include CIA director Allen Dulles. Dulles's brother, Secretary of State John Foster Dulles, had negotiated with Guatemala on behalf of United Fruit in the 1930s. The installation of right-wing dictator Carlos Castillo Armas cemented Guevara's opposition to what

he saw as the capitalist exploitation of the region by the United States. Relocating to Mexico he was introduced to both Fidel Castro and his brother Raúl and traveled to Cuba to participate in the two-year insurgency that eventually toppled the Batista regime. In the interval leading up to the Kennedy assassination he held a variety of important government posts including minister of industries, national bank president, and instructional director of Cuba's armed services; played an important role in implementing land reform and building literacy; and traveled extensively as Cuba's representative. Little wonder then that he would grace the cover of *Time*, who dubbed him the mind behind the revolution and describe him as "guid[ing] Cuba with icy calculation, vast competence, high intelligence, and a perceptive sense of humor." Of course the magazine also saw his every deed as sinister, since by definition Guevara was a Marxist and opposed to US imperial ambitions. See *Time*, "Castro's Brain," August 8, 1960.

35. Correcting "Payne" with "Paine" here and throughout the manuscript. Ruth Paine (1932–present) had been a member of Everett Glover's singing group. Glover invited her to the February 22 party because he knew of her interest in meeting people who spoke Russian.

36. While it makes for a good read this version of the event is contradicted by both the Warren Commission testimony of Ilya A. Mamantov, who Ruth Paine had approached about learning Russian, and Paine herself four years later as part of her grand jury testimony in New Orleans during the Garrison investigation. Mamantov (see note 7 of the Editor's Introduction), when asked to state for the record "the extent of Mrs. Paine's command of the Russian language" (his mother-in-law was acting as Paine's instructor), replied that "for an American" Paine's knowledge of Russian was "fair to good" but that compared to someone fluent in Russian (such as de Mohrenschildt or Marina or himself) her command of the language was "very poor." Paine herself recalled "talking in [Everett Glover's] kitchen with the de Mohrenschildts and not talking with Marina," who was present but simply "listened . . . to the conversation when it was in Russian and Mrs. de Mohrenschildt was helpful to her in translating what was said." When asked if she could speak Russian at the time of Glover's party Paine replied, "Yes, to a degree. I listened [to] Russian better than I spoke it."

37. Paine's husband Michael (1928–present) was an engineer working at the Fort Worth Bell Helicopter plant. He and Ruth separated in September 1963; at the time of the Kennedy assassination he would visit on weekends. He was a member of the Civil Liberties Union and took Oswald to an ACLU meeting on October 25. Oswald joined the ACLU, paying a $2 membership, on November 4, 1963. He listed his occupation as "photographer."

38. Bell Helicopter, founded in 1935, was by the early 1960s a major defense contractor. It would produce the ubiquitous "Huey" helicopters including the UH-1N Twin Huey used during the Vietnam War.

39. The implication here appears to be a lesbian infatuation on the part of Ruth Paine for Marina. The FBI apparently "investigated Ruth Paine's sexual orientation in 1964." See Nancy Wertz, "George de Mohrenschildt, Who Are You?" *The*

Fourth Decade—A Journal of Research on the John F. Kennedy Assassination 5, no. 3 (July 1998): 10. It is true that after the assassination Marina—probably under the influence of Oswald's brother and mother, who viewed Paine as an attention-seeker —broke off contact with Ruth. Despite writing Marina repeatedly, Paine received no reply other than a single Christmas card. The two met once, briefly, in 1964, but since then have never spoken to each other.

40. This description of Oswald's enthusiasm for the film is in stark contrast to de Mohrenschildt's Warren Commission testimony, which describes both Oswalds as bored with the content because neither of them were the outdoors type. In *Marina and Lee* Oswald is described as uninterested because he had seen the film before. See McMillan, *Marina and Lee*, 318.

41. A *guarache* is a Mexican sandal traditionally made of handwoven leather. They began to become popular in the United States in the 1950s. The Beach Boys' 1963 hit "Surfin' USA" refers to them.

42. This is another indication of de Mohrenschildt's devotion to the idea of physical fitness. He had gone so far as to write President Kennedy on February 16, 1963, saying that it was "indeed a pleasure to see an interest displayed by you and your administration in the physical rehabilitation of Washington personnel and of the sedentary American people." Later that year, Kennedy would change the name of the President's Council on Youth Fitness, founded by President Eisenhower in 1955, to the President's Council on Physical Fitness to reflect its role to serve all Americans.

43. A new section heading has been provided given the shift in topic from the de Mohrenschildts' walking trip to Oswald's views of Latin America.

44. Guevara was killed by Mario Terán, a Bolivian army sergeant, who was acting on the orders of Bolivian president Rene Barrientos. The United States had wanted Guevara flown to Panama for interrogation; in a declassified memorandum dated October 11, 1967, President Lyndon Johnson called the decision to kill Guevara "stupid" but "understandable from a Bolivian standpoint." As of 2007 Terán was still very much alive, being married with five children and living in Paraguay under an alias, possibly with CIA protection.

45. The Bay of Pigs Invasion, code-named Operation Zapata, was a large-scale invasion of Cuba using the CIA trained and funded Brigada Asalto 2506 (Assault Brigade 2506, whose base of operations in Guatemala was observed by the de Mohrenschildts during their walking trip through Central America). President Kennedy had inherited the plan from the Eisenhower administration, where it had been overseen by Vice President Nixon. Kennedy, still new on the job, consented to carrying out the plan but introduced changes he believed necessary to decrease the chance of American involvement being discovered. One was changing the landing site from Trinidad to the Bay of Pigs while reducing the number of B-26 bombers supporting the invasion from sixteen to eight. On April 15 the bombers attacked Cuba's small air force but failed to destroy it. This would turn out to be crucial as Cuban planes would attack and destroy two of the three ships supporting the invasion, one of which was carrying extra ammunition. After four days of fighting, hemmed in and nearly out of ammunition, the invaders surrendered. In response to the invasion

Che Guevara, through Richard N. Goodwin, passed a note to President Kennedy in August that read "Thanks for the *Playa Girón*. Before the invasion, the revolution was on shaky ground. Now it's stronger than ever." In December 1962 the Cuban government released 1,113 of the captured rebels in exchange for $53 million in food and medicine raised by private donations within the United States.

46. It is interesting that de Mohrenschildt chooses to mention Lansky rather than other well-known Mafia figures. Lansky (1902–1983) was born Meyer Suchowljansky in Grodno, Belarus, the same general portion of Russia where de Mohrenschildt spent his early childhood. A business partner of Lucky Luciano, Lansky arranged a lucrative deal with Batista, Cuba's dictator, giving the Mafia control over Havana's racetracks and casinos. Lansky then convened the so-called Havana Conference, the first full-scale meeting of underworld bosses since Prohibition. Present were two individuals who would later figure prominently in the CIA's efforts to assassinate Castro after he came to power: Santo Trafficante Jr. and Carlos Marcello. Lansky constructed a 440-room hotel, the Habana Riviera, at a cost of $8 million; completed in 1957, it made millions in profits during its first year of operation. The Mafia's massive enterprise in Cuba came to an end on New Year's Eve, 1958, when Batista resigned and left the country. Lansky fled to the Bahamas, the casinos were shut down, and in October 1960 the island's hotel-casinos were nationalized.

47. Fulgencio Batista y Zaldivar (1901–1973) was a member of the Cuban military and part of the plot that had overthrown Gerardo Machado in 1933. He controlled the government from behind the scenes until 1940, when he was himself elected president on a progressive platform. After his hand-picked successor was defeated at the polls in 1944 Batista fled to the United States before returning to Cuba in 1952 to run for president again. Trailing badly in the polls, he staged a coup with the backing of the army, suspended the constitution, and aligned himself with the country's wealthy landowners and American organized crime, backed by an American government in the grips of Cold War anti-communism. His rule grew increasingly corrupt and repressive, sparking growing popular opposition and then a two-year uprising that ultimately toppled his government at the end of 1958. He fled the country with a considerable fortune on January 1, 1959, and eventually found asylum in Portugal.

48. As a young medical student Guevara traveled throughout South America, where he saw firsthand the extremes of wealth and poverty, gluttony and hunger, health and disease. The diary he kept during this time was published long after his death as *The Motorcycle Diaries*.

49. Costa Rica abolished its army in 1949. It has been a democracy continuously since that time as well, with peaceful and transparent elections.

50. Amending "You can also find refuge there if you steel [*sic*] millions in USA." It is safe to say de Mohrenschildt was comparing Costa Rica to Switzerland as a place one could anonymously hide large sums of money. The text also continues "All these problems are clear and open now but they were not in 1963."

51. A *latifundista* is the owner of a *latifundios*, a large tract of land. El Salvador is the smallest and most densely populated country in Central America. During

de Mohrenschildt's lifetime the population more than doubled, from 1.9 million in 1950 to 4.1 million in 1975.

52. It is not clear where de Mohrenschildt obtained his information but it was substantially correct. A report published by the Organization of American States in 1978 indicates that with "regard to land tenure, according to a 1961 estimate, six families owned 71,923 hectares. In contrast, according to the 1971 census, approximately 305,000 families lived on 42,692 hectares." *Inter-American Commission on Human Rights* (IACHR), "Report on the Situation of Human Rights in El Salvador" (OEA/Ser. L/V/II.46, doc. 23 rev. 1), November 17, 1978.

53. This sentence and the two that follow are relocated here from another portion of the manuscript to provide a transition between the discussions of El Salvador and Nicaragua.

54. The de Mohrenschildts had stumbled upon Brigada Asalto 2506, the CIA-sponsored group of Cuban exiles who were slated to carry out the invasion intended to topple the Castro government. They had been training in the Sierra Madre, near Rethalhueu, in a CIA-run base with the code name JMTrax. The "pilots" de Mohrenschildt mentions must be the Americans present, as the invasion force itself was Cuban. The brigade departed Guatemala on April 13. The text includes two additional sentences that imply Cuba was tipped off about the approaching invasion: "No question that the same idea occurred to all the pro-Castro Guatemalans and the country is full of them. And messages were sent on time to Fidel Castro." The CIA would later pay off the families of American pilots from the Alabama National Guard killed during the failed invasion. The pilots who survived were forbidden to talk about their experiences until the mid-1970s. The CIA did not formally admit that four American pilots had died until 1999. See Jesse Chambers, "The Good Fight: The True Story of the Alabama Air Guard and the Bay of Pigs," *Birmingham Weekly*, September 13, 2007.

55. Anastasio Somoza Debayle (1925–1980) was a graduate of West Point and the president of Nicaragua between 1967–1972 and 1974–1979. He was the last in a family dynasty dating back to 1936 that included his older brother Luis and their father. The family's absolute rule was maintained by corruption and repression but, like numerous other right-wing dictatorships, was deemed acceptable to the United States thanks to its strident anti-communism. See, for example, David Schmitz, *Thank God They're on Our Side: The United States and Right-Wing Dictatorships, 1921–1965* (University of North Carolina Press, 1999). Somoza was overthrown by the Sandinista Revolution in 1979 and fled the country. After being refused entry into the United States by President Carter, he settled in Paraguay. A team of Sandinista operatives assassinated him just over a year later.

56. Replacing "Congress" with "House" so that the text mentions both halves of the US legislature instead of the entire legislature and one of its halves.

57. De Mohrenschildt may have been thinking of the Church Committee, which investigated alleged abuses of law and power by the CIA, FBI, and NSA in 1975 and 1976.

58. New Orleans had a large Cuban refugee community at that time, second only to Miami.

59. The original manuscript has "we spent the entire discussing"—clearly an additional word is needed in order to make the sentence complete.

60. Created in 1886 the Social Register is quite simply a directory of the upper class or power elite in America. To be included as a member signals one is a member of so-called polite society, that is, old money. The Social Register's own website claims that since its inception, "the Social Register has been the only reliable, and trusted, arbiter of Society in America."

61. See the final paragraph of Chapter 2.

62. The sentence in the original manuscript reads "Before busing confusion arose in this country, Lee was keenly aware of the racist cancer eating America's healthy tissues." The material appears to be a garbled allusion to the Montgomery Bus Boycott of 1955–1956, one of the seminal events of the US civil rights movement. De Mohrenschildt might also have been thinking of the desegregation busing controversy that was raging, particularly in Boston, during the months preceding the completion of the manuscript. Oswald, however, appears to have been aware of the "busing confusion" mentioned here so I have chosen to mention Montgomery in the text.

63. It is not completely clear how the quote relates to the previous sentences, though it appears to be saying that moral strength, in the long run, is capable of overcoming brute physical strength.

64. The de Mohrenschildts mentioned the matter of the washing machine in their December 11, 1966, interview "Caught between Two Tragedies: De Mohrenschildts Knew Both Oswalds, Kennedys," published in the *Dallas Times Herald*. Portions of this interview were widely circulated by the Associated Press. In the *Oakland Tribune* the headline read "JFK Alive If There Was a Washing Machine," while the *Arizona Republic* used "Assassination Pinned On Washing Machine." *Esquire* repeated their claims along with twenty-four other largely mocked theories in a May 1967 article "A Second Primer of Assassination Theories." *Esquire* insinuated the de Mohrenschildts' ideas were ridiculous because Lee and Marina "lived close to a Laundromat." The satire doesn't hold water once one has any idea of Marina's explicit and intensifying desire for consumer goods and the impact it was having on her husband's psyche. Her materialism is an oft-repeated theme of de Mohrenschildt's manuscript.

65. Jeanne had been a successful fashion designer in the years prior to the de Mohrenschildts' walking trip through Central America in 1960–1961. From October 11, 1962, until April 27, 1963, she was however working as a salesperson in the hat department at the Preston Center Store of the Sanger-Harris Company, making much less than she was accustomed to. There was little choice as she and George were so destitute they needed the money to survive.

66. The contract he had worked so hard for was signed on March 13, 1963. The sentence "There was a hiatus in our meeting with the Oswalds as I had to fly to Haiti to sign a contract there and then spend some time in New York" has been split into two sentences and the month of the travel, March, inserted. Here again one has to wonder how de Mohrenschildt was "controlling" or "babysitting" Oswald when he was thousands of miles away.

67. Here is another example of de Mohrenschildt merging two small memories into a single event. When the de Mohrenschildts moved to Haiti, Everett Glover was lent most of their furniture because he had recently divorced and forwarded much of his own furniture to his ex-wife and son in Pennsylvania. In January 1964, however, Glover moved into a new house and he, not the de Mohrenschildts, placed most of the furniture into storage. This is probably the reason Glover is present with the de Mohrenschildts in the vignette "A Message from Lee," dated February 1967, in Chapter 5.

68. Henry C. Bruton (1905–1992) graduated from the US Naval Academy in Annapolis, Maryland, in 1926. In the 1930s he earned a master's degree in electrical engineering. During World War II he first commanded the submarine *Greenling* in the Pacific before being promoted to command Submarine Division 82 and Submarine Squadron 2. He also served as chief of staff, Submarine Force, Atlantic Fleet. He did post-graduate coursework in radio and law. During the Korean War he commanded the battleship *Wisconsin* and during February and March of 1952 conducted bombardments of the Korean coast. After retiring in 1960 he was a member of a number of organizations including the Submarine Veterans of World War II and the US Naval Institute.

69. Richard M. Nixon (1913–1994), after a career in Congress and the Senate, had been Eisenhower's vice president between 1952 and 1960 before narrowly losing to Kennedy in the presidential elections. During the weeks the de Mohrenschildts were most frequently seeing the Oswalds, Nixon had been running for governor of California. When he lost to incumbent Democrat Pat Brown, he announced his retirement from politics. On November 21, 1963, he was present in Dallas, attending a meeting with Pepsi Cola executives at a large company convention. He departed the next morning, before Kennedy's arrival. He would reemerge, of course, in 1968, gaining the presidency on a "law and order" platform—only to resign in disgrace after his 1972 reelection amid a multitude of scandals that were sure to see him impeached. The new president, former Warren Commission committee member Gerald Ford, pardoned him and he was spared a criminal trial.

70. In de Mohrenschildt's 1964 Warren Commission testimony, he mentions he had "just recently" received "a letter from Mrs. Bruton in Paris."

71. As commander of the *Greenling* Bruton enjoyed spectacular success against Japanese shipping over the course of three combat tours in 1942 and 1943. In addition to winning three Navy Crosses and a Navy Commendation ribbon, Bruton's decorations included two Legion of Merit medals and a Presidential Unit Citation. Little wonder de Mohrenschildt has trouble remembering the exact number of decorations.

72. De Mohrenschildt's Warren Commission testimony has "we told her that here we have a miserable couple with a child," and Mrs. Bruton said, "fine, bring them along."

73. Written as "linked" in the original manuscript, which is clearly a typo.

74. This sentence does not exist in the original manuscript and has been added to provide some kind of segue to the reference to "diving in" in the sentence that

follows. From all accounts de Mohrenschildt was an avid swimmer and had made use of his friend's pool on past occasions; one can safely assume he didn't go to the Brutons' home on this particular warm spring day in his swimming trunks to *look* at their pool.

75. Written as "and told them" in the original manuscript, which does not fit the surrounding material.

76. Written as "the motor" when "the mother" is clearly what was intended. The meaning of the rest of the sentence is obscure, though one interpretation would read it as a reference to clothes washing with a washboard.

77. Written as "in the tower" but the surrounding context makes it clear that what is being spoken of is a submarine's conning tower, where the commander gives directions to the helmsman. To "conn" or "con" is to control a ship's movements at sea.

78. Written erroneously as "Collins Radow" in the manuscript.

79. Bruton was in fact a vice president in the company, which was based in Richardson, Texas. Collins wasn't just making generic civilian radios, either. According to Richard James DeScocio, "Collins Radio developed classified communication gear for the Navy and did undercover work for the CIA." For example, "Collins Radio was involved in a top secret CIA project to equip a former Navy patrol boat, renamed the *Rex*, to carry commandos and arms into Cuba to assassinate Cuban leaders." The ship and crew were captured by the Cubans on November 1, 1963. See Richard James DeScocio, *Rockefellerocracy: Kennedy Assassinations, Watergate, and Monopoly of the "Philanthropic" Foundations* (AuthorHouse, 2013), 194.

80. I have chosen to fix the manuscript's "I am made to be a salesman" because Bruton would have been talking in English at this point in the conversation and English was his native language.

81. The manuscript fails to indicate who is speaking here, but the surrounding context makes it abundantly clear it is Lee.

82. In de Mohrenschildt's Warren Commission testimony Bruton is quoted as saying "take this guy away from me."

83. The prose, which in the original manuscript reads "as we took her around, the luxury really quite relative of the furnishings, Frannie's paintings (she was an excellent amateur painter)—the whole thing," is badly garbled and has been reconstructed.

84. Adding the word "tales," which seems implied, to the text "told some funny, if slightly derogatory, about his Marine Corps life."

85. This contradicts de Mohrenschildt's Warren Commission testimony, where Mrs. Bruton expresses her shock not in 1967 but in the letter from Paris sent shortly before de Mohrenschildt's testimony in April 1964. It is of course possible the discussion was *repeated* in 1967 and de Mohrenschildt's mind is merging the letter and the later conversation into a single incident, something his memory appears to do on several occasions.

86. Replacing "presumable assassin."

87. In reality de Mohrenschildt *does* discuss the meeting with Bruton in his Warren Commission testimony. Marina, in her testimony, does not, however, and the

manuscript exhibits concern on more than one occasion with correcting *her* version of events. See the vignette "Marina and the Walker Incident" in Chapter 5. Perhaps this is what de Mohrenschildt is hinting at here.

88. De Mohrenschildt's manuscript simply indicates he and his wife were exhausted without explaining why they were in that condition. In his Warren Commission testimony he offers no further explanation: suddenly it was late in the evening and Jeanne is saying they should go drop the toy rabbit off. In Jeanne's testimony, however, we read, "I think we were playing tennis, and then we were somewhere, and then I decided we will be [too] busy tomorrow, and I wanted to take the rabbit to the baby." According to Priscilla Johnson McMillan, who interviewed Marina extensively in the months after the assassination, "George and Jeanne had just come from a party. They were euphoric, on top of the world. . . . George had just returned from a trip to New York, where he had clinched a new job in Haiti [and the de Mohrenschildts] would be leaving within a month for Port-au-Prince." McMillan, *Marina and Lee*, 358–359. The party may be the "somewhere" Jeanne mentions.

89. No color is mentioned in de Mohrenschildt's text, but in Jeanne's Warren Commission testimony the toy rabbit for June is described as being pink.

90. The Oswalds had moved to 214 West Neely Street on March 3, 1963. It is another indication of the ridiculous nature of the thesis that de Mohrenschildt was Oswald's "handler" when you consider this meeting is taking place on April 13, some five weeks after the move, and it is the first time the de Mohrenschildts have visited the address. The monthly rent was $60, not including utilities. Oswald had enrolled in a typing course on January 14 but his attendance fell off and ended altogether by the end of March.

91. A trellis is an architectural structure, usually made from an open framework or lattice of interwoven or intersecting pieces of wood (or bamboo or metal) that is normally made to support and display climbing plants.

92. There was a reason the Oswalds were slow to answer the door. They were expecting the police. "They were not expecting callers and were getting ready for bed when they heard a sudden commotion at the door—the very thing they had been dreading. But instead of police dogs barking, it was George de Mohrenschildt, booming out a loud hello." See McMillan, *Marina and Lee*, 357–358.

93. There is no mention in de Mohrenschildt's manuscript of Marina being three months pregnant, which she surely would have been given that her second daughter was born on October 20. Marina would tell Ruth Paine she was pregnant shortly after this visit by the de Mohrenschildts. Whether Oswald knew at this time is unclear.

94. Apparently de Mohrenschildt was not aware that Oswald had been fired by Jaggars-Chiles-Stovall and was unemployed at the time this conversation took place. Although punctual and always on the job Oswald's performance was so substandard the company released him after ninety days as a matter of policy. The president of Jaggars-Chiles-Stovall in his Warren Commission testimony said that Oswald was an "inept" employee and had been given notice of termination in late March, with his final day on the job being Saturday, April 6. Oswald had sought extra hours, which was why he was working on a weekend. Stovall was contacted shortly there-

after by Ted Gangel, a superintendent at the Padgett Printing and Lithographing Company. Stovall recommended against hiring Oswald. Oswald applied for unemployment benefits on April 12.

95. Replacing "all was not honey in" with "all was not milk and honey for."

96. A reference to the contract mentioned in the chapter's final sentence.

97. In the late eighteenth century the French colony of Saint Dominique (present-day Haiti) was a cornerstone of the French empire. Its plantations produced "the coffee drunk in Paris, the sugar needed to sweeten it, and the cotton and indigo worn by men of fashion." This single colony earned more than Spain's entire overseas empire and generated "more than a third of France's foreign trade." In supporting the American Revolution France saw itself protecting the crown jewel of its colonies. The islanders themselves contributed in multiple ways: soldiers who fought at the Battle of Savannah, gunpowder used at Saratoga, and engineers who contributed to the victory at Yorktown. Ironically, the huge loans France made to the American rebellion weakened its own economy, revolution broke out in France in 1789, and then Saint Dominique declared its independence in 1804. See Ted Widmer, "How Haiti Saved America: Two Centuries Ago, a Glittering Caribbean Island Helped Finance the Revolution," *Boston Globe*, March 21, 2010.

98. The United States occupied Haiti in 1915 and US Marines remained on the island until 1934. In addition to undertaking a large program to improve the country's infrastructure the United States introduced sisal production, which became, along with sugar and cotton, a significant export. It was through a sisal plantation, of course, that de Mohrenschildt was supposed to make most of the money promised in his contract with the Duvalier government.

99. Haiti has 10,715 square miles.

100. His friends unfortunately were right. As reported by the army's 902nd Military Intelligence Group, de Mohrenschildt's friend in the American Embassy—commercial officer Valentin "Teddy" Blaque—had advised him "the forthcoming business venture is hazardous," because after an initial cash payment of $20,000 all of the remaining $285,000 owed to de Mohrenschildt by the Haitian government would be paid through operations of the sisal plantation de Mohrenschildt would be allowed to control. Everything relied on Duvalier honoring the terms of the contract and "Papa Doc" could be trusted only so long as de Mohrenschildt had the weight of the US government behind him. See Joan Mellen, *Our Man in Haiti* (TrineDay, 2012), 421–422. Aristotle Onassis apparently backed out of a partnership of some kind when "he saw the terms of the contract de Mohrenschildt had signed [saying] 'If we had found oil, we wouldn't even have had an explorer's cut.'" Quoted in Evans, *Nemesis*, 137. The plantation's factory was, at least according to a letter de Mohrenschildt wrote to Paul M. Raigorodsky, located "at Mont Rouis." See Warren Commission De Mohrenschildt Exhibit 9. Assuming this is yet another of de Mohrenschildt's phonetic spellings he is probably referring to Montrouis, which would have been an easy drive just slightly more than forty-six miles north along the coast from de Mohrenschildt's office at the Service de Geodesie et de Cartographie (Cartographic and Geodetic Services) on Harry Truman Boulevard.

101. De Mohrenschildt's claim here would appear a bit odd given how badly the business end of things would turn out in Haiti and the bitterness about it expressed elsewhere in the manuscript. After the failure of his Haitian venture de Mohrenschildt was essentially finished as both an entrepreneur and independent petroleum geologist. He would spend the rest of his life as an adjunct teaching French and Russian, first at the University of Texas at Arlington and then Bishop College, all the while unsuccessfully trying to recoup the remainder of the money owed to him by the government of Haiti. On the other hand, before the collapse of the project, "he and Jeanne had some of the grandest times of their lives," according to Sam Ballen. See Ballen, *Without Reservations*, 172.

102. The love de Mohrenschildt shows for the Haitian people seems genuine enough. What he does not seem to grasp, however, is that Haiti was not Mexico, nor Costa Rica, nor Panama, nor even the Haiti he had first visited in the 1950s. By the early 1960s Haiti had become "the archetypical neo-fascist third world dictatorship," and an especially dark, violent, and brutal place. Neil A. Burron, "Michel Martelly: Haiti's New Caesar and the Prospects for Democracy," *New Political Science* 35, no. 2 (June 2013): 167.

103. See Chapter 6, note 21.

104. Replacing "dangling in front" as either a poor or incorrect choice of words. A rifle scope is mounted and would not dangle as described here. De Mohrenschildt is apparently borrowing heavily from his wife's Warren Commission testimony: "something was dangling over [the rifle], and I didn't know what it was. This telescopic sight." See *Warren Commission Hearings and Exhibits*, Vol. 9, 315.

105. At the Polish Military Academy. The entire account here clashes with that of McMillan, who had communicated with and possibly even met the de Mohrenschildts in the late 1960s. She writes that while George was in New York during the first week of April, Jeanne had visited Marina and been shown the rifle *before* the attempt on Walker's life. See McMillan, *Marina and Lee*, 600, n. 16. In her Warren Commission testimony Jeanne is so tense trying to recall events she could not clearly remember whether or not she had been to the home before the Easter visit. In addition Jeanne was no novice around guns. In her testimony she tells Jenner her father had been a gun collector and, while she did not like hunting, she loved skeet shooting.

106. The evidence points to Oswald having ordered the rifle on March 12, 1963, from an ad placed by Klein's Sporting Goods in the magazine *American Rifleman*.

107. In other words this was a classic case of "George being George," precisely the kind of provocative statement de Mohrenschildt made all the time.

108. Major General Edwin A. Walker (1909–1993) was a West Point graduate and veteran of both World War II and Korea, where he had risen to the rank of Major General. In 1957 he was commander of the Arkansas Military District and was called upon by President Eisenhower to quell civil disturbances arising from the federal government's efforts to end school segregation. Walker successfully complied but repeatedly protested the use of federal troops to enforce racial integration. His political views drifted rightward and he came under the influence of the segregation-

ist preacher Reverend Billy James and the right-wing radio program run by Texas oil baron H. L. Hunt, *Life Line*. In 1959 he became acquainted with Robert Welch, an ultra-conservative publisher who had just founded the John Birch Society. Under these influences Walker became convinced that the highest levels of the federal government, along with the civil rights movement for racial equality, were Communist plots to subvert the country. He offered his resignation in August of 1959 but Eisenhower refused, instead offering him the command in Germany that would lead to his dismissal by President Kennedy (see note 111). As a civilian Walker became an increasingly controversial and polarizing figure. He organized a protest at the racially segregated University of Mississippi in September 1962, sparking a fifteen-hour riot on the campus in which two were killed, hundreds wounded, and fifteen federal marshals shot. Attorney General Robert Kennedy attempted to have Walker confined for ninety days of psychiatric examination, but he was released after just five due to public protest. Walker posted bond and returned to Dallas where he was greeted by some two hundred supporters in the picture included in this chapter. A federal grand jury adjourned without pressing charges in January 1963. Little wonder then that Walker would be the subject of much hostile discussion at the parties attended by de Mohrenschildt and Oswald at this time.

109. The original manuscript has simply "Turtle Creek" which might imply Walker was living next to some kind of actual creek, so "Boulevard" has been added for purposes of clarification. The distance from the Stoneleigh Hotel where the de Mohrenschildts lived and the 4011 Turtle Creek Boulevard address given to the Warren Commission by Walker during his testimony is 1.8 miles to 2.2 miles, depending on the route taken. By car, again depending on the route, the distance can be traversed in six to seven minutes.

110. While the recollection about the flags may be true it is worth mentioning that from 1962 to 1967 Walker's front yard contained a large billboard saying "Impeach Earl Warren," the motivation stemming in part from Warren's role in the famous *Brown v. Board of Education* case, which led to the integration of all US public schools.

111. The original manuscript has "General Eisenhower" but Eisenhower was, of course, president when he offered Walker the command in Germany. As commander of the 24th Infantry Division in Germany Walker violated the 1939 Hatch Act, first by requiring his troops to read anti-Communist literature supplied by the founder of the John Birch Society, and second, for instructing them to use the Conservative Voting Index when going to the ballot. He was relieved of command by Kennedy's secretary of defense, Robert McNamara, on April 17, 1961. Before the inquiry could be completed, he resigned in protest on November 2, 1961, and entered politics.

112. Both the year of the election and the name of Walker's opponent have been inserted for informational purposes and clarity. Despite the backing of such high-powered conservatives as John G. Tower and Barry Goldwater, Walker polled last in a field of six candidates but he did garner more than 10 percent of the vote.

113. The humorous implications of "Foker" are unclear, though perhaps it is some sort of obscure reference to the "Fokker Scourge" of World War I, when im-

perial Germany introduced the first combat aircraft possessing synchronization gear that allowed the plane's machine guns to fire through the propeller without hitting it. De Mohrenschildt liked to use teasing nicknames such as calling the very conservative Volkmar Schmidt "Messer Schmidt," a reference to the Messerschmitt Bf 109, one of Nazi Germany's principal fighters during World War II. He called his friend Sam Ballen "Chico Sampson" and was called "Mischka" (Russian for "bear") by his own friends due to his well-honed physique.

114. On April 10, 1963, as Walker was sitting at a desk in his study, a single bullet was fired at him. It struck the frame of the widow and was deflected; fragments of the bullet lightly wounded Walker's forearm.

115. See "Marina and the Walker Incident" in Chapter 5.

116. In fact the husband of Ruth Paine, Dallas engineer Michael Paine, oil engineer Volkmar Schmidt, and de Mohrenschildt himself had *all* made disparaging remarks about Walker in Oswald's presence at one time or another in early 1963. Their comments should not be viewed as overly unusual, though, given the liberal leanings of some the individuals involved and Walker's highly controversial and very visible public profile at the time. Lev Aronson was Jewish and an acquaintance of de Mohrenschildt as well as present at the Ford's holiday party but it is impossible to know if he is the "Jewish man" mentioned here.

117. See Chapter 5.

118. Also discussed in "Marina and the Walker Incident" in Chapter 5.

119. This sentence appears after the joking reference to "General Foker" in the original manuscript. It has been moved here because it sums up the entire incident and is out of place appearing in the middle of it.

120. Edward V. Rickenbacker (1890–1973) was America's leading aerial ace of World War I, winning the Congressional Medal of Honor. He was also an entrepreneur, owning his own car company in the 1920s and forming Eastern Airlines in the 1930s. During World War II he supported the war effort as a civilian, though with sweeping credentials provided by US secretary of war Stimson. In 1943 he conducted a successful fact-finding mission to the Soviet Union. After the war Eastern Airlines was initially an industry leader but then went into decline, and Rickenbacker was forced out of his position as company CEO in late 1959, resigning as chairman of the board at the end of 1963. Politically conservative, he was a staunch opponent of FDR's New Deal.

121. The manuscript contains the following additional matrial: "[Khrushchev] is gone now, God bless his Bible-quoting soul and his earthy personality. His sudden bursts of anger and beating of the table with his shoe are all gone and belong to history. Millions of Russians miss him." Removed from the main text due to being overly tangential.

122. This sentence has been added for factual purposes; the April 19 date is from Jeanne's Warren Commission testimony. In leaving Dallas behind the de Mohrenschildts, as was their habit when they moved, skipped out on their last month's rent. Their landlady, Mrs. J. H. Mayo, indicated to the FBI that other than this one omission they were very good tenants.

123. This sentence has been moved from the beginning of the vignette to the end. In addition, the original text mentions only New York, but de Mohrenschildt's own Warren Commission testimony indicated he visited "New York, Philadelphia, [and] Washington" before briefly returning to Dallas to finish packing. The Oswalds were in New Orleans by that point. There was a farewell celebration in Everett Glover's apartment in Dallas, and then the de Mohrenschildts drove to Miami to catch a plane to Port-au-Prince. The Philadelphia segment involved the continuing custody battle over his daughter Nadya with his third wife, Wynne Sharples, and visiting a longtime acquaintance, Edward Robert Thomas, who was president of the Cobra Petroleum Company, and his wife. What de Mohrenschildt was doing in New York and Washington in April and May of 1963 has only come into sharper focus with the release of newly declassified government documents. In the company of Clémard Joseph Charles, who ran the Banque Commerciale d'Haiti, he attended meetings "with CIA and military intelligence officials," met the top aide to fellow Texan Vice President Johnson, and also met Thomas Devine, who just happened to be a business colleague of George H. W. Bush "at Zapata Offshore, who was doing double duty for the CIA." See Russ Baker, *Family of Secrets: The Bush Dynasty, America's Invisible Government, and the Hidden History of the Last Fifty Years* (Bloomsbury Press, 2009), 70. Dorothe K. Matlack (1906–1991), office of the Army Chief of Staff for Intelligence, and Tony Czaikowski of the CIA met both de Mohrenschildt and Charles in Washington on May 7. See David E. Kaiser, *The Road to Dallas: The Assassination of John F. Kennedy* (Belknap Press, 2009), 187–189. Ostensibly the two men were in the jute business together, but, Matlack told the HSCA in the late 1970s, "I knew the Texan wasn't there to sell hemp." See Mellen, *Our Man in Haiti*, 109. Another jute grower in Haiti, Joseph F. Dryer, informed the HSCA de Mohrenschildt was "always very polite," but despite claiming he was in Haiti to scout for oil Dryer "could never figure out what he did." Dryer suspected de Mohrenschildt had "some intelligence connection." Duvalier's term as president of Haiti was set to expire on May 15. Charles clearly had high-level political aspirations. It seems increasingly clear de Mohrenschildt was hoping for a regime change in Haiti, one that would put his associate Charles in charge of the country. If true, de Mohrenschildt was playing a very dangerous game aligning himself against the likes of Duvalier.

124. Replacing "contract" in the original manuscript. The prose is confused, as de Mohrenschildt had already signed the contract in March. Departing in April to sign an already signed contract would be redundant and has to be an error—at this juncture he is departing to begin work on the long-anticipated project itself. The project had been conceived in the mid-1950s and formal preparation had been proceeding since 1961—seeing it launched was a source of great satisfaction.

125. The details of the contract, signed on March 13, 1963, are described in de Mohrenschildt's Warren Commission testimony in Appendix B.

Chapter 4: Haiti and the Warren Commission
1. Political stability in Haiti had been deteriorating for several months. By the spring and summer of 1963 the situation was extremely volatile. Duvalier's grip on

power was precarious. De Mohrenschildt's arrival on the island corresponded with the so-called Barbot affair. While Duvalier was recovering from the heart attack he suffered on May 24, 1959, he left control of the country in the hands of the head of his Tontons Macoutes, Clément Barbot. Once he had recovered Duvalier accused Barbot of having plotted to replace him and threw him into prison. In April 1963 Barbot was released and immediately instigated a plot to kidnap Duvalier's children and employ them as hostages to force him from power. The plot was carried out on April 26 at the entrance to Collége Bird and was witnessed by French UN representative Jean Richardot: "As I was driving to my office I saw one of the Presidential limousines. . . . It was suddenly attacked by the occupants of a car which had been following. The driver of the limousine and two of the Tontons Macoutes bodyguards were shot, but the children were spared and managed to get to their school."

A countrywide hunt for Barbot and his followers ensued, the violence savage by even Haitian standards. On May 2 the American Embassy informed the State Department it was "difficult to exaggerate the fear, both justified and unreasoning, which now dominates Port-au-Prince." It continues: "Unless Duvalier removed soon from scene (he shows no sign of voluntary departure) I find it difficult to envisage any solution other than intervention." *Foreign Relations of the United States, 1961–1963*, Vol. 12, American Republics, Document 378. American-Haitian relations were also severely strained. A May 3, 1963, column in the British newspaper *The Guardian* noted that a US naval force, including an aircraft carrier, "still stands at alert in international waters off Haiti, ready to evacuate the 1,500 Americans there if the situation deteriorates further." Normal diplomatic relations between the two countries were suspended on May 15, and US Ambassador Raymond L. Thurston recalled on May 26. According to Richardot, himself expelled a few days before Thurston, the fugitive Barbot was "found [by the Tontons] hiding in a cornfield on the edge of the city. They set fire to it and Barbot, forced out, was shot." See Jean Richardot, *Journeys for a Better World: An Inside Story of the United Nations by One of Its First Senior Officials* (University Press of America), 207.

2. Referring to a period of more than five months, leading up to November 22. The text makes almost no mention of what these "delights" consisted of, other than imparting a general sense of living in an idyllic Caribbean setting. Elsewhere in the manuscript there is a single mention of "weekends of skin diving in the beautiful transparent waters of the Caribbean," a pursuit also mentioned in the memoirs of Sam Ballen, who recalls a 1965 excursion to go swimming at the reef at Iboleli (Creole for "dream come true"). See Samuel B. Ballen, *Without Reservations* (Ocean Tree Books, 2001), 174. De Mohrenschildt also was spending many an evening enjoying the same social life described in the memoir of Jean Richardot. "I must admit," Richardot wrote, "that at these receptions at private houses and hotels, often in beautiful flower-filled gardens of tropical ambiance, one could meet the most attractive cosmopolitan people." If you wanted to be in on "the *Télédiol*, the famous Haitian grapevine," you made a point of attending these events. The most famous of these locations was the Hotel Oloffson, "an exotic gingerbread mansion" that "rose up on a small hill at the end of a lane lined with gigantic palm trees." In the Oloffson,

whose cantankerous owner, Al Seitz, was from Queens, one could find "a repeat clientele of well-known American and English jet-setters, including writers, artists, journalists, and some just plain lovers of its picturesque ambiance and famous rum punches." See Richardot, *Journeys for a Better World*, 213–214. Needless to say, de Mohrenschildt spent a lot of time enjoying himself at the Oloffson.

3. A description of the de Mohrenschildts' home in Haiti, the Villa Valbrune, may be found in the Preface, note 8.

4. The American is presumably Alston Boyd, the individual named in the manuscript's preface. The Italian is mentioned in Warren Commission De Mohrenschildt Exhibit 9 (a letter from de Mohrenschildt to Paul M. Raigorodsky dated September 12, 1963) as "a geologist from Florence, Italy." The Swiss participant is described as "a young . . . student" in a December 9, 1963, letter to Dallas life insurance executive Thomas J. Attridge later turned over to the FBI. The fact that at least two members of de Mohrenschildt's team were still students may explain why Sam Ballen would claim the long-term failure of the Haitian venture was the result of the "amateurs involved." The manuscript continues, "Incidentally, I may have gotten this assignment because there were no Haitian geologists in the whole country at the time. There may have been some in exile." Because the material is digressive and almost certainly impossible to document after half a century, it is relocated here.

5. The manuscript continues, cryptically, "But other contacts were not interrupted, including the strangest one, the posthumous, which I will describe later." This sentence is almost certainly meant to foreshadow the discovery of the Oswald "hunter of fascists" photo described in Chapter 5.

6. De Mohrenschildt's surprise appears somewhat contradictory given that it comes after Oswald's talk of "moving away from here after your departure" in the vignette "Rare Meetings in 1963" in Chapter 3. Perhaps he did not expect Oswald to do what he said. In any event the move was truly a surprise for Ruth Paine who, when she visited on April 24, found the Oswalds packed and ready to leave. She convinced Lee to allow Marina to remain behind with her while he found work in New Orleans.

7. The implication here is that Lee and Marina moved to New Orleans at the same time, which, as just noted, is incorrect. Lee left Dallas on April 24, and Marina and the baby joined him on May 11, shortly after his being hired by the Reily Coffee Company. In his Warren Commission testimony de Mohrenschildt correctly indicates, "I did receive a card, a postcard, from Oswald before we left the United States. . . . And I lost the card."

8. It would have been a wise decision, but it does not appear to have been Oswald's primary motivation. Oswald was destitute, had a wife and child with another on the way, and had family connections in New Orleans that might improve his chances of finding work. A letter from Marina to her aunt and uncle in the Soviet Union that surfaced in the early 1990s offers a possible explanation. Dated May 18, 1963, Marina wrote "The whole family has moved to New Orleans. . . . I can brag that I was the first who suggested [Lee] go to New Orleans. Here [he] has relatives and in the end that is better than nothing."

9. This sentence relocated here from a few lines further down in the original manuscript.

10. As just noted Oswald found employment lubricating machines at a company owned by William B. Reily, which produced and sold coffee, on May 9. Since Oswald moved into this apartment on May 10 the postcard the de Mohrenschildts received would have to have been sent after this date. Otherwise the 4905 Magazine Street address could not have been on the postcard. Oswald's monthly rent was $65. He was fired on July 19 for inefficiency and inattention to his work. On July 25 he learned his appeal to reverse his undesirable discharge had been rejected.

11. This is one of several places in the manuscript where de Mohrenschildt seems to exhibit a blind spot to the fact that Oswald dissembled on a significant number of issues, even issues de Mohrenschildt quizzed him personally about, such as the reason for his leaving the Marine Corps.

12. The promise of "new elements" is vague here. Rather than specific evidence de Mohrenschildt may simply be referring to the manuscript in a general sense, its attempts to humanize Oswald through references to his jokes, love for his daughter, strongly held anti-segregationist views, etc.

13. The name of Jack Ruby, Oswald's killer, has been inserted here for clarity.

14. Replacing "over and over and explained constantly" in the original manuscript.

15. This sentence added to provide a transition between those immediately preceding and following it.

16. The assertion here is true. The CIA was so concerned about the behavior of the de Mohrenschildts, from their provocative statements about the assassination to their association with a host of shady characters, most especially Clémard Joseph Charles, that every single piece of mail sent and received by the de Mohrenschildts in Haiti was, quite illegally, being monitored and in some cases opened and photographed. The agency continued to do so until November 22, 1965. The de Mohrenschildts themselves were kept under close observation by the CIA, especially an individual identified in CIA records with the pseudonym Conrad V. Rubricius. Rubricius befriended them, attended their dinner parties, and regularly played tennis against George at the Pétionville Country Club.

17. Janet Lee Auchincloss (1907–1989). Born Janet Norton Lee, she was married three times. Her first husband was John Vernou "Black Jack" Bouvier III, with whom she had two daughters, Caroline Lee Bouvier and future first lady Jacqueline Lee "Jackie" Bouvier. Her husband's womanizing and drinking led to a separation in 1936, a brief reconciliation in 1937, and then a divorce in 1940. She and de Mohrenschildt became acquainted during this time period. She remarried on June 21, 1942, this time to Hugh Dudley Auchincloss Jr., with whom she had another daughter and a son. After Auchincloss's death in 1976, she would remarry in 1979, this time to Bingham Morris; they separated in 1981 but remained married until her death in 1989.

18. Unknown to de Mohrenschildt his good friend Janet had given the letter to *her* good friend: ex-CIA director Allen Dulles, who just so happened to be serving

as one of the seven members selected by President Johnson to lead the Warren Commission investigation into President Kennedy's assassination.

19. The letter is dated December 12, 1963, and was sent from Port-au-Prince. It appears in Appendix A.

20. The letter does not include the exact quote provided by de Mohrenschildt. The content of the letter, however, while exhibiting some skepticism as to Oswald's guilt at the same time paints the accused assassin in an extremely negative light.

21. This sentence inserted for informational purposes using de Mohrenschildt's letter.

22. This sentence has been relocated here from the vignette I have titled "Visiting the Auchincloss Home" later in this chapter.

23. Replacing "motif" in the original manuscript.

24. Wood, who was based in the FBI's Dallas, Texas, field office submitted reports to the Warren Commission on the de Mohrenschildts on at least the following occasions: February 28, 1964 (Jeanne); March 14, 1964 (Jeanne); and twice on March 20, 1964 (George, and both George and Jeanne).

25. Replacing the very awkward "A gray-suited, bulky, Miami suntanned, with false teeths [sic] and an artificial smile, Mr. W. James Wood, an Agent of FBI appeared" in the original manuscript. Wood had flown to Haiti on March 7, 1964. The phrase "gray flannel suit boys" was apparently slang de Mohrenschildt and his friend Sam Ballen used to describe the FBI. When asked during his Warren Commission testimony to recall the name of the FBI agent who had interviewed him a few weeks previously, Ballen responded, "He was one of the agents who interviewed me from California. Had a very nice tan, but I don't know his name." When asked if either of the names "W. James Wood or Raymond P. Yelchek" would refresh his memory, Ballen replied, "The gentleman who came out to my house was Mr. Wood."

26. Replacing "It had contacted" in the original manuscript.

27. J. Walton Moore had been a member of the FBI who in 1948 became part of the fledgling CIA's Domestic Contacts Division. The career switch probably explains why de Mohrenschildt mentions both the FBI and the CIA with a note of uncertainty. It is just the sort of detail he consistently has trouble recalling. Moore may have mentioned both positions over the course of his lunches with the de Mohrenschildts. As was discussed briefly in the Editor's Introduction, these lapses are due to neither a lack of intelligence nor subterfuge on de Mohrenschildt's part but are rather a product of both conversing in a nonnative language and a continental as opposed to an Anglo-American style of reasoning.

28. Moore's duties in Dallas included contacting individuals who had information on foreign topics. He had known the de Mohrenschildts since 1957. He admitted interviewing de Mohrenschildt after his return from Yugoslavia and having "periodic" contact thereafter. Moore would claim their last contact had been in the fall of 1961 when the de Mohrenschildts showed him their film of their walking trip through Latin America. This claim appears somewhat suspect when one considers Colonel Orlov was his handball partner, and Orlov accompanied de Mohrenschildt to the Oswalds' home the first time they met in September of 1962. Jeanne de

Mohrenschildt, in an interview with reporter Bill O'Reilly of WFAA-TV on April 11, 1977 (less than two weeks after her ex-husband's death), would say she and her husband had lunch with Moore several times. After their return from Haiti, however, Moore began refusing their invitations.

29. Ervay Street is in the heart of downtown Dallas. The date of the meeting cannot be pinpointed precisely but must have occurred in either late September or early October of 1962.

30. Moore would continue to vigorously deny the "harmless lunatic" comment attributed to him by de Mohrenschildt, insisting the two of them had never discussed the subject of Oswald. This, too, seems somewhat suspect, given that Everett D. Glover, in an interview with FBI special agent Richard L. Wiehl on February 27, 1964, remembered de Mohrenschildt telling him "late in 1962" that "he had been told by an FBI agent that Oswald was completely harmless." In a letter de Mohrenschildt wrote to Glover from Haiti on January 16 he repeated what he had said earlier: "It's interesting, but before we began to help Marina and the child we asked the FBI man in Dallas or Fort Worth about Lee and he told us he was 'completely harmless.'" Glover turned this letter over to the FBI.

31. Replacing the barely comprehensible "material turpitude behavior pattern" in the original manuscript, as well as "ANSWERED" being capitalized for reasons unknown. The entire sentence has been reconstructed.

32. On the importance of hand shaking to de Mohrenschildt, as a sign of manly respect, see the Editor's Introduction. In spite of all the bluster here, however, de Mohrenschildt *did* sign a retraction. A report filed by Wood on March 14, 1964, indicates de Mohrenschildt "made a complete retraction of his earlier statement." The document was signed on March 7, 1964, and witnessed by both Wood and Norman L. Warner, first secretary of the American Embassy in Haiti. It does not read like a complete retraction, but it was sufficient in that the "harmless lunatic" quote was shifted from J. Walton Moore (CIA, not FBI) to de Mohrenschildt's friend, the lawyer Max Clark, whom he claimed he *thought* was an FBI agent or that George Bouhe had told him Clark had been with the FBI. The fact that Moore kept being mistakenly referred to as an FBI agent irked FBI director J. Edgar Hoover, who knew Moore was CIA, considerably.

33. This appears to be another case where a nonnative English speaker, in this case one who had grown up amid the horrors of the Sino-Japanese War, would have a tendency to read the worst into questions posed by the authorities. Admitting prior political associations could have very real, dire, consequences in a place like Mǎnzhōuguó in the 1930s. Seen this way, the de Mohrenschildts' reactions to Wood's questions appear in a different light.

34. Almost certainly a reference to Ballen's Warren Commission testimony: See *Warren Commission Hearings*, Vol. 9, 59.

MR. LEIBLER: Can you think of any other matter about which you might have knowledge, or anything else that you can think of that you think should be brought to the attention of the commission in connection with [de Mohrenschildt's connection to Oswald]?

MR. BALLEN: I would only add that, in my opinion, George is an extremely discerning person and . . . right now his emotions are kind of tensed up, not because of politics, but because of his personal life and finances and the things concerning prior marriages and his children, and consequently his behavior and conduct right now might not be the best but, despite that, he is an extremely intelligent and fine person and I would think that he should be in a position to contribute as much as anyone on the type of person that Lee Harvey Oswald was.

35. Revising "influenced me very positively in my relationship with Lee" in the original manuscript.

36. The phrase "the latter is more doubtful" is regrettably ambiguous. On the one hand, de Mohrenschildt might be saying that it is even more unlikely that Oswald was an agent of the American government than that he was an agent of the Soviet government *or*, on the other, he might be saying there is more reason to doubt that Oswald wasn't an agent of the American government.

37. The manuscript continues with the humorous aside "Looks like it's a specialty of these government agents to have a capital letter instead of the first name. Purely Anglo-Saxon, you know."

38. Replacing "upon" in the original manuscript.

39. See the Editor's Introduction.

40. Replacing "a mystery man who was close to Lee Harvey Oswald and to Jacqueline Kennedy" in the original manuscript. The articles appear to be one and the same; de Mohrenschildt has simply forgotten the wording of the headline. The article appeared on November 24, 1964.

41. A sadly prophetic observation.

42. Kennedy eliminated most of America's economic assistance to Haiti in mid-1962 due to allegations of millions in misappropriated aid money. Relations between the United States and Haiti would remain tense until after Kennedy's assassination. Thereafter, Duvalier received a modest increase in assistance thanks to his staunchly anti-Communist policies.

43. Boyer was one of the proponents of officially recognizing the Creole language in Haiti. He argued that the power of the mulatto elite could be reduced by "encouraging small peasants to improve their productivity, and by setting up agricultural banks throughout the country to provide credit facilities for these small farmers." See David Nicholls, *From Dessalines to Duvalier: Race, Colour, and National Independence in Haiti* (Macmillan, 1996), 200. At the time of de Mohrenschildt's death Boyer was listed as dean of the faculty of Law and Economics at the Université de Port-au-Prince. See Bernan Associates, Taylor and Francis Group, *The World of Learning, 1977–78* (Europa Publications, 1977), 582.

44. Rankin's letter was dated April 8, 1964. Ambassador Timmons telegrammed

Washington on April 15 "Letter from Warren Commission just received and is being delivered to [the de Mohrenschildts] today." J. Lee Rankin (1907–1996) was a Nebraska-based lawyer who had managed Dwight Eisenhower's campaign in the state in 1952. In 1953 Eisenhower selected Rankin to be the nation's assistant attorney general, Office of Legal Counsel (an office in the Department of Justice that functions as legal adviser to the executive branch, including the president). He argued many cases in front of the Supreme Court, including the landmark *Brown v. Board of Education* case in 1954 where, representing the African American plaintiffs, he argued that the "separate-but-equal" facilities for black and white Americans was unconstitutional. In 1956 he became solicitor general and remained in that position until 1961. Rankin was the unanimous choice of the Warren Committee to serve as general counsel, and it was he who redrafted and edited the *Warren Commission Report* into something resembling a polished argument.

45. The manuscript adds "It was unfortunate that Nero and [our other terrier] were blissfully unaware that this trip was caused by Lee Harvey Oswald, whom they liked so much. For them this expedition was a ball." The use of "unfortunate" may be related to de Mohrenschildt's wistful observation that he wished the dogs could have testified to their love of Lee. Otherwise one would expect "fortunate" and assume "unfortunate" a slip.

46. Located at 1401 Pennsylvania Avenue NW. Designed by architect Henry Janeway Hardenberg in what is known as the Beaux-Arts style (a neoclassical style taught at the École des Beaux-Arts in Paris), it opened in 1901. Located two blocks east of the White House the hotel is still in operation today, under the name Willard InterContinental Washington.

47. Albert E. Jenner Jr. (1907–1988) graduated from the University of Illinois, College of Law in 1930. He excelled as a private practice lawyer and was made the president of the Illinois State Bar Association in 1947. Between 1960 and 1970 he served on the Advisory Committee for the Federal Rules of Civil Procedure, and between 1964 and 1975 he was chairman of the Advisory Committee for the Federal Rules of Evidence. His appointment to the Warren Commission is viewed by some as tainted given his background handling criminal cases involving members of organized crime and as a corporate lawyer whose most important client was Henry Crown, a native of Chicago who was one of the principal shareholders in the nation's largest defense contractor, General Dynamics. After the assassinations of Robert Kennedy and Martin Luther King Jr. in 1968, he participated in the US National Commission on the Causes and Prevention of Violence. He argued cases before the Supreme Court on several occasions in the late 1960s and early 1970s. Serving as minority counsel of the House Judiciary Committee in 1973, Jenner recommended impeaching President Nixon. The Republicans on the committee instigated his removal only to shortly thereafter vote in favor of impeachment. In 1975 Jenner, a longtime opponent of the now infamous House Un-American Activities Committee, participated in its abolishment. His alma mater granted him an honorary doctorate in 1981 and, in return, Jenner endowed the Albert E. Jenner Jr. Professorship in Law in 1982.

48. Replacing "neither" in the original manuscript.

49. Allen W. Dulles (1893–1969) was the first civilian director of Central Intelligence, that is, the head of the CIA. After receiving a law degree from George Washington University Law School he joined his brother, John Foster Dulles, at the law firm of Sullivan and Cromwell. He joined the Council on Foreign Relations in 1927 and was secretary from 1933 to 1944. His early career included experience as a diplomat, with postings in Europe and Turkey. While in Europe he met such leading figures of the era as Hitler, Mussolini, and the Soviet Union's chief representative, Maxim Litvinov. He was an ardent interventionist, collaborating with Hamilton Fish Armstrong, the editor of *Foreign Affairs* magazine, on two books in the late 1930s opposing the policy of American isolation from the world system. During World War II he was stationed in neutral Switzerland as Swiss director of the Office of Strategic Services (OSS), the forerunner to the CIA, and immediately after the war he was OSS station chief in Berlin and Bonn. In 1953 Dulles became CIA director, replacing Rear Admiral Roscoe H. Hillenkoetter; his brother was already serving as President Eisenhower's secretary of state. Dulles is credited with transforming US intelligence into a sprawling and sophisticated worldwide network during the 1950s, but he was also responsible for running everything from mind control programs (MK-Ultra), the U-2 spy plane program, the overthrow of foreign governments (Operation Ajax in Iran, Operation PBSUCCESS in Guatemala), and an ongoing campaign against Fidel Castro's Cuba, Operation 40, that included numerous assassination attempts of Castro carried out with the help of American organized crime. After the failed Bay of Pigs invasion Dulles and other leading members of the CIA were forced to resign by President Kennedy, who vowed to "splinter the CIA into a thousand pieces and scatter it to the winds." Dulles would, oddly enough, be appointed by President Johnson to serve as one of the seven commissioners of the Warren Commission investigating Kennedy's murder in Dallas, a decision that has been widely criticized by historians. Dulles and de Mohrenschildt were both friends of Janet Lee Auchincloss. See the vignette "Visiting the Auchincloss Home" later in this chapter.

50. Adding "former" since Dulles was no longer head of the CIA in 1964. It appears that de Mohrenschildt may be conflating Dulles's role as one of seven committee members heading the President's Commission on the Assassination of President Kennedy (i.e., what has since become known as the Warren Commission) with his former occupation. Or it could simply be one of the many typing mistakes present in the manuscript.

51. Gerald R. Ford (1913–2006) was at the time of the Kennedy assassination a member of the House of Representatives, representing the Grand Rapids district of the state of Michigan. He had initially been elected in 1949, running as a moderate on domestic policy and an internationalist on foreign policy. After his death the *New York Times* noted he was largely a "negotiator and reconciler," who had not authored a single piece of major legislation during his entire quarter century in Congress. He was appointed to the Warren Commission as one of its seven commissioners by President Johnson. He was assigned to prepare a biography of Lee Harvey

Oswald, work that would later lead to the book *Portrait of an Assassin* (Simon & Schuster, 1966). He was House Minority Leader from 1965 until late 1973 when he replaced Vice President Spiro Agnew, who had resigned over bribery allegations. The timing was fortuitous, as President Nixon would resign just months later due to the Watergate scandal. Ford pardoned Nixon, a move that probably cost him the 1976 election against Democratic Party candidate Jimmy Carter. It has since been revealed that Ford was secretly providing the FBI with information about individuals on the Warren Commission who expressed doubts about the lone assassin theory. Ford himself would reveal in a posthumously published book that the CIA destroyed and hid crucial documents from the Warren Commission. Fearing exposure of prior and ongoing operations, the CIA behaved in ways that could "easily be misinterpreted as collusion in JFK's assassination." See Gerald R. Ford, *A Presidential Legacy and the Warren Commission* (FlatSigned Press, 2007).

52. An Italian 6.5-mm Carcano Model 91/38 rifle. It was essentially World War II surplus, having been manufactured in Terni, Italy, in 1940. Anyone acquainted with Italian arms of this era can testify to their inferiority. The side-mounted scope, made by Ordnance Optics, had been attached by the retailer, Klein's Sporting Goods, prior to sale. It fired a copper-jacketed round-nosed bullet. The magazine had a six-round capacity.

53. Replacing "you don't have to be tortured" in the original manuscript.

54. The mention of "the possibility of losing my contract in Haiti" is inserted here using text found in the vignette "Who Were the Real Criminals?" to remind the reader of how important the survey in Haiti was for de Mohrenschildt. His future financial security was in a sense riding on this risky venture. See the excerpt of his Warren Commission testimony in Appendix B. His concern with putting the assassination behind him and returning to Haiti is manifest and palpable.

55. Jenner's exact words are a bit different, and suggest that de Mohrenschildt did not fully understand them. "As you realize, there are rumors and speculations [made by] various people [regarding the de Mohrenschildts] who do not know what the facts are—some of them know bits of the facts—which require us in many instances to inquire into matters that are largely personal. We are not doing so merely because we are curious. I will confine myself to matters that we believe to be relevant. It may not always be apparent to you, because we know a great deal more, of course, than any one witness would know." It is also possible de Mohrenschildt is trying to convey the *general tone* of Jenner's questioning; in that case the assistant counsel's preparation could certainly leave that impression.

56. Throughout the manuscript de Mohrenschildt often refers to the one-volume *Warren Commission Report* published in 1964, not the far larger multivolume *Warren Commission Hearings and Exhibits*—but in that case many *other* testimonies would have been condensed and edited for the *Report* as well, not just those of himself and Jeanne. The complaint rings a bit hollow here.

57. This sentence about de Mohrenschildt's tan is not in the original manuscript but it is simply too amusing not to mention. The precise exchange during his Warren Commission testimony speaks for itself:

MR. JENNER: I think we might at this time see if I can describe you for the record. You are 6' 1", are you not?

MR. DE MOHRENSCHILDT: Yes.

MR. JENNER: And now you weigh, I would say, about 195?

MR. DE MOHRENSCHILDT: That is right.

MR. JENNER: Back in those days you weighed around 180.

MR. DE MOHRENSCHILDT: That is right.

MR. JENNER: You are athletically inclined?

MR. DE MOHRENSCHILDT: That is right.

MR. JENNER: And you have dark hair.

MR. DE MOHRENSCHILDT: No gray hairs yet.

MR. JENNER: And you have a tanned—you are quite tanned, are you not?

MR. DE MOHRENSCHILDT: Yes, sir.

MR. JENNER: And you are an outdoorsman?

MR. DE MOHRENSCHILDT: Yes. I have to tell you—I never expected you to ask me such questions.

58. In another portion of the manuscript de Mohrenschildt claims Jenner's flattery "got me into this talkative mood" to the point he became "drunk with words and descriptions." The sheer length of the deposition itself, some ten hours, "had a soporific effect" because "you get deadly tired of these official proceedings, you begin to agree with the questioner just to get out of this boring room [and] away from [this] annoying, dry individual."

59. This seemingly off-hand comment is not nearly as eccentric as the reader might conclude. In the 1930s, as part of his interest in the Négritude movement of Haitian ethnologist Dr. Jean Price-Mars, Duvalier began an ethnological study of *vodou*. Decades later, as part of his cult of personality, Duvalier revived the practice of voodoo/*vodou* and claimed for himself the title of *houngan*, or priest. He dressed in black suits with narrow black ties, the traditional clothing of Baron Samedi, the *loa* of the graveyard. According to Jean Richardot, Duvalier had employed "a chief *bocor* (a special voodoo priest)" to help him "cast an *ouanga à mort* [a spell or curse meant to harm or kill] on the US President." When Kennedy died, Duvalier "credited his *ouanga* with it" and shortly thereafter "sent an emissary to Arlington National Cemetery to collect some soil from Kennedy's grave in order to protect himself and Haiti from any harm that could come from the dead President's spirit." Quoted in Richardot, *Journeys for a Better World*, 208–209.

60. Replacing "leaking" in the original manuscript.

61. See "First Meetings with Lee" in Chapter 1.

62. This sentence is relocated here from a few paragraphs further down where it is simply a digression in an unrelated discussion.

63. Replacing "Doesn't sound that different" in the original manuscript.

64. Replacing "washup" in the original manuscript.

65. The text continues "Later we shall say whom the Warren Committee tried to cover up, maybe unconsciously." As this topic appears in the last chap-

ter regardless it is deleted here. The idea of an "unconscious" cover up is raised again in Chapter 6.

66. Replacing "the cheek" in the original manuscript. And it is true: Jeanne's questioning drones on for pages without ever broaching the topic of the Oswalds. One suspects the FBI concentrated its inquiries on her husband, leaving the commission no choice but to construct her background on the fly during her testimony in Washington.

67. Replacing "continued recollecting for fiery wife" in the original manuscript. This is just one of many examples where the text has been edited for clarity; the entire quote of Jeanne's recollections at this juncture is especially garbled.

68. Apparently the FBI director actually *was* concerned about protecting "information of a highly personal nature" that had been collected by his agents, but J. Lee Rankin, the general counsel of the Warren Commission, insisted on including everything, perhaps out of fear that deleted material would cast doubt on the integrity of the commission's findings. Quoted in Joan Mellen, *Our Man in Haiti* (TrineDay, 2012), 223.

69. The manuscript has "so we did not discuss further details," which might imply de Mohrenschildt is withholding something from Jenner. He repeatedly emphasizes, however, that he and Jeanne held nothing back when responding to questions and, in fact, were often attempting to contribute *additional*, more favorable observations about Oswald that in their view the commission simply didn't appear interested in.

70. Jeanne's Warren Commission testimony is substantially less confrontational:

MR. JENNER: I show you Commission Exhibit 139. Is that the rifle you saw?
MRS. DE MOHRENSCHILDT: It looks very much like it.

71. This sentence added here as it foreshadows the discussion in Chapter 6.

72. Combining the following two sentences: "We both were investigated the same way. Any time we said anything favorable to Lee, they passed it up."

73. Replacing "jesutitically [*sic*]" in the original manuscript.

74. A reasonable enough assumption.

75. Replacing "misinterpreted" in the original manuscript.

76. Replacing "carrying our mutts" in the original manuscript.

77. Editing for clarity the passage: "We wondered why the Committee paid so much attention to the testimonies of people who had known Lee and Marina in Dallas, long before the assassination or others who had known him long before that? And the answer was—just to fill up the pages and tranquillized American populace."

78. Replacing "mink" in the original manuscript.

79. Another example of paraphrasing.

80. The quote de Mohrenschildt provides is inexact. It combines the first sentence of the letter's second paragraph with the first sentence of the seventh. See Appendix A.

81. Replacing "statement" in the original manuscript.

82. Replacing "here" in the original manuscript.

83. The manuscript continues, "Especially she was not beautiful inside when she married that gangster of international shipping Aristotle Onassis." It is deleted for

being in bad taste. The bitterness de Mohrenschildt displays here toward Onassis will reemerge in more elaborate form later; see Chapter 6. Onassis had his own grandiose yet risky plans for making money in Haiti in the early 1960s, but he fared little better than de Mohrenschildt in his dealings with Duvalier. "Onassis's problems in Haiti began when another player slipped into town," namely, the Egyptian Mohamed Al-Fayed (1929–present) who arrived in Port-au-Prince on June 12, 1964. In a rare display of gullibility Onassis believed Duvalier's assurances while the dictator "found out what [Al-Fayed] had to offer." In the end Duvalier concluded an oil development deal with Al-Fayed and not Onassis. See Peter Evans, *Nemesis: Aristotle Onassis, Jackie, and the Love Triangle That Brought Down the Kennedys* (Harper Collins, 2004), 118–119. Al-Fayed would later abscond with $153,440 he embezzled from Haiti's Port Authority, and go on to purchase London's flagship department store, Harrods, in 1985. His son, Dodi Al-Fayed, would die under mysterious circumstances in 1997 while in the company of Britain's Princess Diana. See Mellen, *Our Man in Haiti*, 208–209, 212–213.

84. Replacing the crudely worded if technically accurate "for organized murder" in the original manuscript.

85. The heading for this section does not exist in the original manuscript. As the text fits neither the material preceding or following it a new heading has been inserted. Hugh D. Auchincloss Jr. (1897–1976) was a Yale Law graduate and veteran of both world wars. During World War II he served in the Office of Naval Intelligence and the War Department. His wealth was inherited; part of it was used to found the Washington, D.C., brokerage firm of Auchincloss, Parker, and Redpath. He helped Jacqueline Bouvier get her first journalist job at the *Washington Times Herald* and gave her away at her wedding to future president John F. Kennedy. He was a longtime supporter of the Republican Party but broke ranks to support Kennedy's run for the White House in 1960.

86. 3044 O Street NW. The Queen Anne–style mansion, built in 1870, contains nine bedrooms, seven bathrooms, and twelve fireplaces. It has been a National Historic Landmark listed on the National Register of Historic Places since 1967.

87. In de Mohrenschildt's December 12, 1963, letter to Janet we find reference to this incident: "Remember our discussion one day on the plane from Dallas to Washington? We spoke of criminal children and of the terrible problem of delinquency in the South. Osvald [sic] was just an expression of that cancer which is eating American youth."

88. Replacing "democratic" in the original manuscript. This claim that he intended to vote for Kennedy in the upcoming election would, however, appear to be somewhat contradicted by his February 2, 1964, letter to Janet, in response to her mistaken belief he was working in Haiti on behalf of the US government: "No, I am not connected with our Foreign Service. I was a consultant for the State Department in 1957/58 (in the geological field) but have not had any consulting jobs for the government and did not mind as I have always been a Republican."

89. De Mohrenschildt may have voted for Kennedy in November 1960, but there is simply no way of knowing for certain.

90. This sentence has been added to clarify what is arguably one of de Mohren-schildt's major points of contention with the official version of events. Recall his earlier mention of European diplomats in Haiti "grumbling" about Oswald's apparent lack of motive.

91. Another portion of the manuscript reads: "Jeanne asked her: 'why don't you, the relatives of our beloved President, you who [are] so wealthy, why don't you conduct a real investigation as to who was the rat who killed him?'"

92. The manuscript continues: "A later chapter dealing with Wellem Oltman's [*sic*] strange adventure, will raise further grave doubts in readers' minds." On Olt-mans see the vignette "A New Friend: Willem Oltmans" in Chapter 6.

93. Replacing the confused text "was a PATSY, a patsy not involved in any revenge arising out of JFK's biggest and costliest mistake—the Bay of Pigs" in the original manuscript.

94. Just over $600,000 in 2013 dollars according to the CPI inflation calculator. The figure may be a low one. See the vignette "Marina after Lee" in Chapter 5.

95. Neither of the de Mohrenschildts appears to have understood that the fact they were not in Dallas in the weeks immediately before the assassination is partially beside the point. The fact that they had interacted with the Oswalds at all made them persons of interest in the assassination investigation. They also had not been casual acquaintants, at least between roughly September and November of 1962. Finally their unrestrained and wild talk of conspiracies at social gatherings in Port-au-Prince more than sufficed to put the spotlight squarely on themselves.

96. Replacing "over eight months" in the original manuscript, which is an inaccuracy. If the de Mohrenschildts saw the Oswalds late in the evening the day before Easter Sunday, which fell on April 14 that year, the interval between this date and the assassination on November 22 would have been a little more than seven months.

97. Replacing "intervening" in the original manuscript.

98. Replacing "despite in later years" in the original manuscript. De Mohren-schildt reported in early 1966 that he "had not received any sisal in return for his services to the GOH [Government of Haiti] in the last year." He would continue to write letters to American government officials appealing for their assistance in recovering the money owed to him by the government of Haiti well into the 1970s. The reactions he received were not without sympathy or denial that his claim had legal standing; rather, by the time de Mohrenschildt left Haiti in late 1966, the United States had more or less resigned itself to Duvalier remaining in power. With Cold War paranoia as rampant as ever and the fear that Haiti might become yet another Cuba, the inquiries made on de Mohrenschildt's behalf simply lacked the sort of vigor needed to solicit a serious response on the Haitian end.

99. This section heading does not exist in the original manuscript. It is inserted here to denote the transition to a new topic.

100. Replacing "grimly the worst suspicions" in the original manuscript.

101. The time span of nine months is a matter of interpretation. The de Mohren-schildts had completed their move to Haiti, including arranging for transportation of their car, on June 2, that is, less than *six* months before Kennedy was assassinated.

George had, however, been in Haiti during the month of March to conclude the contractual arrangements with the Haitian government. Including the visit in March would however still only be a span of *eight* months.

102. Replacing "particularly insisting reporters" in the original manuscript.

103. The heading for this section does not exist in the original manuscript. It is inserted here to denote the transition to a new topic. Replacing the poorly worded "Then there came an officer for us to appear in a televised interview for a program being produced by NBC" in the original manuscript.

104. George McMillan (1913–1987) had reported on the civil rights movement as a freelance journalist, with articles published in leading periodicals such as the *New York Times*, *Saturday Evening Post*, *Washington Post*, *Life*, and *Look*. The June 26, 1964, issue of *Life* had included his article "Klan Scourges St. Augustine: Special Report." His liberal views and success as a writer would have made him naturally attractive to de Mohrenschildt, who was a strong supporter of desegregation and a long-suffering aspiring writer. Because of his interest in the Kennedy assassination, McMillan would later become acquainted with and marry Priscilla Johnson, the future author of *Marina and Lee*.

105. The unnamed mutual friend was Sam Ballen. Ballen would confide in his memoir, "George McMillan had come down to Dallas to produce an NBC television show. . . . I put McMillan in touch with the de Mohrenschildts in Haiti, and a deal was worked out." See Ballen, *Without Reservations*, 175.

106. Replacing "the center of attention" in the original manuscript. Haiti was in the news but hardly the center of the world's attention.

107. In truth these invasions were often by Haitian exiles crossing Haiti's eastern border with the Dominican Republic. For example, a memorandum from Robert M. Sayre of the National Security Council to McGeorge Bundy, the president's special assistant for National Security Affairs, states, "CIA informs me that 28 Haitian exiles did enter Haiti [on July 7, 1964] on the south coast, each armed with an M-1 rifle and about 1,000 rounds of ammunition." See *Foreign Relations of the United States, 1964–1968*, Volume 32, Document 331. The memo dismisses reports "that the exiles may have been trained in Puerto Rico, Miami, or Cuba" as "unfounded." It may be this incursion, or one quite similar, that de Mohrenschildt was referring to. See also Richardot, *Journeys for a Better World*, 206. Richardot, who left the country in May 1963, mentions the invasions as coming from "Florida and across the border with the Dominican Republic." One such invasion frightened Duvalier to the extent that he had packed his bags and was prepared to seek refuge in the Colombian Embassy.

108. According to Jeb Sprague, the act of "leaving the body hanging in public" was an oft-practiced calling-card of the Macoutes, intended to act as "a clear warning to anyone stepping out of line, especially leftists, socialists, and pro-democracy activists." See Jeb Sprague, *Paramilitarism and the Assault on Democracy in Haiti* (Monthly Review Press, 2012), 29.

109. In a letter written on February 2, 1964, for example, de Mohrenschildt extended an invitation to Janet Lee Auchincloss and her husband to visit Jeanne

and himself in Haiti, assuring her she should "not believe the silly reports of the American press about Haiti. It is not a 'hell hole,' no Americans have been molested and the situation at present is peaceful and pleasant." See Warren Commission De Mohrenschildt Exhibit 12.

110. While admittedly just his opinion, de Mohrenschildt's cosmopolitanism often blinded him to the brutal realities of the countries he worked in. As reported by *Life* in March 1963, the per capita income of Haiti's 4 million residents was under $70 per year and the unemployment rate was over 60 percent. See "Voodoo Land in Ferment," *Life* 54, no. 10 (March 3, 1963), 29. Sprague indicates that rather than being an advocate of the impoverished, Duvalier consolidated his power by promoting "a cult of personality around his leadership and blocked the self-empowerment of the poor black majority through violent repression." See Sprague, *Paramilitarism and the Assault on Democracy in Haiti*, 33.

111. A novel first published in 1966 and made into a critically panned movie starring Richard Burton, Elizabeth Taylor, Alec Guinness, and Peter Ustinov a year later. A good contemporary review is G. M. Feigen, "A Triangular Look at the Comedians," *Ramparts* 6, no. 7 (February 1968): 62–65. Predictably, the film enraged Duvalier.

112. The first three sentences of this paragraph are adapted from the memoir of UN representative Jean Richardot, who was staying at the "extraordinary mountaintop home" of Horace and Gordana Ashton, two Americans who had been living on the island since his first visit in 1941. If the Ashtons were not neighbors of the de Mohrenschildts they would appear to have been, given the description, in close proximity. See Richardot, *Journeys for a Better World*, 214.

113. The manuscript continues with the confused prose, "He stopped suddenly as a huge tarantula moved slowly on its long legs close to him, he shuddered. 'Don't worry,' I reassured him, 'these big ones are too dangerous, not the small ones.'"

114. Replacing "diatribe" in the original manuscript. A diatribe is a bitter and abusive speech, whereas there is no bitterness here. It was more a sales pitch.

115. Probably mentioned because de Mohrenschildt was by all accounts an active man and an avid tennis player who would have had few able opponents in a place like Port-au-Prince. In his memoir Sam Ballen writes that throughout their early acquaintance "George and I played tennis at least three times a week." See Ballen, *Without Reservations*, 170.

116. Ballen estimated that NBC "must have given [the de Mohrenschildts] over $15,000" to appear on the program because he had been offered $5,000 by McMillan despite having met Oswald all of once for a total of two hours.

117. Inserting the name of Ballen, who had met George in 1952 and indicated he and de Mohrenschildt talked with each other "at least once a day" for a decade. See Ballen, *Without Reservations*, 165. Ballen had also met Oswald, having interviewed him for a job at de Mohrenschildt's request.

118. Replacing "apartment" in the original manuscript. In de Mohrenschildt's perspective a person who was not living in their own home, regardless of the type of

accommodation, was a renter. Sam Ballen wrote that "NBC paid their expenses to come to a lavish suite in New York." See Ballen, *Without Reservations*, 175.

119. Replacing "drag out of me insidiously some damaging comment to his memory" in the original manuscript. Promoting his book *The Making of an Assassin: The Life of James Earl Ray* on NBC's *Today Show* on October 26, 1976, McMillan would say, "I've worked on three assassinations, and it was my earlier work that made me convinced that the only way, fundamentally, to answer the questions about conspiracies in these assassinations is to prove the motive of the assassin." One could argue however that if one looks only for motives "of the assassin" (singular) one will never discover the possible motives of an assassination conspiracy (plural), and it would appear the program the de Mohrenschildts appeared on in 1964 was based on a similar dubious assumption.

120. Replacing "on wrong premises" in the original manuscript.

121. Inserting "a sudden onset of" here to clarify that the de Mohrenschildts considered Oswald sane up to the time of their last meeting on April 14 but did not rule out the possibility of mental illness arising later, as is indicated in the very next sentence.

122. Replacing "are met every day" in the original manuscript. It would be highly unusual to meet someone mentally ill on the streets every single day.

123. Replacing "groves" in the original manuscript.

124. It is not clear what de Mohrenschildt means here by previewing or the context of his reference to forty minutes. It implies on the one hand his interview was forty minutes long and that he was allowed to view the footage a few days later, but that only the "worst parts" were eventually aired. On the other hand forty minutes could well be the length of the complete program. An hour-long network television broadcast would have had several minutes' worth of commercials. A version of the broadcast available for a time on YouTube (later removed for copyright infringement) was just over forty minutes in length.

125. This sentence added for informational purposes. Remembering George and Jeanne's NBC appearance many years later Sam Ballen would write that "they did not display anything but the distress within them." Ballen, *Without Reservations*, 175.

126. Replacing: "It was like a McCarthy era, the time of the government's witch-hunt against the 'leftists.' This was a general hunt, government's and media's against a defenseless dead man."

127. Replacing "went through customs first," something that seems doubtful.

128. Aubelin Jolicoeur (1924–2005). According to Joan Mellen, Jolicoeur was the mulatto offspring of a French father and a Haitian mother. In addition to being the gossip columnist for *Le Nouvelliste*, a French-language paper printed in Port-au-Prince and distributed to the larger cities of the country, he was a boyhood friend of Haitian dictator Duvalier and worked for Haitian intelligence. See Mellen, *Our Man in Haiti*, 138. He was the basis of the character Petit Pierre in Graham Greene's *The Comedians*. The *New York Times* published Jolicoeur's obituary on March 6, 2005.

129. This sentence does not exist in the manuscript. The greeting is mentioned on

page 138 of Mellen's *Our Man in Haiti*. As de Mohrenschildt was engaged in frequent air travel to and from Haiti, and as he mentions Jolicoeur as being clown-like, it is safe to assume he would have heard this greeting many times.

130. Replacing "surreptitiously" in the original manuscript.

131. Regarding Timmons see the Preface, note 24.

132. Edward Glion Curtis Jr. was the American *chargé d'affaires* in Haiti. See Hal Hendrix, "Grapevine Warned Duvalier—Invasion Plan Known by Haiti in July," *Miami News*, August 11, 1963. Curtis's name comes up in relation to a memorandum prepared for the American Embassy by Paul Johnson, co-director of the Haitian-American Institute in Port-au-Prince. Johnson describes a social gathering hosted by the de Mohrenschildts at the Villa Valbrune on September 12, 1964, shortly before George and Jeanne left for their appearance on NBC television. In this report, declassified in 1994, Johnson describes the de Mohrenschildts as un-American, "unstable and possibly dangerous." When de Mohrenschildt implied Johnson might be connected to the CIA Johnson suggested he might or might not be, which "put an end to his prying." A note by "DCM Curtis" dated September 14 attached to Johnson's report reads "Mr. Johnson was informed that in any future situation such as this he should deny categorically any CIA connection and all knowledge of the organization. . . . He seemed agreeable."

133. Apparently the de Mohrenschildts did make Ambassador Timmons's life a living hell during 1964, everything from wildly accusing the FBI of having assassinated Kennedy at embassy parties, to unauthorized use of the embassy dispensary, to Jeanne following the embassy receptionist into a restroom and slapping her. Timmons described them as "pushy, arrogant, and addicted to name-dropping." For all these reasons the de Mohrenschildts were placed in an adult version of "time out" in October 1964, barred from having contact or association with embassy personnel. Timmons rescinded the restrictions in early December, noting the de Mohrenschildts had apparently learned their lesson. See Mellen, *Our Man in Haiti*, 223–224. Sam Ballen, who visited them in January 1964, found Jeanne "putting together a scenario that [Kennedy's assassination] had been a plot of the CIA and of H. L. Hunt," and he concluded that because of her extreme behavior "George's future in Haiti was now dated." See Ballen, *Without Reservations*, 173.

134. The statement is certainly an odd one given that de Mohrenschildt presents himself elsewhere in the manuscript as an agnostic, a portrait more or less paralleled in the Warren Commission testimony of several members of the Dallas White Russian community. But faced with losing "the deal" the hustler will say anything, so perhaps the statement should not be all that surprising.

135. The sentence would appear to be doubly inaccurate. First, while it is certainly possible *some* of de Mohrenschildt's maps were confiscated in the manner described, it appears that other maps in his possession were stolen by none other than one of his many high-profile acquaintances, Mohamed Al-Fayed, who was busy having his own adventure in the nightmare republic, including a fling with de Mohrenschildt's twenty-one-year-old daughter Alexandra, who was visiting Haiti without her husband. As reported by a CIA informant Al-Fayed attended a party at the de

Mohrenschildts' home on June 20, 1964, and Al-Fayed's bodyguard recalled the de Mohrenschildts were regular dinner guests in the Egyptian's home. Another CIA report cryptically described the relationship between the two men as "professionally necessary but dangerous." On Al-Fayed's time in Haiti see Daniel Sanger and Julian Feldman, "Fayed's Forgotten Years: The Conman, the Dictator, and the CIA Files," *The Daily Telegraph Magazine*, June 20, 1998. Second, de Mohrenschildt is neglecting to inform the reader that after returning from his November 1964 television appearance in New York, he would remain in Haiti for another two years. The manuscript contains almost no material on the December 1964 to November 1966 time period.

136. An indication that de Mohrenschildt did do serious work while in Haiti was his discovery of a large deposit of bauxite "that would turn out to contain fourteen million tons." Quoted in Mellen, *Our Man in Haiti*, 224. Unfortunately he would never profit from the discovery.

137. The de Mohrenschildts did not begin preparing for departure from Haiti until around the end of 1965, more than a year after their appearance on NBC's "The Warren Commission Report." They continued to enjoy themselves. Among their adventures, Sam Ballen recalled, "they chartered a sailboat and spent about two months going around the island to all the most remote spots, living off their fish catches and enjoying native hospitality. No one related easier to native peoples than George and Jeanne." See Ballen, *Without Reservations*, 173. Even having made up their minds to leave, the de Mohrenschildts lingered in Haiti until nearly the end of 1966, hoping to depart with at least $100,000 or, in lieu of cash, Haitian real estate. See Mellen, *Our Man in Haiti*, 225–226.

138. Replacing "looked for" in the original manuscript.

139. Whether or not the story is true this may be a reference not to the presidential palace but rather to Fort-Dimanche, a prison used by Duvalier to torture and murder his political opponents. See Patrick Lemoine, *Fort-Dimanche, Dungeon of Death* (Trafford, 2011). Duvalier sometimes personally observed the torture, which included submersion in baths of sulfuric acid.

140. It is difficult to reconcile this account with the one found in CIA documents declassified in the late 1970s, which have de Mohrenschildt departing on "a Panamanian transport ship called the *Mona I*." See Mellen, *Our Man in Haiti*, 258. It is possible the ship was German but registered under the Panamanian flag.

141. Misspelled "*liasse passe*" in the original manuscript. The *laissez-passer* is a travel document issued by a national government or certain international organizations such as the UN, EU, and the International Committee of the Red Cross. Frequently such a pass would have specific freedom-of-movement limitations.

142. Written as "Incidentally on the manifest of this ship we signed our names as follows: Jeanne—a cook;—reckoned" in the original manuscript. Extrapolating "sailor" based on the work de Mohrenschildt performed and because "sailor" is mentioned in *Our Man in Haiti*.

143. Replacing "an open car" with the make of the de Mohrenschildts' car, mentioned elsewhere in the manuscript as a Galaxie convertible.

144. The precise date has been inserted here. In sum the de Mohrenschildts had been in Haiti roughly three and a half years. They were almost completely broke. Friend Sam Ballen put them up in his guest house for a time. See Ballen, *Without Reservations*, 174–175.

145. Replacing "another situation" in the original manuscript.

146. George and Jeanne's testimony is certainly long but nonetheless it is but a portion of the 476 pages that comprise the *Warren Commission Hearings and Exhibits*, Vol. 9. This volume also includes the testimonies of Paul M. Raigorodsky, Thomas and Natalie Ray, Samuel B. Ballen, Ruth and Michael Paine, and still others.

147. Replacing "interrogation" in the original manuscript.

148. A cynic might argue that it was remarkably naïve for someone so distrusting of government bureaucracy to simply assume a deposition on a presidential assassination would be kept private. Rightly or wrongly, this was de Mohrenschildt's view of the methods of European law enforcement, and he appears to have trusted that the same discretion would apply in the United States.

149. Replacing "shades" in the original manuscript.

150. The manuscript continues, "And never again these patriotic and decent people will expose themselves in the degrading positions of 'informers.'"

151. Inserting "Sam Ballen" here as this is almost certainly who de Mohrenschildt is referring to. First, Ballen was a financial consultant who had completed graduate coursework in banking, geology, and petroleum engineering. Second, he and de Mohrenschildt had been friends since 1952 and would remain in contact until shortly before de Mohrenschildt's death. Third, because Ballen's Warren Commission testimony, while brief, paints Oswald in an even better light than either of the de Mohrenschildts. Ballen indicated it was his impression that Oswald would have viewed President Kennedy "warmly." Of course Ballen's direct exposure to Oswald was limited to a single roughly two-hour employment interview conducted with Oswald as a favor to de Mohrenschildt. Ballen conceded he was unable to help due to an "almost total lack of meaningful training" on Lee's part.

152. The sentence does not appear in the original manuscript. It has been inserted here because the context within the manuscript makes it quite clear these positive comments about Oswald (and at least implicitly de Mohrenschildt himself) in the Warren Commission hearings were not the norm and are meant to be juxtaposed to the more numerous negative views expressed in the next paragraph.

153. Paul M. Raigorodsky (1898–1977) had known de Mohrenschildt for more than fifteen years. His apartment in the Stoneleigh Terrace Hotel (2927 Maple Avenue) was a stone's throw from de Mohrenschildt's Maple Terrace Apartment (3001 Maple Avenue). Jeanne lived briefly in the Stoneleigh before moving in with George at Maple Terrace. Raigorodsky's quote doesn't address *trust*, however, it addresses *truth*. Regardless, one can well imagine de Mohrenschildt's reaction to the sight of the comment: "Well, I'll say there is no other way around this—I don't think his reputation was that of a truthful person." See *Warren Commission Hearings and Exhibits*, Vol. 9, 16. He died of natural causes just two weeks before de Mohrenschildt.

154. Natasha Voshinin (oddly identified only as "Mrs. Igor Vladimir Voshinin"

in her Warren Commission testimony) by her own account worked in de Mohren-schildt's Dallas office for just "2 or 3 weeks maximum . . . no longer than a month," and even then only part time, splitting her hours with another geologist, Henry Rogatz, located in the same building. See *Warren Commission Hearings and Exhibits*, Volume 8, 425–448. She discusses the trips to Houston on pages 438–440. Paul Raigorodsky fills in the blanks to a degree, telling the Warren Commission that de Mohrenschildt was going to Houston "quite often" to see the Brown brothers, Herman (1892–1962) and George (1898–1983). A deal to bring their company in on his Haitian venture was in the works, but apparently fell through when Herman died. When asked about the company itself, Raigorodsky would only answer off the record. The company founded by the Brown brothers, Brown & Root, was one of the largest construction and engineering firms in the world, a major defense contractor, and had pork-barrel ties to Lyndon Johnson dating back to the 1930s. In December 1962 George Brown sold the company to Halliburton Incorporated and served on its board until his retirement. The sale, most likely, ended any chance of a partnership with de Mohrenschildt in Haiti. On the other hand, de Mohrenschildt himself mentions in his Warren Commission testimony visiting "clients" in "the oil business" especially his friend "John Jacobs, Vice President of Texas Eastern [Corp.]" as well as an architect at the Rice Institute (now Rice University) named "Andy Todd." Anderson Todd (1921–present) was an associate professor in 1962, would become professor in 1966 and director of the School of Architecture in 1969.

155. George Bouhe's testimony was taken in Dallas, not Washington. See *Warren Commission Hearings and Exhibits*, Vol. 8, 355–378. Whereas de Mohrenschildt here simply alludes to Bouhe having a low level of intelligence, Igor Voshinin, in his own Warren Commission testimony, is more candid: "George Bouhe is an unusually dumb person." Others in the White Russian community simply considered Bouhe a bit nosy regarding the private affairs of the émigrés he came into contact with. Oddly, however, Bouhe's testimony does not appear to refer to Jeanne's views on religion at all, though certainly her strongly avowed atheism would have been known to him and, being devout, he would have disapproved of them. Helen Leslie, another member of the Dallas Russian émigré community whose testimony in Volume 9 appears immediately before de Mohrenschildt's does say, "Now . . . I will tell you something—that what many people were afraid of, his wife is an atheist. She doesn't believe in God."

156. Possibly Declan P. Ford though these words do not appear in his Warren Commission testimony. Ford and his wife Katya did not like Oswald but respected his political commitments as serious; conversely they liked de Mohrenschildt but considered him all talk, someone who "only wanted to be 'a commissar,' wanted to be 'on top' himself." Quoted in Priscilla Johnson McMillan, *Marina and Lee* (Steerforth, 2013), 299.

157. The manuscript continues: "Of course, in the meantime my daughter had abandoned him and he kept a grudge against me because I had not approved of their teen-age marriage." Gary E. Taylor had married de Mohrenschildt's daughter Alexandra on November 21, 1959, when she would have been sixteen. See *War-*

ren Commission Hearings and Exhibits, Vol. 9, 73–102. The hypothesis that de Mohrenschildt might be behind Oswald's killing of Kennedy is mentioned on page 100 and reads as follows:

> MR. JENNER: . . . We have had some discussion off the record. I will ask you first—is there anything you would like to add that occurs to you that you might think helpful—as an occurrence having taken place or even general thoughts on your part—to the Commission in this important investigation it has undertaken?
>
> MR. TAYLOR: Well, the only thing that occurred to me was that—uh—and I guess it was from the beginning—that if there was any assistance or plotters in the assassination that it was, in my opinion, most probably the De Mohrenschildts.

Taylor indicated his opinion was based on: (1) "their desire . . . to return to Russia at one time"; (2) "they had traveled behind the Iron Curtain"; (3) "they took a trip to Mexico, through Mexico, on the avowed purpose of walking from Laredo, Texas to the tip of South America." Jenner, clearly skeptical, asked some follow-up questions about the factual basis of each opinion and then, finding little, the subject was dropped.

158. The manuscript continues with the following digression: "The story reminds me somewhat of another specimen, Svetlana Stalina, the daughter of [Joseph Stalin] the greatest assassin the world had seen (including Adolf Hitler and Attila the Hun), Communist and daughter of the ferocious Communist, who came to the United States in search of God." Adopting her mother's last name after her father's death in 1953, Svetlana Alliluyeva (1926–2011) defected to the West in 1967. In 1970 she married William Wesley Peters, who had been an apprentice of famed architect Frank Lloyd Wright, and became an American citizen in 1978. It is possible that de Mohrenschildt is here alluding to a 1967 article published in *Esquire* (a magazine he was clearly familiar with), written by Garry Wills and Ovid Demaris, titled "How the Daughter of Stalin Denounced Communism and Embraced God, America, and Apple Pie."

159. The reference to Atlanta is a bit cryptic. A possible explanation is offered by J. P. Phillips, whose *Act of Retribution* provides a detailed account of Oswald's movements during the days immediately after his return from the Soviet Union. On June 14, 1962, using money wired from his brother Robert, the Oswalds purchased airline tickets to Dallas–Fort Worth. Flight 821 "made an unscheduled stopover in Atlanta, Georgia." An Atlanta name and address was found in Oswald's address book after the assassination: "Natasha Davidson, the Russian-speaking mother of Captain Davidson, the resident physician and air attaché at the American embassy in Moscow who performed a physical exam on Marina just prior to the Oswalds' departure from the Soviet Union less than one month earlier." Phillips concludes that exactly "what de Mohrenschildt meant by Oswald's 'activities in Atlanta' can only be conjectured . . . we can reasonably assume that he was most likely referring to the unscheduled Delta 821 stopover." See J. P. Phillips, *Act of Retribution: The*

Military-Industrial-Intelligence Establishment and the Conspiracy to Assassinate President John F. Kennedy, (Xlibris, 2010), 75.

160. On Garrison see Chapter 6. The statement here is a bit of an exaggeration. The Clay Shaw trial ended in acquittal in early 1969, and Garrison remained in office another four years before losing a reelection bid in 1973.

161. Possibly another reference to the Oswald note destroyed by FBI agent Hosty shortly after the assassination, though how that connects with LBJ and his hatred of the Kennedys is unclear.

162. Replacing "and jointly with it his ignorance was also out of the ordinary" in the original manuscript.

163. The manuscript has *Dallas Herald* but the paper ceased using that name in 1888 when it became the *Dallas Times Herald*. The *Dallas Times Herald* won a Pulitzer Prize in 1964 for Robert H. Jackson's photo of Jack Ruby murdering Oswald. Between 1969 and 1986 the newspaper was owned by Times Mirror. It ceased publication in 1991. Notable staff members at the time of the Kennedy assassination were A. C. Greene, who was an editorial page editor, and Jim Lehrer (of later fame as co-host of *The MacNeil/Lehrer NewsHour* on PBS), who was a reporter. Graydon Heartsill (1906–1989) was, primarily, a fashion editor at the *Dallas Times Herald* who had become friends with Jeanne in the 1950s. She had written an article published on November 6, 1960, titled "Pan American Walking Tour" describing the de Mohrenschildts' preparations for their walking trip through Central America. CIA records indicate a letter bearing the return address "Graydon Heartsill, The Dallas Times Herald" and postmarked December 4, 1964, was sent to the de Mohrenschildts in Haiti. A record at the Mary Ferrell Foundation indicates Jeanne lived with, and cared for, the elderly and ailing Heartsill in the late 1980s before placing her "in Traymore Nursing Home on Lemmon Avenue, Dallas."

164. The interview, titled "Caught between Two Tragedies: De Mohrenschildts Knew Both Oswalds, Kennedys," appeared in the *Dallas Times Herald* on December 11, 1966. The story was picked up and reported by the Associated Press in several newspapers including the *New York Times*. These AP stories became the basis of *Esquire*'s lampoon of the de Mohrenschildts as the dimwitted proponents of the "washing machine theory" of Kennedy's assassination mentioned in Chapter 3.

165. Replacing "What is it" in the original manuscript.

166. Arguably one of the high points of the manuscript. The prose here recalls a line from Nietzsche's *Daybreak—Thoughts on the Prejudices of Morality*: "He who is punished is never he who performed the deed. He is always the scapegoat."

Chapter 5: A Ghost Visits: Finding a Photograph

1. Sam Ballen allowed the de Mohrenschildts, who he indicates were all but broke, to stay in his Dallas guest house upon their return from Haiti. Initially all went well but then:

[Jeanne] began drinking excessively and hiding the bottles under her mattress. The two of them started grinding on each other's nerves with daily scenes from a Virginia Woolf script. . . . And so, when I left for a trip to West Texas, I wrote them a note saying it was probably for the best for all of us if they moved out of our guest house. They managed to find another tiny apartment, but Jeanne was furious and started spreading lies about me and falsely claimed that I had cheated a former business partner and god knows what else.

Samuel B. Ballen, *Without Reservations* (Ocean Tree Books, 2001), 174–176. It would be several years before Ballen and his wife would be on speaking terms with the de Mohrenschildts again. Jeanne's drinking and increasingly erratic and belligerent behavior are noted on several occasions in Willem Oltmans's memoirs. "The scenes with Jeanne were terrible," the journalist wrote of a visit he made in November 1972. "It was so embarrassing that I went outside for a walk. When I returned ten minutes later dinner was ready and everything seemed back to normal." De Mohrenschildt downplayed his wife's behavior, telling Oltmans "If I leave her, she will either become a drunkard or end up in a lunatic asylum. I will not do that to her." Willem Oltmans, *Memoires 1972–1973* (Papieren Tijger, 2004), 244–245.

2. George's daughter Alexandra was living in Mexico and Jeanne's daughter Christina was living in California. The report filed by the Palm Beach County Sheriff's Office after de Mohrenschildt's death in 1977 lists Alexandra's address as "Mexico City, Mexico."

3. Replacing "was exactly fitting to us and" in the original manuscript. It is possible that by calling their new home La Citadelle, the de Mohrenschildts were naming it after the Citadelle Laferrière, a large mountaintop stone fortress in northern Haiti. Constructed in the early nineteenth century, it is one of the most popular tourist destinations in the country.

4. One gets the sense that de Mohrenschildt uses the word "exhaust" here and a few other places within the manuscript to convey a financial "drain" rather than "bankruptcy" but knowing for certain is impossible. The original manuscript has "Southwestern Warehouses" in one place and "Southwest Warehouse" in another and has been corrected using declassified records of correspondence between the warehouse and de Mohrenschildt while the latter was in Haiti.

5. The thought trails off here but the implication is clear: the books simply cannot be left behind, regardless of how valueless everything else might be.

6. Replacing "could be eliminated" in the original manuscript. It is an unfortunate choice of words given the prominence of assassination within the surrounding text.

7. See the vignette "Growing Animosity" in Chapter 2.

8. Replacing "punctiously" in the original manuscript.

9. Replacing "had the package to Glover to whom we had loaned some of our furniture" in the original manuscript. Glover, in his Warren Commission testimony, indicated he was in need of furniture, having just moved: "I sent all my furniture to my former wife, all the good furniture, so [de Mohrenschildt] was going to let us use the furniture for as long as we wanted, to save him storage fees and to help us out."

10. The "package" de Mohrenschildt mentions here were the records, which

were wrapped in brown paper, a detail recalled by his and Jeanne's attorney Patrick S. Russell Jr., shortly after George's death in 1977. It is possible however that the records were *mailed* and de Mohrenschildt is forgetting yet another detail. How the photo got there is far less important to him than the fact it was there at all. To complicate matters further, in de Mohrenschildt's Warren Commission testimony Assistant Counsel Jenner mentions instructional records "were found in Mrs. Paine's home" and Glover's own testimony indicates that de Mohrenschildt had loaned him the record player along with the de Mohrenschildts' other furniture and, following de Mohrenschildt's instructions, he had given the record player to Marina in May, and then later in the year Michael Paine returned the record player to Glover, who put it into storage. Glover's testimony is so convoluted on this subject it is not surprising de Mohrenschildt, if he indeed read it, failed to follow it.

11. The manuscript is rather ambiguous regarding Glover's presence/absence. It begins by suggesting Glover was present when the photo was found but then oddly raises a question that is left unanswered, because Glover seemingly was *not* present and had, in fact, moved away without leaving a forwarding address. The only other option would be that Glover was present but the de Mohrenschildts only thought of what is a pretty basic question at a later date, but this would appear to be rather counter-intuitive. Glover as best as can be determined relocated to Wisconsin, joining the Department of Geology and Geophysics at the University of Wisconsin, Madison.

12. Replacing "shrieded" in the original manuscript.

13. The date is added for historical reference. The last issue of the original, weekly version of *Life* magazine was December 29, 1972. The monthly version of *Life* did not begin until 1978, the year after de Mohrenschildt's death. The reference to the "now-defunct" *Life* magazine would appear to date the composition of this portion of the manuscript to 1973 or later.

14. There are credible arguments that the photo of Oswald that appeared on the cover of *Life* bears traces of having been altered. Oswald said as much in his own interrogation. Given de Mohrenschildt's strong distrust of the federal government's law enforcement and national security bureaucracies, one wonders why he wouldn't take the question of photo manipulation more seriously.

15. The inscription is worded "To my dear friend George from Lee" in the original manuscript, which is clearly contradicted by the text on the reverse side of the photo. The correct inscription has been substituted. The date on the back of the photo is "5/IV/1963" which could be read in one of two ways, neither of which supports the idea of de Mohrenschildt being in Haiti at the time. The first would be to read the date as April 5, 1963. The attempt on General Walker's life was April 10. Easter Sunday was April 14, and the de Mohrenschildts visited the Oswalds either late in the evening on Saturday, April 13, or Sunday, April 14 (which is not completely clear). The second is to read the date as May 4, 1963. On that date Oswald was in New Orleans with all of the family's possessions except some of Marina's clothes and a few of baby June's things. This led Priscilla Johnson McMillan to conclude the "package thus appears to have been mailed by Oswald from

New Orleans." See Priscilla Johnson McMillan, *Marina and Lee* (Steerforth Press, 2013), 602, n. 10.

16. Replacing "in several chapters of this book" in the original manuscript.

17. Replacing "enscription" in the original manuscript. The context is Marina's joke, not the fact that she left an inscription. She also made a little doodle of a dog, a tribute to the de Mohrenschildts' two Manchester Terriers.

18. Replacing "considered with suspicion all the visitors at Lee's burial place" and eliminating the multiple uses of "because" and "burial place" in just one sentence.

19. The original manuscript has "who was the making fun of him," which appears to be a typo.

20. Asserting there is "no doubt" here contradicts other portions of the manuscript that seem to doubt Oswald had a part in the attempted shooting of General Walker. Or perhaps de Mohrenschildt simply means no doubt in Marina's own mind.

21. He may not have shown the photograph itself but de Mohrenschildt did contact someone and freely allude to it: freelance writer George McMillan, the man who had come to Haiti to convince him to appear on NBC television in 1964. McMillan's wife in 1967, Priscilla, indicates that in "a letter dated April 17, 1967, George de Mohrenschildt wrote to George McMillan, [my husband], that he had come into possession of some 'very interesting information' about Oswald since his return to the United States, and on June 22, 1968, he invited George McMillan and [myself] to visit him in Dallas to discuss 'some interesting material on Oswald plus a *message* [de Mohrenschildt's italics] from him we discovered in our luggage.'" See McMillan, *Marina and Lee*, 602, n. 9. It is unclear whether the McMillans accepted the invitation and actually visited Dallas. Willem Oltmans's entry in his memoir for September 10, 1972, indicates an unnamed friend of de Mohrenschildt's in the insurance industry had been approached by Priscilla, then "writing a book about Lee and Marina," hoping to get her hands on "the picture that the de Mohrenschildts had found" (Oltmans, *Memoires 1972–1973*, 140–141). De Mohrenschildt indicated to Oltmans he wanted nothing to do with Priscilla and had even sent her a registered letter telling her that "anyone who wrote nonsense about him would be addressed immediately," apparently through "two lawyers in Washington and one in Dallas" that de Mohrenschildt had hired.

22. The "editor" mentioned here appears to have been Richard N. "Dick" Billings (1931–present), the son *Life* magazine's first managing editor, John Shaw Billings (1891–1975), and a staff writer holding the rank of associate editor at the time. For this reason his name is inserted here. After Kennedy's assassination the younger Billings was part of the *Life* magazine team that purchased the Zapruder film.

23. Replacing "makes in doubt" in the original manuscript.

24. The claim made here by de Mohrenschildt is accurate. Although *Life* is best remembered for the 1964 issue that featured one of the Oswald "backyard photos" on its cover, it also published a long article, "A Matter of Reasonable Doubt" on November 25, 1966, that demanded the investigation of Kennedy's assassination be reopened. Richard Billings, having been tipped off by journalist David Chandler that

New Orleans district attorney Jim Garrison had new information on the assassination, arranged to meet Garrison in January 1967. According to Garrison in his 1988 book *On the Trail of the Assassins*:

> In early 1967, we had an unexpected lucky break. Dick Billings, an editor from *Life* magazine, arrived at the office. He was a slender man with a quick mind and a delightful wit. After talking to me at some length, he informed me confidentially that the top management at *Life* had concluded that President Kennedy's assassination had been a conspiracy and that my investigation was moving in the right direction. Inasmuch as *Life* was conducting its own investigation Billings suggested that we work together. The magazine would be able to provide me with technical assistance, and we could develop a mutual exchange of information.

Jim Garrison, *On the Trail of the Assassins: My Investigation and Prosecution of the Murder of President Kennedy* (Sheridan Square Press, 1988), 114. Billings abruptly broke off his relationship with Garrison's investigation in September, accusing him of having links to organized crime. From that point onward *Life* campaigned to discredit Garrison's investigation. Billings himself would resign from *Life* in July 1968, after eleven years with the magazine, to be hired by the *St. Petersburg Times* and the *Congressional Quarterly* shortly thereafter. In the late 1970s G. Robert Blakey, chief counsel of the HSCA, hired Billings as the committee's editorial director; both men concluded Kennedy's killing had been the work of New Orleans Mafia boss Carlos Marcello. They would collaborate to publish a book *The Plot to Kill the President: Organized Crime Assassinated J.F.K.* (Times Books, 1981).

25. It is unclear if the "reporter" mentioned here is associate editor Billings himself or someone working for Billings, but de Mohrenschildt's letter to Billings dated August 29, 1967, mentions "my conversations with you" and "our conversations." See Appendix C.

26. Replacing the awkward and repetitive sentence "Like ourselves, he was at Marina's inscription and gave it the same meaning as ourselves."

27. Replacing "This we found at several occasions" in the original manuscript. It is possible the de Mohrenschildts were being monitored because of Garrison's investigation.

28. It would stretch credulity to believe that, in reaching out to a then-weekly magazine of the stature of *Life*, the de Mohrenschildts were not expecting some kind of remuneration for access to the photo. McMillan had almost certainly paid them handsomely to appear on NBC in 1964, and in the spring of 1967 the de Mohrenschildts were all but broke. George would not begin teaching at the University of Texas, Arlington, until the fall of 1968.

29. A reasonably accurate prophecy given that the flow of declassified materials on the de Mohrenschildts has continued nearly without pause for the better part of the last twenty years.

30. Additional material on the cost of the conflict in Vietnam and how this matter

fits in with de Mohrenschildt's overall view of American foreign and defense policy may be found in Chapter 6.

31. Warren Commission Exhibit 133-A. The de Mohrenschildt photo is what is known as a "first-generation print" of the original. This vignette is perhaps the most mysterious and opaque of the entire manuscript. The timeline is difficult to reconstruct with confidence, because the precise date that *Life* responded to de Mohrenschildt's letter is not specified. The initial phone conversation with Billings appears to have occurred around the middle of August because the two visitors are said to have called "about two weeks" later and de Mohrenschildt's letter to Billings (see Appendix C) dated August 29, 1967, mentions the two strangers as having visited "two days ago," which would have been August 27.

32. Replacing "pause" in the original manuscript.

33. Replacing "Baretta" (a misspelling of Beretta) in the original manuscript, which is incorrect. Oswald did not own a Beretta.

34. The manuscript continues "incidentally he had rather attractive gray eyes." This material has been relocated to the first description of Oswald's physical appearance that appears in Chapter 1.

35. Certainly intriguing but impossible to substantiate due to lack of detail.

36. De Mohrenschildt's August 29 letter to Billings says "one had a Spanish name, another Arthur something." See Appendix C. The names he provides here are most likely made up.

37. Replacing "repetorial" in the original manuscript.

38. Replacing "cameral" in the original manuscript.

39. Why this knowledge would put de Mohrenschildt at ease is unclear. It is possible he knew someone at *Fortune*, or perhaps he simply read the magazine and found it to be trustworthy.

40. Replacing "pumped out" in the original manuscript.

41. This remark, like the one before it relating to *Fortune* magazine, is cryptic. One wonders if this "most admired friend" might have been John Shaw Billings. Billings worked as managing editor for *Time* in the 1930s before becoming the first editorial director of *Life* in 1936. After World War II he was named editor-in-chief of Time-Life and retired in 1955. De Mohrenschildt's letter to Richard Billings written on August 29, 1967, and reproduced here as Appendix C concludes "Both my wife and I are anxious to see you again in Dallas." Source for the letter: James DiEugenio and Lisa Pease, *The Assassinations: Probe Magazine on JFK, MLK, RFK, and Malcolm X* (Feral House, 2003), 449. Given that Billings's son, Richard, was making visits to see the de Mohrenschildts in Dallas, it is possible George and John knew each other.

42. The presence of the visitor, who could not be identified, may explain why de Mohrenschildt did not fear for his physical safety, but it does not explain his naïveté trusting two complete strangers. This is one of several examples in the manuscript where he accepts what is said to him at face value before coming to regret the decision later.

43. The text is ambiguous here. It seems to imply there were twenty different

photos, each with a single individual, but could be read as saying there were a lesser number of photos with groups of individuals adding up to twenty.

44. The answer to the question may be found in de Mohrenschildt's August 29, 1967, letter to Billings. In the letter de Mohrenschildt describes the photos as "pictures of some Cubans involved in the unsuccessful invasion of Haiti." This implies either that "Fernandez" told him who the individuals were or de Mohrenschildt himself recognized them. Even the letter to Billings is mysterious on this count, as there were multiple and repeated invasions during the years the de Mohrenschildts were in Haiti, not just one.

45. Replacing "our Manchesters" in the original manuscript. Nero and Poppaea are present throughout de Mohrenschildt's narrative and deserve to be mentioned here, in their last appearance in the text, by name. Nero apparently passed away in early 1971. The February 16, 1971, entry in Willem Oltmans's memoirs observes that "Jeanne was desolate over the death of the dog Nero. She has already said he will be buried. Beside the grave she wants to plant a few trees." Willem Oltmans, *Memoires 1970–1971* (Papieren Tijger, 2003), 219. His entry for September 10, 1972, reads "Nero was buried an hour outside of Dallas. Jeanne wanted to drive me to the grave of the animal. Fortunately, George did not agree." Noticing the license plate on Jeanne's car read "Nero," after "her favorite dog," the Dutchman wrote "They are getting crazier." Oltmans, *Memoires 1972–1973*, 140, 143.

46. It was in fact just forty-eight hours after the appearance of the two strangers that de Mohrenschildt wrote to Billings (then still cooperating with Garrison) attempting to confirm whether or not two people that been asking questions about Oswald and Haiti were really from *Life*. He does not mention in the letter or the manuscript whether or not he ever checked with *Fortune* about Smith's claim that he worked for that magazine.

47. Replacing "affected" in the original manuscript. There was nothing to "affect" here, really, but the official account could be contradicted.

48. Replacing "swallowed in the mass of our population" in the original manuscript.

49. Deleting "and like the Englishmen said during the war of our GI's: 'overpaid, over-fed, over-sexed and . . . over here'" as overly trite.

50. One of the most moving passages in the manuscript. The regret expressed here is very heartfelt. Jim Garrison, reflecting on his questioning of the de Mohrenschildts, would write "I was particularly affected by the depth of their unhappiness at what had been done not only to John Kennedy but to Lee Oswald as well." Garrison, *On the Trail of the Assassins*, 56.

51. See "The Warren Commission" in Chapter 4.

52. See "Easter of 1963" in Chapter 3.

53. The quote from Marina's testimony is accurate: "Several days after [Oswald's attempt to assassinate General Walker], the de Mohrenschildts came to [visit] us, and as soon as he opened the door he said, 'Lee, how is it possible you missed?'"

54. The full quote is "He asked Lee not because Lee had told him about it, but I think because he is [a] smart enough man to have been able to guess it."

55. The FBI had, of course, investigated the de Mohrenschildts intensely before Marina ever testified due in large part to their wildly imprudent behavior in Haiti after the assassination.

56. Replacing "activated" in the original manuscript.

57. Her precise words were: "I don't know—he is simply a liberal, simply a man. I don't think he is being justly accused of being a Communist."

58. This seems rather unlikely and it should be remembered that Chief Justice Warren had to be convinced by President Johnson to serve on the investigating committee at all.

59. Replacing "Europo-Asiatics" in the original manuscript.

60. It is not clear why de Mohrenschildt considers this a second version. The question and response are not terribly dissimilar to what appears around it:

> MR. RANKIN: You told [us] about the incident of de Mohrenschildt coming to the house and saying something about how your husband happened to miss, and your husband looked at you and looked at him, and seemed to think that you might have told. You have described that. Now, did you have any cause to believe at that time that de Mohrenschildt knew anything about the Walker incident?
>
> MRS. OSWALD: De Mohrenschildt didn't know anything about it. Simply he thought that this was something that Lee was likely to do. He simply made a joke and the joke happened to hit the target.

61. Replacing "all these devious say we came" in the original manuscript.

62. The quote is accurate:

> MR. RANKIN: From your knowledge, were they close enough so that your husband would have made de Mohrenschildt a confidant about anything like that?
>
> MRS. OSWALD: No matter how close Lee might have been to anyone, he would not have confided such things.

63. Adding "had we not left for Haiti" to clarify that the de Mohrenschildts had left the country, leaving Lee and Marina behind.

64. Replacing "follow" in the original manuscript.

65. Oswald had, in fact, left a set of instructions in Russian for Marina indicating what actions to take if he were killed or caught. See Gary W. O'Brien, *Oswald's Politics* (Trafford, 2010), 290.

66. Possibly, but de Mohrenschildt is forgetting Oswald's contempt for the bureaucratic ways of law enforcement and his own observation that the recent move to Neely Street had only heightened the tendency of the Oswalds to live "like hermits." Oswald also left the rifle near the scene of the shooting, and had only recently retrieved it.

67. Replacing "Beckley Street" with the correct location. Oswald was living in a rooming house at 1026 North Beckley Street at the time of Kennedy's assassination.

68. Adding the word "not," which seems to have been an omission.

69. A new section has been created here as it contains most of the manuscript's final assessment of Marina. Much of the first paragraph has been relocated here from the vignette "A Message from Lee" earlier in the chapter.

70. Replacing "this story" in the original manuscript.

71. Replacing "in our testimonies" in the original manuscript, which begs the question of which testimonies.

72. Replacing "come then to a true evaluation" in the original manuscript.

73. See Chapter 2.

74. Replacing "created an appearance" in the original manuscript.

75. A. C. Greene, who was in charge of the editorial page of the *Dallas Times Herald* at the time of the assassination, claimed that the paper received thousands of letters from all over the world, many of them with money enclosed. "From the *Times Herald* through me, from various readers all over the world, I sent Mrs. Tippit over $200,000. I sent Marina Oswald the same amount." Quoted in Cathy Trost and Susan Lewis Bennett, eds., *President Kennedy Has Been Shot* (Sourcebooks Media Fusion, 2004), 272. This is substantially more than the $80,000 amount de Mohrenschildt recalls having been mentioned at the end of his visit to the Auchincloss home in early 1964; see Chapter 4. Whatever the amount was, it is clear that after Lee's death Marina never had to worry about practicing pharmacy again.

76. Replacing "flung the Bible furiously on the floor" which would seem an exaggeration and in any case would have been based on second-hand hearsay.

77. The sentence "Her dreams of America bristling with high buildings, crisscrossed with high-speed roads, blessed with luxury for everyone and especially with fast automobiles for all teenagers and adults" has been revised to better emphasize the materialism expressed in Chapter 2. The manuscript continues with the following digression: "And she was right, some economist calculated fifteen years ago that if the automobiles [k]ept on proliferating at the same rate, each family in America would possess five hundred automobiles at the end of this century. A paradise of [*sic*] earth!"

78. The sentence "Marina lived with her for and off, took advantage of her hospitality" has been reconstructed. The statement may be deemed accurate, however.

79. This reference to the de Mohrenschildts having spoken to Ruth Paine after their return from Haiti is interesting yet devoid of any additional detail. In her grand jury testimony given in New Orleans to the Garrison investigation on April 18, 1968, Paine would testify that "maybe a year ago" the de Mohrenschildts had called and invited her and her ex-husband Michael to dinner and she had spoken with them at that time. The assassination was discussed and Paine recalled that it was the de Mohrenschildts' feeling "that [Oswald] had done it and done it alone."

80. Replacing the overly vague "settled now" in the original manuscript with "remarried now, to a man named Porter." Marina continued to live in Dallas, so it must be her 1965 marriage to Kenneth J. Porter and not her address that de Mohrenschildt is referring to here. Her new marriage got off to a turbulent start. An AP Wirephoto of Marina dated August 18, 1965, contains an image of her leaving "the courtroom of Judge W. E. Richburg . . . after filing a peace bond against her husband, Kenneth Jess Porter. Mrs. Porter swore in a statement that Porter slapped

her and threatened to kill himself. She said he had a gun and it frightened her. Judge Richburg issued a warrant for Porter after talking to him and urging him to come in voluntarily."

81. In a letter that surfaced in the 1990s, written shortly after the attempt on General Walker's life, Marina would write home to her aunt and uncle in the Soviet Union:

> The weather is very good. There are rains and it is not too hot. I have
> been wearing little shorts and we all had time to get tanned. . . . I will
> watch television. Just the other day there was a broadcast from London of
> Princess Alexandra's wedding. It was very festive and beautiful. It was held
> in a big ancient cathedral and the ceremony was very traditional. It was so
> interesting—I got goose-bumps.

The wedding referred to occurred on April 24, 1963. The princess (1936–present) was marrying Sir Angus Ogilvy (1928–2004) in a ceremony viewed by an estimated 200 million worldwide. The letter to Minsk, dated April 27, is indicative of the laziness and lack of substance de Mohrenschildt describes.

Chapter 6: Who Were the Real Criminals?

1. A time span of more than twelve years would suggest that the final portion of the manuscript, presented here as Chapter 6, was composed in the first half of 1976. On May 10, 1976, de Mohrenschildt wrote to Willem Oltmans, "I think the chapter on you will be sensational once I get to it. I will send you the pages for correction or changes, as you suggested." This he did on June 24, 1976. The two typewritten pages are reproduced in Oltmans's memoirs, with the following handwritten message at the top of the first page: "This is a draft. Change it the way you want. [More?] is fine! I hope the facts are correct. Best, George." Willem Oltmans, *Memoires 1976* (Papieren Tijger, 2007), 337–338. During an executive session of the HSCA held on April 1, 1977, Oltmans would confide that the pages de Mohrenschildt sent to him "were so badly written and . . . so incomplete that I rewrote them and sent [them] back to him. And he thanked me very much and said he would include them in the manuscript." Many of the factual details within the vignette I have titled "A New Friend: Willem Oltmans" do indeed appear to have been supplied by Oltmans because they mirror his memoirs quite closely.

2. Replacing "this new focus" in the original manuscript.

3. As noted in prior chapters the crux of de Mohrenschildt's complaint appears to be that the single-volume *Warren Commission Report* did not include the handful of positive statements he made within his terse and largely negative assessment of Oswald in his full deposition. The latter, published within the multivolume *Warren Commission Hearings and Exhibits*, does however contain the positive content.

4. There is reason to believe that Kennedy desired to heal the rift between the two superpowers. His June 10, 1963, speech at American University was a clear olive branch to the people of the Soviet Union. The Limited Test Ban Treaty was

signed with the Soviets on October 7, 1963. There are also indications Kennedy was searching for an early exit from Vietnam, as reflected in his National Security Action Memorandum 263, which called for the withdrawal of 1,000 troops before the end of the year. It is equally apparent that even these small steps alarmed and angered the Cold War establishment in Washington, business conservatives who benefited from military contracts (particularly in the South, and especially in Texas), and staunch anti-Communists. Lyndon Johnson, whose ties to the military-industrial establishment dated back decades, reversed NSAM 263 with his own NSAM 273 on November 26, 1963, just four days after Kennedy's assassination.

5. The manuscript simply says "most of our mishaps," but the material that follows makes explicit that de Mohrenschildt is thinking of foreign and not domestic policy.

6. France received $2.6 billion in American aid between 1945 and 1954. From 1965 to 1975 the United States spent $111 billion on the war ($686 billion in inflation-adjusted dollars in 2008) and suffered 58,000 lives lost and 350,000 total casualties. See Stephen Daggett, "Costs of Major U.S. Wars," *CRS Report for Congress*, July 24, 2008, 2. A line in a holiday greeting card penned by de Mohrenschildt and sent to Willem Oltmans around the end of 1972 contains the humorous line "Lee H. Oswald is delighted with the fall of the $ [and] our victories in V.-Nam and the admission of Red China." Willem Oltmans, *Memoires 1971–1972* (Papieren Tijger, 2003), 320.

7. Inserting "late" here because Hunt had recently passed away. Haroldson Lafayette Hunt Jr. (1889–1974), known throughout his life as "H. L. Hunt," was at the time of the Kennedy assassination a Texas oil tycoon and close to if not the wealthiest man in America. In 1957 *Fortune* magazine estimated his fortune as between $400 and $700 million; after his death in 1974, his estate was valued at close to $5 billion. He was an ultra-conservative who was a member of the John Birch Society, supported Joseph McCarthy's antiCommunist witch hunts in the Senate, and funded two right-wing radio programs. He was also a close friend of General Edwin Walker, who had been removed by Kennedy and later allegedly shot at by Oswald. On the other hand Hunt disliked the CIA and rebuffed their efforts to recruit his assistance. On Hunt and the CIA see Joan Mellen, *Our Man in Haiti* (TrineDay, 2012), 335–386. Some conspiracy theories link Hunt to Kennedy's assassination on the basis of Kennedy's plan to change tax policy regarding the oil industry's depletion allowance.

8. The precise origin of the quote cannot be determined. It is probably made up and meant to be taken ironically, as a demonstration of how much of an outlier Hunt's extremist right-wing political views were.

9. Replacing "in the future" in the original manuscript.

10. Replacing "In this he was so different and so noble compared with" in the original manuscript.

11. Here as in most other places of the manuscript de Mohrenschildt is almost certainly speaking of the abridged one-volume *Warren Commission Report*, not his testimony in Volume 9 of the multivolume *Warren Commission Hearings and Exhibits*.

12. This sentence has been relocated here from the vignette "Visiting the Auchincloss Home" in Chapter 4, where it is simply out of place, to amplify the rest of this paragraph.

13. Perhaps de Mohrenschildt was on to something. "Both of Nixon's chief aids, Bob Haldeman and John Ehrlichman, noted in their memoirs that the president seemed obsessed with what he called the 'Bay of Pigs thing.' Both were convinced that when Nixon used the phrase, it was shorthand for something bigger and more disturbing. Nixon did not tell even those closest to him what he meant." Both Haldeman and Ehrlichman concluded Nixon was referring to the Kennedy assassination. See Russ Baker, *Family of Secrets: The Bush Dynasty, America's Invisible Government, and the Hidden History of the Last Fifty Years* (Bloomsbury Press, 2009), 179–182.

14. Members of the Mafia who had worked with the CIA to assassinate Castro included Sam Giancana (1908–1975), Carlos Marcello (1910–1993), Santo Trafficante Jr. (1914–1987), and John Roselli (1905–1975). These career criminals were none too happy to see the Bay of Pigs invasion fail, nor were they happy about the continued legal heat being applied by Kennedy's attorney general, his brother Robert.

15. Oswald attended a meeting on October 23, 1963, where General Walker was a speaker.

16. Changing "play with" in the original manuscript to "manipulate." The description here might apply as much if not more to de Mohrenschildt himself.

17. Earling Carothers "Jim" Garrison (1921–1992) was the city of New Orleans district attorney between 1962 and 1973. A graduate of Tulane University in 1949, Garrison worked in the FBI for two years and served in the National Guard. He joined a law firm in New Orleans in 1954 and practiced law before becoming an assistant district attorney in 1958. After losing a 1959 bid to become a criminal court judge, he ran for district attorney in 1961, beating the incumbent during the Democratic primaries. He gained national attention in the early 1960s for cracking down on prostitution and making frequent raids on the city's French Quarter. He was reelected in 1965 with 60 percent of the vote. Late in 1966 he began investigating the possibility of a conspiracy to assassinate President Kennedy, resulting in the 1967 arrest of prominent New Orleans businessman Clay Shaw. Garrison's contention was that Shaw and other right-wing individuals, along with elements of the CIA, had carried out the assassination. Shaw denied any involvement with the CIA. Garrison's case was weak but was made weaker by both government interference and a remarkably hostile mainstream media. The trial, which took place between January and February of 1969, ended in acquittal after less than one hour of jury deliberation. Over time it has since been revealed that Shaw was a CIA contact, and a highly paid one at that.

18. Garrison was defeated at the polls by Harry Connick Sr. in 1973. In April 1978, however, he defeated Republican Thomas F. Jordan for a judgeship on the state Circuit Court of Appeals and remained in that office until his death.

19. The manuscript does not mention the title by name, but it is almost certainly a reference to the book written by Garrison and published by McGraw-Hill in April

1976 titled *The Star-Spangled Contract*. In the story a former CIA agent, Colin Mc-Ferrin, discovers the president has been targeted from within, and that the assassination plot is part of an even larger conspiracy. The work received a scathing review by novelist Larry McMurtry in the *New York Times* on May 9, 1976. Regardless McGraw-Hill paid a quarter of a million dollars for the manuscript, making the then nearly broke Garrison a wealthy man. While de Mohrenschildt calls Garrison's book "a fiction," he means this in the sense that the book is fictional, not in the sense it is false.

20. This version of the manuscript does not elaborate on the nature of the warning. The draft pages sent to Willem Oltmans in late June 1976 contain the following almost certainly fabricated exchange between Oltmans and RFK:

> The day before our agreed appointment, [Oltmans] went to see Attorney Gen. Robert Kennedy on some matter. Mr. Kennedy asked him if it were true that he intended to come and see "the de Mohrenschildts" in Dallas.
>
> "Yes, I do," said Oltmans. "Tomorrow, as a matter of fact. I want to have filmed interview with them."
>
> "Well, I strongly advise you, don't do it!"
>
> "But why?" insisted Oltmans.
>
> "Believe me, just don't do it! They have dangerous ideas."

Oltmans, *Memoires 1976*, 337–338. Oltmans's memoirs indicate he told de Mohrenschildt of a meeting he had with Robert Kennedy prior to their becoming acquainted. Kennedy allegedly told Oltmans that the de Mohrenschildts were "dangerous people" and advised him not to meet them. In the spring of 1967, immediately after the failure of his Haitian venture, de Mohrenschildt had phoned Aristotle Onassis from Texas demanding a meeting in Europe because he had some kind of valuable information. Onassis declined but sent a proxy to Dallas, who returned to tell him some disturbing news about his extensive holdings in the country of Monaco. It may be possible RFK saw de Mohrenschildt as a threat due to his association with Onassis. See Peter Evans, *Nemesis: Aristotle Onassis, Jackie O, and the Love Triangle That Brought Down the Kennedys* (HarperCollins, 2004), 137–141. See also the vignette in this chapter titled "A New Friend: Willem Oltmans," which is devoted entirely to Oltmans.

21. Martin Luther King Jr. (1929–1968), American clergyman, activist, and leading figure of the African American civil rights movement. In the last year of his life he became increasingly outspoken about the issue of poverty in America and the Vietnam War. He was assassinated in Memphis, Tennessee, on April 4, 1968. In addition to the 1964 Nobel Peace Prize, he was posthumously awarded the Presidential Medal of Freedom in 1977 and the Congressional Gold Metal in 2004.

22. James Earl Ray (1928–1998), a small-time criminal, initially entered a guilty plea admitting to having assassinated King but then fired his attorney and recanted his admission three days later. Sentenced to ninety-nine years in prison, he spent the remainder of his life trying to withdraw his original plea and secure a trial. The King

family became convinced Ray was not involved and supported his efforts to win a trial.

23. Regarding Hoover's desire to destroy King's reputation, de Mohrenschildt is correct. The civil rights movement was a major target of the now infamous COINTELPRO program the FBI ran between 1950 and 1971. Jacqueline Kennedy, speaking in the months after her husband's assassination, said in an interview that Hoover had told the president that King tried to arrange a sex party while in town for the March on Washington in August 1963 and later told Robert Kennedy that King had made derogatory comments during the president's November funeral. The actual tapes of King recorded by the FBI will not be released until 2027.

24. This sentence added to the text to establish and clarify the amount of time that passed between the deaths of King and Robert Kennedy and the death of Hoover.

25. The last two sentences of this paragraph have been relocated here from the vignette "Contrasts between Lee and Marina," in Chapter 2 due to their having the subject of Hoover in common with the preceding material.

26. Replacing "shrews" in the original manuscript.

27. Replacing "assembled" in the original manuscript.

28. There is a remote possibility this a reference to the 1972 book *The Politics of Heroin in Southeast Asia* (Harper and Row, 1972) by Alfred W. McCoy, which discussed Air America, an airline that the CIA covertly owned and operated in Laos for more than thirteen years. Laos was, according to an article written by professor of history William M. Leary and displayed at the CIA website (www.cia.gov), the largest paramilitary operation ever undertaken by the agency. The CIA continues to deny connections between its activities in Laos and the Southeast Asian opium trade, despite a preponderance of independent research and evidence of the agency's involvement in drug smuggling both in Southeast Asia and in other parts of the world such as Afghanistan and Central America. More recently see, for example, Alexander Cockburn and Jeffrey St. Clair, *Whiteout: The CIA, Drugs and the Press* (Verso, 1998).

29. What de Mohrenschildt means here by "Chinese money" is difficult to decipher with any certainty. He might be implying American money will become worthless, or that the United States itself will become more like, or possibly subservient to, Communist China, but there is no way of knowing.

30. See Chapter 1.

31. A massive three-volume narrative about the Soviet forced labor camp system utilizing eyewitness testimony, primary research material, and Solzhenitsyn's own experiences as a prisoner. Its central arguments were that the Soviet regime could not govern without the threat of the camps and that the Soviet economy depended on the productivity of camp labor. The effect of the trilogy was shattering, as it called into doubt the moral standing of the Soviet regime and the Soviet brand of communism. Written between 1958 and 1968, it was first published in English and French in 1973. Publication in the Soviet Union had to wait until 1989; it is now mandatory classroom reading in the new Russian Federation. If de Mohrenschildt read the text

it would have been in either English or French; as he was fluent in both languages which version is not clear.

32. Replacing "espoused" in the original manuscript.

33. De Mohrenschildt is being rather ungenerous here. The death of a second Kennedy brother by assassination in June 1968 prompted quite understandable fear in Jacqueline that her late husband's children might also be at risk. She is quoted as having said, "If they're killing Kennedys, then my children are targets." Quoted in J. Randy Taraborrelli, *After Camelot: A Personal History of the Kennedy Family, 1968 to the Present* (Grand Central Publishing, 2012), 12. It would be understandable that she would turn to Onassis for privacy and protection; she hardly needed to marry him for his money.

34. The alumni news section of the September 1968 issue of the University of Texas at Austin's *Department of Geological Sciences Newsletter* mentions de Mohrenschildt "lecturing three days a week at UT-Arlington" so this recollection is probably an honest one. In reply to my June 2013 inquiry, Mark Permenter, executive director of university publications at the University of Texas, Arlington, informed me the dean of women in the fall of 1968 was named Nancy Thorpe. Further research indicated she had become dean of women in 1967. It is true that Jacqueline's marriage with the much older and, to many, vulgar and disreputable Onassis produced a considerable public backlash, particularly in the European press, who knew the sleazier aspects of Onassis's life in greater detail than the American press.

35. Aristotle Socrates Onassis (1906–1975), a wealthy shipping magnate, is perhaps best known for having married President Kennedy's widow, Jacqueline Bouvier Kennedy, in October 1968. His life had numerous similarities to de Mohrenschildt's: multilingual, multiple marriages, an immense social network of often famous friends and business contacts, rampant womanizing, a streak of sadism, behind-the-scenes dealing with governments, and an intense entrepreneurial drive. In the case of Onassis, however, he was able to translate that drive into lasting business arrangements that made huge sums of money: tobacco, whaling, shipping, an airline, real estate, and more.

36. Stating this just lines after "I am sure the discoveries will continue to be forthcoming" is certainly intriguing, not least of all where de Mohrenschildt himself is concerned. Is he being coy? Perhaps. Onassis, who had his own interests in Haiti, had backed out of potential partnership with de Mohrenschildt when he saw the terms of the contract de Mohrenschildt had signed with the country's dictator, President Duvalier.

37. This sentence certainly suggests that de Mohrenschildt and Onassis had met each other. Why else would he be aware of details such as how Onassis danced or what languages he sang in? Onassis made his first million selling cigarettes in Argentina during the late 1920s and early 1930s. The two brands he produced were made of milder Turkish rather than Cuban tobacco and were marketed to an emerging female market. He branched out into shipping as a way to reduce the cost of importing tobacco from Turkey. Onassis would eventually hold dual Argentine and Greek citizenships.

38. A newspaper (*The Chained Duck* or *The Chained Paper*) published weekly in France, featuring investigative journalism, humor, and satire. On December 3, 1973, members of France's Directorate of Territorial Surveillance (DST) were caught trying to install a listening device in one of *Le Canard*'s offices. A scandal ensued leading to the resignation of Interior Minister Raymond Marcellin (1914–2004) on February 27, 1974. The article de Mohrenschildt refers to appears to have been published on March 17, 1975, just days after Onassis's death. That de Mohrenschildt would rely on *Le Canard* rather than a more serious French newspaper such as *Le Monde* casts at least some suspicion on his comments about Onassis.

39. Onassis did indeed work out an agreement to save his fleet at the start of World War II, but de Mohrenschildt exaggerates the nature of the deal. Some of the vessels had already been seized in neutral ports or captured by the rapid German *Blitzkrieg*, which had occupied much of Europe, including France and Greece, in 1940–1941. Onassis rented out those ships still remaining under his control to the Allies; in exchange ships lost at sea due to enemy action were replaced with war-surplus vessels at the end of the war at favorable prices. An example of this is Onassis's own yacht, the 325-foot *Christina*. It was originally a Canadian anti-submarine River-class frigate launched in 1943 that had participated in the battle of the Atlantic and the Normandy D-Day invasion. Onassis was allowed to purchase the vessel for its scrap value of $34,000 and then spent $4 million refitting it. Onassis may not have been a saint, but his actions here were simply good business.

40. Possibly a reference to Onassis's joint venture with the Saudi government that would have allowed him to monopolize the transport of Saudi oil, the so-called Jeddah Agreement of January 1954. The deal, which would have made Onassis one of the most powerful men in the world and seriously undermined American influenced in the Middle East, was sabotaged by the United States. Robert Aime Maheu (1917–2008), an American businessman and lawyer who worked for the FBI, CIA, and Howard Hughes, was recruited by Vice President Nixon to instigate a campaign of dirty tricks to wreck the agreement. In 1960 Maheu was recruited by the CIA to participate as its go-between with organized crime in the plot to assassinate Cuba leader Fidel Castro, a role he confirmed to the Church Committee in 1975.

41. Apparently a rather callous reference to the myasthenia gravis Onassis was suffering from during the final years of his life. It is an autoimmune neuromuscular disease. Its symptoms include fatigue as muscles become progressively weaker, particularly muscles that control the eye and eyelid movement, facial expressions, talking, and swallowing. It can lead to slurred speech, an unstable or waddling gait, and shortness of breath.

42. While much has been made of this sentence in some quarters over the years, its placement here seems to be the product of little more than simple bitterness; de Mohrenschildt's relation with the Auchincloss family became strained after the Kennedy assassination and Onassis had withdrawn from the Haitian project de Mohrenschildt valued so highly.

43. This paragraph and the one that follows were, in the original manuscript, the conclusion to the vignette I have titled "Marina after Lee" in Chapter 5. Clearly

this material is unconnected to the discussion of Marina's life after the death of her husband and for that reason it is added here where the discussion is clearly political.

44. Remembering that the futures of the FBI, CIA, and other federal agencies were in some doubt during the mid-1970s and some modest reforms were proposed and enacted.

45. Replacing "Surete General" in the original manuscript. The text appears to be referring to the Sûreté nationale, one of the two national police forces (the other being the military Gendarmerie) in France between 1944 and 1966. How the tactics of the Sûreté nationale would have been a preferable alternative to the FBI is not specified.

46. Replacing the unintentionally amusing "boogie men" in the original manuscript.

47. Replacing "for all its size and expense" in the original manuscript.

48. Replacing "And FBI could not protect the lives of the President John F. Kennedy, of his brother Robert nor, the most important, the life of Dr. Martin Luther King," in the original manuscript. The bloated FBI budget is mentioned elsewhere in the manuscript but is included here since de Mohrenschildt is calling for reform of the agency.

49. On de Mohrenschildt's contact with the CIA's J. Walton Moore in Dallas, see Chapter 4 and Appendix B.

50. Replacing "had pried too much into my private life" in the original manuscript. It is clear that de Mohrenschildt is talking about one particular aspect of his private life here, not his private life in general.

51. The manuscript switches topic here and discusses de Mohrenschildt's relationship with Willem Oltmans for several paragraphs. The original vignette title, "Willem Oltmans and His Clairvoyant," does not reflect the friendship the two men obviously shared. For this reason a new subheading has been introduced. The original draft that de Mohrenschildt sent to Oltmans for review had the even stranger title "America, the Land of Violence."

52. Willem L. Oltmans (1925–2004) was a Dutch investigative journalist whose career often crossed the boundary between observer and participant. While living in Rome in 1954, he befriended Indonesian president Sukarno. In 1956 he interviewed Sukarno, against the wishes of the Dutch government. While Oltmans tried to convince the Dutch public of the legitimacy of Sukarno's policies, the Dutch minister of foreign affairs effectively sabotaged his career. He moved to the United States and worked as a freelance reporter for Dutch television. In October of 1961 the *Dallas Morning News* included him among a list of names scheduled to speak before the Dallas Women's Club. He testified before the US Congress in 1963. The title of the hearings was "Attempts of Pro-Castro Forces to Pervert the American Press." He was on his way to another speaking engagement at the Dallas Women's Club when the events de Mohrenschildt describes happened. He maintained contact with Jim Garrison as well as de Mohrenschildt, and interviewed Garrison for Dutch television on March 1, 1968. Oltmans sued the Dutch government for lost income and after nearly a decade of litigation finally prevailed in 1991, being awarded $8 million

guilders ($4 million dollars). Oltmans made a cameo appearance as none other than de Mohrenschildt in Oliver Stone's 1992 movie *JFK*.

53. Oltmans attended Yale in 1948, at the same time William F. Buckley Jr. was in attendance, but he did not graduate.

54. Wichita Falls, Texas, is about 140 miles northwest of Dallas. The airport encounter and subsequent conversation during the flight are described in Oltmans's memoirs. See Willem Oltmans, *Memoires, 1963–1964* (Papieren Tijger, 2000), 181–183.

55. Deleting "When the Warren Commission asked the Dallas police official whether they didn't think Oswald an important enough subject to borrow a tape-recorder for the investigation of the murder of the president of the United States, the answer had been negative." The exact same information is mentioned a second time just a few paragraphs further on.

56. Gerard Croiset (1909–1980) was a Dutch-born psychic sometimes consulted by police to assist in cases involving missing persons or murder. While enjoying a number of successes that attracted intense media attention, Croiset also experienced a number of well-publicized failures.

57. Written by Jack Harrison Pollack (1914–1984). Pollack was primarily a magazine writer, covering topics including travel, education, medicine, law, and the occult. His work was published in *Life*, *Look*, *Harpers*, and the *Saturday Evening Post*. His other books were *Dr. Sam: An American Tragedy* (Henry Regnery, 1972) and *Earl Warren: The Judge Who Changed America* (Prentice Hall, 1978). For the book on Croiset Pollack relied heavily on the input of Wilhelm Heinrich Carl Tenhaeff, who since 1953 had held the unique position of professor of parapsychology at the University of Utrecht.

58. The meeting with Croiset took place on February 5, 1967, and was also attended by Carel Enkelaar and Croiset's son Henry. As remembered by Oltmans Croiset's "vision"—which also contained details about the assassination itself—included the following:

> The suspected assassin, Oswald, he told us, had a special friend in Dallas who, in turn, had become friends with the family of Jacqueline Kennedy. The friend was in India. He would have received $900,000 for organizing the attack on JFK. He was middle-aged and moved prominently in circles of the Texas oil industry, possibly a geologist. He had to be of European origin and had a duplicate name with both a "de" and a "sch." He was a kind of father figure for Oswald.

Willem Oltmans, *Memoires 1966–1967* (Papieren Tijger, 2002), 231–232. De Mohrenschildt in truth had met Jacqueline long before he met Oswald and was not in India. His brother, Dimitri, stayed in that country for extended periods of time. Many of Croiset's other details appear surprisingly accurate.

59. Oltmans would hardly need to "consult" with Enkelaar given that both men were present at the meeting with Croiset on February 5. The assignment to track

down "the man in the petroleum industry with the double name" was given to Oltmans by Enkelaar on February 9. Oltmans, *Memoires 1966–1967*, 232. Reading through Oltmans's memoirs from the late 1960s and early 1970s one gets the distinct impression Enkelaar embraced what Croiset had to say more enthusiastically than Oltmans did.

60. Oltmans's memoirs indicate his 1967 visit to see Marguerite occurred on March 10 rather than March 11. The error here is most likely Oltmans's as he extensively revised the draft of this vignette after de Mohrenschildt sent it to him.

61. The manuscript erroneously mentions a date of April 22 for the interview, which has been deleted. Oltmans's memoirs indicate he phoned de Mohrenschildt on March 31, 1967, and George had replied to his interview request by responding "I would be delighted to appear in your television program." Oltmans, *Memoires 1966–1967*, 275–276.

62. The Seventh World Petroleum Congress in Mexico City occurred between Sunday, April 2, and Sunday, April 9, 1967. It was attended by 3,500 delegates from 80 different countries, who presented a total of 408 papers. The World Petroleum Congress was first held in 1933 and met once every four years until 1991, when it began to be held every three years. It is the premier conference organized by the World Petroleum Council, bringing together thousands of top-level executives in the oil and gas industry.

63. Replacing "two weeds" in the original manuscript. The September 1967 issue of the *Department of Geology, The University of Texas [at Austin] Newsletter* (No. 16) quotes directly from a letter written by de Mohrenschildt on page 42: "George writes 'Still Director of the Geological & Mineralogical Survey of Haiti. Spending more time in the USA now—after four years in the Caribbean, Texas is hotter, but less dangerous than Haiti. Was a delegate of Haiti at the Seventh World Petroleum Congress.'" By the time of the congress in the spring of 1967 de Mohrenschildt had permanently abandoned his work in Haiti; if he was a director or delegate of anything it would appear to be only wishful thinking.

64. In response to my inquiry a member of the Textual Archives at the John F. Kennedy Presidential Library indicated that, at least in their files, Senator Robert Kennedy had made three speeches in Albany. The first was on March 1, 1965, before the Women's Division of the State Democratic Convention. The second was on March 20, 1965, at the Legislative Correspondents' Dinner. The third was July 26, 1967, before the Committee on Economic Development, New York Constitutional Convention. Willem Oltmans's memoirs, however, indicate the speech was April 3, 1967, before the state legislature. Oltmans, *Memoires 1966–1967*, 277.

65. Located in the borough of Queens, roughly a half hour east of Manhattan's Central Park.

66. April 4, 1967. Oltmans refers to the accident "yesterday afternoon" in his entry for April 5. Oltmans, *Memoires 1966–1967*, 279–280.

67. Oltmans wrote quite extensively about the former Indonesian leader. The exact title of the book in question, probably written in Dutch, is unclear. In the photo included here he may be seen holding a copy of his 1973 book *Den Vaderland*

getrouwe: uit het dagboek van een journalist, which may be loosely translated as *The True Homeland: The Diary of a Journalist*. Replacing "late President Sukarno of Indonesia" in de Mohrenschildt's text, which implies Sukarno (1901–1970) was already deceased. Sukarno had, however, been forced out of power by rivals in 1967, and it is this that the manuscript is probably referring to.

68. Smith was an attorney and later a Miami municipal judge whose home was a yacht at Fort Myers. Oltmans's memoirs indicate the date was June 11, 1967, and it was a telegram, not a phone call "from the mysterious lawyer from Fort Lauderdale, Glenn Bryan Smith [Jr.]" that led to the meeting in Utrecht. Smith bragged about being involved in the manhunt in Bolivia for Che Guevara; Oltmans wrote "I felt this Smith represented U.S. intelligence and was wary." The account of the meeting provided here by de Mohrenschildt is however substantially the same as Oltmans's account in his own memoirs.

69. The manuscript does not include Moore's name, just the title of his book. Published in 1965, the paperback became a best-seller in 1966 and a movie with the same title, starring John Wayne, was released in 1968. Oltmans's memoirs describe Moore introducing him to Glenn Byran Smith Jr. at a cocktail party given by Moore's publisher on May 10, 1967. Oltmans, *Memoires 1966–1967*, 288.

70. Now part of HP/De Tijd after having merged with another publication, *De Tijd*, in 1990. The magazine is also a monthly now rather than being a weekly. The September 30 date has been inserted using Oltmans's memoirs.

71. On October 9 de Mohrenschildt indicated to Oltmans he was willing to do a filmed interview for $250. Oltmans wrote in his memoirs that during this 45-minute interview "George sometimes read notes for the camera, and sometimes he improvised." He also mentions someone else as being present during the recording, "a West German geologist who was working for an oil company" and who had also met Oswald. This individual was almost certainly de Mohrenschildt's friend Volkmar Schmidt. Oltmans noted that this other individual had a "different view" than the de Mohrenschildts, regarding Oswald as "an idiot" who wanted "to change the world" without any wherewithal for accomplishing such a goal. The suspicious Oltmans commented that the words of this "so-called West German" did not "seem quite kosher." Willem Oltmans, *Memoires, 1967–1968* (Papieren Tijger, 2002), 137.

72. Replacing "still deadly convinced" in the original manuscript.

73. It is important to note the presence of this scenario in the manuscript. After his mental breakdown and hospitalization in the fall of 1976, de Mohrenschildt began to tell others, including Oltmans, that this was the *true* version of events, going so far as to say—according to Oltmans at least—that he had both discussed the idea of assassinating Kennedy with Oswald and had even helped him plan out the act. Oltmans then said de Mohrenschildt had confessed to being the middleman between Oswald and the ultra-conservative Texas oil baron H. L. Hunt. A few have taken Oltmans seriously, but the self-serving tale is clearly ridiculous; in the winter and spring of 1977 de Mohrenschildt was obviously a very disturbed man. His Dallas lawyer Patrick S. Russell Jr. said "He began to have bizarre hallucinations and distortions. He believed people were following him." Frankly, Oltmans ought

to have known better. His memoirs make clear that he knew de Mohrenschildt's mental health was seriously impaired. Instead he chose to exploit their early 1977 conversations for all the public attention he could squeeze, getting his name in *Time*, *Newsweek*, and *New Times*, publishing several articles, appearing on NBC's *Today Show*, and testifying in Washington. He wasn't quite the friend de Mohrenschildt thought he was, and perhaps he never was. De Mohrenschildt tended to distrust those at a physical distance and trust those in immediate proximity too readily and without question.

74. It should be clear from this sentence that de Mohrenschildt had reached no firm conclusions regarding the identity of the "real criminals" and was willing to leave the matter to future research.

75. The preceding two sentences, slightly modified, have been relocated here from the vignette "Further Conversations with Lee, 1962" in Chapter 1.

76. Compare the view expressed here with a story recounted by Dick Russell, who in the autumn of 1975 tracked down de Mohrenschildt on the Bishop College campus, hoping to learn more about Oswald, and was told, "It is all in the *Warren Commission [Report]*. All this new talk is so much lies and bullshit. Nothing will ever be solved, unless somebody comes up with a confession." See Dick Russell, *The Man Who Knew Too Much: Inquest, Counterplot, and Legend* (Carroll & Graf, 2003), 170. De Mohrenschildt would mention Russell's visit in a letter written to Willem Oltmans shortly thereafter: "He is writing a book about Oswald. I did not want to talk too much about him, although the guy was humble and very nice." Willem Oltmans, *Memoires, 1975–1976* (Papieren Tijger, 2006), 104. Oltmans, too, would recount after de Mohrenschildt's death that "when we were alone, on long walks for instance, he would say that someday someone would confess, and only then would the world learn what really happened on November, 22, 1963 in Dallas." Willem Oltmans, *Memoires 1978* (Papieren Tijger, 2008), 312.

77. The manuscript does not name the lawyer, but de Mohrenschildt could be referring to none other than Specter. Arlen J. Specter (1930–2012), himself the son of émigré Russian parents, was assigned to the Warren Commission as an assistant counsel thanks to a recommendation by Representative Gerald R. Ford. Specter was a co-author of the "single-bullet theory"—see the following note. Initially a Democrat, he switched to the Republican Party in 1965 and was elected district attorney of Philadelphia that same year. He served two terms before being defeated in 1973 in a bid for a third. After practicing law privately for several years, he was elected to the Senate in 1980. In 2009 he switched back to the Democratic Party and was defeated in the 2010 primary.

78. Replacing "killed Kennedy" in the original manuscript with "passed through Kennedy" as this is a more accurate description of the damage inflicted by the bullet in question. De Mohrenschildt is probably referring to the "single-bullet theory" posited by the Warren Commission. According to the theory, a single 6.5-mm round passed through President Kennedy's upper back, exited his neck, struck Texas Governor Connally, exited his chest, passed through his wrist, and lodged itself in his thigh. The bullet was then found, virtually intact, on a gurney at Parkland Hospital

where it supposedly fell out of Connally's thigh. Critics have dubbed this the "magic bullet theory," pointing out the implausibility of a bullet emerging in such pristine condition after passing through both men, destroying a five inch section of one of Connally's ribs and breaking the radius bone in his wrist. Metal fragments both recovered from and left inside Connally's body after surgery also cast doubt on the bullet's authenticity. The origins of this passage may lie in a November 27, 1973, meeting Willem Oltmans arranged between de Mohrenschildt and forensic pathologist Cyril Wecht (1931–present). Oltmans would write in his memoirs "George welcomed Wecht with the words: 'So, you found me'" and that after initially being reluctant to meet Wecht "George liked him immediately." Willem Oltmans, *Memoires 1972–1973* (Papieren Tijger, 2004), 243. In 1978, as part of the House Select Committee on Assassinations, Wecht was the lone dissenting member of a nine member medical panel who concurred with the Warren Commission's "single–bullet theory."

79. Connally caused a furor when, after viewing frame-by-frame blow-ups of the Zapruder film for *Life* magazine in 1966, he reiterated his belief he was struck by a separate bullet. In a classic case of "damage control" he then called a press conference to defend the findings of the Warren Commission, only to contradict the single-bullet theory yet again when he inadvertently mentioned there were still fragments of the bullet in his thigh.

80. This sentence and the one immediately following have been relocated here from the vignette "Our Return to the United States," in Chapter 4. The original material reads:

> Lee became the subject of articles and books—and will be for a long time—by scavengers from a poor man's death. I would not dare to call our dear President Gerald Ford a scavenger, but his book was the first one, directly accusing Lee Harvey Oswald—on his 'Portrait of the Assassin.' Naturally the book was ghost written, inept and uninteresting, yet he was the first one (he or his ghost-writer) to have the information assembled by the Warren Committee. Again, I have to give credit to the American people, the book was a failure.

This material fits perfectly here, whereas in the earlier vignette it is out of place. The November 19, 1975, entry in Willem Oltmans's memoirs quotes a letter from de Mohrenschildt: "The whole Dallas thing is fucked up. It's like that moron Gerald Ford. *Les bêtises se sont des Américains Incomparables!*" Oltmans, *Memoires 1975–1976*, 104.

81. Replacing "in our luggage" in the original manuscript. Prior chapters indicate that what was left behind in Dallas consisted of furniture and boxes of other items deemed not essential to the de Mohrenschildts' move to Haiti. It is also safe to assume the de Mohrenschildts would have taken their luggage to Haiti, not put it in storage.

82. An important and largely overlooked statement. While the manuscript is extremely critical of how the Warren Commission conducted its interview with him and his wife, its seeming (and unseemly) obsession with ferreting out vast amounts of

minutia of little or no relevance to the assassination investigation itself, de Mohren-schildt did not in the end believe the members of the commission were covering up the existence of a conspiracy. Earl Warren himself would write the very year that de Mohrenschildt died that the alternative conclusion "would mean the whole struc-ture [of the American government] was absolutely corrupt from top to bottom," willing to suppress, neglect, and overlook evidence of a conspiracy, "with not one person of high or low rank willing to come forward to expose the villainy." See Earl Warren, *Memoirs of Chief Justice Warren* (Doubleday, 1977), 367.

83. Replacing "of condemnation" in the original manuscript.

84. The manuscript continues with the digression "It's the same self-illusion as throwing Prince [Norodom] Sihanouk out of Cambodia, accusing him of being a 'red prince.' Then financing and supporting to the bitter end his enemies. Fortunately for the 'Red Prince' he is well and back in his country, while his enemies are either dead or exiled." Sihanouk (1922–2012) had been the effective ruler of Cambodia from 1953 until 1970, when he was deposed by General Lon Nol and the National Assembly. The new government was immediately recognized by the United States. Sihanouk fled to Beijing, formed the National United Front of Kampuchea, and supported the Khmer Rouge in their struggle to overthrow the government formed by Nol. When Pol Pot seized power in April 1975 Sihanouk returned and served as the symbolic head of state briefly before being forced into retirement on April 4, 1976. The consummate political survivor, he outlasted the Khmer Rouge and would remain a major force in Cambodia's politics until his death.

85. The text mistakenly identifies Fritz as both captain and "chief" of the Dallas police but in truth this was another individual, Jesse E. Curry. Captain John Will Fritz (1895–1984) joined the Dallas Police Department in 1921, advancing through the ranks to become captain in 1934. He retired in 1970.

86. While it sounds dramatic and he may well have *thought* it, Warren does not appear to have actually said this. There is no mention of a tape recorder during the Warren Commission testimony of Dallas chief of police Curry. Fritz was asked about a tape recorder, but the question was posed by Assistant Counsel Joseph A. Ball, not Warren:

MR. BALL: Did you have any tape recorder?
MR. FRITZ: No sir; I don't have a tape recorder. We need one, if we had had one at this time we could have handled these conversations [with Oswald] far better.
MR. BALL: The Dallas Police Department didn't have one?
MR. FRITZ: No sir; I have requested one several times but so far they haven't gotten one.

87. The notes of Captain Fritz, written several days after the assassination, did eventually surface. Five pages were discovered among his belongings after his death. They were released by the Assassination Records Review Board in 1997. Earlier that same year the board had released the notes of FBI agent James P. Hosty Jr. Combined

they help fill in what for decades had appeared to be a rather suspicious lack of documentation regarding Oswald's time in Dallas police custody.

88. Replacing simply "Jones" in the original manuscript with his full name. On Jones and the role he may have played in de Mohrenschildt choosing the original title of the manuscript see the Editor's Introduction.

89. Jones was the owner of the *Midlothian Mirror*, not just an editor.

90. Replacing "Midlothian" in the original manuscript with the full name of the newspaper.

91. Replacing "cracked down" in the original manuscript, which is clearly a conflation of "cracked up" and "broken down."

92. Oswald's statement about being a patsy was said just once, rather than twice. See the Editor's Introduction. Regarding the de Mohrenschildts, Jones would write, "[The paper] asked for an interview shortly after he and his wife returned from Haiti in early 1967. He was most cordial, but refused to answer any questions." See William Penn Jones Jr., *Forgive My Grief II* (Midlothian Mirror, 1967), 125.

93. Strangely, with but one exception de Mohrenschildt refuses to consider that Oswald might try to kill Texas governor John Connally, the man he saw as being responsible for changing his Marine Corps discharge from honorable to undesirable. There is clear hostility expressed toward Connally by Oswald at several points within the manuscript.

94. The meaning here is obscure but seems to imply that as horrible as President Kennedy's death was, his ascent to martyrdom was political capital the surviving Kennedys could use to their own profit. If that is correct, de Mohrenschildt is being more than a bit ungenerous again, much as he was a few paragraphs earlier regarding Jacqueline Kennedy's reasons for marrying Aristotle Onassis.

95. This sentence and the one immediately preceding it are relocated here from the vignette titled "The Warren Commission" in Chapter 4. De Mohrenschildt's understanding of the bicameral nature of the US legislative branch—or at least his ability to describe it in English—was a bit shaky. Elsewhere in the manuscript he mentions the "Senate" and "Congress" as if they were different institutions rather than the former being one-half of the latter. So it may well be this is yet another slip and he is referring to the Senate when what he truly means is the House of Representatives. The House, after months of debate, authorized the creation of the House Select Committee on Assassinations by a vote of 280 to 65 on September 17, 1976, so this line penned in the early summer of 1976 appears to have been written before that vote. On the other hand, the Senate's Select Committee to Study Governmental Operations with Respect to Intelligence Activities (i.e., the Church Committee) had released its final report in April 1976. In any event the material is *forward looking* and for that reason has been moved here, to what is essentially the conclusion of de Mohrenschildt's narrative.

96. The preceding five sentences have been relocated here from the vignette "Contrasts between Lee and Marina" in Chapter 2 to provide a final summation of how de Mohrenschildt perceived Oswald's Russian language abilities. That Oswald spoke Russian better than professional language instructors would have to be

deemed an exaggeration. Recall the description of Oswald becoming irritated when Marina would correct his mistakes in Chapter 2.

97. Replacing the awkward "anti any people" in the original manuscript.

98. Founded in 1922. While other satirical magazines disappeared from the scene *Krokodil* continued, lampooning Soviet bureaucrats, the problems of drinking on the job by Soviet workers, as well as ridiculing capitalist countries and the various opponents of the Soviet Communist system. It was discontinued after the dissolution of the Soviet Union in 1991 but reappeared in 2005, deliberately printed on old Soviet-style paper.

99. Ivan Andreyevich Krylov (1769–1844), writer of many well-known fables in the manner of Aesop such as *The Mice in Council* and *Wolves and Sheep*.

100. The election of Ronald Reagan in the fall of 1980 reflected a sharp rightward shift in the public mood of the country as the 1970s ended, one that has continued largely unabated for the last three decades. Reagan embarked on a program of military Keynesianism and belligerent anti-Soviet rhetoric not seen since the height of the Cold War twenty years earlier. For a primer on the emergence of the New Right, see Mike Davis, *Prisoners of the American Dream: Politics and Economy in the History of the US Working Class* (Verso, 1986), 157–180.

101. Henry Kissinger (1923–present) was born in Germany, his Jewish family moving to the United States in 1938 to escape Nazi persecution. He became a naturalized American citizen in 1943 and received a doctorate in political science from Harvard in 1954. He gained the attention of nonacademics after the publication of *Nuclear Weapons and Foreign Policy*, a work that argued that a limited nuclear war could be fought and won. He supported Nelson Rockefeller's failed White House bids in 1960, 1964, and 1968, then was appointed national security advisor by Richard Nixon in 1969. Kissinger is credited with extending the policy of détente, leading to reduced tensions with the world's biggest Communist powers, the Soviet Union and China. He was heavily involved in the brokered ceasefire that led to the end of American involvement in Vietnam, which led to his being named (along with President Nixon) *Time* magazine's Man of the Year in 1972 and co-recipient (along with Le Duc Tho of North Vietnam's Politburo) of the 1973 Nobel Peace Prize. At the same time Kissinger's involvement in foreign policy decisions supporting brutal authoritarian regimes in Argentina, Chile, Cyprus, East Timor, and Indochina, among others, have been viewed by some as worthy of prosecution for war crimes and crimes against humanity. Kissinger, like George H. W. Bush, made an inquiry on de Mohrenschildt's behalf in the early 1970s. In a message to the American Embassy in Haiti titled "Case of George de Mohrenschildt," dated June 10, 1974, he wrote:

The [State] Department has reviewed the matter and concluded that Mr. de Mohrenschildt has an equitable case but not one valid under principles of international law as it has not been established that all judicial and administrative remedies have been exhausted with a resulting denial of justice or that it would be futile to exhaust available remedies.

Kissinger then requested that the embassy "discuss the case informally with appropriate officials of the Government of Haiti." While some discussions did occur, it was clear that "Baby Doc" had no intention of paying the money owed to de Mohrenschildt under the terms of his March 1963 contract.

102. Replacing "thrived" in the original manuscript.

103. As the holocaust referred to here is clearly one triggered by a thermonuclear exchange the word "nuclear" has been inserted here.

104. Replacing "a détente" in the original manuscript. Oswald may have dreamed of peace, but he would not dream of a concept that only came into wide use years after his death.

105. This sentence was originally found between the vignettes "Separation and More Trouble" and "Reconciliation" in Chapter 2. In addition to being out of place there it fits perfectly here, as an illustration of de Mohrenschildt's assertion that Oswald did not dogmatically side with either superpower.

106. Replacing "all of us" in the original manuscript. The material is discussing the relations of nation-states, not peoples. The emotion behind the appeal is, however, understandable.

107. Replacing "dummies" in the original manuscript. The material suggests foolishness rather than stupidity.

108. Oswald made two appearances on WDSU radio in New Orleans in the summer of 1963. The first was on the program *Latin Listening Post* on August 17. The second was on the program *Conversation Carte Blanche* on August 19. The transcripts of both programs in their entirety may be found in Gary W. O'Brien, *Oswald's Politics* (Trafford, 2010), 342–371.

109. The bullet fired at Walker could not be identified in 1963, but using a new technique, neutron activation analysis (NAA), the HSCA would conclude just two years after de Mohrenschildt's death that the bullet fired at Walker was probably from a Mannlicher-Carcano such as the gun Oswald owned. More recent research has cast serious doubt on the veracity of the NAA technique, however.

110. Nixon was Eisenhower's vice president from 1953 until 1961. The statement here, referring to an event in 1963, appears to be in error. Nixon had, however, been to the state of Texas in the spring of 1963. Perhaps it is this that de Mohrenschildt was thinking of.

111. It was more than just speculation. On April 21, just eleven days after the attempt on Walker's life, the *Dallas Morning News* had run a headline and lead story about a speech former vice president Nixon had given in New York accusing President Kennedy of being soft on Castro's Cuba. Oswald armed himself with his pistol and announced, "Nixon is coming to town. I'm going to have a look." Before he could leave, Marina locked him in the bathroom and kept him there for several hours until he agreed to abandon his plans. A full account of this strange incident—Nixon was not even in Dallas at the time—may be found in Priscilla Johnson McMillan, *Marina and Lee* (Steerforth Press, 2013), 366–369.

112. Replacing "connections" in the original manuscript.

113. An essentially accurate assessment. See, for example, O'Brien's *Oswald's Politics*.

114. The preceding dialogue between Jeanne and Lee has been relocated here from the end of the vignette "The Oswalds in Minsk."

115. Earlier in the original manuscript, in the middle of the vignette "The Warren Commission," de Mohrenschildt comments "Poor fellow, even his tomb was stolen and desecrated from the public cemetery in Arlington, Texas." The desecration may have actually occurred but Oswald's grave is in Rose Hill Memorial Burial Park in Fort Worth.

116. See for example Jones Jr., *Forgive My Grief II*, 125–155, which is little more than extended excerpts from the *Warren Commission Hearings and Exhibits*. The book's unpaginated introduction by Maxwell Geismar describes the de Mohrenschildts as "baffling figures" who "were friends and perhaps sponsors" of Oswald "in a very curious relationship." Geismar also describes de Mohrenschildt as moving "in some high, and highly ambiguous, social circles" in addition to having given the Warren Commission testimony that "was very shadowy." Oddly enough de Mohrenschildt's manuscript presents Jones Jr. in a positive light.

117. The manuscript continues:

One theory had it that Lee was operated by me via long distance, from Haiti to Dallas. Impulses were transmitted very deviously because I, a geologist and a famous scientist, had previously inserted a transistor in Lee's skull (either under the skin or implanted deeper, I do not remember). A book was published in New York describing this whole operation in detail. Since Papa Doc disliked President Kennedy, we would sit in his office, surrounded by his "Tonoon-Mascouts"—and would operate poor Lee, who would blindly obey us. As a credit to the American reader, I may say that this book didn't have much success and I seldom meet anyone who had bothered to read it.

It is impossible to know for certain what "book published in New York" de Mohrenschildt is talking about here but it would have been a work similar to one published by Lincoln Lawrence titled *Mind Control, Oswald & JFK: Were We Controlled* (University Books, 1967). While de Mohrenschildt is mentioned in the book, the material relates to his having "hidden" his Germanic/pro-Nazi past and says nothing about Haiti or controlling Oswald long-distance in the manner described here. Before blogging the pulp paperback was the *de rigueur* method of communication for literary crackpots everywhere, so there may well have been not one but several such books.

118. Replacing "infraction" in the original manuscript. The stories in question began circulating in February of 1975. De Mohrenschildt was supposed to have gone to the Bahamas to receive $250,000 for carrying out his part in Kennedy's assassination.

119. An earlier portion of the manuscript mentions the same two newspapers

in addition to Fensterwald. The sentence mentioning Fensterwald is relocated here. Bernard "Bud" Fensterwald Jr. (1921–1991) was an American-born lawyer who defended, among others, accused assassin James Earl Ray and James W. McCord Jr. of CIA/Watergate fame. In 1969 he and Richard E. Sprague founded the "Committee to Investigate Assassinations." Fensterwald contacted Willem Oltmans on several occasions in the early 1970s hoping to secure information about de Mohrenschildt and Oswald. In particular he wanted a copy of the tapes Oltmans made with de Mohrenschildt in the late 1960s. A letter from Fensterwald to Oltmans dated April 11, 1973, reads "We are most anxious to hear your tapes of George. . . . This is important as George becomes of increasing interest." Oltmans duly informed de Mohrenschildt, who replied by letter on June 3: "I am sending this letter 'registered' so it won't get lost. *Please* under no conditions release the tapes to any gov't commission. They caused me and Jeanne enough harm and I am contemplating a lawsuit for a large amount. We should ask them for a large amount of money to make the tapes available (for instance, $10,000) and in any case do not agree on anything without our agreement, OK?" Oltmans, *Memoires 1972–1973*, 320–321. De Mohrenschildt and his lawyer contemplated suing Fensterwald about the Bahamas allegations during the winter of 1975, telling Oltmans on February 17, 1975, "Patrick says to circulate this story is a criminal offense. I could sue the bastard, which would be fun, you know." Willem Oltmans, *Memoires 1974–1975* (Papieren Tijger, 2005), 160. Fensterwald was later among the names under consideration for chief counsel for the House Select Committee on Assassinations but withdrew his name after opposition by Congressman Henry B. Gonzalez.

120. In fact suing was very much de Mohrenschildt's style. In early 1972, for example, he filed suit in US district court against the Phillips Petroleum company, claiming he "contacted Phillips officials about oil potential in Nigeria in 1963, and sent them some information on where they might drill." See "Oil Suit Asks for $6 Million," *Lawton Constitution*, February 11, 1972. De Mohrenschildt was asking Phillips to pay "$5 million in damages and $1 million in attorneys' fees." See "Geologist Files Whopping Suit against Phillips," *Ada Evening News*, February 11, 1972, and "Phillips Named in Court Case," *Daily Ardmoreite*, February 11, 1972.

121. See Chapter 4. De Mohrenschildt's criticism is perhaps a bit too harsh regarding the mainstream print media. The *Washington Post*, fresh off its Pulitzer Prize for its coverage of the Watergate scandal and cover-up, was in May 1975 considering a two-year partnership with the *Boston Globe* and *Chicago Tribune* to investigate the deaths of both President and Senator Kennedy. It was the brainchild of executive editor Ben Bradlee (1921–present), who held a closed-door meeting with his editor Harry Rosenfeld (1929–present). Bradlee, who had been a close friend of then-Senator John F. Kennedy, noted it was "a mystery that just won't go away and we should commit large resources to it." Rosenfeld pointed out the logistical difficulties of coordinating with other newspapers as well as finding "a good editor or reporter [with] the psychic stamina to endure not being published for two years." Rosenfeld was also skeptical about what their investigation might uncover, since so many of the key witnesses found in "the supposedly definitive . . . twenty–six volumes [of

the *Warren Commission Hearings and Exhibits*] . . . had died." The investigation might turn up something, but it "had to be more than table talk." Bradlee asked him not to be against the project, to which Rosenfeld replied, "I am not against it, but I want to know what we could expect from our investment." Apparently the project fell through, not because the topic was unworthy of investigation but because Rosenfeld felt it was too difficult to "translate [Bradlee's] enthusiasms into practical terms." See Harry Rosenfeld, *From Kristallnacht to Watergate* (SUNY Press, 2013), 262–264.

122. An alternative translation of the French title would be *America Burns*. The book was originally published by Frontiers Publishing Company located in Voduz, Liechtenstein, and was 410 pages long. In 2002 the book was republished in English by Penmarin Books as "the long-suppressed European best-seller" with the title *Farewell America: The Plot to Kill JFK*. Penmarin indicated that efforts "to contact Frontiers Publishing Company regarding reproduction have proved fruitless."

123. In Chapter 7 of *Rearview Mirror: Looking Back at the FBI, CIA and Other Tails*, which is titled "The *Farewell America* Plot," William W. Turner contends the authors were members of French intelligence acting with at least implicit cooperation from the Kennedy inner circle. He also indicates that in spite of the book's European success Frontiers Publishing disappeared shortly after the book was published.

124. Replacing "chapter" in the original manuscript. This is another example of de Mohrenschildt's tendency to conflate two English words; what is clearly meant here is a passage within a single chapter, not an entire chapter. A near identical passage from *L'Amérique Brûle* appears in an earlier portion of the manuscript; de Mohrenschildt indicates in the earlier quote that the material was found on page 356 and complains that if he "were a CIA agent" he "would not have been treated so miserably by the American Embassy in Port-au-Prince, and especially by the [American] Ambassador."

125. The manuscript continues to quote in English from *L'Amérique Brûle*:

His nickname was "the Chinaman" and he pretended to have been born in the Ukraine and was an ex-officer in the Polish Cavalry. He was recruited during the war by the OSS and was inscribed in 1944 at the University of Texas where he obtained a degree of a geological engineer, specializing in petroleum geology. The CIA utilized him in Iran, Indonesia, Egypt, Panama, Nicaragua, San Salvador, Honduras, Ghana, Togoland and finally in Haiti, where he worked "in principle" with [the] Sinclair Oil Company. De Mohrenschildt was closely connected with or mixed up with oil circles and was a member of [the] Dallas Petroleum Club, Abilene Country Club, [and the] Dallas Society of Petroleum Geologists. He had very close relations with [the] manager of [the] Kerr-McGee Oil Company, Continental Oil Company, Coswell Oil Equipment, Texas-Eastern Corporation and also with John Mecom of Houston. He was a distinguished and cultured man, who was part of the establishment and member of the social register. His White-Russian wife, born in China, often operated with him. Another of his covers was [the] ICA, Washington D.C.

In response to this passage, de Mohrenschildt replies: "I have never been to some of the countries mentioned here (for example Egypt and Indonesia) and I lived and worked in many other countries this [passage] did not mention. In each case I either worked for myself or for some oil companies, but I never, ever worked for [the] CIA. And I do not think [the] CIA will hire me in the future! As for the I.C.A. mentioned above, this was the name of the division of the State Department, a shortening of International Cooperation Administration which dealt with economic help abroad. I was hired as a petroleum technician in that capacity [and] worked for a year in Yugoslavia."

126. While it seems unlikely that de Mohrenschildt was anything more than a minor and occasional source of information for American intelligence agencies, someone who was willing to "merge his own business interests with an additional money-making opportunity providing appropriate feedback to governments in the need to know," the paragraph ends not with an emphatic statement of innocence but rather almost a sly hint that at some still unknown date in the future the identity of former CIA agents will be dragged into the light. Including his name? Or is this all meant in jest, another dose of the famous de Mohrenschildt humor? A chameleon and hustler right to the end. See Nancy Wertz, "George de Mohrenschildt, Who Are You?" *The Fourth Decade: A Journal of Research on the John F. Kennedy Assassination* 5, no. 5 (July 1998): 9.

127. Possibly a reference to the Rockefeller Commission, formally known as the United States President's Commission on CIA Activities within the United States. The commission had been created in response to an article published in the *New York Times* on December 22, 1974, indicating that the CIA had conducted illegal domestic activities. David Belin, who had been a Warren Commission staffer, was the Commission's Executive Director. In the single report issued in 1975 the Rockefeller Commission touched upon abuses including the opening of mail and surveillance of domestic opposition groups such as the anti-war movement, as well as MKULTRA, the CIA's mind control study. Other possibilities are the Senate's Church Committee, or the House's Pike Committee, both of which began conducting investigations during the 1975–76 time period. The final report of the Pike Committee was never officially completed but much of the final draft was later published in the *Village Voice*.

128. De Mohrenschildt's famously robust health had started to decline in the eighteen months preceding the completion of the manuscript. A holiday card sent to Willem Oltmans around the end of 1974 mentions having gone "to the hospital for seven days, actually it was a pneumonia with heart complications," and on March 13, 1975, he would add in a letter "I'm still suffering some effects of my bronchial pneumonia, I guess it will go away with warmer weather." Oltmans, *Memoires 1974–1975*, 315, 345. George would have another, even more severe, case of bronchitis in the spring of 1976. It is probably for this reason that he speaks of being "fairly healthy."

129. The prose here is noticeably reminiscent of text in de Mohrenschildt's 1973 letter to Republican National Committee chairman George H. W. Bush: "As you

know I've been happily teaching at Bishop College for the last four years. . . . I lost interest in just 'making money' and found more satisfaction in teaching." In a letter composed just a few days after Nixon's landslide reelection in 1972 he would tell Willem Oltmans "Life is great—not because of Nixon, but because of my black students and exciting faculty members." Oltmans, *Memoires 1972–1973*, 337. Happy as he may have been, teaching had not stopped de Mohrenschildt from continuing to lobby the federal government at regular intervals to aid him in recovering the money owed to him under the terms of his contract with the government of Haiti.

130. Replacing "life in a very different way" in the original manuscript. De Mohrenschildt explains his love for young people elsewhere in the manuscript as: "We like young people who search to solve some problems which bother them." He says this in the context of his relationship with Oswald, someone that "disliked many aspects of American life" but who at the same time "thought maybe somewhere else it was better."

131. Assuming the passage was written in 1976, which seems likely, de Mohrenschildt had been teaching French and Russian in the Literature Department of Bishop College since the beginning of the decade. By the spring 1977 semester, the school's financial problems had led it to eliminate its program in Russian, and de Mohrenschildt was teaching a single course in French. It was not enough for a couple to live off of, so in January 1977 Jeanne had gone to California to stay with relatives and hopefully find work. George was to have joined her once she found employment. Until Oltmans appeared in Dallas in late February and lured George to Europe they communicated by phone almost daily.

132. Bohemian Club co-founders Sam Ballen and Bruce Calder, for example. Ballen would speak kindly about his friend a few years before his own death in February 2007. From the start, Ballen wrote, he and George were "brothers under the skin." See Samuel B. Ballen, *Without Reservations* (Ocean Tree Books, 2001), 161–162. Ballen would relocate from Texas to New Mexico where, in 1968, he became owner of Santa Fe's famous La Fonda hotel. The Ballen family still maintains a majority ownership. On learning of de Mohrenschildt's death, Calder told Ballen, "George was bound to end up as he did. He was a rebellious child who would not submit to the conformity of society. There should be a national fund to take care of the material needs of such people since they add so much to the joy of others." Quoted in Ballen, *Without Reservations*, 259.

133. Replacing "good" in the original manuscript. Clearly the good changes referred to here are the socially progressive ones mentioned throughout the manuscript, like the end of the South's system of racial segregation.

134. Most likely a reference to the series of tapes recorded in the company of Willem Oltmans on February 14–15, 1969. There were ongoing discussions between de Mohrenschildt and Oltmans about how best to profit from a sale of the tapes but ultimately no sale ever occurred. In a letter written to Oltmans dated May 10, 1976, de Mohrenschildt would mention listening to these tapes again and trying "to transcribe them" as part of his effort to "reconstruct Lee's personality." Oltmans, *Memoires 1976*, 321. Similarly Jeanne would tell the FBI in an interview given April

27, 1977, that "a couple of years ago" her husband "started writing a manuscript based on the information that was on these tape recordings."

135. Replacing "presented on a dish" in the original manuscript.

136. The original manuscript, as the reader knows from the Editor's Introduction, does not conclude with this powerful line but rather with the defensive: "Let us hope that this book, poorly written and disjointed, but sincere, will help to clear up our relationship with our dear, dead friend Lee." As an editor I found this sentence a far more effective means to open the narrative than to conclude it. As for dying too young, much the same could be said of de Mohrenschildt. His older brother Dmitri lived to be one hundred, passing away in 2002; George's suicide at age sixty-five saddened many.

Selected
Bibliography

EDITOR'S NOTE: An asterisk (*) denotes sources mentioned either by title, publisher, and/or author within the de Mohrenschildt manuscript; a dagger (†) indicates sources that appear to be alluded to within the same text.

Anonymous. "A Primer of Assassination Theories." *Esquire*. December, 1966, pp. 205–210.

*Anonymous. "A Second Primer of Assassination Theories." *Esquire*. May, 1967, 104–107.

†Anonymous. "Voodoo Land in Ferment. Time Runs Out for a Caribbean Dictator Who Rules by Bullets and Black Magic." *Life* 54, no. 10 (March 8, 1963), 28–35.

Baker, Judith Vary. *Lee and Me: How I Came to Know, Love, and Lose Lee Harvey Oswald*. Walterville, OR: TrineDay, 2011.

Baker, Russ. *Family of Secrets: The Bush Dynasty, America's Invisible Government, and the Hidden History of the Last Fifty Years*. New York: Bloomsbury Press, 2009.

Ballen, Samuel B. *Without Reservations: From Harlem to the End of the Santa Fe Trail*. Santa Fe, NM: Ocean Tree Books, 2001.

Bernan Associates, Taylor and Francis Group. *The World of Learning, 1977–78*. London: Europa Publications, 1977.

Blakey, George Robert, and Richard N. Billings. *The Plot to Kill the President: Organized Crime Assassinated J.F.K.* New York: Times Books, 1981.

Braudel, Fernand. *Civilization and Capitalism, 15th–18th Century, Volume 1: The*

Structures of Everyday Life—The Limits of the Possible. Translated by Sian Reynolds. New York: Harper and Row, 1981.

Bugliosi, Vincent. *Reclaiming History: The Assassination of President John F. Kennedy.* New York: W. W. Norton, 2007.

Burron, Neil A. "Michel Martelly: Haiti's New Caesar and the Prospects for Democracy." *New Political Science* 35, no. 2 (June 2013): 161–181.

Burrough, Bryan. *The Big Rich: The Rise and Fall of the Greatest Texas Oil Fortunes.* New York: Penguin, 2009.

Byrne, Jeb. *Out in Front: Preparing the Way for JFK and LBJ.* Albany, NY: SUNY Press, 2009.

Chambers, Jesse. "The Good Fight: The True Story of the Alabama Air Guard and the Bay of Pigs." *Birmingham Weekly*, September 13, 2007.

Cockburn, Alexander, and Jeffrey St. Clair. *Whiteout: The CIA, Drugs, and the Press.* London: Verso, 1998.

Daggett, Stephen. "Costs of Major US Wars." *CRS Report for Congress*, July 24, 2008.

Davis, Mike. *Prisoners of the American Dream: Politics and Economy in the History of the US Working Class.* London: Verso, 1986.

Diderot, Denis. *Rameau's Nephew / D'Alembert's Dream.* Translated by Leonard Tancock. New York: Penguin, 1966.

Diederich, Bernard, and Al Burt. *Papa Doc and the Tontons Macoutes.* Princeton, NJ: Markus Weiner, 2005.

DiEugenio, James, and Lisa Pease. *The Assassinations: Probe Magazine on JFK, MLK, RFK, and Malcolm X.* Port Townsend, WA: Feral House, 2003.

Epstein, Edward J. *The Assassination Chronicles.* New York: Carroll and Graf, 1992.

Evans, Peter. *Nemesis: Aristotle Onassis, Jackie, and the Love Triangle That Brought Down the Kennedys.* New York: Harper Collins, 2004.

Fanning, Leonard M. *Foreign Oil and the Free World.* New York: McGraw-Hill, 1954.

Feigen, G. M. "A Triangular Look at *The Comedians.*" *Ramparts* 6, no. 7 (February 1968): 62–65.

Fensterwald, Bernard Jr. *Assassination of JFK by Coincidence or Conspiracy?* New York: Zebra Books, 1977.

Ford, Gerald R. *A Presidential Legacy and the Warren Commission.* Clarksville, TN: FlatSigned Press, 2007.

*Ford, Gerald R., with John R. Stiles. *Portrait of an Assassin.* New York: Simon & Schuster, 1966.

Foucault, Michel. "Nietzsche, Genealogy, History." In *The Foucault Reader*, edited by Paul Rabinow, 76–100. New York: Pantheon Books, 1984.

*Garrison, Jim. *The Star-Spangled Contract.* New York: McGraw-Hill, 1976.

———. *On the Trail of the Assassins: My Investigation and Prosecution of the Murder of President Kennedy.* New York: Sheridan Square Press, 1988.

Gold, Herbert. *Haiti: Best Nightmare on Earth.* Piscataway, NJ: Transaction Publishers, 2004.

Golz, Earl. "Oswald Friend Vowed Suicide, Psychiatrist Claimed." *Dallas Times Herald*, April 1, 1977.

*Greene, Graham. *The Comedians*. London: Bodley Head, 1966.

*Hearings before the President's Commission on the Assassination of President Kennedy (Warren Commission Hearings and Exhibits). 26 volumes. Washington, DC: US Government Printing Office, 1964.

Heartsill, Graydon. "Pan American Walking Tour." *Dallas Times Herald*, November 6, 1960.

*———. "Caught between Two Tragedies: De Mohrenschildts Knew Both Oswalds, Kennedys." *Dallas Times Herald*, December 11, 1966.

Hendrix, Hal. "Grapevine Warned Duvalier—Invasion Plan Known by Haiti in July." *Miami News*, August 11, 1963.

*Hepburn, James. *L'Amérique Brûle (America is Burning)*. Vaduz, Liechtenstein: Frontiers Publishing, 1968.

†Jones Jr., William Penn. *Forgive My Grief II*. Midlothian, TX: Midlothian Mirror, 1967.

Kaiser, David. *The Road to Dallas: The Assassination of President Kennedy*. Belknap Press, 2009.

Kelso, Iris. "Garrison Planned to Link General to JFK Slaying." *Washington Post*, September 16, 1973.

Kornbluh, Peter, ed. "The ULTRASENSITIVE Bay of Pigs: Newly Released Portions of Taylor Commission Report Provide Critical New Details on Operation Zapata." *National Security Archive Electronic Briefing Book No. 29*, May 3, 2000.

La Fontaine, Ray, and Mary La Fontaine. *Oswald Talked: The New Evidence in the JFK Assassination*. Gretna, LA: Pelican Publishing, 1996.

Lane, Mark. *Rush to Judgment: A Critique of the Warren Commission's Inquiry into the Murders of President John F. Kennedy, Officer J. D. Tippit and Lee Harvey Oswald*. New York: Holt Rinehart Winston, 1966.

Lemoine, Patrick. *Fort-Dimanche, Dungeon of Death*. Bloomington, IN: Trafford Publishing, 2011.

Mailer, Norman. *Oswald's Tale: An American Mystery*. New York: Random House, 1995.

Mathews, John Burt. *The Bases of United States–Venezuela Relations, 1900–1950*. Madison: University of Wisconsin Press, 1953.

†McCoy, Alfred W. *The Politics of Heroin in Southeast Asia*. New York: Harper and Row, 1972.

McMillan, George. *The Making of an Assassin: The Life of James Earl Ray*. New York: Little & Brown, 1976.

———. "The Man Who Knew Oswald." *Washington Post*, April 3, 1977.

McMillan, Priscilla Johnson. *Marina and Lee: The Tormented Love and Fatal Obsession behind Lee Harvey Oswald's Assassination of John F. Kennedy*. Hanover, NH: Steerforth Press, 2013.

Mellen, Joan. *Our Man in Haiti: George de Mohrenschildt and the CIA in the Nightmare Republic*. Waterville, OR: TrineDay, 2012.

Minutaglio, Bill, and Steven L. Davis. *Dallas 1963*. New York: Grand Central Publishing, 2013.

†Moody, Sid. "A Look at Lives Touched by the Assassination. For Some the Terrible Day is not Over Yet." *Sarasota Herald–Tribune*, November 15, 1964.

Nietzsche, Friedrich. *Beyond Good and Evil: Prelude to a Philosophy of the Future*. Translated by Walter Kaufman. New York: Vintage Books, 1989.

———. *On the Genealogy of Morals and Ecce Homo*. Translated by Walter Kaufman. New York: Vintage Books, 1989.

———. *Daybreak: Thoughts on the Prejudices of Morality*. Edited by Maudmarie Clark and Brian Leiter. Translated by R. J. Hollingdale. New York: Cambridge University Press, 1997.

O'Brien, Gary. *Oswald's Politics*. Bloomington, IN: Trafford Publishing, 2010.

O'Leary, Jeremiah. "The de Mohrenschildt-JFK Enigma." *Washington Star*, March 31, 1977.

———. "Oswald Cohort Death Raises Questions." *Washington Star*, April 1, 1977.

Oltmans, Willem. "New Mysteries in the Kennedy Assassination?" *Nieuwe Revu* (translated in *Atlas World Press Review*), May 1977, 13–15.

———. *Memoires 1964–1966*. Breda: Papieren Tijger, 2001.

———. *Memoires 1966–1967*. Breda: Papieren Tijger, 2002.

———. *Memoires 1967–1968*. Breda: Papieren Tijger, 2002.

———. *Memoires 1968–1970*. Breda: Papieren Tijger, 2003.

———. *Memoires 1970–1971*. Breda: Papieren Tijger, 2003.

———. *Memoires 1971–1972*. Breda: Papieren Tijger, 2003.

———. *Memoires 1972–1973*. Breda: Papieren Tijger, 2004.

———. *Memoires 1973*. Breda: Papieren Tijger, 2004.

———. *Memoires 1973–1974*. Breda: Papieren Tijger, 2004.

———. *Memoires 1974*. Breda: Papieren Tijger, 2005.

———. *Memoires 1974–1975*. Breda: Papieren Tijger, 2005.

———. *Memoires 1975*. Breda: Papieren Tijger, 2006.

———. *Memoires 1975–1976*. Breda: Papieren Tijger, 2006.

———. *Memoires 1976*. Breda: Papieren Tijger, 2007.

———. *Memoires 1976–1977*. Breda: Papieren Tijger, 2007.

———. *Memoires 1977–1978*. Breda: Papieren Tijger, 2008.

———. *Memoires 1978*. Breda: Papieren Tijger, 2008.

———. *Memoires 1978–1979*. Breda: Papieren Tijger, 2009.

———. *Memoires 1979–A*. Breda: Papieren Tijger, 2010.

———. *Memoires 1979–1980*. Breda: Papieren Tijger, 2011.

———. *Memoires 1979–B*. Breda: Papieren Tijger, 2011.

———. *Memoires 1980*. Breda: Papieren Tijger, 2011.

———. *Memoires 1980–1981*. Breda: Papieren Tijger, 2012.

———. *Memoires 1981*. Breda: Papieren Tijger, 2012.

O'Reilly, Bill. *Killing Kennedy: The End of Camelot*. New York: Henry Holt, 2012.

Ortiz, Frank V. *Ambassador Ortiz: Lessons from a Life of Service*. Edited by Don J. Usner. Albuquerque: University of New Mexico Press, 2005.

Pease, Lisa. "Martin Luther King's Son Says: James Earl Ray Didn't Kill MLK." *Probe* 4, no. 4 (May–June): 1997.

Phillips, J. P. *Act of Retribution: The Military-Industrial-Intelligence Establishment and the Conspiracy to Assassinate President John F. Kennedy.* Bloomington, IN: Xlibris, 2010.

*Pollack, Jack Harrison. *Croiset the Clairvoyant.* New York: Doubleday, 1965.

†Pond, Elizabeth. "Soviet Wife of U.S. Citizen Not Allowed to Join Husband." *Christian Science Monitor,* July 14, 1976.

Posner, Gerald. *Case Closed.* New York: Anchor/Doubleday, 2003.

Potter, Matt. "Oil and Politics in La Jolla." *San Diego Reader,* January 5, 2011.

Rabe, Stephen G. *The Most Dangerous Area in the World: John F. Kennedy Confronts Communist Revolution in Latin America.* Chapel Hill: University of North Carolina Press, 1999.

Report of the President's Commission on the Assassination of President John F. Kennedy (The Warren Report). Washington, DC: US Government Printing Office, 1964.

Reston, James Jr. *The Accidental Victim: JFK, Lee Harvey Oswald, and the Real Target in Dallas.* New York: Zola Books, 2013.

Richardot, Jean. *Journeys for a Better World: An Inside Story of the United Nations by One of Its First Senior Officials.* Lanham, MD: University Press of America, 1994.

Rommel, Erwin. *The Rommel Papers.* Edited by B. H. Liddell-Hart. New York: Da Capo Press, 1953.

Rosenfeld, Harry. *From Kristallnacht to Watergate: Memoirs of a Newspaperman.* Albany, NY: SUNY Press, 2013.

Russell, Bertrand. "Sixteen Questions on the Assassination." *Minority of One* 6, no. 9 (September 1964): 6–8.

Russell, Dick. *The Man Who Knew Too Much: Inquest, Counterplot, and Legend.* New York: Carroll & Graf, 1992.

Sanger, Daniel, and Julian Feldman. "Fayed's Forgotten Years: The Conman, the Dictator, and the CIA Files." *The Daily Telegraph Magazine,* June 20, 1998.

Savage, Sean. *JFK, LBJ, and the Democratic Party.* Albany, NY: SUNY Press, 2005.

Schmitz, David. *Thank God They're on Our Side: The United States and Right-Wing Dictatorships, 1921–1965.* Chapel Hill: University of North Carolina Press, 1999.

Scott, Peter Dale. *Deep Politics and the Death of JFK.* Berkeley: University of California Press, 1996.

Sprague, Jeb. *Paramilitarism and the Assault on Democracy in Haiti.* New York: Monthly Review Press, 2012.

Stephens, Joe. "Ford Told FBI of Skeptics on Warren Commission." *Washington Post,* August 8, 2008.

Swindle, Howard, and Hugh Aynesworth. "Photo and Manuscript Given to Investigators." *Dallas Times Herald,* April 2, 1977.

†Szulc, Tad. "Friend of Oswalds Knew Mrs. Kennedy." *New York Times,* November 24, 1964.

Taraborrelli, J. Randy. *After Camelot: A Personal History of the Kennedy Family 1968 to the Present*. New York: Grand Central Publishing, 2012.

Timmons, Benson E. L., III. "Telegram from the Embassy in Haiti to the Department of State." *Foreign Relations of the United States*, 1964–1968, Volume 32, *Dominican Republic; Cuba; Haiti; Guyana*; Document 325, 762–764.

Trost, Cathy, and Susan Lewis Bennett, eds. *President Kennedy Has Been Shot*. Naperville, IL: Sourcebooks MediaFusion, 2003.

Tulcin, Doris F. *Memoirs of a Monarch: A Chronicle of My Life*. Bloomington, IN: iUniverse, 2008; New York: Grand Central Publishing, 2012.

Tunzelmann, Alex von. *Red Heat: Conspiracy, Murder, and the Cold War in the Caribbean*. New York: Henry Holt, 2011.

Turner, William W. "The Inquest." *Ramparts* 5, no. 12 (June 1967): 17–29.

———. "Assassinations: Epstein's Garrison." *Ramparts* 7 (September 7, 1967): 8–11.

———. "The Garrison Commission on the Assassination of President Kennedy." *Ramparts* 6, no. 6 (January 1968): 43–68.

———. *Review Mirror: Looking Back at the FBI, the CIA and Other Tails*. Roseville, CA: Penmarin Books, 2001.

US Congress, House of Representatives, *Appendix to Hearings before the Select Committee on Assassinations of the House of U.S. Representatives*, Vol. 12 (US Government Printing Office, 1979), 69–315.

Vorontsov, Vladimir, ed. *Words of the Wise: A Book of Russian Quotations*. Moscow: Progress Publishers, 1979.

Waldron, Lamar. *Ultimate Sacrifice: John and Robert Kennedy, the Plan for a Coup in Cuba, and the Murder of JFK*. New York: Carroll & Graf, 2006.

Warren, Earl. *Memoirs of Chief Justice Earl Warren*. New York: Doubleday, 1977.

Weiford, Nancy Wertz. "A Last Wild Ride for George de Mohrenschildt." *Dealey Plaza Echo*, 15, no. 1 (March 2011): 39–45.

Weiss, Murray, and William Hoffman. "The Oswald Connection." *Sun Sentinel*, November 21, 1993.

Wertz, Nancy. "George de Mohrenschildt, Who Are You?" *The Fourth Decade—A Journal of Research on the John F. Kennedy Assassination* 5, no. 5 (July, 1998): 8–19.

Widmer, Ted. "How Haiti Saved America: Two Centuries Ago, A Glittering Caribbean Island Helped Finance the Revolution." *Boston Globe*, March 21, 2010.

Williamson, Charles T. *The U.S. Naval Mission to Haiti, 1959–1963*. Annapolis, MD: Naval Institute Press, 1999.

Wilson, Theodore. "Oral History Interview with Benson E. L. Timmons III." Transcript of interview conducted on July 8, 1970. Independence, MO: Harry Truman Library.

About the Editor

Dr. Michael A. Rinella received his Ph.D. in political science in 1997. Since 1999 he has been an acquiring editor at the State University of New York Press, where he has seen through to publication over 400 works in the humanities and social sciences, more than a dozen of which have won recognitions and awards for excellence. Notable among these are the nonfiction works *JFK, LBJ, and the Democratic Party* and *The Senator from New England: John F. Kennedy, 1952–1960*. In addition he collaborated with former Kennedy/Johnson advance man Jeb Byrne in publishing his memoir *Out in Front: Preparing the Way for JFK and LBJ*. His efforts have been acknowledged in well over 100 published scholarly works. He is also a freelance writer and occasional teacher of political theory, philosophy, international political economy, and military history. In the spring of 2012 he was the NEH Distinguished Visiting Professor, Philosophy, at the State University of New York, Potsdam.

Index

Blaque, Valentin "Teddy," 2, 84, 251n15, 251n16, 297n100
Bloom, George A., 279n72
Boethius, 285n20
Bogoiavlensky, Valentin, 257n17
Bouhe, George A.,
    angry at de Mohrenschildt, 142, 281n91
    assistance to Marina Oswald, 134–139, 154, 268n92, 275n48, 277n59, 281n90
    attends Christmas party, 161
    becomes disgusted with Oswald, 139–140
    biography, 254n3
    de Mohrenschildt and, 5–6, 129–132, 145–146
    fear of Oswald, 151–152, 268n91, 276n50
    intelligence of, 92, 321n155
    supports segregation, 170
    Warren Commission testimony of, 255n4, 256n12, 259n32, 267n83, 274n25, 321n155
Bouvier, John V. "Black Jack" III, 60, 75, 282n97, 304n17
Boyd, Alston, 1, 248n3, 303n4
Boyer, Hervé, 76, 307n43
Breitman, Michael, 55, 287n31
Brown, George R., 321n154
Brown, Herman, 321n154
Brown, Pat, 294n69
Bruton, Frannie, 61–64, 295n85
Bruton, Henry C.,
    biography, 294n68
    commander of the Greenling, 294n71
    employed by Collins Radio, 295n79
    entertains Oswalds 61–64, 175
Buckley, William F. Sr., 22, 267n84
Buckley, William F. Jr., 267n84, 340n53
Bundy, McGeorge, 315n107
Bush, Barbara, 234
Bush, George H. W.,
    George I. Bloom and, 279n72
    letters from de Mohrenschildt, 229–30, 352n129
    letter to de Mohrenschildt, xxvi, 231–233

Thomas J. Divine and, 239n13, 301n123
Bush, George W., 257n14
Byrd, Harold, 252n19

Cabell, Charles, 252n19
Cabell, Earle,
    mayor of Dallas, 2, 252n19
    member of Congress, 233
Castro, Fidel,
    Biography, 288n33
    Mafia attempts to assassinate, 291n46, 309n49, 334n14, 338n40
    Oswald's admiration of, 55, 57, 198
Castro, Raúl, 288n33
Chandler, David, 326n24
Charles, Clémard Joseph
    business with de Mohrenschildt, 220
    political ambitions of, 301n123
    United States visit, 214–216
Clark, Gali, 129, 254n3
Clark, Max,
    consulted by de Mohrenschildt, 145–146, 306n32
    discovers Oswalds, 129
    Oswald rude to, 152
    Warren Commission testimony of, 271n12, 284n19,
Clark, Tom C., 262n48
Connally, John,
    biography, 260n37
    governor's race and, 67
    Oswald's hatred of, 11, 40, 42, 117, 346n93
    single bullet theory and, 116, 343n78, 344n79
Coolidge, Calvin, 261n48
Contessa (mule), 55
Croiset, Gerard,
    biography, 340n56
    vision of de Mohrenschildt 340n58
    Willem Oltmans and, 113, 116, 241n27
Curry, Jesse E., 345n85
Curtis, Edward Glion Jr., 89, 318n132

d'Alembert, Jean Le Rond, 238n4
Davidson, Natasha, 322n159
Dealey, E. M. "Ted," 252n19

Kennedy, John F.,
  assassination of, xiii, xvi
  assists filming of *Seven Days in May*,
    278n69
  Bay of Pigs and, 83, 110, 245n58,
    290n45
  fires Alan Dulles, 309n49
  jokes about, 18
  martyrdom of, 118, 245n58, 346n94
  media coverage after death, 72
  on cover of *Time*, 41, 278n63
  Oswald's attitude toward, 41, 58
  personal life, xxix
  plans to replace FBI Director Hoover,
    262n48
Kennedy, Joseph P.,
  business with James Roosevelt,
    278n64
  fortune of, 41
Kennedy, Robert F.,
  assassination of, 110, 112
  J. Edgar Hoover and, 336n23
  personal life, xxix
  speech in Albany, 341n64
  Willem Oltmans and, 113–14,
    335n20
Khrushchev, Nikita,
  biography, 275n40
  baby June's resemblance to, 34, 69,
    133
  death of, 300n121
King, Martin Luther Jr.,
  biography, 335n21
  assassination of, 110
  Oswald's admiration for, 66
  targeted by COINTELPRO, 336n23
Kissinger, Henry,
  biography, 347n101
  détente and, 119
  de Mohrenschildt and, 233
Kitchel, George, 224, 242n41
Koestler, Arthur, 40
  novel *Darkness at Noon*, 277n61
Korth, Fred, 260n37

Lansky, Meyer, 58, 291n46
Lawrence, Lincoln, 349n117
Leffelaar, Henk, 123

Lehrer, Jim, 323n163
LeMay, Curtis E., 278n69
Leslie, Helen, 321n155

MacArthur, Douglas, 258n20
Machado, Decio de Paulo "King of
  Bananas," 15, 200, 263n57
MacNaughton, Lewis W., 254n3
Maheu, Robert Aime, 338n40
Mallon, H. Neil,
  Dallas Council of World Affairs
    organizer and president, 198
Mamantov, Ilya A.
  biography, 238n7
  Ruth Paine and, 289n36
Mann, James Robert, 16, 264n61
Marcus, Stanley,
  Dallas Council of World Affairs
    president, 198
Marx, Karl, 9
  Das Capital, 258n27
Matlack, Dorothe, 251n15, 301n123
McCarthy, Eugene, 46, 280n78
McGee, Dean,
  Dallas Council of World Affairs
    president, 198
McGhee, George, 239n15
McMillan, George,
  biography, 315n104
  interviews de Mohrenschidlts, 88
  visits Haiti, 85–88, 249n8
McMillan, Priscilla Johnson,
  communication with de
    Mohrenschildt, 326n21
Medvedev, Alexandr Ivanovich, 26
Meller, Anna, xxvii, 37, 39, 141, 161,
    177, 195, 255n4, 258n27
Meller, Teofil, 37, 276n51
Moore, J. Walton,
  career of, 305n27
  knows Lawrence Orlov, 255n5
  knows de Mohrenschildts, 73, 112,
    146–147
  mistaken as being FBI, 306n32
  views de Mohrenschildt's home movie,
    305n28
Moore, Robin, 115
Morel, George, 2

Murchison, Clint, 242n41
  co-owner of the Hotel del Charro,
    262n51

Nero (dog), xxxiv, 8, 37, 91, 100–101,
    258n22
  death of, 329n45
  walking trip and, 55, 239n13
  Warren Commission appearance,
    77–79, 308n45
Nietzsche, Friedrich, xxv, 247n65,
    323n166
  admiration for Dostoyevsky, 273n20
  author of Ecce Homo, 242n43
Nixon, Richard M.,
  alludes to Kennedy assassination,
    334n13
  Bay of Pigs and, 290n45
  biography, 294n69
  creation of DEA and, 286n26
  enemy of Admiral Bruton, 61, 64
  Kennedy assassination and, 334n13
  Oswald wants to shoot, 120, 178
  presidential election of 1960 and, 82
  resignation of, 310n51
  sabotages Jeddah Agreement, 338n39
  vice-president, 348n110
Nobel, Robert, 268n86

Okui, Yaeko, 51–53, 57, 163, 283n10
  conversation with Oswald, 284n13
  Marina's distrust of, 284n14
Oltmans, Willem,
  biography, 339n52
  appears in movie JFK, 340n52
  car accident of, 113–115
  contracted by Bernard Fensterwald Jr.,
    350n119
  de Mohrenschildt discusses Oswald
    with, 279n77
  doubts about de Mohrenschildt,
    241n29
  education of, 112, 340n53
  friendship with de Mohrenschildt,
    115–116, 241n27, 245n58,
    342n76, 352n128
  Gerald Croiset and, 340n58
  interviews de Mohrenschildts, 342n71

opportunism of, 242n35, 342n73
origins of manuscript and, 332n1,
    353n134
President Sukarno and, 341n67
Robert Kennedy and, 110, 335n20
threatened by Glenn Byran Smith Jr.,
    342n68
Onassis, Aristotle,
  biography, 337n35
  contact with de Mohrenschildt,
    297n100, 335n20, 337n37
  death of, 111, 338n41
  Duvalier and, 313n83
  fortune of, 111, 338n39
  Jeddah Agreement sabotaged, 338n40
O'Reilly, Bill, 306n28
Orlov, Lawrence, 5–6, 130–132, 259n32
  associate of J. Walton Moore, 255n5
Oswald, Audrey Marina Rachel,
  birth, 256n8
  baptism, 279n75
Oswald, June Lee, 6, 8, 18, 23, 29, 36–
    39, 51, 56, 61, 106
  baptism, 32, 44, 274n31
  birth of 256n8
  care of, 35, 136, 208
  Oswald's fondness for, 6, 10, 34, 39
  resemblance to Nikita Khrushchev, 34,
    69–70, 133
Oswald, Lee Harvey, throughout, but
    especially,
  Admiral Bruton and, 62–63
  admiration for President Kennedy, 82,
    108
  anger about discharge, 11, 42, 260n36
  appearance described, 6, 19
  backyard photo of, 95–97
  camera equipment of, 18, 265n69,
    275n38
  conspiracy scapegoat, 83, 93, 102,
    112, 121
  contrasted with Marina, 29–32
  death and, 19, 44
  first meets de Mohrenschildt, 6
  humor of, 9–10, 17–18
  interviewed by Sam Ballen, 18, 92
  Kennedy administration policies and,
    41, 58, 108